ΛDΛMS
FastLetter™
User's Manual

Visit our home page at http://www.adamsmedia.com

ADAMS MEDIA CORPORATION
Holbrook, Massachusetts

TABLE OF CONTENTS

Introduction 3
   Welcome to Adams FastLetter! 3
   Documentation Structure 3
   Choosing Strategies 3
   Accessing the Online Help System. 4
   Conventions 4
   How to Contact Adams Media Corporation 5
      Before Calling Technical Support 5
1. Setup and Program Requirements 6
   System Requirements 6
   Installing Adams FastLetter 6
   Starting Adams FastLetter 7
   Computer Setup 7
2. Creating a Cover Letter 8
   Invoking FastLetter. 8
   Selecting a Type of Letter. 8
   Constructing Your Letter 8
   Providing Common Cover Letter Data. 9
   Naming Your Cover Letter 9
   Selecting Contacts for Your Letter 9
   Making Final Edits 10
   Saving Your Work 10
   Exiting from FastLetter. 10
   Accessing Your Cover Letters 10
      Accessing a Partially-Created Cover Letter. 10
3. Using the Word Processor 11
   Getting Online Help 11
   Saving Your Work 11
      Exporting Your Document to Another Word Processor 11
   Managing Your Files 12
4. Tutorial. 13
   Cover Letter Tutorial 13
Appendix 14
   Increasing Performance. 14
   Troubleshooting 15
Software Licensing Agreement 16

INTRODUCTION

WELCOME TO ADAMS FASTLETTER!

Congratulations! You've made a great choice in purchasing Adams FastLetter. It is one of the most comprehensive job-search tools on the market today.

DOCUMENTATION STRUCTURE

This manual covers the following topics:

Setup and Program Requirements

This chapter walks you through the setup procedure that installs Adams FastLetter onto your computer. It also lists program requirements and tells you how to start Adams FastLetter.

Creating Cover Letters

This chapter presents a step-by-step approach to creating cover letters with FastLetter. You simply walk through a series of screens and dialog boxes that prompt you to choose various options, such as letter type and content, and provide information, such as personal work history and contact information, to create your cover letter.

Using the Word Processor

Adams FastLetter has a built-in word processor that you can use to create all kinds of documents. This chapter describes how to access the word processor online help system and how to save and manage your files.

Tutorial

Adams FastLetter includes a colorful slide show to assist you in creating cover letters that make an impact. This chapter describes how to use the tutorial.

CHOOSING STRATEGIES

In this competitive job market, your cover letter is more than likely the first contact you will have with a potential employer. If it is well written, your letter will lead the reader to the other part of your application—your resume. If your letter is poorly written, the employer may not even take the time to review your resume, and your application has a good chance of ending up in the "circular file." Therefore, choosing a strategy for writing your cover letters and resume is essential.

Tutorial

Adams FastLetter provides a tutorial that covers critical information on the role of cover letters in seeking employment.

Advisor

Adams FastLetter also provides extensive information on various topics, including the following:

▲   Marketing your skills

▲   What employers look for in a cover letter

▲   Choosing cover letters that best suit your particular needs

ACCESSING THE ONLINE HELP SYSTEM

Adams FastLetter comes with a complete online help system that includes step-by-step instructions that you can follow as you work and get information on every available command.

You can access online help in several ways:

▲   **Help Menu**

To display the Contents menu for either the main window or the word processor, choose Contents. To get help on a specific topic in the help system, choose Search. To get help on using help, choose How to Use Help from the Help menu within the help system.

▲   **Advisor Button**

Click on the Advisor button to access valuable information on topics related to the task you are performing at any given point. The Advisor also gives you extensive information on all essential aspects of cover letters.

▲   **F1 Key**

To get help on a command within a menu, press F1 while the command is highlighted. To display the Contents menu, press F1 anywhere on the screen.

CONVENTIONS

This documentation uses the following conventions:

This	Represents
ALL CAPITALS	Indicates filenames, directory names, keyboard keys, and acronyms. For example, Change the AUTOEXEC.BAT file.
bold	Indicates text that you type directly into the computer. For example, Type **A:SETUP** in the Run dialog box.
[ ]	Indicates the type of text you must supply. For example, Type in [contact person].
Shortcut keys	Keys can be used in combination or sequences as shortcut keys. For example, SHIFT/TAB means to hold down the SHIFT key while pressing TAB.
underline	Indicates menus on the menu bar. For example, Use the Help menu.
>	Indicates a submenu choice or a series of choices. For example, Choose Cover Letters > Letter Samples.

How to Contact Adams Media Corporation

You can contact Adams Media Corporation in several different ways, as follows:

Mailing Address:
Adams Media Corporation
260 Center Street
Holbrook, MA 02343 USA

Main Number:
617-767-8100

Technical Support:
617-767-4128

Fax:
617-767-2055

Email:
For technical support: Internet (support@adamsonline.com);
America Online (AM supp); or CompuServe (102132,1646)

Before Calling Technical Support

We understand that there will be times when you might encounter some problems in running Adams FastLetter. Before contacting us, take a few minutes to review the following to see if you can solve the problem yourself:

▲ Make sure that your system complies with the requirements outlined in the System Requirements section of this manual.

▲ Make sure that your computer functions properly without Adams FastLetter.

▲ Review the troubleshooting section in the manual first, as well as any tips in the Technical Support folder on Adams JobBank Online.

If these steps do not provide you with a satisfactory solution, contact Adams New Media Technical Support.

Technical Support Hours: Monday through Friday, between
9 A.M. and 6 P.M., Eastern Standard Time.

Before you call, make sure you have your computer turned on and Adams FastLetter loaded and up on the screen. When you reach an Adams New Media Technical Support Specialist, be sure to give the specialist the following information:

▲ The version of Adams FastLetter

▲ The type of PC you are using (386, 486, Pentium)

▲ The version of Windows and DOS you are using

1 SETUP AND PROGRAM REQUIREMENTS

This chapter explains how to run Setup to install Adams FastLetter on your hard disk. It also provides information on system requirements and how to start up Adams FastLetter.

SYSTEM REQUIREMENTS

Adams FastLetter requires the following:

Computer

▲   386 PC-compatible computer (486 recommended)

▲   256 color VGA monitor, SVGA recommended

▲   Mouse

Resources

▲   2 MB RAM, 4 MB recommended

▲   2.8 MB of free hard disk space

Operating System

▲   MS-DOS® 3.1 or higher

▲   Windows® 95, Windows® 3.1, or Windows for Workgroups® 3.11

INSTALLING ADAMS FASTLETTER

The setup procedure installs all components of Adams FastLetter onto your computer hard disk.

To start the setup procedure, do the following:

1.   Insert the Adams FastLetter diskette into a floppy drive.

2.   From the Windows Program Manager, choose Run from the <u>F</u>ile menu.

3.   Type **A:SETUP** in the Run dialog box. If you are using the B drive, substitute **B:** for **A:**.

4.   The Adams FastLetter setup procedure begins by notifying you that this program will install the software onto your computer. Click on OK.

5.   Select the drive on your computer where you want Adams FastLetter installed. The default drive is C:. Click on OK. Setup displays the following screen:

6. Select the main subdirectory path where you want Adams FastLetter to be installed. The default is \FCOVER. Click on OK.

7. Setup will continue by copying all appropriate files from the installation diskette.

8. Setup gives you the option of viewing the README file after the installation. Select Yes if you want to view the file at this time. Select No if you do not want to view it at this time. Click on OK.

9. Adams FastLetter has successfully been installed on your system. Click on OK to continue.

If you selected Yes to view the README file, that file will appear in Windows Help. If not, you will see the Adams New Media group displayed on your computer.

Starting Adams Fastletter

To start Adams FastLetter, do the following:

1. Open the Adams New Media group in the Windows Program Manager.

2. Double click on the Adams FastLetter icon.

Computer Setup

Adams FastLetter works best with the color monitor set to 256 colors or higher. Monitors set at sixteen colors will function, but they will not display the full range of colors.

2 CREATING A COVER LETTER

When writing your cover letter, think of it as a marketing took, much like a television or radio commercial. Too many commercials are a fast-talking, mind-numbing blur of seemingly useless information. Effective commercials catch your attention by high-lighting only the most attractive features of a product.

This chapter is designed to get you started on using FastLetter to create your own cover letter "commercial" in which you highlight your most attractive features as a potential employee. Invoke Adams FastLetter and follow along!

INVOKING FASTLETTER

To display a series of dialog boxes to help you create a cover letter, do the following:

1. Click on the FastLetter button or choose the FastLetter command from the Techniques menu.

SELECTING A TYPE OF LETTER

The FastLetter screen appears where you can select many different types of cover let-ters. When you click on a letter type, valuable information about that letter type is dis-played in the dialog box to help you choose the appropriate cover letter type.

1. Click on the type of letter you want to create.

2. Click on Next to start to construct your letter.

CONSTRUCTING YOUR LETTER

The following screen shows the Response to a Classified Advertisement dialog box.

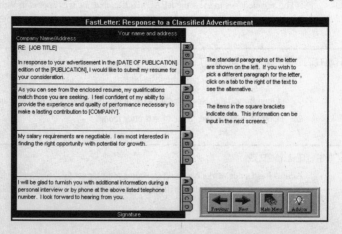

The standard paragraphs of the letter appear separated by lines. Each paragraph has four tabs to the right that allow you to change paragraphs.

1. Click on each tab to select the appropriate paragraph.

2. Continue this process for each paragraph until you finish constructing your letter.

PROVIDING COMMON COVER LETTER DATA

You will notice that some paragraphs contain items in square brackets. These items indicate areas where data will automatically be added to your letter. When you finish constructing your letter, the Letter Data screen appears where you provide the information for these items.

1. Click on Next to display the Letter Data screen as follows:

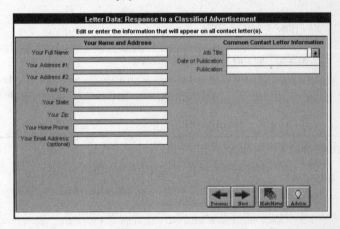

2. Type in the appropriate information into the fields provided in the screen.

3. Click on Next. This displays the Cover Letter Name dialog box.

NAMING YOUR COVER LETTER

While in the Cover Letter Name dialog box, do the following:

1. Click on OK to use the name provided (for example, Cover001) or type in another name for your cover letter.

2. Click on OK.

SELECTING CONTACTS FOR YOUR LETTER

While in the Contact Data screen, do the following:

1. To enter contact data, type in a new contact person in the Contact #1 fields. To enter a second contact, click on Contact #2, and enter the information in the corresponding fields.

2. Click on Next to finish creating your cover letter.

Making Final Edits

Your completed letter appears in the word processor for you to review and edit as necessary.

Saving Your Work

Once you are satisfied with your work, choose Save from the word processor File menu to save your cover letter. Adams FastLetter automatically saves cover letters in the \COVER subdirectory

If you want to change the name of your cover letter or save the file in another directory, choose Save As.

Exiting from FastLetter

When you have completed your work and saved your cover letter, and you want to return to the main window, click on Main Menu.

If you click on Main Menu before saving changes to your document, Adams FastLetter displays a dialog box that asks you if you want to save your changes before exiting. Click on Yes.

Accessing Your Cover Letters

To access your completed cover letters, do the following:

1.   Choose Open Cover Letter from the File menu in the Main window. This displays the Open File dialog box.

2.   Click on the cover letter you want from the Files list, or type in the cover letter name in the File name box.

3.   Click on OK.

If you chose a different subdirectory in which to save your cover letter, you must select that directory in the Directories list before specifying the cover letter name.

Accessing a Partially-Created Cover Letter

If for any reason you exited out of FastLetter before completing your cover letter, you must invoke FastLetter to retrieve your work. Note: This only applies to the last cover letter you started.

To finish creating your cover letter, do the following:

1.   Click on FastLetter or choose FastLetter from the Techniques menu. This displays a dialog box asking you if you want to continue on a cover letter that you worked on previously.

2.   Click on Yes. FastLetter takes you to the point where you previously exited out of FastLetter.

3.   Continue the process of creating your cover letter.

3 USING THE WORD PROCESSOR

The Adams word processor provides robust editing features so that you can create all types of documents.

When you use FastLetter to create your cover letters, they are placed in the word processor so that you can review and make final edits to them as needed.

You can also invoke the word processor directly to create any document you want by choosing the Adams Word Processor command on the File menu.

GETTING ONLINE HELP

The word processor also provides extensive online help that you can access in several different ways.

▲ To get help on any menu item, select the menu item and press F1.

▲ To access the help contents, press F1 anywhere in the word processor or choose Contents from the Help menu.

▲ To search through the help contents to find the topics you want, click on Search while in the Contents topic or choose Search from the Help menu.

You can also click on Advisor to get help on topics related to the tasks you are performing at any given point.

SAVING YOUR WORK

Once you are satisfied with your document, choose Save from the File menu to save your document. Choose Save As if you want to change the name of your file or save the file in another subdirectory.

Exporting Your Document to Another Word Processor

If you want to use your document in another type of word processor, you must save your document in Rich Text Format (RTF). Once you open the document in the other word processor, you can save the document in any format you want.

To save your document in RTF, do the following:

1. Choose the Export to Word Processor command from the File menu.

2. In the File Export dialog box, specify the name of the file you want to export.

3. Select the subdirectory where you want your document saved. You can specify your word-processor subdirectory or any other subdirectory as necessary.

4. Click on Export.

Managing Your Files

When you create cover letters, your files are automatically saved in various Adams FastLetter subdirectories.

For example, if you accepted \FLETTER as the default directory when you installed the product, the subdirectories will be C:\FLETTER\COVER.

All cover letters you create using FastLetter are saved in the \COVER subdirectory.

You can store your files in any subdirectory you want. To override the default, use Save As to specify to which directory you want your file saved.

4 TUTORIAL

Adams FastLetter provides a ten-minute slide show covering important facts about the power of well-written cover letters. To start the tutorial, do the following:

1. Click on Cover Letter Tutorial to begin the slide show.

2. Click on the Previous and Next buttons to move through the tutorial.

3. Click on Exit at any time to leave the tutorial.

COVER LETTER TUTORIAL

The cover letter tutorial contains crucial information on the following topics:

▲   General tips

▲   Paragraph construction

▲   Questions to ask yourself before you begin writing

▲   Writing your cover letter

▲   Formatting your cover letter

▲   Using paper and envelopes

▲   Choosing a printer

▲   Editing tips

APPENDIX

INCREASING PERFORMANCE

Some commonly asked questions about improving system performance are answered below. Note that the instructions for Windows 95 are often different than those for Windows for Workgroups 3.11 and Windows 3.1.

Question: Is there anything I can do to improve performance so it runs faster?

Answer: Here are a few suggestions you can try to improve the speed and performance.

▲ Always keep a certain amount of hard disk space free. Always having 10 to 15 MB free will help the program move files back and forth between RAM (memory) and your hard drive. Do the following to make your computer's hard drive work best with memory.

Windows 95 — Choose Programs > Accessories > System Tools > Scandisk to check out your hard disk. Use Standard to do a basic check or Thorough to do a complete surface scan. Then use Programs > Accessories > System Tools > Disk Defragmenter to optimize your hard drive. **Note: Do not run Scandisk from DOS when running Windows 95.**

Windows for Workgroups or Windows 3.1 — Exit Windows, and at the DOS prompt, type "Scandisk." After Scandisk has checked and fixed your hard drive, return to the DOS prompt and type "Defrag." If your drive is badly fragmented, choose "fully optimize." If your computer needs minor defragmentation, select "optimize" to do the job. Use the Defrag utility to defragment and optimize your hard drive.

Note: We strongly recommend that you back up your hard drive before proceeding with Defrag.

▲ Make sure your computer's memory settings are set as follows.

Windows 95 — Choose Settings > Control Panel > System > Performance > Virtual Memory to select "Let Windows manage my virtual memory settings." Then choose Settings > Control Panel > Performance > File System > Hard Disk to set "Read Ahead Optimization" to "full."

Windows for Workgroups and Windows 3.1 — Make sure that 32 bit file and Disk access are enabled. To do this, choose Main > Control Panel > Enhanced. Click on the "Virtual Memory" button. Click on the "change" button, and check off the boxes next to "Use 32 bit Disk Access" and "Use 32 bit File Access." Next, choose a "permanent swap file setting" of at least 5 MB. Click "OK," and restart Windows for changes to take effect.

Important: Be sure to save any vital work before restarting Windows.

▲ Add more RAM (memory). You will notice improved performance, especially if your computer has 2 to 4 MB of RAM.

Here is a list of troubleshooting questions and answers to help you solve possible problems.

Question: How do I improve the graphics so that the screen image does not look grainy or fuzzy?

Answer: The program works best with the color monitor set to 256 colors or higher. Monitors set at 16 colors will function, but they will not display the full range of colors. Note that newer, more advanced computers and monitors may have their own icon in Program Manager where you can make the change. Otherwise, change the number of colors thus:

Windows 95 — Choose Settings > Control Panel > Display

Windows for Workgroups and Windows 3.1 — Choose Main > Control Panel > Drivers

Question: The fonts look wrong on the screen and on the printer. How do I fix them?

Answer: TrueType fonts must be activated to get the best results in screen and printed output. Activate the fonts from the Program Manager by choosing Main > Control Panel > Fonts. If you have other font managers installed on your computer, be sure to turn them off.

Software Licensing Agreement

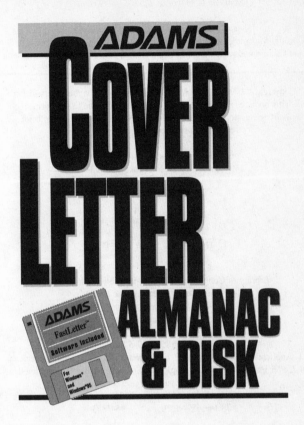

ADAMS
COVER
LETTER
ALMANAC
& DISK

ADAMS FastLetter™ Software Included

For Windows® and Windows®95

ADAMS MEDIA CORPORATION
Holbrook, Massachusetts

Credits
Robert L. Adams, *Senior Editor*
Laura Morin, *Managing Editor*
Robert Galligan, *Editorial Assistant*
Christina M. Hodge, *Editorial Assistant*
Maureen E. O'Toole, *Editorial Assistant*

Special thanks to the following contributors:
Dorothy Malcolm, *Career Pro*, Copley Square, Boston, Massachusetts
Deborah Shapiro, *Parnell Personnel Consultants, Inc.*, Newton, Massachusetts

---

Published by Adams Media Corporation
260 Center Street, Holbrook, MA 02343

ISBN: 1-55850-619-5

Printed in Canada

J I H G F E D C B

Library of Congress Cataloging-in-Publication Data
The Adams cover letter almanac & disk.
p.   cm.
Includes Adams FastLetter user's manual.
Includes index.
ISBN 1-55850-619-5 (pb)
1. Applications for positions. 2. Cover letters. 3. Adams FastLetter.
4. Cover letters—Computer programs. I. Adams Media Corporation.
II. Title: Adams FastLetter user's manual.
HF5383.A263   1996
808'.06665—dc20   96-7853
CIP

This publication is designed to provide accurate and authoritative information with regard to the subject matter covered. It is sold with the understanding that the publisher is not engaged in rendering legal, accounting, or other professional advice. If legal advice or other expert assistance is required, the services of a competent professional person should be sought.

— From a *Declaration of Principles* jointly adopted by a Committee of the American Bar Association and a Committee of Publishers and Associations

Product or brand names used in this book may be trademarks or registered trademarks. For readability, they may appear in initial capitalization or have been capitalized in the style used by the name claimant. Any use of these names is editorial and does not convey endorsement of or other affiliation with the name claimant. The publisher does not intend to express any judgment as to the validity or legal status of any such proprietary claims.

This book is available at quantity discounts for bulk purchases.
For information, call 1-800-872-5627 (in Massachusetts, call 617-767-8100) .

Visit our home page at http://www.adamsmedia.com

Table of Contents

How to Use This Book 21

Part I
All about Cover Letters

Chapter 1
Introduction to Cover Letters 25

Chapter 2
The Anatomy of a Cover Letter 29

Chapter 3
A Question of Style 35

Chapter 4
Twenty Cover Letter Blunders to Avoid 41

Part II
All about Job Hunting

Chapter 5
Planning Your Job-Search Campaign 51

Chapter 6
The Best and Worst Ways to Find Jobs 57

Chapter 7
Contacting Companies Directly 63

Chapter 8
Networking Your Way to a Job 71

Part III
Sample Cover Letters

Chapter 9
    Cover Letters for Special Situations **79**
    50-Plus Job Candidate (Product Manager) 80
    All Employment at One Company (Inventory Control Manager) . 81
    All Employment at One Company (Materials Manager) 82
    Application for In-House Position (District Supervisor) 83
    At-Home Parent Reentering the Work Force (Graphic Designer) . 84
    At-Home Parent Reentering the Work Force (Salesperson)...... 85
    Career Changer (Advertising Assistant) 86
    Career Changer (Business Consultant) 87
    Career Changer (Casino Dealer) 88
    Career Changer (Computer Programmer) 89
    Career Changer (Credit Analyst)........................... 90
    Career Changer (Marketing Executive) 91
    Career Changer (Nurse) 92
    Career Changer (Product and Services Developer)............. 93
    Career Changer (Real Estate Developer) 94
    Career Changer (Sales Representative)...................... 95
    Displaced Homemaker (Administrator) 96
    Fired/Laid Off (Recruiter)................................. 97
    Fired/Laid Off (Sales Director)............................. 98
    Former Small Business Owner (Environmental Advocate) 99
    Freelancer (Production Assistant)......................... 100
    Freelancer (Writer) 101
    Frequent Job Changer (Marketing Assistant) 102
    Gaps in Employment History (Assistant Curator) 103
    Gaps in Employment History (Editor) 104
    Immigrant (Accountant) 105
    Military Background (Electronics Supervisor) 106
    Military Background (Transportation Operator)............... 107
    No Clear Career Path (Account Manager) 108
    Overseas Employment History (Marketing Assistant) 109
    Part-Time Employment History (Art Instructor) 110
    Part-Time Employment History (Store Manager).............. 111
    Physically Challenged (Meeting Planner).................... 112
    Physically Challenged (Telemarketer) 113
    Recent Graduate (Airline Caterer) 114
    Recent Graduate (Assistant Museum Director) 115
    Recent Graduate (English Teacher) 116
    Recent Graduate (Environmental Campaigner) 117
    Recent Graduate (Forester)............................... 118
    Recent Graduate (Gerontologist) 119
    Recent Graduate (Legal Assistant) 120

Recent Graduate (Physicist) 121
Recent Graduate (Set Designer) 122
Recent Graduate (Translator) 123
Retiree Reentering the Work Force (Math Instructor) 124
Temporary Employment History (Administrative Assistant).... 125
Temporary Employment History (Publisher's Assistant)....... 126
Weak Educational Background (Parking Supervisor) 127
Weak Employment Background (Finance Broker)............ 128
Weak Employment Background (Sales Manager) 129

Chapter 10
Response to a Classified Advertisement **131**
Administrative Assistant 132
Administrative Judge.................................... 133
Analyst 134
Assistant Curator...................................... 135
Assistant Editor....................................... 136
Assistant Hospital Supervisor 137
Associate Desktop Publisher............................. 138
Athletic Director 139
Business Consultant 140
Campus Police Officer 142
Canine Science Instructor 143
Case Manager 144
Chief Financial Officer 145
Child Care Director.................................... 146
Claims Adjuster....................................... 147
Clinical Research Nurse 148
Conference Coordinator 149
Contracted Typist 150
Cosmetologist 151
Customer Service Representative 152
Dental Hygienist 153
Dentistry Department Manager.......................... 154
Director of Public Works 155
Editorial Assistant..................................... 156
Events Planner.. 157
Features Reporter 158
Field Finance Manager 159
Film Archivist 160
Fundraiser 161
Gemologist 162
Home Economist/Coordinator........................... 163
Hospital Administrator 164
Hotel Manager.. 165
International Buyer 166

Legal Assistant 167
Librarian 168
Loan Officer 169
Masonry Supply Manager............................... 171
Meeting Planner 172
Multimedia Specialist 173
Newspaper Intern 175
Occupational Health Manager........................... 176
Office Receptionist 177
Park Maintenance Supervisor 178
Photographer/Writer 179
Political Staffer 180
Preschool Director...................................... 181
Product Developer....................................... 182
Production Assistant 183
Production Controller 184
Program Coordinator.................................... 185
Project Manager 186
Public Relations Associate 187
Publicist... 188
Publisher's Assistant................................... 189
Purchasing Agent 190
Real Estate Sales Associate............................. 191
Regional Manager...................................... 192
Researcher.. 193
Restaurant Manager Trainee............................ 194
Sales Representative 195
Senior HVAC Technician 196
Site Location Supervisor................................ 197
Social Worker 198
State Administrator..................................... 199
Store Manager... 200
Systems Trainer.. 201
Technical Writer 202
Telemarketer 203
Television Camera Operator 204
Translator 205
Travel Agent 206
Writing Instructor 207
Yacht Salesperson...................................... 208
Youth Center Director.................................. 209

Chapter 11

Response to a "Blind" Advertisement.................... **211**
Administrator: Parks and Recreation Department 212
Applications Programmer 213

Assistant Personnel Officer............................214
Business Consultant 215
Case Manager 216
Catering Manager 217
Chief Executive Officer 218
Editorial/Computer Production Manager 219
Executive Sous Chef................................220
Field Finance Manager 221
Labor Relations Specialist.............................222
Legal Associate.....................................223
Librarian 224
Major Account Manager..............................225
Manufacturing Test Technician 226
Marketing Analyst...................................227
Medical Assistant 228
Nurse's Aide 229
Operations Manager 230
Optical Manufacturer 231
Payroll Supervisor...................................232
Pharmaceutical Administrator.........................233
Production/Materials Control Manager...................234
Sales Manager......................................235
Staff Photographer...................................236
Teacher 237
Technical Sales Associate.............................238
Typist..239
Underwriter..240
Writer/Researcher 241

Chapter 12
"Cold" Letter to a Potential Employer..................243
Accountant 244
Accounts Receivable Clerk............................245
Administrative Assistant..............................246
Administrative Director...............................247
Advertising Executive................................248
Advertising Sales Associate 249
Alumni Relations Coordinator 250
Architectural Engineer 251
Art Director..252
Arts Administrator...................................253
Associate Editor 254
Audio-Visual Specialist...............................255
Automated Systems Specialist 256
Aviation Specialist 257
Banking/Finance Professional..........................258

Business Consultant 259
Buyer... 260
Campaign Manager..................................... 261
Chef.. 262
Civil Engineer 263
Clinical Psychologist.................................. 264
Clinical Researcher 265
Clinical Service Administrator 266
Communications Consultant............................. 267
Computer Applications Programmer 268
Computer Programmer 269
Computer Software Designer 270
Consulting/Management Specialist....................... 271
Controller 272
Country Club Manager 273
Editorial Assistant..................................... 274
Electrician 275
Electromechanical Drafter............................... 276
Elementary School Teacher 277
Engineer 278
Engineering Instructor.................................. 279
Esthetician.. 280
Executive Secretary.................................... 281
Facilities Specialist 282
Field Coordinator 283
Financial Associate 284
Financial Consultant 285
Financial Planner...................................... 286
Flight Attendant....................................... 287
Foreperson/Ironworker 288
Fundraiser 289
Graphic Artist 290
Head Nurse 291
Health Services Coordinator 292
Human Resources Professional........................... 293
Human Services Coordinator 294
Insurance Salesperson.................................. 295
Interior Designer 296
International Sales Associate 297
Jewelry Designer....................................... 298
Jewelry Sales/Buyer 299
Landscape Designer 300
Lawyer.. 301
Legal Assistant 302
Legal Associate.. 303
Librarian 304

Manufacturer...305
Marketing Director 306
Marketing/Development Executive......................307
Marketing Intern 308
Massage Therapist....................................309
Mechanical Engineer..................................310
Multimedia Manager...................................311
Mutual Funds Broker 312
Nurse..313
Nurse: Anesthesia 314
Office Manager 315
Operations Executive 316
Operations Manager 317
Pharmacy Director....................................318
Plant Manager 319
Printer 320
Production Manager 321
Project Manager 322
Property Manager 323
Public Relations Assistant...........................324
Quality Control Specialist...........................325
Real Estate Banker 326
Repair Technician 327
Research Assistant...................................328
Retail Sales Manager.................................329
Retail Salesperson...................................330
Sales Executive 331
School Administrator: Secondary Level................332
Security Specialist..................................333
Social Worker: Counseling............................334
Social Worker: Geriatrics 335
Social Worker: Medical 336
Telemarketer 337
Television Production Assistant 338
Textile Specialist...................................339
Underwriter..340
Upper-Level Manager: Accounting 341
Veterinarian...342
Visual Media Production Assistant....................343

Chapter 13
Letter to an Employment Agency 345
Accounting Manager...................................346
Administrative Assistant 347
Advertising/Graphic Design Assistant 348
Bookkeeper 349

Chemist 350
Claims Processor 351
Computer Operations Supervisor 352
Cook 353
Cosmetologist 354
Dental Assistant 355
Director of Operations 356
Director of Pharmacy 357
Executive Assistant 358
Hotel Administrator 359
Housekeeper 360
Insurance Account Manager 361
Insurance Underwriter 362
Legal Administrator 363
Medical Assistant 364
Office Manager 365
Operations Manager 366
Property Manager 367
Purchasing Agent 368
Quality Control Specialist 369
Retail Manager 370
Sales/Customer Service Representative 371
Secretary 372
Security Guard 373
Stenographer 374
Wait Person 375

Chapter 14

Letter to an Executive Search Firm 377
Buyer 378
Chief Executive Officer 379
Commercial Transportation Specialist 380
Corporate President 381
Director of Administration 382
Director of Information Services 383
Engineering Administrator 384
Executive Administrator 385
Financial Administrator 386
Labor Relations Specialist 387
Lawyer: International Law 388
Management Consultant 389
Operations Manager 390
Plant Manager 391
President/CEO 392
Senior Accountant 393
Senior Business Analyst 395

Vice-President of Banking 396
Vice-President of Nursing. 397
Vice-President of Sales 398

Chapter 15
Networking Letter **399**
Administrative Assistant 400
Advertising Executive 401
Advisor 402
Architectural Designer 403
Assistant Hospital Administrator 404
Auto Salesperson. 405
Bank Manager 406
Beverage Manager. 407
Broadcast Manager 408
Business Consultant 409
Business Manager 410
Chief Financial Officer 411
Commercial Real Estate Sales Executive 412
Community Relations Specialist. 413
Construction Engineer. 414
Construction Manager. 415
Consultant 416
Corporate Treasurer. 417
Credit Officer 418
Customer Support Representative. 419
Director of College Development 420
Director of Information Services. 421
Driver 422
Editor. 423
Electrical Engineer 424
Elementary Teacher. 425
Environmental Services Director 426
Executive Nonprofit Director 427
Field Service Manager 428
Finance Assistant. 429
Finance Executive 430
Finance Manager. 431
Genetic Research Technician 432
Golf Instructor. 433
Human Resources Manager 434
Insurance Manager 435
International Controller. 436
International Marketing Specialist 437
Inventory Control Supervisor 438
Legal Assistant 439

Leisure Trainer 440
Maintenance Supervisor 441
Marketing Assistant. 442
Marketing Specialist 443
Medical Sales Representative 444
Microwave Technician 445
Mortgage/Loan Officer 446
Nurse 447
Paralegal 448
Payroll Supervisor 449
Power Systems Designer 450
Production Manager 451
Program Coordinator. 452
Project Manager 453
Promotions Representative 454
Property Manager 455
Publicist 456
Publishing Intern 457
Quality Control Engineer 458
Record Manager 459
Research Assistant. 460
Restaurant Manager. 461
Retail Sales Manager. 462
Sales Director 463
Sanitarian. 464
Secretary 465
Special Agent 466
Staff Accountant 467
Teacher: Secondary Level. 468
Telecommunications Specialist. 469
Telemarketer 470
Transportation Coordinator. 471
Victim Witness Advocate 472
Writer/Reporter 473
X-Ray Technician 474

Chapter 16

Broadcast Letter 475
Account Executive 476
Account Manager 477
Chiropractor 478
Corporate Salesperson. 479
Credit Manager 480
Entrepreneur 481
Fashion Designer. 482
Financial Consultant 483

Fleet and Transportation Manager 484
Freight Supervisor...................................... 485
Legal Associate.. 486
Marketing/Sales Executive 487
Multimedia Specialist 488
Program Manager 489
Real Estate Executive 490
Senior Vice-President 491
Senior-Level MIS Operator.............................. 492
Vice-President of Administration 493
Warehouse Operator 494
Zoologist 495

Chapter 17
Resume Letter **497**
Business Manager 498
Cardiologist... 500
Community Center Director 501
Construction Manager.................................. 503
Director of Information Services......................... 505
District Manager 506
Hospital Administrator 507
Manufacturing Manager 508
Real Estate Director 510
Vice-President, Sales and Marketing 512

Chapter 18
Follow-Up Letter (After Telephone Conversation) **515**
Acquisitions Manager 516
Arbitrator... 517
Assistant Engineer..................................... 518
Assistant Portfolio Manager 519
Associate Editor 520
COBOL Programmer 521
Concierge 522
Department Manager................................... 523
Executive Marketing Director........................... 524
Export Manager....................................... 525
Flight Attendant....................................... 526
Head Coach... 527
Laboratory Technician 528
Magazine Publishing Intern 529
Mailroom Supervisor................................... 530
Manager of Patient Services 531
Nanny 532
Precision Inspector 533

Principal 534
Production Assistant 535
Protection Professional 536
Psychiatric Nurse...................................... 537
Purchasing Agent 538
Regional Sales/Product Trainer......................... 539
Teacher 540

Chapter 19

Follow-Up Letter (After Job Interview) **541**
Administrative Assistant 542
Assistant Editor....................................... 543
Bank Manager... 544
Business Manager 545
Computer Operator 546
Conference Coordinator 547
Distribution Coordinator.............................. 548
District Sales Supervisor.............................. 549
Doctor 550
Editorial Assistant 551
Engineering Consultant................................ 552
Executive Assistant................................... 553
Export Manager....................................... 554
Finance Executive 555
Fundraiser 556
Hotel Manager.. 558
Human Resources Representative....................... 559
Inventory Control Analyst............................. 560
Legal Intern.. 561
Materials Manager.................................... 562
Personal Secretary.................................... 563
Personnel Manager 564
Product Design Engineer.............................. 565
Production Assistant 566
Public Records Analyst................................ 567
Publisher's Assistant.................................. 568
Real Estate Salesperson............................... 569
Recycling Manager 570
Restaurant Manager................................... 571
Retail Sales Associate 572
Sales Representative 573
Staff Accountant 574
Talent Agent 575
Teacher 576
Writer/Researcher 577

Chapter 20

Information Request **579**

Alumni Network 580

Annual Report 581

Career Planning Services 582

Company Catalog 583

Course Registration 584

Grants Listing 585

Industry Directory 586

Industry Newsletter 587

Membership Listing 588

Subscription Information 589

Chapter 21

Address/Phone Number Change **591**

Laboratory Assistant 592

Musician 593

Pet Groomer 594

Staff Nutritionist 595

Wholesale Buyer 596

Chapter 22

Thank You Letter (For Good Reference) **597**

Biomedical Researcher 598

Bookkeeper 599

Broker 600

Fashion Designer 601

Government Intern 602

Nurse 603

Retail Store Manager 604

Surgeon 605

Teacher 606

Technical Writer 607

Chapter 23

Thank You Letter (For Letter of Recommendation) **609**

Accountant 610

Art History Student 611

Chemical Engineer 612

Human Resources Representative 613

Restaurant Manager 614

Chapter 24

Thank You Letter (For Referral) **615**

Acquisitions Editor 616

Bank Manager 617

Computer Application Programmer 618
Fitness Instructor....................................... 619
Medical Assistant 620
Nurse... 621
Photographer.. 622
Publicist.. 623
Software Technician 624
Teacher 625

Chapter 25
Thank You Letter (After Informational Interview)......... **627**
Art Designer 628
Benefits Coordinator................................... 629
Child Psychologist..................................... 630
High School Administrator 631
Hotel Clerk 632
Marketing Assistant.................................... 633
Mechanical Engineer................................... 634
Meteorologist 635
Occupational Therapist 636
Social Worker 637

Chapter 26
Resurrection Letter.................................... **639**
Advertising Assistant 640
Assistant Regional Manager 641
Bank Administrator.................................... 643
Billings Clerk 644
Business Manager 645
Commercial Photographer.............................. 646
Computer Programmer 647
Correctional Officer 648
Field Engineer... 649
Foreign Language Teacher 650
Freelance Copy Editor................................. 651
Fundraising Coordinator 652
Jewelry Designer....................................... 653
Physical Therapist..................................... 654
Purchasing Agent 655
Radio Announcer....................................... 656
Sales Representative 657
Sanitation Inspector................................... 658
Shipping/Receiving Expediter........................... 659
Social Worker 660
Staff Accountant 661
Systems Analyst 662

Telemarketer 663
Translator 664
Typist. 665

Chapter 27
Response to Rejection **667**
Administrative Assistant 668
Architect 669
Assistant Editor 670
Counselor 671
Telemarketer 672

Chapter 28
Withdrawal from Consideration **673**
Coach. 674
Firefighter 675
Freelance Textbook Editor 676
Hair Stylist. 677
Legal Assistant 678
Nurse's Aide 679
Preschool Instructor. 680
Regional Sales Manager 681
Systems Analyst 682
Travel Agent 683

Chapter 29
Rejection of Offer **685**
Archivist 686
Assistant Art Director 687
Dental Hygienist 688
Editor. 689
Law Enforcement Officer 690
Marine Biologist 691
Paralegal 692
Production Assistant 693
Program Coordinator. 694
Publishing Intern 695
Researcher. 696
Sales Representative 697
Systems Representative. 698
Teacher 699
Veterinary Assistant 700

Chapter 30
Resignation Letter **701**
Architect 702

Environmental Consultant............................... 703
Forester 704
Hotel Manager....................................... 705
Marketing Director 706
Medical Technologist 707
Production Assistant 708
Speech Pathologist 709
Transaction Processing Supervisor....................... 710
Vice-President, Sales................................. 711

Chapter 31
Acceptance Letter 713
Accountant 714
Benefits Administrator 715
Contractor 716
Customer Service Representative 717
Editorial Assistant.................................... 718
Geographer 719
Group Leader.. 720
Statistician.. 721
Underwriter... 722

Chapter 32
Resumes and Cover Letters in the Electronic Age.......... 723

Index 729

How to Use This Book

The *Adams Cover Letter Almanac* is a comprehensive guide to crafting a job-winning cover letter. To get the most from this book, we recommend that you begin by looking over Part I: "All about Cover Letters." Here you will find everything you need to know about writing your cover letter, from piecing together an introduction to choosing the right format. Are you wondering how to personalize each letter? Should you mention personal preferences, like a salary range? Are there any common blunders you should avoid? Part I will answer all your cover letter questions, and more!

Part II: "All about Job Hunting" addresses more general job-search issues such as how to network effectively and how to determine the best companies to contact. If you're having trouble designing an effective strategy for finding employment in today's tough job market, look no further. Part II provides a step-by-step guide for job hunters.

Once you're ready to begin writing, we suggest you turn to Part III: "Sample Cover Letters." This section contains six hundred examples of cover letters used by real people to win real jobs. The letters address twenty-three types of situations including responses to classified advertisements, information requests, and thank you letters. Choose the chapters that are applicable to your special circumstances and start writing, using the samples as guidelines.

Remember, there is no one way to write a cover letter. The advantage of having so many different styles and formats is that you can pick and choose elements from numerous samples and custom-design each cover letter to fit your needs.

PART I
All about Cover Letters

1
Introduction to Cover Letters

Purpose of the Cover Letter

Your cover letter is more than likely the first contact you will have with a potential employer. If it is well written, your letter will lead the reader to the other part of your application—your resume. If your letter is poorly written, the employer may not even take the time to review your resume, and your application has a good chance of ending up in the trash.

Put yourself in the boss's shoes. If you were doing the hiring, what attributes would the ideal candidate for employment possess? You probably would prefer that the person has work experience similar to, or at least applicable to, the position he or she is applying for. You would want the candidate to be ambitious and anxious to contribute his or her energy and skills to the success of your company. The perfect candidate would demonstrate interest in, and knowledge about, your industry *and* your specific organization. (An applicant's prior knowledge of an industry or a particular company suggests that he or she has a compelling interest in the firm, and is not looking at the current opening as "just another job.") In short, if you were doing the hiring, you probably would want to hire an energetic, dedicated, and skilled candidate.

Your cover letter affords the opportunity for you to present yourself as the perfect candidate. You can begin by learning how to create an effective sales pitch.

The Sales Pitch

Imagine your cover letter as a marketing tool, much like a television or a radio commercial. Too many commercials are a fast-talking, mind-numbing blur of seemingly useless information. Effective commercials catch your attention by highlighting only the most attractive features of a product.

Your cover letter should be your commercial, in which you highlight your most attractive features as a potential employee. Remember, employers typically receive hundreds of applications for each job opening. No one is going to waste time reading through a long letter crammed with text. Be brief. You should avoid detailing your entire work history in your cover letter—save that information for your resume. The best way to distinguish yourself is to highlight one or two of your accomplishments or abilities that show you are an above-average candidate for the position. Stressing only one or two unique attributes increases your chances of being remembered by the recruiter and getting to the interview stage, where you can elaborate on the rest of your accomplishments.

In addition, the cover letter allows you to carefully select one or two accomplishments or special skills that reflect your suitability for the desired position. If you are applying for a job that doesn't fit directly into your experience, make sure you explain how your background and qualifications match the position's requirements. For example, imagine you are a bank accountant seeking an applications programmer position in a computer software developing company. Throughout your career, you have used computers on a daily basis, and even helped design the bookkeeping software your bank uses. A well-crafted cover letter would emphasize your relevant computer experience, and de-emphasize your accounting experience.

Personalize Each Letter

The success of your job-hunting campaign relies on the *quality* of your contacts and how well you maintain them, not on the *quantity* of applications you send out. Taking time to research each employer promises to be much more effective than sending out hundreds of form letters. In effect, you are saying to an employer, "This is where I want to work. I have done my research and I am confident of my decision." Also, the employer will view your interest as an indication that you are likely to stay with the company for a substantial period of time if hired. (For more information on researching a potential employer, see Chapter 7.)

First, try to determine the appropriate person to whom you should address your cover letter. In general, the more influential your contact is, the better. Try to contact the head of the department in which you are interested. This will be easiest in mid- and small-size companies where the head of the department is likely to have an active role in initial screening. If you are applying to a larger corporation, it is likely that your application will be screened by a human resources or personnel department. If you are instructed to direct your inquiry to this division, attempt to find out the name of the senior human resources manager. This way, you may be able to cut down on the amount of hands your resume passes through on its way to the final decision-maker. At any rate, be sure to include your contact's name and title on both your letter and the envelope. This will ensure that your letter will get through to the proper person, even if a new person occupies this position.

When to Send a Cover Letter

Every time you make contact with a potential employer, send a cover letter. Whether your resume is sent as an initial inquiry, or whether you are following up on a phone conversation, job interview, or position offering, write a carefully composed, polished letter. If you have recently contacted a hiring manager, sending another copy of your resume may not be necessary. In general, a resume does not have to accompany every cover letter you send, but a cover letter must be enclosed every time you send a resume. Even if you are following up on an advertisement that reads simply "send resume," be sure to include your letter. It is not professional to send out a resume without one.

2
The Anatomy of a Cover Letter

Before a potential employer reads a word of your cover letter, he or she has probably already made an assessment of your organizational skills and attention to detail simply by observing its appearance. How your correspondence looks to a reader—its format, letter quality, and the size, color, and quality of paper—can mean the difference between serious consideration and a negative response. You just can't afford to settle for a less than perfect presentation of your credentials. This chapter not only outlines the basic format you should follow when writing, but shows you how to put the finishing touches on a top-notch product.

Length of the Cover Letter
Four short paragraphs on one page is the ideal length for a cover letter. A longer letter is unlikely to be read.

Paper Size
Use standard 8½-by-11-inch paper for your cover letter. If you use a smaller size, the correspondence will appear more personal than professional; a larger size would simply look awkward. Also, paper other than the standard size is easily lost in an employer's files if too small or discarded for not fitting with other documents if too large.

Paper Color
Like your resume, white and ivory are the only acceptable paper colors for a cover letter.

Paper Quality
As with resumes, standard, inexpensive office paper (twenty-pound bond) is generally acceptable for most positions. Executive and top-level positions may require more expensive stationery papers, such as ivory laid.

Preprinted Stationery
Unless you're a top-level executive with years of experience, you should avoid using preprinted stationery. Also, never use the stationery of your current employer.

Typing and Printing

Your best bet is to use a word processor with letter-quality type or a word processing program on a computer with a letter-quality printer. If these options are not available to you, a high-quality office typewriter or a good, clean home typewriter is a satisfactory alternative for your cover letter. Handwritten letters are not acceptable.

The Envelope

Your cover letter should always be mailed in a standard, business-sized envelope. Unless your handwriting is *extremely* neat and easy to read, you should always type your envelopes. Also, address your envelope, by full name and title, specifically to the contact person you identified in your cover letter.

Ten Key Ingredients to Successful Cover Letters

Your cover letter may be printed on the highest quality paper and typed on a state-of-the-art computer, but if it isn't arranged according to the proper format, you probably won't come across as the best candidate for the position you are applying for. Certain basic guidelines should be followed when composing the actual contents of your letter.

1. **Return address.** Your return address and phone number should appear in the top right-hand corner, without your name. As a general rule, you should avoid abbreviations in the addresses of your cover letters, although abbreviating the state is increasingly common in all business correspondence.

2. **The date.** The date should appear two lines beneath your return address on the right hand side of the page. Write out the date; do not use the abbreviated format.

    Example: May 12, 1996

3. **The addressee.** Always try to find out the name and proper title of the addressee before you send out a cover letter. Two lines beneath the date, list the full name of the addressee. On the next line, list the individual's formal business title; on the subsequent line, list the name of the company. This is followed by the company's address, which generally takes two lines. Occasionally, the individual's full title or the company name and address will be very long, and can appear awkward on the usual number of lines allocated. In this case, you may prefer using an extra line.

4. **The salutation.** The salutation should be typed two lines beneath the company's address. It should begin with "Dear Mr." or "Dear Ms.," followed by the individual's last name and a colon. Even if you have previously spoken with an addressee who has asked to be called by his

or her first name, you should never use a first name in the salutation.

In some cases, such as when you are responding to "blind" advertisements, it may be necessary to adopt a general salutation. In such a circumstance, salutations such as "Dear Hiring Manager" or "Good Morning" may be stronger choices than "Dear Sir or Madam" or "To whom it may concern." In any case, avoid potentially offensive salutations like "Dear Gentlemen," or "Dear Sirs."

5. **First paragraph.** State immediately and concisely which position you wish to be considered for and what makes you the best candidate for that position. If you are responding to a classified ad, be sure to reference the name of the publication and the date the ad appeared. Keep the first paragraph short and hard-hitting.

   Example: Having majored in mathematics at Boston University, where I also worked as a Research Assistant, I am confident that I would make a very successful Research Trainee in your economics research department.

6. **Second paragraph.** Detail what you could contribute to this company, and show how your qualifications will benefit this firm. If you're responding to a classified ad, specifically discuss how your skills relate to the job's requirements. Remember, keep it brief!

   Example: In addition to my strong background in mathematics, I also offer significant business experience, having worked in a data processing firm, a bookstore, and a restaurant. I am sure that my courses in statistics and computer programming would prove particularly useful in the position of Trainee.

7. **Third paragraph.** Describe your interest in the corporation. Subtly emphasize your knowledge about this firm (the result of your research effort) and your familiarity with the industry. You should present yourself as eager to work for any company where you apply for a position.

   Example: I am attracted to City Bank by your recent rapid growth and the superior reputation of your economic research department. After studying different commercial banks, I have concluded that City Bank will be in a strong competitive position to benefit from upcoming changes in the industry, such as the phasing out of Regulation Q.

8. **Final paragraph.** In the closing paragraph, specifically request an interview. Include your phone number and the hours you can be reached, or mention that you will follow up with a phone call within several days to arrange an interview at a mutually convenient time.

   Example: I would like to interview with you at your earliest convenience. I am best reached between 3:00 and 5:00 P.M. at (617) 555-5555.

9. **The closing.** The closing should be two lines beneath the body of the letter and should be aligned with your return address and the date (toward the right of the page). Keep the closing simple—"Sincerely" suffices. Four lines underneath this, type in your full name as it appears on your resume.

   Sign above your typed name in black ink. Don't forget to sign the letter! As silly as it sounds, people often forget this seemingly obvious detail. An oversight such as this suggests that you don't take care with your work.

10. **The enclosure line.** If you are enclosing a resume or other materials with your letter, include an enclosure line, flush left, at the bottom of the letter.

    Example: Enc. resume

General Model for a Cover Letter

Your Address
Your Phone

Date

Contact Person Name
Title
Company
Address

Dear Mr./Ms._____:

Immediately explain why your background makes you the best candidate for the position you are applying for. Keep the first paragraph short and hard-hitting.

Detail what you could contribute to this company. Show how your qualifications will benefit this firm. Remember to keep this letter short; few employers will read a cover letter over one page.

Describe your interest in the corporation. Subtly emphasize your knowledge about this firm (the result of your research effort) and your familiarity with the industry. You should present yourself as eager to work for any company which you interview with.

In the closing paragraph, you should specifically request an interview. Include your phone number and the hours when you can be reached. Alternatively, you might prefer to mention that you will follow up with a phone call (to arrange an interview at a mutually convenient time within several days).

Sincerely,

Your full name
(typed)

Enc. resume

General Model for a Follow-Up Letter

Your Address
Your Phone

Date

Contact Person
Title
Company
Address

Dear Mr./Ms._____:

Remind the interviewer of the position for which you were interviewed, as well as the date. Thank him or her for the interview.

Confirm your interest in the opening and the organization. Use specifics to emphasize both that you have researched the firm in detail and considered how you would fit into the company and the position.

Like in your cover letter, emphasize one or two of your strongest qualifications and slant them toward the various points that the interviewer considered the most important for the position. Keep the letter brief; a half-page is plenty.

If appropriate, close with a suggestion for further action, such as a desire to have additional interviews. Mention your phone number and the hours you can best be reached. Alternatively, you may prefer to mention that you will follow up with a phone call in several days.

Sincerely,

Your full name
(typed)

Enc. resume

3
A Question of Style

 After you have chosen a career path, written your resume, and researched prospective employers, you are ready to begin composing your cover letter. Unlike a resume, a cover letter shouldn't just summarize your credentials. Your aim is to demonstrate why your skills and your background make you a perfect match for the specific position you seek. Choosing the best writing style will help your cover letter stand out from other job seekers in a positive way. This chapter covers everything you need to know before and after you begin writing.

What Writing Style Is Appropriate?

In general, your cover letter should adopt a polite, formal style that balances your confidence in yourself with a sense of respect for the potential employer. Keep the style clear, objective, and persuasive rather than narrative. In other words, don't waste precious space boasting personal information instead of presenting relevant qualifications. Consider these approaches from two marketing directors responding to the same classified advertisement:

Candidate A: "In 1988, I graduated from college, and moved to Boston because my sister lived there. When I couldn't find a job, I ended up back in graduate school in New York, where I stayed until 1990. Once graduated, I flew back to my favorite city, Boston, and have been successful in marketing ever since."

Candidate B: "In addition to a Bachelor of Arts degree in Business Administration, I recently received a Master's degree, cum laude, in International Marketing from Brown University. This educational experience is supported by two years' part-time experience with J&D Products, where my marketing efforts resulted in increased annual product sales of 25 percent."

Candidate A focuses on irrelevant information, and fails to relate his or her qualifications to the desired position. Candidate B, in turn, successfully highlights only pertinent data, including educational training and specific accomplishments. The result is a targeted and cohesive statement that will win the reader's attention.

Tone

Think of how you would sell your qualifications in a job interview. You probably would (or probably should) think harder about what to say and how to say it than you would during an informal conversation. Above all, you would want to sound polite, confident, and professional. Adopt a similar tone when you draft your cover letter. Your letter should immediately communicate your eagerness to join the firm and confidence in your abilities. The trick, however, is to sound enthusiastic without becoming melodramatic. Take, for example, the candidate who expressed his desire to enter the advertising field as "the single, most important thing I have ever wanted in my entire twenty-three years of existence." The candidate who was actually offered the position began her letter: "My extensive research into the industry, coupled with my internship and educational training, have confirmed my interest in pursuing an entry-level position in advertising."

Tone may vary somewhat according to profession: A comedian and a chemist probably would choose dissimilar tones. While it would be perfectly fitting for a comedian to adopt a light-hearted, familiar tone that highlighted his or her sense of humor, the chemist would be best served by a more formal voice. Remember, use your best judgment when establishing tone, and err on the side of caution. Place yourself in the employer's frame of mind: Is there the slightest chance that he or she might be turned off by your tone? If so, adopt a more moderate voice.

The tone of your letter may also vary depending on what stage your career is in. A recent college graduate might focus on his or her eagerness to enter the workplace, whereas a seasoned executive may choose to display a reserved confidence in his or her extensive experience.

State Your Purpose

To begin, don't make the employer guess your purpose for writing. Immediately explain the purpose of your letter, whether it is to request a company bulletin or to respond to an advertisement for an opening. Your reader will not have the time or desire to search for a delayed explication.

Bear in mind that your cover letter is an advertisement for yourself, not an affidavit. Do not feel compelled to describe every job you've ever had. If you are applying for an entry-level bank teller position, it is not advantageous to include detailed descriptions of your summers as camp counselor or lifeguard. More than likely, the hiring manager doesn't need to know the entire journey of your career; what matters is your pertinent experience.

Present Yourself as an Industry Insider

No matter what stage you are at in your career, you can sell yourself as an industry insider and a desirable employee. Indicate the industry knowledge you gathered during your preliminary research and cite some of the company's recent achievements or goings-on. Not only will you appear well prepared, but your letter will stand above those who have forgotten this crucial tip!

Emphasize Concrete Examples

Your resume details what duties you have performed in your jobs. In contrast, your cover letter should highlight your most significant accomplishments. Instead of stating something like, "My career is highlighted by several major achievements," use concrete examples:

- "While Sales Manager at Corpco, I supervised a team which increased revenues by 35 percent in eighteen months."

- "I published four articles in the *New England Journal of Medicine*."

- "At EarthFriends, I advanced from telephone fundraiser, to Field Manager, to Canvas Director within two years."

List tangible, relevant skills rather than personal attributes. A sentence such as "I am fluent in C+, Pascal, and COBOL programming languages" is a good substitute for a vague statement like "I am a goal-oriented, highly skilled Computer Programmer."

Use Powerful Language

Your language should be hard-hitting and easy to understand. Make your letters interesting by using action verbs such as "designed," "implemented," and "increased," rather than passive verbs like "was" and "did." Use simple, common language and avoid abbreviations and slang. Also steer clear of language that is too technical or jargon-heavy. Keep in mind that the first person who reads your cover letter may not possess the same breadth of knowledge as your future boss.

In the course of a job search, it is tempting to use catch phrases that you may have picked up from various job-search reference materials, phrases that sound as though they *should* go in a cover letter. Be assured that almost every person who applies for the position presents him- or herself as a "self-starter" with "excellent interpersonal skills." Improve upon these self-descriptions wherever possible by listing actual projects and goals. "I am a determined achiever with proven leadership skills" can be rephrased "While at MoneyWorks, I successfully increased the number of projects completed before deadline, while supervising a staff of fifteen." Once you begin working, employers will discover your personal attributes for themselves. While still under consideration for a position, concrete experiences are more valuable than vague phrases or obscure promises.

Action verbs make a cover letter come alive. Which are right for your cover letter?

accelerated	evaluated	prepared
accomplished	examined	presented
achieved	executed	prioritized
administered	expanded	processed
advised	expedited	produced
analyzed	extracted	programmed
appointed	facilitated	promoted
arranged	formulated	proposed
assisted	founded	provided
attained	generated	published
balanced	headed	recruited
budgeted	helped	regulated
built	identified	reorganized
calculated	illustrated	represented
catalogued	implemented	researched
chaired	improved	resolved
collaborated	increased	restored
compiled	initiated	restructured
composed	innovated	retrieved
computed	instructed	reviewed
conducted	integrated	revised
constructed	interpreted	scheduled
consulted	launched	shaped
created	maintained	sold
delegated	managed	solved
demonstrated	marketed	streamlined
designed	mediated	summarized
developed	monitored	supervised
devised	negotiated	taught
directed	operated	trained
edited	organized	upgraded
educated	performed	utilized
encouraged	persuaded	worked
established	planned	wrote

Vary Your Sentence Length

Initially, your cover letter will be scanned, not read. Short, concise sentences are much more effective than long-winded ones. Paragraphs should be no longer than three sentences. If necessary, you can break up the material into two or more paragraphs.

Including Personal Preferences

Candidates often worry if, and how, they should include their own working environment preferences, their availability to travel and/or relocate, and salary demands. The best bet is to mention work preferences only if you are confident they match the job description your potential employer offers. For instance, don't state that you work best independently in a formal office setting if you are applying for a position that requires group interaction and extensive travel. If you are applying to an out-of-state firm, indicate a willingness to relocate; otherwise, a hiring manager will question your purpose in writing and may not take the initiative to inquire.

Also, refrain from offering salary information unless the advertisement you are responding to requires it. If you must include salary requirements, give a salary range rather than a number. Another option is to simply indicate that salary concerns are negotiable.

Don't Forget to Proofread!

As with your resume, mistakes in cover letters can be embarrassing, particularly when something critical (such as your name) is misspelled. So proofread it as carefully as possible. Get a friend to help you—read your draft aloud as your friend checks the proof copy. Then have your friend read aloud while you check. Next, read it word by word, checking for spelling and punctuation.

If you wrote your cover letter on a word processing program, use that program's built-in spelling checker to double-check for spelling errors. Most quality word processors include this convenient feature; however, a spelling checker is not a substitute for proofreading your cover letter—it still must be proofread to ensure that there are no errors. (Bear in mind that a spelling checker cannot flag errors such as "to" for "two," or "bills" for "skills.")

4
Twenty Cover Letter Blunders to Avoid

 So far, we've seen what makes a successful cover letter. However, there are certain errors that promise to diminish your hard work. From typographical mishaps to erroneous employer information, *all* mistakes have a negative impact on the application process. Serious errors will land your application in the wastebasket. Be forewarned: Carefully read your cover letter at least twice.

The following list outlines some of the most common cover letter mistakes and, more importantly, suggests ways to correct them. These examples have been adapted from real-life cover letters gathered during the course of our research. Although some of these blunders may seem obvious, they occur far more often than you might think. Needless to say, none of the inquiries that included these mistakes met with positive results.

1. **Unrelated career goals:** Tailor your cover letter to the specific position applied for. A hiring manager is only interested in what you can do for the company, not what you hope to accomplish for yourself. Your letter should convey a genuine interest in the position and a long-term pledge to fulfilling its duties. Consider the difference between these two real-life examples:

   Example A (wrong way): "While my true goal is to become a Professional Dancer, I am exploring the option of taking on proofreading work while continuing to train for the Boston Ballet's next audition."

   Example B (right way): "I am very interested in this proofreading position, and I am confident of my ability to make a long-term contribution to your capable staff."

2. **Comparisons and clichés:** Avoid obvious comparisons and overused clichés; such expressions distract from your letter's purpose: to highlight your most impressive skills and accomplishments.

   Here are a few real-life blunders we encountered: "My word processor runs like the wind," "I am a people person," "Teamwork is my middle name," "Your company is known as the crème de la crème of accounting firms," "I am as smart as a whip," "Among the responses you receive for this position, I hope my qualifications make me leader of the pack." So, remember to adopt a formal, professional writing style.

3. **Wasted space:** Since cover letters are generally four paragraphs long, every word of every sentence should be directly related to your purpose for writing. In other words, if you are applying for a position as a chemist, include only those skills and experiences most applicable to that field. Any other information weakens your application. Some real-life blunders we've seen include:

Example: "As my enclosed resume reveals, I possess the technical experience and educational background to succeed as your newest Civil Engineer. In addition, I am a certified Gymnastics Instructor who has won several local competitions."

Example: "I am writing in response to your advertisement for an Accounting Clerk. Currently, I am finishing an associate degree at Fisher Junior College. My courses have included Medieval Architecture, Film Theory, American History before 1900, and Nutrition."

4. **Form letters:** Mass mailings, in which you send a general form letter to a large number of employers, are not recommended. This approach does not allow you to personalize each application. Every cover letter that you write should be tailored to the position you are seeking and demonstrate both your commitment to a specific industry and familiarity with each particular employer. Mass mailings may indicate to a hiring manager that you are not truly interested in joining his or her organization.

There are certain formats and phrases that signal to an employer that you are using a form letter. In one real-life mass mailing mishap, the candidate created a form letter with blank spaces where he penned in the employer's name and position applied for. Another applicant who was indecisive about her field of interest created a list of possible positions in her letter. She then circled the most appropriate job description depending on the targeted company.

5. **Inappropriate stationery:** As we mentioned in Chapter 2, white and ivory are the only acceptable paper colors for a cover letter. We've seen letters in every shade from hot pink to electric blue and, to be honest, the color was the *only* thing we noticed. Also, we recommend standard office stationery; steer clear of transparent typing paper or personal stationery.

In any case, the stationery you choose should not distract from the contents of your cover letter. A cat enthusiast who applied to our company "enhanced" her letter with several images of her favorite felines. A musician applying for an office position sent a letter decorated with a border of musical notes and instruments. Remember, don't rely on graphics to "improve" your cover letter; let your qualifications speak for themselves.

6. **"Amusing" anecdotes:** In general, if you desire serious consideration, your cover letter should adopt a serious, professional tone. Imagine yourself in an interview setting. Since you do not know your interviewer, you would not joke with him or her until you have determined what demeanor is appropriate. Likewise, when writing to a potential employer you have not met, you should remain polite and professional. Avoid blunders like the one this job hunter made:

Example: "I feel I am especially qualified to join your staff, as my name, Chris Smith, almost rhymes with your company, **Christmas**, company."

7. **Erroneous company information:** If you were the employer, would you want to hire a candidate who confuses your company's products and services or misquotes recent goings-on? To avoid such errors, be sure to verify the accuracy of any company information that you mention in your cover letter. On the other hand, if you haven't researched the company, don't bluff. Statements like "I know something about your company" or "I am familiar with your products" signal to an employer that you haven't done your homework.

When citing information about a company, be specific. The following is an example of an effective way to use company information in your cover letter. "I have been following Any Corporation's growth for many months and I was excited to learn of your recent acquisition of C&M, Inc. Congratulations on successfully entering the international market!"

8. **Desperation:** In your cover letter, you should sound determined, not desperate. While an employer appreciates enthusiasm, he or she may be turned off by a desperate plea for employment. However, a fine line often separates the two, so the best advice would be to follow your instincts. Here are a few blunders to avoid: "I am desperately eager to start, as I have been out of work for six months," "Please call today! I'll be waiting by the phone," "I really, really need this job to pay off medical bills." In one letter we came across, the candidate even dramatically enlarged the type of this closing statement, "I AM VERY BADLY IN NEED OF MONEY!"

9. **Personal photos:** During the course of our research, we found actual photographs of candidates enclosed in job applications. We opened one letter to find an 8-by-10-inch glossy of a doctor surrounded by her patients. Another candidate used his computer to electronically scan his image onto the cover letter stationery. A third blew up a picture of his face to cover the entire page, then handwrote his letter over it!

   Unless you are seeking employment in modeling, acting, or other performance industries, it is not appropriate to send a photograph. An employer will see what you look like should you reach the interview stage. Until then, even the cutest baby face won't help you get a foot in the door!

10. **Confessed shortcomings:** Some job-hunters mistakenly call attention to their weaknesses in their cover letters, hoping to ward off an employer's objections. This is a mistake because the letter emphasizes your flaws rather than your strengths. For example, avoid statements such as these: "Although I have no related experience, I remain very interested in the Management Consultant position" and "I may not be well qualified for this position but it has always been my dream to work in the publishing field." Instead, emphasize your strengths, including valuable skills, related experience, and company knowledge.

11. **Misrepresentation:** In any stage of the job-search process, never, *ever*, misrepresent yourself. In many companies, erroneous information contained in a cover letter or resume will be grounds for dismissal as soon as the inaccuracy is discovered. Protect yourself by sticking to the facts. You are selling your skills and accomplishments in your cover letter. If you achieve something, say so, and put it in the best possible light. Don't hold back or be modest—no one else will. At the same time, however, don't exaggerate to the point of misrepresentation.

    Example: "In June, I graduated with honors from American University. In the course of my studies, I played two varsity sports while concurrently holding five jobs."

    Example: "Since beginning my career four years ago, I have won hundreds of competitions and awards, and am considered by many to be the best Hair Stylist on the East Coast."

12. **Demanding statements:** Keep in mind that your cover letter should demonstrate what you can do for an employer, not what he or she can do for you. For example, instead of stating, "I am looking for a unique opportunity in which I will be adequately challenged and compensated," say "I am confident that I could make a significant contribution to your organization, specifically by expanding your

customer base in the Northwest region and instituting a discount offer for new accounts."

Also, since you are requesting an employer's consideration, your letter shouldn't include personal preferences or demands. Statements such as "It would be an overwhelmingly smart idea for you to hire me" or "Let's meet next Wednesday at 4:00 P.M., when I will be available to discuss my candidacy further" often put the potential employer on the defensive. Job candidates' demands are rarely met with an enthusiastic response.

13. **Missing resume:** Have you ever forgotten to enclose all the materials you refer to in your cover letter? On numerous occasions, we've received letters with no resumes. Writing samples have been promised but not delivered. Not only is this a disappointment, but a fatal oversight. No employer is going to take the time to remind you of your mistake; he or she has already moved on to the next application.

14. **Personal information:** Do not include your age, weight, height, marital status, race, religion, or any other personal information unless you feel that it directly pertains to the position that you're seeking. For instance, age might be relevant if you are seeking a job at a seniors' organization and height and weight may be important if you are applying to an athletic team.

Similarly, you should list your personal interests and hobbies only if they are directly relevant to the type of job you are seeking. If you are applying to a company that greatly values teamwork, for instance, citing that you organized a community fundraiser or played on a basketball team will probably be advantageous. When in doubt, however, leave it out.

15. **Choice of pronouns:** Your cover letter necessarily requires a thorough discussion of your qualifications. Although some applicants might choose the third person ("he or she") as a creative approach to presenting their qualifications, potential employers sometimes find this voice disconcerting. In general, using the first person ("I") voice is preferable.

Example A (wrong way): "Chris Smith is a highly qualified Public Relations Executive with over seven years of relevant experience in the field. She possesses strong verbal and written communication skills and her client base is extensive."

Example B (right way): "I am a highly qualified Public Relations Executive with over seven years of relevant experience in the field. I possess strong verbal and written communication skills and my client base is extensive."

16. **Tone trouble:** Tone problems are subtle, and may be hard to detect. When you are reading your cover letter back to yourself, patrol for tone problems by asking yourself after each sentence: Does that statement enhance my candidacy? Could a hiring manager interpret that last statement in an unfavorable way? Have a second reader review your letter. If the letter's wording is questionable, by all means rewrite it. Always phrase your statements in a positive way!

17. **Gimmicks:** Gimmicks such as sending a home video or a singing telegram to replace the conventional cover letter may seem attractive. No matter how creative these ideas may sound, the majority of employers will be more impressed with a simple, well-crafted letter. In the worst case scenario, gimmicks can even work against you, eliminating you from consideration. Examples we've seen include sending a poster-size cover letter by courier service or baseball hat with a note attached, "I'm throwing my hat into the ring!" Avoid such big risks; most hiring decisions are based on qualifications not gimmicks.

18. **Typographical errors:** It is very easy to make mistakes in your letters, particularly when you are writing many in succession. But it is also very easy for a hiring manager to reject out of hand any cover letter that contains errors, even those that seem minor at first glance. Don't make the mistake that one job-hunting editor recently made, citing his attention to detail while misspelling his own name!

    Here are a few common technical mistakes to watch out for when proofreading your letter:

    ● Misspelling the hiring contact's name or title in the address, in the greeting, or on the envelope.

    ● Forgetting to change the name of the organization you're applying to each time it appears in your application, especially in the body of the letter. For example, if you are applying to Boots and Bags, in your closing don't express enthusiasm for a position at Shoe City.

    ● Indicating application for one position and mentioning a different position in the body of the letter. For instance, one candidate applying for a telemarketing position included the following statement, "I possess fifteen years' experience related to the Marketing Analyst availability."

19. **Messy corrections:** Your cover letter should contain *all* pertinent information. If, for any reason, you forget to communicate something to your addressee, retype the letter. Including a supplementary note, either typed or handwritten, will be viewed as unprofessional or, worse, lazy. For example, one candidate attached a "post-it" note to

his cover letter, stating his willingness to travel and/or relocate. This, and all other information, must be included in your final draft.

Also, try to avoid using correction fluid or penning in any corrections. It's always a better idea to take the time to retype the letter perfectly.

20. **Omitted signature:** However obvious this might sound, don't forget to sign your name at the close of your cover letter. Far too many letters that we've seen had a typed name, but no signature. An employer might interpret this oversight as carelessness.

Also, your signature allows you the chance to personalize your letter. Don't blow it by using a script font or a draw program on your word processor. Although there is a rainbow of colors to choose from, always sign your name neatly in blue or black ink.

PART II
All about Job Hunting

5
Planning Your Job-Search Campaign

Sunday	Monday	Tuesday	Wednesday	Thursday	Friday	Saturday
			1	2	3	4
5	6	7	8	9	10	11
12	13	14	15	16	17	18
19	20	21	22	23	24	25
26	27	28	29	30		

No matter how terrific they may be, your resume and cover letter alone will not land you a job. You will need a comprehensive and well-defined plan in order to go job hunting effectively. A plan will help you keep up the vigorous pace of the job-search process and keep you from becoming frustrated or unmotivated. It will also enable you to pace yourself and monitor your progress against predetermined goals. If your plan is not an effective one, you will be able to see problems more clearly and tackle them head-on by changing direction or using different techniques.

Your job-search plan should incorporate a number of different job-finding methods. Decide which of the strategies described in Chapter 6 you want to try first. If you plan to pursue classified ads, decide which newspapers are worth monitoring. If you want to contact companies directly, find out which sources of company listings will best suit your needs. If you plan on networking (which experts strongly recommend), make a list of people you plan on contacting first.

Predict how much time you are going to spend pursuing these different avenues and set up a specific weekly schedule for yourself. It's important not to overlook this step; it will help you be more productive and make it more difficult to fall behind.

Getting Organized
Organization will make your job search more efficient and less stressful. Obviously, you should try to keep your desk or work area free of clutter. Make a to-do list at the beginning of each day and try to accomplish each of your goals by the end of that day. Also, use an organizer notebook that includes a pen and a daily calendar for recording appointments. Be sure to take it with you to interviews.

It's also important to create a chart or similar system that shows where and to whom you've sent your resume. Use it to track whether or not companies have responded and when and if you need to follow up with a phone call.

Oversized index cards are another useful way to organize your job search. Keep each contact's name, position, company, address, telephone number, contact method, follow-up date, status, and other important details on individual cards for quick and easy reference. If you are responding to an advertisement in a newspaper, clip the ad and paste it onto the card, along with the name of the newspaper and the date. If an employer or networking contact gives you his or her business card, you can staple it to an index card, and jot down any other pertinent information as well. Keep all of your cards in a index card box in alphabetical order for easy reference.

How Long Should Your Job Search Take?

As you may have already discovered, finding a job is not easy. It takes a lot of energy and a tremendous amount of effort. Current statistics show that the average job search lasts approximately one week for every $2,000 of income sought. For example, if your goal is a position that pays in the $30,000 range, your search will take approximately fifteen weeks. However, this statistic and others like it obscure one very important fact: You are the person who ultimately controls what kind of job you end up with and how long it takes to find it.

If you are like most job-hunters, you will have to contact several hundred companies before you find the right job. If you put tremendous effort into your job search and contact many companies each week, you will probably get a job much sooner than someone who is only searching casually and sending out one or two resumes a week.

Job Hunting Full-Time

Ideally, for the first few months of your job search, you should try to look for a job full-time. If you're able to afford this luxury, be sure to work from a vigorous, intense job-search plan that allows you to invest a minimum of forty hours per week.

Vary your activities a little bit from day to day—otherwise your job search may quickly become tedious. For example, every Sunday you could look through the classified ads and determine which jobs are appropriate for you. On Monday, follow up on these ads by sending out your resume and cover letter and making some phone calls. For the rest of the week, you could spend your time doing other things besides following up on specific job openings. On Tuesday, for instance, you might decide to focus on contacting companies directly. On Wednesday, you could do more research to find listings of other companies to contact. Thursday and Friday might be spent networking, as you try to set up appointments to meet with people and develop more contacts.

Every few weeks you should evaluate your progress and fine-tune your search accordingly. If you find that, after putting in a great deal of effort over a period of several months, you aren't even close to getting a job, then it's probably time to reconsider your options. Are the job-search methods you've chosen working well for you? Are you spending too much time responding to newspaper ads and not enough time networking and "cold" contacting? Could you be more aggressive in your job search?

The key to an effective job-search campaign is knowing when to persist in the current direction that your job hunt is taking and when to give up what you're doing and start over. It isn't easy. Often, talking with other job hunters and knowing the current state of the job market in your industry of interest will help you to draw this fine line.

Job Hunting While You're Still Employed

Looking for a new job while you're still employed can be a sticky situation. Time, or the lack thereof, can be a major problem and you may find yourself feeling more than a bit overwhelmed. Also, there is the very real concern that your current employer will find out that you're looking for a new job before you're ready to tell him or her. But there are ways to maximize time and minimize stress during your job search.

First, set aside blocks of your days and/or evenings specifically dedicated to your job search. You may choose to bag your lunch and spend your lunch hour making networking calls or following up on resumes you've sent out. Plan to spend several hours on weeknights and on Saturdays mailing out resumes and tracking down job leads. Whatever schedule you decide upon, try to stick to it.

Executive recruiters and employment agencies that don't charge job hunters a fee may be particularly helpful to the employed job seeker. Not only will they do the footwork for you, but they can help you uncover job leads you may not otherwise be able to find.

There is also a wide range of services that can help you save time by handling some tasks while you're at work, such as a telephone answering service or a resume service that mails out your resume to job leads you supply. These services can be extremely useful to the harried job hunter, but some are not what they seem. Be an informed consumer and shop wisely.

Organization will also play a key role in the success and the length of your job search. It may be worth your while to reread the section on getting organized at the beginning of this chapter.

Of course, time management and organization are probably not your only concerns. You may worry that you'll be found out by your current employer or wonder about the ethical issues involved. To dispel any concerns you may have, you should not feel obligated to inform your current employer that you are job searching until you are ready to give your notice. Revealing this information too soon may very well cost you your job. Remember, employers would rather lose you at their convenience than at your own.

To ensure that your job hunt is kept quiet, you should never tell any of your co-workers or colleagues of your plans. This may sound obvious, but it's a mistake that's too often made—at the expense of the job seeker. Also you may choose to head your resume with a phrase like "Confidential Resume of . . ." or make some similar mention of confidentiality in your cover letter. Most recruiters will understand and honor this request for discretion. Ask hiring managers not to contact you at work but instead leave a message on your home answering machine, which you can check regularly during the day. Sometimes, though, hiring managers will overlook such a request and contact you at work anyway. If you find this happening to you, you may choose to use your voice-mail rather than routing your calls through the receptionist.

It's important for job hunters to view their situation realistically. The days when employees dedicated their entire careers to a single employer are long gone. It is expected that people will change jobs several times during their career, and it would be foolish to leave a current position without having something else lined up. So if you have a misdirected sense of guilt, you shouldn't. Channel that energy into your job-search efforts instead.

Long-Distance Job Hunting

As if finding a job isn't tough enough, long-distance job hunting can be very difficult. There are several steps you can take to make this transition as smooth as possible. First, call or write your new city's Chamber of Commerce to get information on the city's major employers. Subscribe to a local newspaper and sign up with local employment agencies. Inform your networking contacts of your plans and ask them for any leads or suggestions they can give you in this new location. Do they know of anyone who works in that area who can give you suggestions? Also, be sure to check with your national trade or professional association. Most large associations offer members access to a national network. Contact the national office for a list of chapters in your new city.

If you are relocating to a new city because your spouse has been transferred, be sure to ask your spouse's company about spouse relocation assistance. Some larger companies may offer free career counseling and other job-hunting services to you. If your spouse's employer does not offer this service, consider contacting a career counseling center for guidance. You may be able to negotiate with your future employer to pay the center's fees.

Planning Your Finances

In addition to being stressful, looking for a new job can be costly. Expenses relating to your job hunt, in addition to everyday living expenses, can mount to a formidable sum in the face of a reduced income. Following are some guidelines to help you make this aspect of your job search somewhat smoother.

First of all, if you are laid off, you should know that most companies offer one week's to one month's severance pay for every year of service. Get a written copy of your company's policy. Immediately file for unemployment benefits and, if you can afford it, extend your health insurance. Some larger companies will also offer outplacement services to help employees in their transition to another job. Find out if your company offers any such assistance.

Next, assess your financial fitness. Make a detailed list of all your expenses, separating them into three categories: priority one, priority two and priority three. Priority one expenses should include the bare essentials such as rent/mortgage, utilities, groceries, and car payment. Be sure to figure job-search expenses in your priority one list. Priority two expenses should include important but not necessarily essential items such as credit card bills (which can be paid at a later date), home maintenance, and automotive maintenance. Priority three expenses should include more frivolous items that can be sacrificed temporarily, such as cable television, magazine subscriptions, leisure activities, and miscellaneous luxury purchases. Total your estimated expenses in each of these three categories.

Now, make a detailed list of your income and assets. This should include any income from part-time, temporary, and freelance work, unemployment insurance, severance pay, savings, investments, spouse's income, and alimony.

If you estimate that it will take you six months to find a new job (not a bad measure for today's market), multiply the total of your priority one expenses by six and subtract it from your current income and/or savings for that same period of time. You may find that some budgeting is in order. Perhaps you can cut down or eliminate some of those priority two and three expenses. Determine what is absolutely essential and what can be sacrificed for the time being.

You may also decide to write your creditors to request a reduced payment schedule in light of your employment situation. This may not always be possible, and it can affect your credit rating. But many creditors, when given a choice between receiving a partial payment or no payment at all, will agree to work out an acceptable plan with you. Be sure to ask your creditors to help preserve your good credit rating.

You should also know that some job-hunting expenses are tax deductible if you are looking for a new position in your current line of work. (Unfortunately, no tax relief is available if you switch careers or if you are a first-time job seeker.) All expenses associated with your job-hunting campaign are generally deductible, including resume typing, printing, postage, telephone costs, travel costs, and employment agency fees. If your new job is at least fifty miles further from your home than your old job was, you will also be able to deduct up to $3,000 of your total moving expenses. Of course, you'll need to accurately document all your expenses so be sure to save all your receipts.

To generate additional income for yourself during this time, consider taking on part-time, freelance, or temporary work. You may choose to borrow against your life insurance or retirement policy, if you have one, or accept a loan from a friend or relative.

Now that you've determined how much money you have and how much you'll need, establish a realistic budget. It should be very detailed and laid out on paper. Be sure to monitor your budget on a regular basis so you don't suddenly find yourself overwhelmed by a financial predicament that could otherwise have been avoided.

6
The Best and Worst Ways to Find Jobs

 You may be surprised to learn that some of the most popular job-search methods are quite unsuccessful for most of the people who use them. In this chapter you'll have a chance to take a look at the real value of the services and techniques at your disposal.

Employment Agencies

Employment agencies are commissioned by employers to find qualified candidates for job openings. However, you should know that the agency's main responsibility is to meet the needs of the employer—not to find a suitable job for you.

This is not to say that you should rule them out altogether. There are employment agencies that specialize in specific industries or industry functions that can be useful for experienced professionals. However, employment agencies are not a good choice for entry-level job-seekers. They often try to steer inexperienced candidates in a direction they're not interested in and often place them in clerical positions.

If you decide to register with an agency, your best bet is to find one that is recommended by a friend or associate. Barring that, you can find names of agencies in *The JobBank Guide to Employment Services* (Bob Adams, Inc., 1994) found in your local public library, or by contacting:

National Association of Personnel Consultants (NAPC)
3133 Mount Vernon Avenue
Alexandria, VA 22305
(703) 684-0180

Be aware, though, that there are an increasing number of bogus employment service firms, usually advertising in newspapers and magazines. These companies promise even inexperienced job seekers top salaries in exciting careers—all for a sizable fee. Others use expensive 900 numbers that job seekers are encouraged to call. Unfortunately, most people find out too late that the jobs they are promised don't exist.

As a general rule, most legitimate employment agencies will never guarantee you a job and will not seek payment until after you've been placed. Even so, you should check every agency you're interested in with your local chapter of the Better Business Bureau (BBB). Find out if it is licensed and has been in business for a reasonable amount of time. Have any valid complaints been registered against the agency recently? Has the firm been responsive to these complaints?

Then, if all checks out with the BBB, call the firm to find out if it specializes in your area of expertise and how it will go about marketing you. If you are asked to sign a contract, have an attorney look at it first. Find out who will pay the agency's fee. You should avoid any firms that are not company "fee paid."

After you have selected a few agencies (three to five is best), send them your resume with a cover letter. Make a follow-up phone call a week or two later, and try to schedule an interview. Be prepared to be asked to take a battery of tests on the day of your interview.

Above all, though, do not expect too much. Only a small percentage of all professional, managerial, and executive jobs are listed with these agencies, so they are not a terrific source of opportunities. Use them as an addition to your job-search campaign, but focus your efforts on other, more promising methods.

Executive Search Firms

Also known as headhunters, these firms are somewhat similar to professional employment agencies. They seek out and screen candidates for high-paying executive and managerial positions and are paid by the employer. Unlike employment agencies, they typically approach viable candidates directly, rather than waiting for candidates to approach them. Many prefer to deal with already employed candidates and will not accept "blind" inquires from job hunters.

These organizations are not licensed, so if you decide to go with an executive search firm, make sure it has a solid reputation. You can find names of search firms in *The JobBank Guide to Employment Services* or by contacting the following:

Association of Executive Search Consultants (AESC)
500 5th Avenue, Suite 930
New York, NY 10110
(212) 398-9556

American Management Association (AMA)
Management Services Department
135 West 50th Street
New York, NY 10020
(212) 586-8100

As with employment agencies, do not let an executive search firm become a critical element of your job-search campaign—no matter how encouraging it may sound. Continue to actively seek out your own opportunities and keep all of your options open.

Temporary Agencies

Temporary or "temp" agencies (such as Kelly Services and Manpower) can be a viable option. Usually these agencies specialize in clerical and support work but it's becoming increasingly common to find temporary assignments in other areas like accounting, computer programming, and management consulting. Working on temporary assignment will provide you with additional income during your job search and will add experience to your resume. It may also provide valuable business contacts or lead to job opportunities.

You can find temporary agencies listed in the *Yellow Pages*. Send your resume and cover letter and later call to schedule an interview. Be prepared to be asked to take a battery of tests on the day of your interview.

Newspaper Classified Ads

Contrary to popular belief, newspaper classified ads are not a good source of opportunities for job hunters. Few people find jobs, although many spend a tremendous amount of time and effort pouring through newspaper after newspaper.

According to career development consultant Charles Logue, less than 3 percent of all job openings are advertised in classified ads. Worse, so many applicants respond to these ads that the competition is extremely fierce. Even if your qualifications are good, your chances of getting an interview are not. If you plan on using classified ads as a source for seeking employment, be sure to focus only a small portion of your job-search efforts in this direction.

"Blind" Ads

"Blind" ads are newspaper advertisements that don't identify the employer. Job-seekers are usually instructed to send their resumes to a post office box number. Although they may seem suspicious, blind ads can be a source of legitimate job opportunities. A firm may choose to run blind advertisement because it does not wish to be deluged with phone calls, or it may be trying to replace someone who hasn't been terminated yet.

You should be aware, though, that blind ads are sometimes used for deceitful purposes, such as selling employment marketing services and sexually harassing unsuspecting job hunters. The best advice is to trust your instincts and don't allow yourself to be put in a situation that makes you feel uncomfortable.

Public Employment Service

Your state employment service, sometimes called the Job Service, has about 1,700 local offices (also called employment service centers) nationwide, which provide job placement assistance and career counseling. With so many white collar workers out of work, these agencies are doing more and more to accommodate professional and managerial personnel. Check your local phone book for the office nearest you.

Job Counseling Services

The job counseling services offered by your city or town are another useful option. You can find them listed in your local phone book or by writing:

National Board for Certified Counselors
3D Terrace Way
Greensboro, NC 27403
(910) 547-0607

You may also wish to consult *The JobBank Guide to Employment Services*, which lists career counseling services as well as executive search firms, employment agencies, and temporary help services located throughout the United States.

Nonprofit Agencies

It may be worthwhile to find out what services are provided by nonprofit agencies in your local community. Many of these organizations offer counseling, career development, and job placement services to specific groups such as women and minorities. Also, try contacting the national organizations below for information on career planning, job training, or public policy support.

For Women:
U.S. Department of Labor
Women's Bureau
200 Constitution Avenue NW
Washington, DC 20210
(202) 219-6606

Wider Opportunities for Women
815 15th Street N.W.
Suite 916
Washington, DC 20005
(202) 638-3143

For Minorities:
National Association for the Advancement of Colored People (NAACP)
Attn: Job Services
4805 Mount Hope Drive
Baltimore, MD 21215-3197
(410) 358-8900

National Urban League
Employment Department
500 East 62nd Street
New York, NY 10021
(212) 310-9000

National Urban League
Washington Operations
1111 14th Street N.W., 6th Floor
Washington, DC 20005
(202) 898-1604

For the Blind:
Job Opportunities for the Blind Program
National Federation for the Blind
1800 Johnson Street
Baltimore, MD 21230
(800) 638-7518

For the Physically Challenged:
President's Committee on Employment of People with Disabilities
1331 F Street N.W., Third Floor
Washington, DC 20004-1107
(202) 376-6200

College Career Centers

If you're a recent college grad, your school's career center is a great place for you to start your job search. Your college career center can help you identify and evaluate your interests, work values, and skills. Most offer workshops on topics like job-search strategy, resume writing, letter writing, and effective interviewing, or job fairs for meeting with prospective employers. Yours should also have a career resource library where you can find job leads and an alumni network to help you get started on networking.

Even if you've long since graduated, your college's career center may be able to provide you with valuable networking contacts. You should call to find out if your alma mater offers this or other services to alumni.

Electronic Data Bases

Electronic data bases compile information on job seekers to be scanned and searched by hiring companies. They may be the new wave for job seekers of the future, but right now they are primarily used by college students and recent grads, often with limited results.

These services usually charge between $30 and $50 to list your resume for one year. If you decide to go this route, be sure to make it only one small part of your job-search plan.

Direct Contact

One of the best ways to find a job is by direct contact. Direct contact means introducing yourself to potential employers, usually by way of a resume and cover letter, without a prior referral. This type of "cold contact" can be very effective if done the right way. Chapter 7 explains just how to do this.

Networking

Another excellent method of finding work is through networking, a strategy that focuses primarily on developing a network of "insider" contacts. This is a great approach to use even if you don't have any professional contacts. Networking takes many forms; with a little skill and a lot of effort, it can be a very productive tool for you. Chapter 8 takes you through the networking process step by step.

7
Contacting Companies Directly

 Direct contact (also called "cold contact") means making a professional, personal approach to a select group of companies. Done well, it can be an excellent method for most job-seekers, leading to many opportunities, and possibly, job offers. However, if you're an experienced professional looking for a high-level managerial or executive spot, you may find that this approach does not work well for you. If you find that this is the case, your best bet will probably be networking (see Chapter 8).

The Best Companies to Contact

One of the most common mistakes that job-hunters make is focusing their search on very large, Fortune 500-type companies. Despite the fact that most of these giants are dramatically downsizing their work force, big corporations still look good to many, who flood human resources departments with resumes. According to a recent article in *Fortune*, IBM receives about one million resumes a year!

But don't give up hope! There are countless midsize companies with anywhere from one hundred to one thousand employees where the competition is much less fierce. These companies are large enough to have a number of job openings at any given time. In fact, experts predict that as many as one-third of all new jobs will be created by midsize firms over the next two years. At the same time, these companies are small enough that they are often overlooked by other job hunters, meaning there will be less competition for job openings.

But the best source of job opportunities today is small companies—those with one hundred or less employees. A recent Dun and Bradstreet report predicts small companies will be responsible for almost 80 percent of the 2.1 million new jobs created in America this year. These companies are not very visible to the general public, meaning that there will generally be less competition for job openings. An additional advantage is that most smaller firms offer significant room for career growth. There are drawbacks, though: small companies generally offer less job security than midsize firms and fewer employee benefits.

Do Your Homework

If you are trying to enter a new field, your first order of business is to do a little background research. Find out the current trends in the industry and become familiar with names of the major and up-and-coming players. Your industry's trade journal and informational interviews are two terrific ways to find this kind of "insider" information. Check your local library for *The Encyclopedia of Business Information Sources* or *Predicasts F&S Index* to identify publications in your field of interest.

If you're a veteran of the field you're looking in, make sure that you keep up with current industry trends by talking with your associates, attending your professional association's functions, and reading your industry's trade journals.

What to Look For

Now you should be ready to look for information about individual employers. But rather than going into great detail in your search at this point, you should be trying to find out only basic information about many different companies, including:

- Company name, address, phone, and fax number.
- Names and job titles of key contacts.
- Is the company privately or publicly held?
- Its products and/or services.
- The year of its incorporation.
- Its number of employees.

Plan on doing further, more detailed research later on as you start to schedule interviews.

Where to Find It

Where can you find this kind information about potential employers? One good place to start is the *JobBank* books, a series of employment directories listing almost all companies with fifty or more employees in larger cities and metropolitan areas in the U.S. Each *JobBank* provides up-to-date information including key contacts, common positions the company hires for, educational backgrounds sought, and fringe benefits offered. There is also a section on that particular region's economic outlook, as well as a section listing addresses of professional associations, Chambers of Commerce, and executive search firms and job placement agencies.

You can find the following *JobBank* books at your local bookstore: Atlanta; Boston; Carolina; Chicago; Dallas/Fort Worth; Denver; Detroit; Florida; Houston; Los Angeles; Minneapolis/St. Paul; Missouri; New York; Ohio; Philadelphia; Phoenix; San Francisco; Seattle; Tennessee; and Washington DC.

There are many other resources you can use to find listings of companies, most of which can be found at your local library. Ask the reference librarian to help you locate the many directories available that list basic information about companies in your field of interest. Be sure not to overlook these great tools:

Dun and Bradstreet's *Million Dollar Directory* is a good place to begin your research. It lists approximately 160,000 companies that are both publicly and privately held and is updated annually.

Standard & Poor's Register of Corporations lists fewer companies than the *Million Dollar Directory* (about 45,000), but provides valuable biographical information on thousands of company officials.

Corporate Technology Directory (Corporate Technology Information Services) focuses on the products produced by approximately 35,000 companies. This is a great resource for job seekers interested in high-tech industries, including computers, biotechnology, environmental engineering, chemical and pharmaceutical, and transportation.

Personnel Executives Contactbook (Gale Research) lists key personnel and other contacts at 30,000 publicly and privately held companies and government agencies.

The National JobBank (Adams Media Corporation) lists key contacts at over 17,000 small and large companies. It includes information on common positions filled and educational backgrounds desired and is updated annually.

Directory of Human Resources Executives (Hunt-Scanlon) names human resource executives and provides information on the number of employees and area of specialization of 5,000 public and private companies.

Directory of Corporate Affiliations (National Register) is one of the few places where you can find information on a company's divisions and subsidiaries. This particular book lists information on approximately 4,000 parent companies.

Many of these resources can also be found on CD-ROM at your library. These "books on disk" are easy to use and can save you a lot of time. They are often attached to printers so you can print the information you need. Usually, libraries will provide free access to CD-ROM data bases.

Also, don't overlook the countless industry-specific directories that are available, such as *Dun's Directory of Service Companies*, *Martindale-Hubbell Law Directory*, and *Standard Directory of Advertisers*. These are a terrific place to find potential employers and often include information on professional associations and industry trends. Ask your reference librarian for help in identifying the directories that specialize in your field of interest.

Think Big

As a general rule, you should always *try* to contact a department head or president of any company you consider working for. This will probably be easier to do at smaller companies where the president of the company may be directly involved in the hiring process. However, as you apply to larger and larger companies, more and more you will find yourself bumped back to the personnel office. If this happens to you, try to contact a key decision-maker within personnel.

The first step you should take in contacting a company directly is to mail your resume, accompanied by a personalized cover letter, and a self-addressed stamped envelope. Part I of this book shows you how to write an attention-grabbing cover letter.

The 60-Second Pitch

Approximately one week after you have sent your letter to a key decision-maker, you should follow up with a phone call. Don't simply ask if your inquiry has been received—this can be frustrating to employers who are inundated with hundreds of resumes and you probably won't get the response you're hoping for. A better approach is to state that you've sent your resume and explain, in 60 seconds or less, why you think you're the best candidate for the position. We call this the "60-second pitch."

Your 60-second pitch should be a clear and concise summary about yourself. It should include three important elements:

1. What kind of work you do (or want to do);
2. What your strongest skills and accomplishments are;
3. What kind of position you are seeking.

Your resume is probably the best and easiest place to find this information. One communications professional used her resume to create her 60-second pitch:

> *"Hello. My name is Elaine O'Connor. I'm a production assistant with a B.A. in Communications and three years of solid broadcasting and public relations background. I have extensive experience developing and researching topics, pre-interviewing guests, and producing on-location video tapings.*
>
> *"I've been watching your station for some time now and I've been impressed with your innovative approach and your fast growth. I recently sent you my resume and was wondering if you anticipate any openings that might be appropriate for someone with my experience?"*

Mike, a father who was returning to a full-time position when his daughter began the first grade, also had a terrific 60-second pitch:

> *"My name is Mike Johnson. I sent you my resume last week and I'd like to take a moment to introduce myself. I've been working part-time as an accounts receivable supervisor for the past five years and have expertise in payables, receivables, and credit. I'm looking for a full-time accounting position.*

"I read the article about your firm's recent expansion in last Sunday's business section and think that we might make a great match. Do you have a few minutes?"

As you can see, tailoring your pitch to the needs of each particular employer will make your 60-second pitch stronger. At the same time, you should memorize the "core" of your pitch—the part about your qualifications that you will recite to every potential employer. This will help you feel more confident and sound more natural. Also be sure to speak slowly and clearly.

If you are invited to an interview after you've "pitched" yourself to the employer, great! If not, don't let it end there! Ask if there are any particular qualifications that he or she is looking for in a candidate. Is there anything else you can do or any additional information that you can send (writing samples, clippings, a portfolio) to help the employer make his or her decision? Even if the employer says no, that your initial application is sufficient, he or she may be impressed by your interest and enthusiasm.

Then, if you have not already done so, specifically ask the employer if he/she would have a few minutes to meet with you. If that doesn't work, ask if the employer knows anyone who might be interested in speaking with someone with your qualifications. If you are unable to arrange an interview or get a referral, ask the employer if he/she would mind if you called back in three to four weeks. The goal is to get a positive result from the phone call—whether it's an interview or simply a scrap of job-hunting advice. Don't give up too easily, but be professional and courteous at all times.

Getting Past Gatekeepers

Gatekeepers are those receptionists, assistants, and other workers who try to screen all calls, making sure only the most important ones go through to the top. You should expect to encounter many gatekeepers throughout your job search—and how you handle them can make a big difference in your campaign.

If your call is screened by a gatekeeper, don't request a call in return unless the contact will recognize your name. Simply give your name and ask when it's best to call back. Call again the next day at the time he or she suggested. Keep calling once a day for at least five days before you change tactics.

Another alternative is to try asking for your contact by her first name. You could say, for example, "This is Susan Thomas. Is Sharon in?" If you say this with an air of confidence and authority, you might just get through.

If you're asked what the call is about, try saying that you've been in correspondence with Sharon and she's expecting your call (if you sent your resume and cover letter, mentioning that you'd be calling). If you're pressed to be more specific, you can say, "I would like Sharon's expertise on a sales and marketing issue." Or use an implied referral, "I was just talking with John Barker at ACME Industries about something that might interest Sharon. Would you put me through, please?"

Whatever approach you choose to take, never say that your call is personal—this sends up a red flag to most gatekeepers and will hurt your chances of getting through.

If none of these approaches work, try calling when the gatekeeper is least likely to be there—before or after hours and during lunch. Employers will often answer their own phone during off hours.

Another technique that works well is to call the office of the president and say something like, "Hi. I don't think I really need to speak with the president—I'm just trying to find out who's in charge of sales and marketing. Could you help me with that?" Then be sure to thank the person and jot down his or her full name. Then you can get past that person's gatekeeper by saying something like, "Bill Warner in the president's office suggested I speak with Sharon Rice. Is she in?"

If none of these suggestions work for you, as a last resort you should ask for the gatekeeper's help. You could say, "Joe, I've been trying to reach your boss for some time now and I haven't had much luck. Do you have any suggestions on how I might be more effective?" A sincere and polite request for help will often either get you through to your contact or at least win a useful bit of advice.

If you've exhausted all of these techniques and feel as if you'll never get through, don't waste your time. Simply move on to other, more promising contacts and opportunities.

Contacting the Same Firm Twice

One approach that can be very effective is calling some of the firms you contacted a few months previously. This shows that you are genuinely interested in the firm and will certainly make you stand out in the contact's mind. You could say something like:

> "My name is Robert Shustak and I contacted your firm several months ago about an entry-level position in advertising. I've been talking with other firms and I'm very much committed to this industry. I recently saw your firm mentioned in the local newspaper, and I'm more convinced than ever that your company is a terrific place to work.
>
> "I feel I have a lot to offer you and I'd like for you to reconsider my application."

The technique works especially well when you contact firms you interviewed with. Only a fraction of those applying for a position get to the interview stage; if you were one of them, the firm was obviously impressed with your qualifications. Chances are good that you would still be considered for another position at that company.

You don't have to telephone, of course; you might prefer to write a letter. Part III of this book contains twenty-five samples of resurrection letters you could send to a company that interviewed you but did not offer you a position.

Don't Give Up!

Cold contact is challenging and often frustrating. But no matter how frustrated you may become, it's important to be polite to your contacts (and their gate-keepers!) at all times. Like anyone else, they will be more willing to help out a professional, friendly caller than someone who sounds frustrated or unpleasant.

Job searching is not easy for anyone. If you go into it expecting some rejection, it will be easier to take when it happens. This is when attitude becomes crucial. If you're optimistic and you believe in yourself, you have the most important ingredients of a successful job search.

8
Networking Your Way to a Job

Networking is the most effective of all job-hunting tools. In fact, experts indicate that as many as 86 percent of all jobs are found through networking. This chapter is designed to dispel the mystery and confusion that often surrounds this job-search method. As you read on, you will see that networking is not just for people with lots of professional experience. It can work for anyone—even people with few or no contacts in the business world.

Overcoming Hesitation

If you feel hesitant about networking, you're not alone. Many job-seekers mistakenly think that networking is somehow degrading or manipulative. They suspect that networking really means pestering strangers for a job and begging for scraps of help and sympathy. They opt not to use this important tool and end up needlessly limiting their opportunities.

The problem is that these people don't understand what networking really is. Networking means letting people you know—personally and professionally—that you are looking for a job. You simply ask them to keep you in mind if they hear of any appropriate openings or know anyone who might need someone with your skills.

It will probably feel awkward at first, but with practice you'll feel much more comfortable and confident making calls. Keep in mind that this is a time-honored practice—in fact, it's how most job seekers get jobs. And, once you find the right job, you can "give something back" by lending a hand to other networking job seekers.

Present Yourself as an Industry "Insider"

One of the secrets of networking is knowing what you want—or at least appearing to know what you want. For instance, if you are trying to break into a field where you don't have any experience, tell your networking contacts that you are interested in the industry they work in and show them that you are knowledgeable about that industry. This way, you will be perceived more or less as an "industry insider." Better yet, if you can cite some work experience in that industry and a referral, people will be interested in talking with you.

So—how do you start? Keep up to date with your industry of choice by reading its trade journals. Check your local library for *The Encyclopedia of Business Information Sources* or *Predicasts F&S Index* to identify publications in your field of interest. Be sure to read your industry's publications on a regular basis.

In addition, you should keep an eye out for information about your chosen industry that appears in the mainstream media: your daily newspaper, magazines like *Time* and *Business Week*, news broadcasts, books, and other sources.

Tracking Down Leads

Who should you contact? Obviously, if you have experience in your industry of choice, you need only leaf through your Rolodex and call up some of your already established contacts. But how do you network if you don't already have prior experience and contacts?

The answer is simple: Start with the people you already know. Friends, relatives, neighbors, your doctor, your hairdresser—even your plumber can be a source of important business contacts. These people might not work in the industry you're interested in, but they may know someone you should contact. Someone who knows someone who . . . you get the idea.

At first, you might not think you have many contacts at your disposal—but if you think carefully you'll realize you do. Let's say that there are thirty people you can initially contact, but none of them work in the industry you're interested in. They may, as a group, know sixty people who do work in that industry, work in a related industry, or are in a position to know someone who works in the industry. That's a lot of people.

But don't stop there. Contact the people you know on a professional or academic basis, such as former teachers, past employers and co-workers, and established business contacts. Find out if your college, graduate, or prep school offers networking services for alumni; if not, they will probably have an alumni directory that you can use.

Consider joining a professional organization. If you don't know the associations in your field and their locations and publications, consult the *Encyclopedia of Associations* or *National Trade and Professional Associations of the United States*. Your local library should have these books on hand.

Lastly, you should make a point of getting out and talking to people in your industry through informational interviews, at seminars, even at social events—anywhere you might expect to find "insiders."

What Should I Say and Do?

First you should tell your contact a little bit about your qualifications and what kind of job you're looking for. If the contact is not someone who already knows you well, you should cite the name of the person who referred you and then introduce yourself with your 60-second pitch (as described in Chapter 7). Be sure at some point to ask the contact if he or she knows of anyone who might be looking for someone with your qualifications. Then ask for the name of anyone who might know anyone looking for someone with your qualifications.

If the conversation is going well, you may decide to ask your contact if he or she would have a few minutes to meet with you. If you are unable to arrange an interview or get a referral, ask the employer if it would be all right to call back in three or four weeks.

> *"Anthony Barrett? Hello, my name is Leslie Pellham. Jason Randall at Computing Associates was telling me yesterday about your company's recent innovations in applications and recommended that I speak with you. Do you have a minute to talk with me? Great.*
>
> *"I've been a programmer for eleven years at PC Systems and I'm looking for a change of pace. I was hoping you could tell me a little more about your firm and the qualities you look for in job candidates.*
>
> *"I see. Well, I have a thorough knowledge of COBOL, Pascal, Fortran, and C++ in a Windows and DOS environment. I also have experience in information mapping. It sounds as if we might make a good match. Could I come in and meet with you for a few minutes at your convenience?"*

Now, if Anthony agrees, Leslie should schedule an appointment and thank him for his time. If Anthony declines, however, Leslie should politely persist:

> *"Oh, I understand—you don't have any openings right now. Is there someone you can think of who might be looking for somebody with my qualifications? Also, I'd like to send you my resume anyway, in case a position opens up in the near future."*

If Anthony says he can't think of anyone, Leslie should ask him for a referral. Chances are that her polite persistence will pay off and she'll come away with at least one new contact.

Networking for Those Entering a New Field

If you are trying to enter a new field, it's a good idea to ask your contacts for information about the industry in general and about their particular position. Are there any specific qualifications or training that makes some candidates more competitive than others? Tell each of your contacts a little bit about your situation and ask for advice.

This is how Jim, a recent college graduate, "pitched" himself to a potential employer:

> *"Ms. Silva, my name is Jim Philipps and my uncle, Joe Adams, suggested that I call you. I've just graduated from City University with a degree in English. I've been working part-time as a bank teller for two years and I very much want to pursue a career as a loan officer. I realize that you may not have any openings at this time but I was hoping that you would be able to meet with me for a few minutes to discuss the banking industry."*

Ms. Silva then says she's very busy and she doesn't have the time to meet with Jim. Jim politely persists:

> *"I understand that you're busy—that's why I'll only ask for one more minute of your time. As you know, I have some part-time work experience in banking. Are there any other specific qualifications or training you could recommend that would help me get a job as a loan officer?"*

Ms. Silva then gives Jim some advice on how to get a job in the banking industry.

> *"Thank you for that suggestion—I'm sure it will be very helpful. Now, would you be able to refer me to someone who might be looking for someone with my qualifications?"*

If Ms. Silva says no, Jim should ask if she knows anyone who might know anyone looking for a job in the banking industry. The point is to get at least one referral or job lead from each contact.

> *"Thank you for referring me to Ms. Lehman at Center Bank—I'll be sure to call her today. In the meantime, though, could I send you my resume for your files? Great. Thank you again for all your help. By the way, Uncle Joe says 'hello!'"*

The Informational Interview

Informational interviews are an important way of building your network and can lead to valuable information and opportunities. If you tell a contact that all you want is advice, make sure you mean it. Never approach an informational interview as though it were a job interview—just stick to gathering information and leads and see what happens.

Tell your contact right away that all you would like is to learn more about the industry or company in question, and that you'll be the one asking all the questions. Also, unless it's specifically requested, sending your resume to someone you'd like to meet for an informational interview will probably give the wrong impression.

> *"My name is Jim Philipps and David Silva suggested I call you. I've just graduated from City University with a degree in English and I'm interested in beginning a career as a loan officer.*
> *"I know that you may not have any openings at this time, but I would like to come by and talk with you for a couple of minutes about the opportunities that might be available in banking."*

Sometimes an employer will mistake your intentions and tell you that he or she has no jobs available. If this happens, you can say something like:

"I understand that you might not have any openings right now, but I'd like to have a chance to meet with you for a couple of minutes anyway, just to discuss the banking industry in this city and the opportunities one might expect at those places that might be hiring. Would this be possible?"

You might find that the straightforward approach sometimes works better:

"My name is Jim Philipps and David Silva suggested I call you. I've just graduated from City University with a degree in English and I'm interested in beginning a career as a loan officer.
"I assure you I won't ask you for a job, but I was hoping that you would be able to meet with me briefly to discuss the banking industry."

Now that you've scheduled an informational interview, make sure that you're prepared to take the lead. After all, you're the one doing the interviewing—not vice versa. Have some specific questions ready, such as:

- How did you get started in this business?
- What do you like most about your job, your company, and your industry?
- What do you dislike most about your job, your company, and your industry?
- What would you say are the current career opportunities for someone with my qualifications in the industry?
- What are the basic requirements for an entry-level position in the industry?
- Is there a trade association or a trade publication that might aid me in my job search?
- Where do you see the industry heading in the near future?
- What advice would you give to someone looking for a job in the industry?
- Is there anything else I should know about the industry?
- Do you know of anyone who might be looking for someone with my qualifications?
- Do you know of anyone who might know of anyone looking for someone with my qualifications?

Send a Thank You Letter

If a networking contact has been particularly helpful to you, by all means send a thank you note. Not only is this courteous, it keeps your contacts current. Part III provides a complete "how-to" in order to create an outstanding thank you letter.

More Networking?

Go back and call once again those people you already contacted for leads several months ago. You could say something like:

> *"As you may remember, we spoke several months ago about my interest in a career in banking. I was hoping that you might know of some other people who might be looking for someone with my qualifications."*

You may be pleasantly surprised. It's not uncommon to catch a contact in a different frame of mind and learn of someone new. Or perhaps your contact has met someone in your industry of interest since you last spoke.

PART III
Sample Cover Letters

9
Cover Letters for Special Situations

Writing a cover letter can seem like an even more formidable task when you find yourself in what we call "special situations." Perhaps you lack paid job experience, have been out of the workplace to raise children, are concerned about possible discrimination due to age or disability, or are trying to enter a field in which you have no practical experience. Not to worry! The key to improving your cover letter in these special situations is to emphasize your strengths. Focus on your marketable skills (whether they were acquired in the workplace or elsewhere), and highlight impressive achievements, relevant education and training, and/or related interests. And, of course, you should take care to downplay or eliminate any information that may be construed as a weakness.

For example, if you are a "displaced homemaker" (a homemaker entering the job market for the first time), you can structure your cover letter to highlight the special skills you've acquired over the years while downplaying your lack of paid experience. If you are an older job candidate, use your age as a selling point. Emphasize the depth of your experience, your maturity, your sense of responsibility, and your positive outlook. Changing careers? No problem! Instead of focusing on your job history you should emphasize the marketable skills you've acquired that are considered valuable in the position you are seeking. For example, let's say your career has been real estate and, in your spare time, you like to run marathons. Recently, you heard about an opening in the sales and marketing department at an athletic shoe manufacturer. What you need to do is emphasize the skills you have that the employer is looking for. Not only do you have strong sales experience, you're familiar with the needs of the company's market, and that's a powerful combination!

Throughout this chapter you'll find creative solutions for even the most daunting career obstacles. Use them as a guideline for creating your own job-winning cover letters.

50-PLUS JOB CANDIDATE
(Product Manager)

178 Green Street
Fort Worth, TX 76111
(817) 555-5555

April 11, 1996

Pat Cummings
Vice-President
Any Corporation
1140 Main Street
Fort Worth, TX 76101

Dear Mr. Cummings:

Is your corporation in need of a motivated professional with comprehensive product management experience? If so, I would like to present my qualifications for your consideration.

In my vast experience, I have gained valuable insight into all aspects of product/protocol development and management to obtain FDA product approval. As Product Manager for Estrade, Inc., I provided extensive coordination of all product development activities for a large medical supply corporation. This acquired knowledge of clinical research would be especially beneficial to your development team.

I have consistently maintained a strong motivation for developing innovative product design and management, as well as a flexibility to new approaches and marketing techniques. I am thoroughly proficient in most major computer applications, including E-Mail and Internet Services. Much of my work has necessitated collaboration with systems consultants on the design and implementation of data management systems, including remote access.

I would be happy to further outline my skills during the course of a personal interview. After you have reviewed my qualifications, please contact me to schedule a time that is convenient for you to meet.

I appreciate your consideration and look forward to speaking with you.

Sincerely,

Chris Smith

Enc. resume

■ Summary of experience accentuates candidate's acquired professional skills and impressive track record.

■ Valuable computer skills are highlighted.

ALL EMPLOYMENT AT ONE COMPANY
(Inventory Control Manager)

178 Green Street
Minot, ND 58702
(701) 555-5555

April 4, 1996

Pat Cummings
President
Any Corporation
1140 Main Street
Grand Forks, ND 58201

Dear Ms. Cummings:

I am currently searching for a position in inventory control and administration, and would like to inquire about suitable opportunities at Any Corporation.

As a member of your staff, I would offer over twelve years' experience in inventory control management, in positions ranging from Office Manager to Vice-President of Inventory Management/Administrative Services. I possess a strong background in customer service, excellent interpersonal skills, and a strong motivation to successfully complete any task before me. These qualifications are supported by a Master of Business Administration degree, and a Bachelor of Science in Management.

If given the chance, I am confident I could cost-effectively direct your inventory control. Please contact me at your convenience to schedule a meeting. The opportunity to further prove my capabilities is of great interest to me.

I look forward to your reply.

Sincerely,

Chris Smith

Enc. resume

■ Letter outlines series of promotions.

■ Candidate's highest educational achievement is shown before other less significant degrees.

ALL EMPLOYMENT AT ONE COMPANY
(Materials Manager)

178 Green Street
Daytona Beach, FL 32115

August 18, 1996

Pat Cummings
Vice-President, Fiscal Affairs
Any Hospital
1140 Main Street
Orlando, FL 32816

Dear Mr. Cummings:

During the past eighteen years, I have progressed rapidly in positions of
responsibility from Supervisor of Patient Transportation to Manager of
Warehousing/Distribution to my current position as Senior Buyer and Manager of
Inventory Control.

Although my prior associations have been growing and challenging experiences, I
would like to make a position change and move into materials management within
the health care field. I am in search of an opportunity for my skills to achieve the
same meaningful results, in a broader scope of responsibility, as I have in my past
positions.

Through cost-effective negotiations, purchasing, and control, I have been able to
reduce the expenditures of all in-house medical and nonmedical supplies,
substantially, each year as Manager of Inventory Control. In addition, I played a
key role in automating inventories and providing a functional layout for warehouse
locations which effectively reduced the selection and distribution process for
warehoused materials. This also enabled me to provide more stringent controls,
thereby reducing shrinkage, damage, and obsolescence—common problems
causing great concern in the health care field.

Enclosed is my resume. I would very much like to schedule a mutually convenient
interview time. I can be reached at the above address or by phone at (904) 555-
5555. The opportunity to join your management team is of great interest to me,
and I look forward to meeting with you for further discussion.

Sincerely,

Chris Smith

Enc. resume

■ Candidate omits past employer's name.

■ Letter indicates how candidate contributed to previous employer.

APPLICATION FOR IN-HOUSE POSITION
(District Supervisor)

178 Green Street
Big Stone Gap, VA 24219
(703) 555-5555

September 17, 1996

Pat Cummings
Personnel Director
Any Gas Company
1140 Main Street
Norfolk, VA 23510

RE: Management Job Posting
District Supervisor (Grade 25)

Dear Ms. Cummings:

In keeping with the management job posting for the above position, I am enclosing my resume summarizing my experience with Any Gas Company, as well as other employers in the gas distribution-related industry.

All of these positions required my ability to provide technical support, retain personnel, and supervise outside contractors, and work with developers and public officials during the joint work programs and projects. I am extremely well organized, am a good time manager, and have the technical capability to work with and direct company and contractor personnel on all phases of gas distribution systems, from new construction to replacement and operation.

In addition, I believe my previous accomplishments with Any Gas attest to my strong communication skills and my ability to work harmoniously with people at all levels of responsibility within departments. During my five years of service, I feel that I have sought to, and have succeeded in, making a substantial contribution here. The position of District Supervisor would offer me the opportunity to extend that contribution, and I feel well prepared to handle its challenges and responsibilities.

I look forward to meeting with you in a personal interview to discuss my interest in this position. Thank you for your consideration.

Sincerely,

Chris Smith

Enc. resume

■ Candidate chronicles career progression within firm.

■ Four short paragraphs is the ideal length for a cover letter.

AT-HOME PARENT REENTERING THE WORK FORCE
(Graphic Designer)

178 Green Street
Mountain View, CA 92715
(415) 555-5555

July 23, 1996

Pat Cummings
Director
Any Advertising Agency
1140 Main Street
Sausalito, CA 94966

Dear Mr. Cummings:

I am very interested in a freelance or part-time position in graphic design or advertising production. I forward the attached resume for your evaluation.

Please note that in addition to a Bachelor of Arts degree and current enrollment in the Massachusetts College of Art's Graphic Design Certificate Program, I offer more than seven years of valuable experience in production and traffic areas of print and graphic design, and in related fields including fundraising and direct and mass mailings.

As you can see from my resume, I left the field three years ago with excellent references to raise a family and manage a household. Now, with a family well established, I am highly motivated to return to the work force and contribute the valuable experience gained before and during my hiatus.

I would like the opportunity to make a significant contribution to the success of Any Advertising Agency. I am available at the above address and phone number should you have any further questions.

I look forward to hearing from you.

Sincerely,

Chris Smith

Enc. resume

■ Letter focuses on candidate's past job experience while incorporating functional qualifications.

■ Continuing education demonstrates candidate's dedication to his/her field.

AT-HOME PARENT REENTERING THE WORK FORCE
(Salesperson)

178 Green Street
Fort Collins, CO 80525
(303) 555-5555

August 15, 1996

Pat Cummings
Department Manager
Any Store
1140 Main Street
Aurora, CO 80012

Dear Ms. Cummings:

Emmett Puffin recently informed me that you are seeking a full-time addition to your children's department sales staff. I have been observing some very positive changes developing at Any Store, especially your new campaign to promote back-to-school sportswear. I am anxious to join such a successful sales team.

As my resume indicates, I possess over three years' experience within the retail and wholesale arenas. I am committed to quality sales and service standards and am eager to continue my record of success with Any Store. As your newest Sales Associate, I would contribute strong interpersonal skills and an enthusiastic selling approach.

I will contact you next Wednesday to schedule a personal interview. I look forward to discussing how my capabilities could be guided to suit your needs.

Thank you for your time and consideration.

Sincerely,

Chris Smith

Enc. resume

■ Letter omits mention of employment gaps.

■ Candidate expresses interest in returning to full-time employment.

CAREER CHANGER
(Advertising Assistant)

178 Green Street
Daytona Beach, FL 32115
(904) 555-5555

August 18, 1996

Pat Cummings
Hiring Manager
Any Advertising Agency
1140 Main Street
Orlando, FL 32816

Dear Mr. Cummings:

I am very interested in pursuing my career in the advertising industry at Any Advertising Agency. While researching area firms, I read an exciting piece in *Ad World* about your recent campaign for Homeloving soups. Congratulations on receiving a Cleo Award for your efforts!

I would love to join your winning team in an entry-level, administrative position. I can offer over eight years of administration, promotion, and communication experience. The following achievements would be especially beneficial to your firm:

Administration: Recordkeeping and file maintenance. Data processing and computer operations, accounts receivable, accounts payable, accounting research and reports. Order fulfillment, inventory control, and customer relations. Scheduling, office management, and telephone reception.

Promotion: Composing, editing, and proofreading correspondence and PR materials for own house cleaning service.

Communication: Instruction, curriculum and lesson planning, student evaluation, parent-teacher conferences, development of educational materials. Training and supervising clerks.

Computer Skills: Proficient in Microsoft Word, Lotus 1-2-3, Excel, Filemaker Pro, and ADDS Accounting System.

I would like to request a personal interview to further outline my skills, and how they could be immediately applicable to an administrative position at Any Advertising Agency. I will call your office on August 23 to schedule a convenient meeting time.

Thank you, Mr. Cummings. I look forward to our conversation.

Sincerely,

Chris Smith

Enc. resume

■ Categorizing qualifications adds strength to cover letter.

■ Introduction expresses candidate's knowledge of firm.

CAREER CHANGER
(Business Consultant)

178 Green Street
Arkadelphia, AR 71999
(501) 555-5555

March 12, 1996

Pat Cummings
Human Resources Director
Any Corporation
1140 Main Street
Pine Bluff, AR 71601

Dear Ms. Cummings:

I am responding to your recent request in the *Arkansas Democratic-Gazette* for a Business Consultant.

Currently, I am a faculty member in the Department of Management and Aviation Science at Henderson State University. I am also engaged in several temporary assignments involving the installation, conversion, and maintenance of automated accounting systems, troubleshooting, and training. I have working knowledge of, and have taught several applications and operating systems. This includes, but is not limited to, the use of electronic spreadsheets (1-2-3, Excel, Quattro, etc.), and word processing and accounting (Peachtree, AccPac, Great Plains, MYOB, Quicken, Quickbooks, One-Write Plus, etc.) in Windows, Mac, and traditional DOS (IBM/PC) environments.

In strategic market development, the ability to assess customer needs relative to overall market conditions and to respond to them rapidly is critical for successful business development. Let me provide you with innovative approaches to getting the job done based on action, not words.

I would like the opportunity to help you increase your value-added services and profitability. I look forward to discussing this further.

Sincerely,

Chris Smith

Enc. resume

■ Related work experience is accentuated.

■ Computer experience calls attention to candidate's technical knowledge.

CAREER CHANGER
(Casino Dealer)

178 Green Street
Carson City, NV 89706

August 26, 1996

Pat Cummings
Hiring Manager
Any Casino
1140 Main Street
Las Vegas, NV 89109

Dear Mr. Cummings:

Although I have spent the past two years as a medical student and my work experience has been focused in medical research and direct patient care, I am interested in a career change. I am in search of a position where I can use my skills to deal effectively with people, in an exciting and fast-paced environment such as Any Casino.

My work experience and educational discipline have provided me with the ability to rapidly learn new skills and produce solid returns with minimal instruction or supervision. I realize that to become a competent Casino Dealer requires training and experience, and I am willing to devote the time and effort necessary to become a professional in the field.

My professional profile is enclosed. I would like to convince you that I am qualified and strongly dedicated to becoming an effective Dealer for your casino. Can we schedule an interview?

Should you require additional information, please contact me at the above address or by phone at (702) 555-5555. May I hear from you?

Yours sincerely,

Chris Smith

Enc. professional profile

■ Letter emphasizes qualifications pertaining to candidate's job objective.

■ Phrasing request in question form is a strong closing.

CAREER CHANGER
(Computer Programmer)

178 Green Street
Yanton, SD 57078
(605) 555-5555

February 2, 1996

Pat Cummings
Director of Information Systems
Any Corporation
1140 Main Street
Sioux Falls, SD 57117

Dear Ms. Cummings:

After eighteen years in a successful practice of general dentistry, I decided on a career change. To make the transition into computer programming, I sold my practice and have spent the last four years preparing as both a full-time student of computer programming and a Customer Service Representative and computer operator with the products division of CMZ Incorporated.

Although my present position is interesting and has provided me with the opportunity to apply my technical and computer skills, I am looking for a position with room for merit advancement based on my personal performance and contribution to the cost-effective efficiency of your systems.

The enclosed resume summarizes my background and experience. I am available to discuss my qualifications in a personal meeting. I can be reached at the above address or by phone at (605) 555-5555.

Sincerely,

Chris Smith

Enc. resume

■ Unrelated work experience is omitted.

■ Continuing education indicates candidate's ongoing commitment to his/her field.

CAREER CHANGER
(Credit Analyst)

178 Green Street
Laie, HI 96762
(808) 555-5555

April 6, 1996

Pat Cummings
Credit Supervisor
Any Corporation
1140 Main Street
Honolulu, HI 96816

Dear Mr. Cummings:

Please accept the enclosed resume as an expressed interest in joining Any
Corporation to contribute and develop my skills.

My experience lies in customer service and sales, where I have dealt with the
public in a sales and assistance capacity in a financial environment. I would now
like to expand and advance my career by applying my developed skills to a
position as a Credit Analyst. Relevant skills and experience include:

- Bachelor of Science degree in Business Administration.
- Extensive experience in researching, compiling, and analyzing financial
  reports.
- Exclusively responsible for customer service for over 1,000 accounts.
- Opened and serviced 85 new accounts over one-year period.

I would welcome the opportunity to meet with you to discuss ways in which my
capabilities may suit your needs. Please consider my application and direct your
response to the above address.

Your time and consideration is very much appreciated. I look forward to hearing
from you.

Sincerely,

Chris Smith

Enc. resume

■ Letter emphasizes qualifications
pertaining to candidate's job
objective.

■ Bullets make cover letter easy to
read.

CAREER CHANGER
(Marketing Executive)

178 Green Street
Boise, ID 83725
(208) 555-5555

August 5, 1996

Pat Cummings
Vice-President
Any Corporation
1140 Main Street
Chicago, IL 60605

Dear Ms. Cummings:

I am forwarding my resume with regard to the opening in your marketing department as advertised in the August 4 edition of the *Chicago Tribune*.

Although I am currently employed in a management position, I am interested in a career change, especially one where I can combine a thorough knowledge of boating with my sales, marketing, and communication skills. I am an imaginative, well organized self-starter with a strong interest in boating. As a semiprofessional sailboat racer, I twice won national honors and participated in the races at Cape Cod. In addition, I have made lasting contacts with owners and officials.

After you have had the chance to review my resume, please contact me so that we can further discuss the possibility of my joining your staff. I am confident that my business background and knowledge of boats will enable me to have a favorable impact on both your sales and image.

Thank you for your attention, and I look forward to speaking with you again to learn more about this opportunity.

Sincerely yours,

Chris Smith

Enc. resume

■ Awards draw attention to candidate's significant accomplishments.

■ Candidate expresses knowledge in his/her field of interest.

CAREER CHANGER
(Nurse)

178 Green Street
Statesboro, GA 30458

February 22, 1996

Pat Cummings
Nursing Supervisor
Any Hospital
1140 Main Street
Gainesville, GA 30503

Dear Mr. Cummings:

Six years ago, I started a career in nursing. I subsequently left to enter business, and later opted to resign from a lucrative position to pursue my first career, nursing.

During the past four years, I have been employed as a Patient Care Technician while concurrently completing my degree requirements and all associated clinical rotations at the Medway, City Veteran's, and St. Luke's Hospitals. I will receive my Associate degree in Nursing, May 1996, and I am interested in joining a professional nursing staff where I can continue to develop my clinical experience to advance within the profession.

The enclosed resume is a brief summary of my education, clinical training, and experience. However, the opportunity to meet with you will enable me to further detail my qualifications and dedication to quality patient care. Should you require additional information prior to our meeting, please contact me at the above address or by phone at (912) 555-5555. I am interested in available opportunities with your hospital and look forward to a positive response.

Yours sincerely,

Chris Smith

Enc. resume

- ■ Only relevant educational training is included.
- ■ Candidate tailors letter to his/her field of interest.

CAREER CHANGER
(Product and Services Developer)

178 Green Street
Wichita, KS 67202

February 4, 1996

Pat Cummings
Vice-President
Any Bank
1140 Main Street
Topeka, KS 66607

Dear Ms. Cummings:

During the past eight years, I have been actively involved as Vice-President and Director of Operations of an established, quality, $1.4 million function/recreation complex with total responsibility for creating effective sales programs and assuring the quality of services provided.

Currently, I am seeking a career change and opportunity to associate with a progressive bank where I can effectively apply my creative and innovative talents and capability for developing or increasing new service products.

I am flexible, highly energetic, and adept at initiating promotional advertising and marketing programs that will stimulate growth and profits. I am not afraid of the risk or extra time required to gain valuable banking experience at Any Bank, and I would welcome the challenge.

The enclosed resume summarizes my background and experience. Should you require additional information, please contact me at the above address or phone me at (316) 555-5555. I will contact your office next week to schedule a mutually convenient time to meet.

I appreciate your consideration.

Yours sincerely,

Chris Smith

Enc. resume

■ Powerful adjectives, when used sparingly, ensure maximum impact.

■ Interest in new field is emphasized.

CAREER CHANGER
(Real Estate Developer)

178 Green Street
Norfolk, VA 23529
(804) 555-5555

July 20, 1996

Pat Cummings
Director of Real Estate Development
Any Corporation
1140 Main Street
Alexandria, VA 22312

Dear Mr. Cummings:

After several years of diverse and successful experience as a Municipal Bond
Broker, I decided to pursue a career change encompassing a broader scope of real
estate development. To achieve this objective and establish myself as a
professional in the field of real estate development, I spent the past year
completing a comprehensive graduate program and earned a Master's degree in
Real Estate Development from the University of Virginia.

Presently, I am investigating career opportunities with a progressive developer
emphasizing the financial and field aspects of project management. My
experience, prior to entering said graduate program, required extensive
involvement in the purchase and sale of bonds for financing public and private
developments. These included private and public construction developments and
business ventures that required the ability to work with decision makers and
financial/investment professionals in the field of real estate development.

I am a dedicated, energetic self-starter who can recognize opportunities and has
always been willing to devote the time necessary to complete any task thoroughly.
With this attitude, I feel confident that I can readily become a valuable asset as a
member of your management team.

I am presently available for an interview, and will be glad to meet with you at a
mutually convenient time. My resume is enclosed for your review.

I appreciate your consideration.

Yours sincerely,

Chris Smith

Enc. resume

- Impressive educational background strengthens cover letter.

- Closing informs addressee that resume is enclosed.

CAREER CHANGER
(Sales Representative)

178 Green Street
Belle, WV 25015

February 24, 1996

Pat Cummings
Sales Manager
Any Corporation
1140 Main Street
Clarksburg, WV 26302

Dear Ms. Cummings:

If you are in need of a highly motivated achiever skilled in selling products and services and developing client relationships and new business, then we have good reason to meet.

During the past six years, I have owned and operated a photography studio and photo processing laboratory, both of which require the ability to manage inside production while producing enough outside sales to keep the business profitable. Since accomplishing my objective, I am interested in associating with a firm, such as Any Corporation, that can benefit from my ability to sell, manage, and train others to do a quality job.

I am confident of my ability to handle a sales position requiring innovative thinking for positive results. I would welcome the opportunity to convince you of my enthusiasm and skill in a personal interview. When would be a good time for you to meet?

I can be reached at the above address or by phone at (304) 555-5555.

Sincerely,

Chris Smith

Enc. business profile

■ Related work experience is accentuated.

■ Closing reiterates candidate's qualifications for position.

DISPLACED HOMEMAKER
(Administrator)

178 Green Street
Solon, OH 44139

February 25, 1996

Pat Cummings
Human Resources Director
Any Corporation
1140 Main Street
Cleveland, OH 44111

Dear Mr. Cummings:

I would like to offer my skills and experience for your consideration regarding administrative positions available at Any Corporation.

As an addition to your staff, I would bring extensive, varied experience in administration, including staff supervision, meeting planning and direction, and activities scheduling. I have the ability to speak effectively before groups, and communicate well through phone contact or the written word. Additionally, my skills include fund-raising, promotion, and bookkeeping.

I am very interested in contributing to the continued success at Any Corporation, and am sure I would meet your expectations. Could we meet for further discussion? Please contact me at the above address or by phone at (216) 555-5555.

Thank you for your time.

Sincerely,

Chris Smith

Enc. resume

- Letter focuses on the needs of the employer, not the job candidate.
- Letter emphasizes qualifications pertaining to candidate's job objective.

FIRED/LAID OFF
(Recruiter)

178 Green Street
Pennesauken, NJ 08110
(609) 555-5555

July 23, 1996

Pat Cummings
President
Any Executive Search Firm
1140 Main Street
Pleasantville, NJ 08232

Dear Ms. Cummings:

My interest in applying for a position as Recruiter at your firm has prompted me to forward the attached professional profile for your consideration.

My expertise was gained over seven years while recruiting high technology, support staff, and marketing personnel. Much of this experience involved extensive travel, training program development, and networking prospective clients. I possess valuable contacts within the management information systems, software development, and engineering industries that would prove to be a valuable asset to your client base.

I would very much like to apply my skills and knowledge as a member of your recruiting staff. I believe that, in a very short time, I could significantly contribute to your success.

I will follow up this inquiry with a phone call in several days. Thank you for your time.

Sincerely,

Chris Smith

Enc. professional profile

■ Letter omits reason for departure from last job.

■ Unrelated work experience is omitted.

FIRED/LAID OFF
(Sales Director)

178 Green Street
Provo, UT 84603
(801) 555-5555

November 19, 1996

Pat Cummings
Chief Executive Officer
Any Corporation
1140 Main Street
Salt Lake City, UT 84110

Dear Mr. Cummings:

Todd Duncan, of your operations department, suggested I contact you concerning employment opportunities. Todd mentioned that you were considering expanding your sales staff, and thought you might benefit from a professional with my qualifications.

I offer more than twenty years of progressively responsible experience in sales, culminating in my most recent position of Director of Sales and Pricing with a $750 million, 120-store chain. As a senior-level manager, I have been responsible for all aspects of store operations, including merchandising management, buying, strategic planning, marketing, and staff development and management.

Although I have thoroughly enjoyed my present position, corporate downsizing has prompted me to search for a new association. I feel that my years of successful management experience can be more advantageously utilized by a growing and diversifying firm such as Any Corporation.

If you are looking for a well organized, innovative individual with the ability to garner results, please contact me. I would be happy to meet with you at your convenience.

Sincerely,

Chris Smith

Enc. resume

■ Letter briefly suggests reason for departure and emphasizes skills and accomplishments.

■ Candidate immediately introduces purpose for writing.

FORMER SMALL BUSINESS OWNER
(Environmental Advocate)

178 Green Street
Cambridge, MA 02142

May 18, 1996

Pat Cummings
Director
Any Agency
1140 Main Street
Boston, MA 02118

Dear Ms. Cummings:

I am seeking a challenging position in the promotion of environmental awareness.
I read about your agency in the May edition of *Save Our Earth*, and was impressed
by your Stop and Think! campaign to educate Boston in the way of
environmentally safe alternatives to everyday living. I would like to become a part
of your dedicated team.

I possess both a passion for environmental concerns and experience in the
practical application of related programs. For the past four years, I have been
operating my own business, Recycling Renegades, in Cambridge. To begin, I
successfully acquired the first recycling permit in the city of Cambridge for
ferrous and non-ferrous metal, aluminum, high-grade paper, and plastic. As Owner
and Manager, I conducted research, developed pilot programs, formulated
networks for voluntary recycling, picked up and processed materials, and
distributed proceeds to community associations.

Although still extremely committed to recycling efforts, I feel it is time to shift to
a wider focus. I would like to apply my skills to developing innovative programs
for the promotion of all environmental concerns.

Would it be possible to meet for a personal interview? I have several fresh ideas I
would like to share with you. Please contact me at (617) 555-5555 at your
convenience.

Sincerely,

Chris Smith

Enc. resume

■ Candidate emphasizes how past
business experience can benefit
potential employer.

■ Introduction states candidate's
desire to join specific organization.

FREELANCER
(Production Assistant)

178 Green Street
Miami, FL 33132

September 21, 1996

Pat Cummings
Executive Producer
Any Production Company
1140 Main Street
Hialeah, FL 33012

Dear Mr. Cummings:

I am writing to express my keen interest in the Production Assistant position, as advertised in the September 20 edition of the *Miami Herald*.

I possess extensive experience in all aspects of video production, including positions as Writer, Researcher, Director, and Editor. For the past three years, I have been a freelance Production Assistant working on several commercial and documentary pieces. As Chief Assistant on "Milk Carton Kids: An American Crisis," I assisted in preliminary research/writing, scheduling location shooting, and screening potential interview candidates. I also helped in the completion of two public service announcements for Miami Child Services, where my duties also involved camera operation and heavy editing work.

My freelance experience has been diverse and very rewarding, and yet, I would like a permanent production position where my skills can be utilized to a greater advantage. I have admired Any Production Company's work for some time, and attended your screening of "Silent Victims" at the Miami Rape Awareness Convention last month. I would like the opportunity to contribute to such remarkable work.

Please contact me at (305) 555-5555 or (305) 444-4444 evenings, if you need any additional information or if you would like to arrange a meeting.

I look forward to hearing from you.

Sincerely,

Chris Smith

Enc. resume

■ Candidate clearly indicates type of position desired.

■ Candidate's most relevant work experience is prioritized.

FREELANCER
(Writer)

178 Green Street
Oklahoma City, OK 73125
(918) 555-5555

January 6, 1996

Pat Cummings
Publisher
Any Publishing Company
1140 Main Street
Toledo, OH 43660

Dear Ms. Cummings:

I am a Freelance Writer well versed in educational and reference materials for
college students and adults. I am particularly experienced in the areas of careers,
self-help, and parenting. I have frequently noticed such books published by Any
Publishing Company appearing on the best-seller lists, and am especially
interested in learning more about your freelance needs.

Over the past ten years I have developed a writing style that is precise, clear, and
accurate. Whether creating textbook materials, teacher apparatus, or ancillary
activities and worksheets, I am capable of tailoring tone and approach to a variety
of purposes and audiences. I have become quite adept at synthesizing information
and conveying it in a creative and well organized way.

I am sure that our mutual interests will be served by discussing your projects in
greater detail. I would be happy to provide writing samples and references
testifying to the quality of my work.

Thank you for your consideration. I look forward to hearing from you.

Sincerely,

Chris Smith

Enc. resume

■ Letter emphasizes candidate's
strong work history.

■ Letter incorporates company
knowledge into discussion of
qualifications.

FREQUENT JOB CHANGER
(Marketing Assistant)

178 Green Street
El Segundo, CA 90245
(213) 555-5555

December 14, 1996

Pat Cummings
Director of Marketing
Any Corporation
1140 Main Street
Los Angeles, CA 90089

Dear Mr. Cummings:

I am currently seeking an entry-level opportunity in a successful marketing department, and have learned about Any Corporation through the *L.A. Top Sellers Guide*. Congratulations on such an outstanding year!

As you can see from the enclosed resume, since completion of my Bachelor of Science degree, my professional associations have been extensive and diverse. Throughout my experiences, I have developed several important skills that I believe could benefit your marketing department. I possess solid communication skills, both in person and by phone. I am proficient with Macintosh, PC, and spreadsheet applications, and I can effectively manage all aspects of daily business operations, including inventory management and account maintenance. Above all, I possess a strong work ethic and enthusiasm to learn.

Last month I took an intensive seminar entitled "Marketing for Success!" This investment conclusively confirmed my desire to pursue marketing as a career. I know that, if given the chance, I could quickly prove my worth as a member of your staff. Would you permit me that chance?

I look forward to your response.

Sincerely,

Chris Smith

Enc. resume

■ Letter expresses commitment to field of interest.

■ Letter focuses on acquired skills rather than detailing past employers.

GAPS IN EMPLOYMENT HISTORY
(Assistant Curator)

178 Green Street
Tallahassee, AL 36078

June 3, 1996

Pat Cummings
Curator
Any Museum
1140 Main Street
Mobile, AL 36633

Dear Ms. Cummings:

If you are in need of a skilled individual to assist you in museum operations, I would like to offer the enclosed resume for your consideration. I am currently seeking a full-time position in which I can apply both museum and gallery experience and a keen interest in fine art.

As you will note from my resume, I have completed two extensive internships for successful art galleries in the greater Alabama area. In each position, I was exposed to all aspects of operations, from sales to clerical duties. My responsibilities also included assisting customers, setting up displays, and completing mailings for exhibitions. I also possess a Bachelor of Art degree in Art History, and have participated in several related seminars.

In addition, I have spent the last year traveling extensively through Europe and visiting some of the finest museums in the world. This experience has greatly intensified my interest in securing a position in the art world.

I would be available for an interview at your convenience to discuss my qualifications further. Please contact me at the above address or by phone at (205) 555-5555.

Sincerely,

Chris Smith

Enc. resume

■ Candidate expresses interest in returning to full-time employment.

■ Letter briefly explains reason for employment gaps.

GAPS IN EMPLOYMENT HISTORY
(Editor)

178 Green Street
Seymour, CT 06483
(203) 555-5555

August 21, 1996

Pat Cummings
Executive Editor
Any Magazine
1140 Main Street
Shelton, CT 06484

Dear Mr. Cummings:

During a recent telephone conversation, Ellen Marquis, Editor of *On The Town*, recommended that I contact you regarding employment opportunities. I am an experienced Editor interested in continuing a successful career in the field of magazine publishing. A summary of my qualifications includes:

- More than ten years of combined experience writing and editing.
- Adept at managing multiple responsibilities simultaneously.
- Experienced at delegating authority and motivating others to ensure efficiency and productivity.
- Computer knowledge, including Lotus 1-2-3, Microsoft Word, WordPerfect, and Pagemaker.

Specifically in the area of magazine publishing, my responsibilities have also included selecting submissions, assisting in layout and design, recruiting writers, and writing headlines. I possess a Bachelor of Arts degree in English and additional coursework completion in Desktop Publishing and Feature Writing.

I would welcome the opportunity to meet with you in a personal interview to discuss my qualifications in relation to your needs. I will call you on Monday, August 26, to follow up on this inquiry.

I appreciate your time, Mr. Cummings.

Sincerely yours,

Chris Smith

Enc. resume

■ Letter omits mention of employment gaps.

■ Continuing education demonstrates candidate's dedication to his/her field.

IMMIGRANT
(Accountant)

178 Green Street
Eagan, MN 55122
(612) 555-5555

September 12, 1996

Pat Cummings
Senior Accountant
Any Corporation
1140 Main Street
Bloomington, MN 55438

Dear Ms. Cummings:

I am currently searching for an accounting position in which to contribute financial expertise as well as the ability to interface effectively with the business community on an international scale.

I offer over twelve years of comprehensive accounting experience, in both public and private firms. My skills include audits, Chapter 11 filings and bank reconciliation, preparation of financial reports, and accounts payable/receivable. In my most recent position as Senior Accountant, I was solely responsible for the setup and modification of a new computer system, and leading a steering committee to select a general ledger package currently in use.

As you will note from my resume, the majority of my work experience has been focused in Madrid, Spain. Last year, I made the decision to permanently move to the United States with my family, and am very interested in securing a long-term association with a firm such as Any Corporation. Please be assured that although English is my second language, I have been speaking it fluently for over twenty years. As a Staff Accountant at your firm, I could provide translation services to your international department if needed, and an extensive knowledge of European financial dealings.

I would very much like to meet with you for further discussion. I will call your office next week to confirm a meeting time that fits your schedule. In the interim, please contact me if I can provide you with any additional information.

Sincerely,

Chris Smith

Enc. resume

■ Work permit information is optional in a cover letter.

■ Foreign language skills strengthen candidate's qualifications.

MILITARY BACKGROUND
(Electronics Supervisor)

178 Green Street
Laramie, WY 82071
(307) 555-5555

March 23, 1996

Pat Cummings
Personnel Supervisor
Any Corporation
1140 Main Street
Whitewater, WI 53190

Dear Mr. Cummings:

For eighteen years, I have been actively involved in electronic
communication operations, equipment maintenance and documentation, and
personnel training and supervision with the United States Navy.

I am currently investigating opportunities in the civilian electronics industry
in which I can apply this training and experience. I am especially interested in
joining an organization where there is a need for experienced supervision. My
strongest assets include achieving full manpower utilization, working cooperation,
and a high degree of employee morale and production through better management
techniques.

My experience extends itself to civilian as well as military personnel and
encompasses human resources management and other personnel programs. My
experience in line-supervision involved large technical as well as clerical stages in
the operation and maintenance of highly complex equipment and communication
systems.

My qualifications are broad and can be effectively utilized in the
management of personnel programs, human resource management instruction,
and/or line supervision. I am confident that my joining Any Corporation in any of
these areas of responsibility would be mutually beneficial. I will call you next
week to discuss further your needs in relation to my qualifications.

I am willing to relocate, and future compensation packages are negotiable.
I appreciate your consideration.

Sincerely,

Chris Smith

Enc. resume

■ Including a military record can be advantageous if it relates to candidate's job objective.

■ Willingness to relocate can be advantageous.

MILITARY BACKGROUND
(Transportation Operator)

178 Green Street
Provo, UT 84602
(801) 555-5555

January 10, 1996

Pat Cummings
Controller
Any Corporation
1140 Main Street
Provo, UT 84602

Dear Ms. Cummings:

During the past twelve years, my experience has been focused in transportation and sales, and seven of these were spent with the United States Army. Although my recent experience has been in the sale of intangibles, I am interested in resuming a civilian career in transportation operations or in the sale of products or equipment allied to the transportation field.

I have a Bachelor of Science degree, and I am a graduate officer of the U.S. Army Transportation School—the equivalent of a graduate school. In addition to managing all phases of complete civilian and tactical transportation operations (vehicles from two-and-one-half-ton cargo trucks to ten-ton tractor trailers and petroleum tankers), I have taught courses and have trained troops in the total transportation cycle in the United States and abroad.

The enclosed resume summarizes my educational background and experience in the above areas. I feel confident that with my qualifications in the transportation field, I can contribute substantially toward the efficient operation of an in-house traffic, transportation, and distribution function, and/or commercial transportation depot.

I would appreciate the opportunity to further discuss my qualifications in the transportation field and the immediate and long-term contribution I could make to Any Corporation.

If my qualifications interest you, please contact me. I will be glad to furnish any additional information you require.

Sincerely,

Chris Smith

Enc. resume

- Qualifications call attention to candidate's relevant supervisory and administrative experience.

- Candidate details how past military experience will benefit potential employer.

NO CLEAR CAREER PATH
(Account Manager)

178 Green Street
Gallup, NM 87301
(505) 555-5555

July 21, 1996

Pat Cummings
Hiring Manager
Any Accounting Firm
1140 Main Street
Albuquerque, NM 87103

Dear Mr. Cummings:

I am seeking an entry-level position in accounting in which I can apply expertise in both financial management and customer service. While researching area firms, I became very interested in Any Accounting Firm's esteemed training and development program. To such a program, I would bring:

- Bachelor of Science degree, cum laude, in Finance.
- Four years of collections experience.
- Successfully collected 90 percent of company's overdue accounts.
- Experience in accounts payable and accounts receivable.
- Computers: Lotus 1-2-3, Microsoft Word, and MASS-11.
- Knowledge of spreadsheets and accounting software.
- Excellent interpersonal skills.
- Strong leadership qualities.

I am a highly motivated self-starter who has the ability and drive to make a significant contribution to your firm. My resume is enclosed for your review. Would your schedule permit a meeting next week to further discuss my desire to join Any Accounting Firm's staff? I will call you on Friday, July 26, to follow up on this inquiry.

Thank you for your consideration. I look forward to speaking with you.

Sincerely,

Chris Smith

Enc. resume

■ Letter focuses on functional skills applicable to potential employer.

■ Educational honors indicate candidate's potential to excel.

OVERSEAS EMPLOYMENT HISTORY
(Marketing Assistant)

178 Rue Vert
Paris, France
011-331-45-55-55

January 7, 1996

Pat Cummings
Director of Human Resources
Any Corporation
1140 Main Street
New York, NY 10028

Dear Ms. Cummings:

I am looking for a new association with an international service-oriented organization which can benefit from my multilingual and organizational skills in a marketing position.

I have a Bachelor of Arts degree in French (summa cum laude), am fluent in French and Italian, and have strong proficiency in Spanish. In addition, I have experience as an Interpreter and Translator working on international market research with the International Marketing Department at the University of Paris, Sorbonne. I concurrently worked as an Administrative Assistant to professors and business executives.

Since 1992, I have been tutoring individuals in foreign languages and English as a Second Language. I am familiar with various cultures and work well with multilingual, multicultural individuals and groups.

The enclosed resume summarizes my experience. I will be in New York from February 14 through February 28 to secure permanent housing arrangements. I would appreciate the opportunity to meet during that time so that we may discuss the mutual benefits of my joining your firm.

I will call the week of February 5 to confirm receipt of my application and to schedule an interview. Thank you for your time.

Sincerely,

Chris Smith

Enc. resume

■ Candidate emphasizes international work experience and how it might benefit potential employer.

■ Candidate indicates time frame for follow-up contact.

PART-TIME EMPLOYMENT HISTORY
(Art Instructor)

178 Green Street
Marysville, OH 43040
(513) 555-5555

January 28, 1996

Pat Cummings
Principal
Any Elementary School
1140 Main Street
Dayton, OH 45404

Dear Mr. Cummings:

I would like to express my interest in applying for the part-time Art Instructor position advertised in the *Dayton Daily News*.

I am a trained Elementary Art Instructor with expertise in arts and crafts instruction as well as program conception and coordination. For four years, I taught art classes on a part-time basis for the Roosevelt School in Marysville. In addition to my teaching and program management activities, I arranged field excursions and produced an annual district-wide arts competition. Also, I hold a State of Ohio Elementary Education Certificate in Art, and a Bachelor of Fine Arts in Art Education.

For the past year, I have been spending weekends as Arts and Crafts Program Director for the Dayton Parks and Recreational Association. I create and facilitate programs for children, control a budget, select and purchase supplies, and supervise aides in various duties. Since this work is restricted to weekends, my weeks would be completely open to fulfill my responsibilities as your Art Instructor. I am confident that I could create and maintain an exciting program at Any Elementary School.

My resume is enclosed for your review. I would welcome the opportunity to discuss my relevant experience further in a personal interview. As such a time, I could provide you with several excellent references attesting to my skills, as well as a portfolio of past implemented programs.

I look forward to hearing from you.

Sincerely,

Chris Smith

Enc. resume

■ Candidate indicates type of employment desired.

■ Part-time employment history indicates candidate's ability to handle multiple responsibilities.

PART-TIME EMPLOYMENT HISTORY
(Store Manager)

178 Green Street
Brooklyn, NY 11735
(516) 555-5555

April 30, 1996

Pat Cummings
District Manager
Any Retail Chain
1140 Main Street
New York, NY 10016

Dear Ms. Cummings:

My interest in joining your dynamic staff in a full-time management position has prompted me to forward the enclosed resume for your consideration.

During the past seven years, I have held progressively responsible positions in retail sales, from Salesperson to Manager. In my most recent position as Store Manager for Raintree Designs, I assumed responsibility for branch sales from $.5 to $1.2 million in one year. I possess hands-on experience in sales, inventory control, and product promotion. As Assistant Manager for Rips, Inc. in Brooklyn, I supervised a staff of twelve, oversaw the production of a promotional video, and assisted in the selection of chain-wide promotion techniques.

As my resume reveals, the majority of my retail management experience has been on a part-time basis. At this point in my career, I am ready to apply acquired skills to a long-term, more permanent association. As an employee of Any Retail Chain, I would extend every effort to increase sales and promotion, and assure smooth store operations.

After you have had the opportunity to review my qualifications, I would appreciate hearing from you to schedule a personal interview. I would like to learn more about your needs, and discuss my ability to contribute to your goals.

Thank you for your time.

Sincerely,

Chris Smith

Enc. resume

- Part-time experience is relevant to full-time employment.
- Specifically citing number of personnel supervised draws attention to candidate's leadership abilities.

PHYSICALLY CHALLENGED
(Meeting Planner)

178 Green Street
Muckilteo, WA 98275
(206) 555-5555

October 3, 1996

Pat Cummings
Director of Human Resources
Any Corporation
1140 Main Street
St. Charles, MO 63302

Dear Mr. Cummings:

I recently learned from your Vice-President of Operations, Marsha Ponnif, that you might be in need of a Meeting Planner to join your management structure. I am submitting the enclosed business profile for your review.

During the past sixteen years, I have successfully demonstrated solid troubleshooting and problem resolution skills in management, marketing, and sales. My progressively responsible experience includes:

- Corporate/institutional meeting planning.
- Hospitality service coordination.
- Destination management/program coordination.
- Employee/client incentive programs.
- Sales/customer service.

Although my positions have been fast-paced and broad in scope, I would like to make a change and am very impressed by the products and services offered by Any Corporation. Could we meet for an interview? I will contact you next week to schedule a convenient time for further discussion.

Thank you, Mr. Cummings. I look forward to our next conversation.

Sincerely,

Chris Smith

Enc. business profile

■ Unless it is immediately relevant to a candidate's job objective, indicating a physical handicap is unnecessary.

■ Basis for referral is immediately established.

PHYSICALLY CHALLENGED
(Telemarketer)

178 Green Street
West Lafayette, IN 47906
(317) 555-5555

March 14, 1996

Pat Cummings
Telemarketing Director
Any Corporation
1140 Main Street
Lafayette, IN 47902

Dear Ms. Cummings:

I am writing to inquire about possible telemarketing opportunities available at Any Corporation.

During the past five years of direct telemarketing experience, I have acquired a proven track record of outstanding selling and closing capabilities. In my recent position at EPS Telecommunications, my efforts consistently achieved at least 10 percent of sales records through cold-calling techniques. I am an excellent listener who is patient and sensitive to clients' needs, and I am calm under pressure.

Although I have enjoyed my past positions, my true desire has always been to enter the realm of sports-related telemarketing. I have maintained a wide general knowledge of, as well as active participation in, sports activities. Each year I participate in the Indiana State Marathon, and last year placed fourth in the Wheelchair Division.

I am confident of my ability to apply this combined interest and capability to successfully meet all sales quotas at Any Corporation. Please contact me after you have had a chance to review my enclosed resume. I would be very interested in talking with you further regarding suitable telemarketing opportunities.

Thank you for your time.

Sincerely,

Chris Smith

Enc. resume

■ Job descriptions emphasize candidate's accomplishments.

■ Interest in new field is emphasized.

RECENT GRADUATE
(Airline Caterer)

178 Green Street
Providence, RI 02902
(401) 555-5555

October 4, 1996

Pat Cummings
College Relations Representative
Any Service
1140 Main Street
Hartford, CT 06115

Dear Mr. Cummings:

I am writing and enclosing my resume to apprise you of my interest in working for your airline catering service.

I will receive my Bachelor of Science degree in Food Service from Johnson and Wales University in January. In addition to studying such valuable courses as Chemical Science, Organic Chemistry, Nutrition, and Food Service Administration, I have learned a great deal about the food industry as an active member of the Student Association for Agricultural Science. Further, I offer solid experience in the food industry through working as an Assistant Manager for two summers at a local yogurt shop.

I would be very interested in securing an entry-level position with Any Service. If you feel that my qualifications might meet your needs, please contact me at (401) 444-4444. Otherwise, a message may be left at my above-listed phone number.

Thank you for your attention, and I look forward to your response.

Sincerely,

Chris Smith

Enc. resume

■ Letter includes course work that corresponds to position desired.

■ College activities are related to candidate's field of study and career objective.

RECENT GRADUATE
(Assisant Museum Director)

178 Green Street
Vermillion, SD 57069

June 26, 1996

Pat Cummings
Museum Director
Any Museum
1140 Main Street
Rapid City, SD 57701

Dear Ms. Cummings:

I am a recent graduate of the University of South Dakota with a well-rounded art history background. I would like to put my skills and knowledge to use in an entry-level position at your prestigious museum, perhaps as an Assistant Director to the Curator.

As my resume indicates, I participated in an exclusive summer program for art history majors at Le Louvre in Paris. There, I studied some of the most significant works in European art and attended a very interesting seminar about the workings of the Louvre itself. I also worked for two summers at the Metropolitan Museum of Art in New York City, where I served as a Museum Assistant at the information booth. My coursework in African-American art, modern art, and museum science has also prepared me well for an entry-level position in a fine arts museum.

I have long been a lover of art and art museums. I have been visiting your museum ever since I was a small child and would be thrilled at the opportunity to become a part of your excellent staff.

Enclosed is my resume for your consideration. I may be reached at (605) 555-5555 after 3:00 p.m. and on weekends. I hope to hear from you soon.

Sincerely,

Chris Smith

Enc. resume

■ Letter conveys polite enthusiasm.   ■ Applicable coursework, workshops, and seminars are highlighted.

RECENT GRADUATE
(English Teacher)

178 Green Street
Plymouth, MA 02360
(508) 555-5555

April 8, 1996

Pat Cummings
Human Resources Manager
Any School District
1140 Main Street
Newton, MA 02164

Dear Mr. Cummings:

In response to last week's advertisement in the *New England Journal of Higher Education* for an English Teacher, I have enclosed my resume for your consideration.

I have recently graduated from Boston College with a Bachelor's degree in Secondary Education. I am certified to teach both English and Special Education. In addition to fulfilling my practice teaching requirement in your district, I participated in a volunteer literacy program to tutor both youth and adults struggling with reading difficulties. I also organized and performed in a variety show at Newton High School that benefited special needs students.

As I fulfilled my practice teaching requirement in District 5, I was continually impressed by its high educational standards and its long-standing record of producing students whose SAT scores are among the highest in the nation. I would consider it a great opportunity to teach in such an accomplished district.

I will be calling you on Monday, April 13, to confirm that you received my resume and answer any questions you may have. I look forward to speaking with you.

Sincerely,

Chris Smith

Enc. resume

- ■ Position applied for is clearly and immediately defined.
- ■ Volunteer experience gives candidate a competitive edge.

RECENT GRADUATE
(Environmental Campaigner)

178 Green Street
New London, CT 06320

July 17, 1996

Pat Cummings
Regional Program Director
Any Environmental Campaign
1140 Main Street
Danbury, CT 06810

Dear Ms. Cummings:

As a recent graduate of Tufts University Environmental Leadership Training Program and a 1993 graduate of Mesa State College with a degree in Biology, I am currently launching my career as an Environmental Campaigner in areas of concern that affect local, national, or world communities.

For the past several years, my elective studies concentrated on biology, chemistry, and the scientific, management, and political issues associated with the environment. In addition, I have organized recycling programs in my hometown and on my college campuses. Now I aim to make environmental campaigning my full-time profession. I am anxious to devote my energy to Any Environmental Campaign, and am confident I can make a significant contribution.

I can be reached at the above address or by phone at (203) 555-5555.

Looking forward to your return response for a better world.

Sincerely,

Chris Smith

Enc. resume

- ■ Activities highlight candidate's involvement in local community.
- ■ Relevant course work adds depth to candidate's educational background.

RECENT GRADUATE
(Forester)

178 Green Street
Los Angeles, CA 90053
(213) 555-5555

July 30, 1996

Pat Cummings
Director
Any Bureau
1140 Main Street
Oakland, CA 94612

Dear Mr. Cummings:

I am a recent college graduate with a degree in Earth Science and Forestry and am seeking a position in Forestry in the Pacific states.

In June, I graduated from the University of Southern California with a Bachelor's degree in Earth Science and Forestry. I have studied many relevant courses including Forest Economics, Range Management, Ecology, Soil Science, Hydrology, Wildlife, and Agronomy. In 1991, I was recognized for outstanding achievement in the natural sciences when I was awarded the prestigious Lukestrom Badge.

I also offer on-site work experience, having interned last summer for the California State Soil Conservation Service. In this position, I was exposed to all aspects of applied soil science. I provided technical assistance primarily to farmers and ranchers to promote the conservation of soil, water, and related natural resources. Equally important, I helped to develop programs to combat soil erosion and maximize land productivity without damaging the environment.

I gained valuable experience in forestry when I attended Southern California University's Field Camp in Walgreen Falls. I planted and maintained trees and rare natural vegetation and recorded and charted their growth. In addition to testing soil and water samples, I tracked wildlife species and worked to preserve natural habitats for endangered species.

If you feel that I am suitable for a position with Any Bureau, I would greatly appreciate an interview. I may be reached at the above listed number during the morning hours. Thank you for your consideration!

Sincerely,

Chris Smith

Enc. resume

■ Relevant internship bolsters otherwise limited work experience.

■ Extracurricular and school-related awards add weight to candidate's letter.

RECENT GRADUATE
(Gerontologist)

178 Green Street
Worcester, MA 01610
(508) 555-5555

June 23, 1996

Pat Cummings
Director
Any Agency
1140 Main Street
Salem, MA 01970

Dear Ms. Cummings:

Thank you for taking the time to speak with me today. As I mentioned on the phone, I am interested in beginning a career in the field of gerontology.

I am currently a senior at the College of the Holy Cross, majoring in Sociology. I have studied a variety of subjects including gerontology, where I first became interested in this field. Other related courses I have taken include Poverty and Crisis, the Political Economy of Health Care in the United States, Race Relations, and Women in Society. My current grade point average is 3.64 and I am a member of the Phi Beta Kappa honor society.

In addition to my school work, I am an active member of the student-run Volunteers for a Better World Program. Some of the experiences I have gained through this organization include serving Thanksgiving dinner to the homeless at a local soup kitchen, tutoring underprivileged junior high students in math and English, and codirecting a very successful annual campus food drive. As a contributing writer for the *Angora*, I wrote many articles and editorials concerning various social issues, including the plight of the elderly.

As a result of my classroom studies and my volunteer experience, I feel that I have an excellent grasp of the social and political issues that affect older adults in the United States. I feel that, at your agency, I could make a real difference in the lives of older people.

I've enclosed my resume and a sample article for your perusal. Thank you for your attention to this matter and I look forward to your response.

Sincerely,

Chris Smith

Enc. resume

■ Educational honors are emphasized.

■ Personal interests and activities are relevant to candidate's field of interest.

RECENT GRADUATE
(Legal Assistant)

178 Green Street
Aston, PA 19014
(215) 555-5555

April 4, 1996

Pat Cummings
Attorney-at-Law
Any Firm
1140 Main Street
Erie, PA 16563

Dear Mr. Cummings:

Justice Ellen Malone, of Allentown Courthouse, suggested that I contact you
regarding an opening you may soon have for a Legal Assistant.

I will be graduating this May from Temple University with a Bachelor of Arts
degree in African-American Studies. In addition to my core studies, I have studied
in a variety of areas including business administration and computer applications.
In 1991, I was awarded the prestigious Lieberman Scholarship.

I also offer a strong background in law, having worked in a variety of legal
settings throughout my college years. I was a volunteer for Temple's Student
Legal Aid, helping students with a variety of legal problems. I worked part-time
over the past three years as a Volunteer Probation Officer for the Allentown
juvenile court. And in addition to being an Outside Media Contact for an Aston
Outreach Unified Neighborhood Team, I spent one summer as a Research
Assistant for the Chief County Clerk of Allentown.

All of these positions have given me a strong sense of the law and the American
legal system. Moreover, this experience convinced me that I would like to pursue
the law as a career. Justice Malone highly recommends your firm as one which
might be a good match for my goals and qualifications.

Enclosed is my resume. I will contact you within the week to further discuss the
possibilities of securing this position. Thank you for your time.

Sincerely,

Chris Smith

Enc. resume

■ Part-time work experience during
school indicates candidate's
strong work ethic.

■ Impressive credentials and
awards further enhance
candidate's qualifications.

RECENT GRADUATE
(Physicist)

178 Green Street
White Plains, NY 10604
(914) 555-5555

March 16, 1996

Pat Cummings
Professional Recruiter
Any Photographic Institute
1140 Main Street
Long Island, NY 11747

Dear Ms. Cummings:

Perhaps you are seeking an addition to your excellent team of physicists? A new person can provide innovative approaches and ideas to the challenges of research and development.

As you can see from my resume, I will be graduating in June from New York University with a Bachelor's degree in Physics. I also have studied related fields such as chemical engineering, mathematics, and systems applications, all of which I am sure would help me as a physicist with Any Photographic Institute. I offer solid experience, having worked for two summers for the physics department at NYU, both as an intern and a laboratory technician.

Additionally, I have a personal interest in photography, having been an avid amateur photographer for many years. I built my own darkroom and have won several awards for my photographs. Because of this, I feel that Any Photographic Institute is an especially good match for my skills and interests.

Please advise me of any positions that may become available. Your consideration of my credentials is greatly appreciated.

Sincerely,

Chris Smith

Enc. resume

■ Use of concrete examples highlights candidate's achievements.

■ Internships strengthen candidate's short work history.

RECENT GRADUATE
(Set Designer)

178 Green Street
Columbia, SC 29202
(803) 555-5555

August 14, 1996

Pat Cummings
Stage Director
Any Production Company
1140 Main Street
Columbia, SC 29202

Dear Mr. Cummings:

Lynne Winchester recently indicated that you may have an opening for a Set
Designer and suggested that I contact you. I seek a creative position involving
stage design in television.

I graduated last December from Clemson University with a Bachelor of Arts
degree in Theatre Arts and a concentration in Studio Art. In addition to modern
drama, and music and sound in theatre, I completed courses in set creation and
design, intermediate painting, and woodworking. As a member of the drama club,
I designed and helped create props for numerous campus productions including
The Tempest and *Marco Polo Sings A Solo.*

As for my work experience, I co-designed and co-created the props and
decorations for a new miniature golf course with a tropical island theme, which
turned out to be a big hit. I also gained valuable skills working as an apprentice to
a busy carpenter and painting houses for a large company.

Enclosed is my resume as well as some photographs of my work. I have some
great ideas for the sets of "Trivia Tunes" and "Videos After Dark" which I would
like to discuss with you in a personal interview. I may be reached at the above
listed number before 1:00 p.m. weekdays. Thank you for your consideration of my
application.

Sincerely,

Chris Smith

Enc. resume
    photographs

- Courses listed are related to candidate's field of interest.

- Enclosure line refers to all attached materials.

RECENT GRADUATE
(Translator)

178 Green Street
Chicago Heights, IL 60411
(708) 555-5555

July 5, 1996

Pat Cummings
Director
Any Council
1140 Main Street
Denver, CO 80204

Dear Ms. Cummings:

I am writing with the hope that you will consider me for the position of Translator as advertised in today's *Rocky Mountain News*.

I graduated last month with a Bachelor of Arts degree in International Relations and French Language from Northwestern University. Consistently on the dean's list and graduating one year early with honors and advanced standing, I was recognized throughout my career for excellent scholarship. I was also very active in many extracurricular events and organizations, including a residential honors program studying ethics and politics. By my junior year, I had become a Model United Nations Advisor, an Alumni Ambassador, and President of the International Affairs Society.

In addition, I have some work experience in the field of international affairs, having worked as an interpreter and translator for a Parisian film corporation. In this position, I interpreted for negotiations over film coproductions and translated agreements, film scripts, scenarios, and foreign correspondence. I also worked as the Assistant to the Parisian Correspondent for Desliases Associates, a prestigious import/export company.

I feel confident that an interview would determine that my expertise in international affairs and the French language and culture makes me well qualified for this position. I am not limited by location and would enjoy the opportunity to live and work in Denver for Any Council.

I look forward to meeting you, Ms. Cummings, and will give you a call to follow up on this letter toward the end of next week.

Sincerely,

Chris Smith

Enc. resume

■ For recent graduates, extracurricular activities demonstrate potential for productivity.

■ Educational honors indicate candidate's potential to excel.

RETIREE REENTERING THE WORK FORCE
(Math Instructor)

178 Green Street
Bartow, FL 33830
(813) 555-5555

August 2, 1996

Pat Cummings
Principal
Any Junior High School
1140 Main Street
St. Petersburg, FL 33716

Dear Mr. Cummings:

Recently I bumped into long-time friend and colleague, Harry Nestor, Superintendent of St. Petersburg Schools. Harry tells me that Any High School is currently searching for a part-time Math Instructor for the upcoming school year. I would like to express my interest in assuming such a position.

As my enclosed professional profile reflects, I possess over thirty-three years of experience in junior high and high school education. Before assuming my most recent position as Principal of Sacred Heart Junior High School in St. Petersburg, I taught math and science courses to middle school children for thirteen years. My expertise ranges from remedial math to precalculus for advanced students. In addition to my Master's degree in Education, I hold a Florida State Teacher Certification.

Although retired for over a year, I feel I still have much to offer in the field of education, and would once again like to apply my skills to the personal and intellectual advancement of all students.

I look forward to hearing from you further regarding this position.

Sincerely yours,

Chris Smith

Enc. professional profile

- Candidate explains how extensive experience will benefit potential employer.
- Professional certification and strong educational background add strength to cover letter.

TEMPORARY EMPLOYMENT HISTORY
(Administrative Assistant)

178 Green Street
Van Nuys, CA 91411

October 1, 1996

Pat Cummings
Director
Any Temporary Agency
1140 Main Street
Van Nuys, CA 91411

Dear Ms. Cummings:

I am forwarding the enclosed resume for your consideration regarding suitable temporary assignment positions.

My five years of consecutive temporary assignment work have provided me with skills and qualifications applicable to many different fields. In short, I would offer a potential employer:

- Three years accounting, financial, and administrative experience.
- Computer knowledge including IBM, Macintosh, and Honeywell systems.
- Proficiency in word processing programs and spreadsheet applications.
- Outstanding communication and organizational skills.

Should you require any additional information after reviewing my qualifications, please do not hesitate to contact me at the above address or by phone at (818) 555-5555. I would prefer to receive an assignment in the Van Nuys area, and compensation requirements are negotiable.

Sincerely,

Chris Smith

Enc. resume

■ Candidate informs agency contact of all relevant information, including travel availability and salary requirements.

■ Letter focuses on acquired skills relevant to field of interest.

TEMPORARY EMPLOYMENT HISTORY
(Publisher's Assistant)

178 Green Street
Wilmington, DE 19899
(302) 555-5555

February 22, 1996

Pat Cummings
Editor
Any Publishing Company
1140 Main Street
New Castle, DE 19720

Dear Mr. Cummings:

I would like to take this opportunity to express my interest in the Publisher's Assistant position advertised in the February 21 edition of the *News-Journal*.

I am a 1994 graduate of Johns Hopkins University, holding a Bachelor of Arts degree in English. Since my graduation, I have accepted several temporary positions with area businesses in order to gain a wide range of skills to apply to an entry-level position in publishing. While at Curran, Moylan, and Hudson, I developed strong written and interpersonal communication skills. My responsibilities included sorting mail, interfacing with management and clients, and inputing data. As a temporary Marketing Assistant at Finner and Grant Publishers, I assisted in special project work in the editorial department and assisted with administrative responsibilities.

Each of my experiences has provided me with excellent computer and general office skills which I could apply to the position of Publisher's Assistant. I would appreciate the chance to discuss my qualifications with you, and to learn more about current projects at Any Publishing Company. I plan to call you within the next several days to arrange a meeting.

Thank you for your consideration.

Sincerely,

Chris Smith

Enc. resume

- ■ Candidate immediately specifies position being applied for.
- ■ Temporary experience is relevant to full-time employment.

WEAK EDUCATIONAL BACKGROUND
(Parking Supervisor)

178 Green Street
Scottsdale, AZ 85254
(602) 555-5555

May 13, 1996

Pat Cummings
Manager of Operations
Any Airport
1140 Main Street
Phoenix, AR 85021

Dear Ms. Cummings:

I am currently investigating opportunities to which I can apply my knowledge of, and extensive experience in, the management of large parking facilities.

In my most recent position at Parkinson Hotel, my proven abilities and tireless work ethic resulted in rapid advancement to a management position after only one year of service as a Parking Attendant. As Supervisor of Parking Facilities, I oversaw all financial collections, maintained customer service standards, effectively troubleshooted, and managed a large staff. Additionally, I administered work schedules and payroll, assigned duties, and interfaced with hotel management.

I am a self-motivated, people-oriented, responsible individual capable of meeting your expectations for quality supervision. I look forward to a personal interview to further discuss how I can contribute to your parking staff.

Sincerely,

Chris Smith

Enc. resume

- Listing educational background is optional if candidate possesses extensive work experience.

- Qualifications highlight candidate's problem-solving ability.

WEAK EMPLOYMENT BACKGROUND
(Finance Broker)

178 Green Street
Irving, TX 75038
(803) 555-5555

December 14, 1996

Pat Cummings
Broker
Any Corporation
1140 Main Street
El Paso, TX 79998

Dear Mr. Cummings:

During the past seven years, I have held positions ranging from Supervisor of field operations to Sales and Marketing Manager of jewelry and specialty products, and am comfortable in both wholesale and retail markets.

Currently, I am seeking a position change where I can utilize my experience in telemarketing, inside sales management, and dealings with commodity brokers in sales with an established security brokerage or related financial service.

During the course of my research into the field, I was impressed by the innovative sales techniques and increasing market share held by Any Corporation. I would love to begin a long-term association with your firm, and I am willing to start at entry level and participate in your formal registered-representative training program. I am confident that I have the ability to quickly establish contact with customers and develop sales-producing accounts.

The enclosed resume summarizes my background and experience in the above areas. I would welcome the chance to discuss the possibility of our joining forces. I will call you next Tuesday to schedule a mutually convenient time to meet.

Thank you, Mr. Cummings, for your consideration. I look forward to speaking with you.

Sincerely yours,

Chris Smith

Enc. resume

- Letter emphasizes valuable skills.
- Candidate's practical experience outweighs his/her education.

WEAK EMPLOYMENT BACKGROUND
(Sales Manager)

178 Green Street
Kalamazoo, MI 49006
(616) 555-5555

June 20, 1996

Pat Cummings
On-Site Sales Manager
Any Corporation
1140 Main Street
Roscommon, MI 48653

Dear Ms. Cummings:

If your company is looking for a self-motivated person who can work well with people, grasp and expand on new ideas, tackle and follow through on difficult projects, and achieve set objectives, then I feel we have good reason to meet.

Confident in my ability to succeed, I offer you a Bachelor of Science degree in Economics (cum laude), a graduate degree in Urban Affairs, experience in sales, and the desire to apply all or part of this background to a structured management training program in your firm.

The enclosed resume summarizes my background. I am not afraid of hard work, can work under pressure, and honestly feel that within a short time I could be contributing a profitable return on your company's training investment. I am available any time to learn more about Any Corporation and convince you of my desire to join your ranks.

I look forward to meeting with you. Thank you for your time.

Sincerely,

Chris Smith

Enc. resume

- Impressive educational experience and qualifications helps compensate for candidate's short employment history.

- Candidate refers to attached resume in closing.

10
Response to a Classified Advertisement

Response letters are written for job openings advertised in the classified ads. When writing your cover letter, you should keep the specifics of the advertisement in mind. If the job requires travel or relocation, make sure to specify your availability in your response. Only address salary preference if requested, phrasing it in a range so you don't limit your opportunities.

Be sure to tailor your letter to the specific requirements outlined in the ad. For instance, Marsha Z. recently reworked her cover letter to respond to an opening for a Computer Programmer. Although she had been working in retail, she de-emphasized her sales accomplishments to highlight computer courses she had taken, applications she was proficient in, and her experience working as an intern for an IBM computer design team. As a result, Marsha landed an interview!

It is important to keep in mind, though, that classifieds should be responded to quickly. The faster your inquiry reaches an employer's desk, the more individual attention it will receive.

RESPONSE TO A CLASSIFIED ADVERTISEMENT
(Administrative Assistant)

178 Green Street
Ecru, MS 38842
(601) 555-5555

November 1, 1996

Pat Cummings
Office Manager
Any Corporation
1140 Main Street
Chicago, IL 60605

Dear Mr. Cummings:

Your October 30 advertisement in the *Jackson Review* calls for an Assistant with a background rich in a variety of administrative skills, such as mine.

As an organized and detail-oriented individual with five years' experience in administration, I believe my qualifications match your requirements. My strengths also include independent working habits and superb computer skills. As an Administrative Assistant at Lambert Hospital, I was in charge of all computer support, word processing and data base, spreadsheet, and administrative functions. Duties included all purchasing, equipment maintenance, daily office operations, supervising of staff and volunteers, and coordinating various projects with staff and outside vendors.

I would appreciate the opportunity to discuss this position with you at your convenience, as it sounds like an exciting opportunity. If you have any questions, do not hesitate to contact me at the above-listed phone number or at (601) 444-4444.

Sincerely,

Chris Smith

Enc. resume

- Introduction is brief and attention-grabbing.
- Candidate details applicable work experience.

RESPONSE TO A CLASSIFIED ADVERTISEMENT
(Administrative Judge)

178 Green Street
Fox, OR 97831
(503) 555-5555

May 23, 1996

Pat Cummings
Chairperson
Chicago Municipal Court
1140 Main Street
Chicago, IL 60605

Dear Ms. Cummings:

Your advertisement in the May 30th issue of *Lawyers Monthly* is of great interest to me. I feel that I have the qualifications necessary to effectively handle the responsibilities of Administrative Judge.

During the past four years as Assistant Attorney General, I have gained broad experience in the litigation of personal injury actions and workers' compensation claims. In this position, I made extensive use of my legal knowledge as well as my research, analytical, writing, and judgmental skills. I am confident of my ability to provide the expertise necessary for the professional representation of an Administrative Judge.

The enclosed resume describes my qualifications for the position advertised. I would welcome the opportunity to personally discuss my qualifications with you at your convenience.

Sincerely,

Chris Smith

Enc. resume

- Closing is brief and to the point.
- Letter cites advertisement's specific publication and date.

RESPONSE TO A CLASSIFIED ADVERTISEMENT
(Analyst)

178 Green Street
Henniker, NH 03242
(603) 555-5555

December 30, 1996

Pat Cummings
Director, Financial Planning
Any Corporation
1140 Main Street
Nashua, NH 03061

Dear Mr. Cummings:

I write in response to your advertisement for an Analyst in the December 28 edition of the *Telegraph*. During the past several years I have been actively involved, in both academic and workplace settings, with financial and business analysis as well as support activities involving corporate business and finance.

Although my present position has provided me with the opportunity for quality professional development as an Analyst and interesting challenges through diverse assignments, I am ready for a change. I am interested in joining a firm in which I can offer my analytical and qualitative skills toward making a substantial contribution to its overall success and reputation.

The enclosed employment profile is a summary of my experience. I would be glad to schedule an interview to discuss your requirements and my ability to handle the responsibilities of the position offered.

Should you require additional information prior to our meeting, please feel free to contact me at the above address and daytime number, or during the evenings at (603) 444-4444.

In the interim, I will look forward to your return response.

Yours sincerely,

Chris Smith

Enc. employment profile

- Position applied for is clearly and immediately defined.
- Including an evening telephone number is optional in a cover letter.

RESPONSE TO A CLASSIFIED ADVERTISEMENT
(Assistant Curator)

178 Green Street
Bensonville, IL 60106
(708) 555-5555

June 21, 1996

Pat Cummings
Curator
Any Music Library
1140 Main Street
Evansville, IL 47713

Dear Ms. Cummings:

    I wish to be considered for the position of Assistant Curator of your music library as advertised in last Friday's *Evansville Courier*.

    My experience includes working as the Assistant Editor of *Classics Quarterly*, writing classical music reviews for the *Complete Record Guide*, conducting interviews and writing concert reviews for *Chicago Rock*, and writing rock and country album reviews for *Inside Edge*. I was also employed as the Classical Music Listings Coordinator for the *Complete Musical Almanac* summer and fall supplements. Currently, I am proofreading and copyediting part-time for *Art Illinois*, and am doing evening announcements (two nights per week) at WKEM in Belleville.

    In addition, I offer a Bachelor of Arts degree in Music, a Master's degree in Musicology from DePaul University, a year at Cambridge University (England) studying music and the arts, and doctoral studies at the University of Chicago.

    I am very interested in resuming regular, full-time employment with a facility in need of a skilled professional knowledgeable in all aspects of musicology. I have often visited and relied on the resources available at Any Music Library, and would welcome the opportunity to join your ranks. I am confident my experience could be applied to a successful career as your Assistant Curator.

    I would be happy to meet with you to further discuss the position and my ability to meet your needs. I will be in the Evansville area during the week of July 3, and will call your office to schedule a convenient interview time.

    Thank you for your time.

Sincerely,

Chris Smith

Enc. resume

■ Candidate includes all relevant experience to advertised position.

■ Impressive educational background strengthens cover letter.

RESPONSE TO A CLASSIFIED ADVERTISEMENT
(Assistant Editor)

178 Green Street
Worcester, MA 01610
(508) 555-5555

June 28, 1996

Pat Cummings
Editor
Any Corporation
1140 Main Street
Boston, MA 02215

RE: Assistant Editor

Dear Mr. Cummings:

I recently read your advertisement in the *Boston Globe* for the position of
Assistant Editor, and am highly interested in learning more about the job's specific
requirements.

I possess strong written and verbal communication skills, as well as computer and
desktop publishing experience. My accomplishments include:

- Winning the Columbia Scholastic Press Association's First Place Gold
  Circle Award for graphic art.
- Serving as feature editor, art editor, graphic artist, and reporter for various
  college publications.
- Completing a course in advertising art/desktop publishing, which focused
  on the use of Pagemaker software.
- Proficiency in IBM compatible WordPerfect and Lotus 1-2-3 software.

Please find my resume attached for your review. I would appreciate the
opportunity to discuss my specific abilities in relation to your needs. I will call you
next Monday to schedule a mutually convenient time to meet.

Thank you for your consideration.

Sincerely,

Chris Smith

Enc, resume

■ Setting desired position apart from body of letter may be advantageous when responding to classified advertisement.

■ Letter uses bullets to highlight candidate's achievements related to advertised position.

RESPONSE TO A CLASSIFIED ADVERTISEMENT
(Assistant Hospital Supervisor)

178 Green Street
Stoughton, MA 02072
(617) 555-5555

July 27, 1996

Pat Cummings
Administrator
Any Corporation
1140 Main Street
Chicago, IL 60605

RE: Assistant Hospital Supervisor position

Dear Ms. Cummings:

I am writing in response to your advertisement in this past week's *Boston Phoenix*.

I recently took a sabbatical and finished my Bachelor of Arts degree in May at Emerson College. I am currently seeking full-time employment.

My employment background consists of twelve years at the Deaconess Hospital, where I provided a wide range of administrative, financial, and research support to the Chief Executive Officer. I have a strong aptitude for working with numbers and extensive experience with computer software applications.

I would be interested in speaking with you further regarding this position. I am hopeful that you will consider my background in administrative support, as well as my word processing, data base, and spreadsheet skills an asset to Any Corporation.

Thank you in advance for your consideration.

Sincerely,

Chris Smith

Enc. resume

■ Candidate expresses interest in returning to full-time employment.

■ Candidate uses closing to suggest possibility of interview.

RESPONSE TO A CLASSIFIED ADVERTISEMENT
(Associate Desktop Publisher)

178 Green Street
Tacoma, WA 98447
(206) 555-5555

March 10, 1996

Pat Cummings
Managing Editor
Any Corporation
1140 Main Street
Richmond, VA 23225

Dear Mr. Cummings:

In response to your advertisement for an Associate Desktop Publisher, I am
sending my resume for your review.

My ten years of computer experience include researching, developing, and
documenting the operational procedures of a software seller. I was responsible for
all aspects of the manual, from conceptualization to publication. I also coordinated
and published the sales and marketing of a newsletter distributed to key accounts
and sales representatives.

Successful completion of such projects requires skills in researching, organizing,
writing, and editing. I am proficient in several desktop publishing and word
processing applications, including WordPerfect, Microsoft Word, and Corel
Ventura.

I will be moving to the Richmond area next week and would be happy to meet
with you at your convenience. I will call your office during the week of March 17.
Thank you.

Sincerely,

Chris Smith

Enc. resume

- Computer experience calls
  attention to candidate's technical
  knowledge.
- Candidate immediately specifies
  position being applied for.

RESPONSE TO A CLASSIFIED ADVERTISEMENT
(Athletic Director)

178 Green Street
La Crosse, WI 54601
(608) 555-5555

September 23, 1996

Pat Cummings
Headmaster
Any School
1140 Main Street
Brownsville, TX 78520

Dear Ms. Cummings:

I am writing to you regarding the opening for the position of Athletic Director, as advertised in the *Wisconsin State Journal*. I believe that, with my background in athletics and science, I have the technical knowledge, work ethic, and organizational skills to contribute to your team.

For the past nine years I have been coaching rowing. I feel strongly that the qualities embodied in rowing have made me successful in my various business and athletic endeavors. Goal setting, discipline, determination, and teamwork are applicable to any field.

I admire Any School's unique educational philosophy, which stresses the utility of athletics to instill discipline in young minds. I feel that I can contribute to your school's achievement-oriented environment.

Due to a change in the position of Head Crew Coach at Yale University, I was put in an interim position of responsibility for the smooth running of the boathouse. For the 1995-1996 season, I dealt with all the ordering, budgeting, donation solicitation, spare parts inventory, and travel arrangements for the crews. I was, in effect, the administrative head of the boathouse.

I will call in approximately two weeks to discuss how I hope to contribute to your school. A resume is enclosed for your consideration.

Sincerely,

Chris Smith

Enc. resume

■ Candidate's most recent position is outlined in detail.

■ Since company name and information is provided in advertisement, candidate promises to follow up inquiry.

RESPONSE TO A CLASSIFIED ADVERTISEMENT
(Business Consultant)

178 Green Street
Payne Gap, KY 41537
(606) 555-5555

June 3, 1996

Pat Cummings
Director of Recruiting
Any Corporation
1140 Main Street
Payne Gap, KY 41537

RE: Business Consultant; *Lexington Herald-Leader*; May 27, 1996

Dear Mr. Cummings:

I am a new MBA graduate from Spain's premiere business school, la Universidad de Negocios. Although I have lived in Spain for most of my life, I am an American citizen and have just recently moved to Kentucky to seek permanent employment.

Your advertisement captured my attention because I am very interested in pursuing a career as a software consultant. Please allow me to highlight my qualifications as they relate to your stated requirements.

Your Requirements
- Experience consulting to small businesses
- Experience working in small businesses
- Marketing experience
- Enjoy using computers
- Assist in the development and implementation of new software producers for small businesses

My Experience
- Graduated with an M.B.A. Immersed in case study method, in which students act as consultants, analyzing and solving business problems.
- Founded Widgetsoft, a software development business. Worked in small departments of larger companies. Enjoy handling multiple responsibilities and working closely with others.
- 4-1/2 years of progressive marketing experience. Possess strong writing, editing, and desktop publishing abilities.

- Fluency in Lotus 1-2-3, Microsoft Word, Word for Windows, dBase. Programming experience in C+, Fortran, COBOL.
- At John Whitmore & Sons, I participated in the development of a new CD-ROM Atlas. Assisted with marketing, content, and user interface issues.

I believe my qualifications are commensurate with your requirements for this position. I would welcome the opportunity for an interview to discuss with you how I can help develop outstanding software products for Any Corporation.

Sincerely,

Chris Smith

Enc. resume

■ Unique format demonstrates candidate's ability to meet advertised job requirements.

■ International work experience adds weight to candidate's qualifications.

RESPONSE TO A CLASSIFIED ADVERTISEMENT
(Campus Police Officer)

178 Green Street
Stanford, CA 94305
(415) 555-5555

February 23, 1996

Pat Cummings
Director of Security
Any College
1140 Main Street
Whittier, CA 92608

RE: Campus Police Officer

Dear Ms. Cummings:

My interest in pursuing and expanding my professional career in law enforcement
and security management has prompted me to respond to your advertisement in
the March issue of *Careers in Law Enforcement*.

For the past twelve years, my background has been concentrated in security and
law enforcement. In my present position, I am responsible for maintaining the
highest possible site and operations security for a key United States government
defense contractor. From 1982 to 1990, I served in the United States Army where I
was responsible for maintaining peak law enforcement/security alertness and the
welfare of all personnel. In that capacity, I received numerous letters of
commendation for superior job performance. I am a graduate of military police
school, I have completed additional law enforcement seminars, and I am enrolled
in a criminal justice degree program.

Through practical experience, I am well versed in military and international law as
well as United States law and procedures. If we could meet in a personal
interview, I could discuss further my qualifications and outline the potential
contribution I could make to your security office.

I look forward to your response.

Sincerely,

Chris Smith

Enc. resume

- Including a military record can be advantageous if it relates to candidate's job objective.

- Continuing education indicates candidate's ongoing commitment to his/her field.

RESPONSE TO A CLASSIFIED ADVERTISEMENT
(Canine Science Instructor)

178 Green Street
Winesburg, OH 44690
(614) 555-5555

February 25, 1996

Pat Cummings
Academic Administrator
Any College
1140 Main Street
Cincinnati, OH 45202

RE: Canine Science Instructor

Dear Mr. Cummings:

My interest in the position of part-time Instructor for courses in animal grooming and behavior training advertised in the February 24 edition of the *Cincinnati Post* has prompted me to forward my resume for your review.

In addition to a Bachelor of Arts degree in Behavioral Sciences, I hold certificates in Kennel Management, Dog Grooming, Training, and continue to attend seminars in adult dog and puppy training. Beyond my academic pursuits, I have more than six years of hands-on experience teaching group obedience classes for dogs and puppies. I also provide private lessons, behavioral consultations, and training for AKC Titles.

After you have had the opportunity to review my qualifications, I would appreciate meeting with you to further discuss this position. I am well qualified to teach future instructors in courses on animal grooming and behavior training, and feel confident that I can provide the kind of student support expected by Any College.

Yours sincerely,

Chris Smith

Enc. resume

■ Including professional accreditation and licensure may be advantageous for certain kinds of work.

■ Experience reinforces candidate's suitability for advertised position.

RESPONSE TO A CLASSIFIED ADVERTISEMENT
(Case Manager)

178 Green Street
White Plains, NY 10606
(914) 555-5555

December 17, 1996

Pat Cummings
Director of Social Services
Any Agency
1140 Main Street
Hoboken, NJ 07030

Dear Ms. Cummings:

I am responding to your advertisement in the *Star Ledger* in search of a Case Manager. My interest is in pursuing and expanding my professional career in the motivation and guidance of juveniles to achieve positive objectives and personal dignity. It is this goal that has prompted me to forward the attached resume for your review and consideration.

Please note that I have directed and dedicated my efforts, both academically and through the co-op program at Fordham University, to working with juveniles and prison inmates, guiding them through innovative programs in self-preservation. These programs required extensive communication and interaction with boards of trustees, agency personnel, and the Neighborhood Watch campaign. In addition, I have acquired excellent customer/client relations and communications skills, as well as sound knowledge of office procedures, in a variety of full-time and part-time positions.

I would welcome a meeting to learn more about your work at Any Agency and how I could contribute to your success. I will call next Monday to follow up on my inquiry.

Yours sincerely,

Chris Smith

Enc. resume

- Activities highlight candidate's involvement in local community.
- Unrelated work experience is omitted from response letter.

RESPONSE TO A CLASSIFIED ADVERTISEMENT
(Chief Financial Officer)

178 Green Street
Rigby, ID 83442

June 25, 1996

Pat Cummings
Controller
Any Corporation
1140 Main Street
Boise, ID 83706

RE: Chief Financial Officer

Dear Mr. Cummings:

With reference to the above-advertised position, the attached resume is submitted
for your evaluation.

I have a record of outstanding success in the management of corporate financial
operations for fast-paced manufacturing companies and associated commercial
operations in multilocation, multistate, and international environments.

My sixteen years of progressively responsible experience encompassed
management of all aspects of the financial and treasury functions, in a range from
Cost Accounting Manager to Chief Financial Officer and Vice-President, Finance.
This experience has encompassed the successful management of corporate real
estate, human resources, and general operations. In addition to holding a M.B.A.
in Finance and a Bachelor of Arts degree in Accounting, I have been a Certified
Public Accountant since 1978.

My resume is a good summary of my background and general experience. Please
contact me at the above address or call (208) 555-5555 (home) or (208) 444-4444
(office), as I would like to arrange a mutually convenient time for a meeting,
during which we can further discuss your current or anticipated openings. May I
hear from you?

Yours sincerely,

Chris Smith

Enc. resume

■ Letter illustrates continual career
progression.

■ Candidate's highest educational
achievement is shown before
other less significant degrees.

RESPONSE TO A CLASSIFIED ADVERTISEMENT
(Child Care Director)

178 Green Street
Lime, OH 45804
(419) 555-5555

July 18, 1996

Pat Cummings
Director
Any Center
1140 Main Street
Toledo, OH 43660

RE: Assistant Center Director

Dear Ms. Cummings:

I am responding to your advertisement in the July 18 edition to the *Toledo Blade*.

I am a licensed Child Care Provider in the state of Ohio with three years' experience working in a private center facilitating the care of over forty children. In this capacity, I have been solely responsible for the supervision of ten children, ranging in age from six months to five years. My duties include distributing meals and snacks, monitoring "playtime," and creating, and instructing children in, diverse educational activities.

In addition, I have experience working with children in various settings, and have held positions such as private nanny, tutor, camp counselor, and gymnastics instructor. I also wrote a children's book, which included many hours of research and interaction with children of all ages.

I would appreciate the opportunity to provide you with several diverse, very favorable references regarding my capabilities to fill this position. I will follow up on this inquiry in several days to schedule a meeting.

With best regards,

Chris Smith

Enc. resume

■ Qualifications highlight candidate's leadership skills.

■ Introduction immediately refers to publication where advertisement appeared.

RESPONSE TO A CLASSIFIED ADVERTISEMENT
(Claims Adjuster)

178 Green Street
Salisbury, NC 28145
(704) 555-5555

August 26, 1996

Pat Cummings
Claims Supervisor
Any Insurance Agency
1140 Main Street
Asheville, NC 28802

Dear Mr. Cummings:

Yesterday I read, with interest, your advertised opening for a Claims Adjuster in the *Citizen Times*. During the past fifteen years, I have been employed by a major insurance company where my primary area of concentration has been in workers' compensation claims handling.

Due to my company's consolidation, I am currently seeking to join an organization in need of a highly productive individual with a sound background in claims handling, cost containment, customer relations/service, employee training, and administrative support.

I am well organized, am capable of researching and coordinating detailed data, and can work effectively with professionals as well as corporate management to arrive at mutually favorable solutions.

Are you interested in filling your availability with an individual who, in previous positions, has cost-effectively negotiated over one hundred claims in a six-month period? If so, I would love to meet with you in a personal interview. I have enclosed my business profile for your review and am confident I can make an immediate and successful contribution to Any Agency.

Sincerely,

Chris Smith

Enc. business profile

■ Phrasing interview request in question form is a strong closing.

■ Four short paragraphs is the ideal length for a cover letter.

RESPONSE TO A CLASSIFIED ADVERTISEMENT
(Clinical Research Nurse)

178 Green Street
Marietta, GA 30060

August 20, 1996

Pat Cummings, R.N.
Head Nurse
Any Hospital
1140 Main Street
Savannah, GA 31404

Dear Ms. Cummings:

I believe I have the combined clinical nursing and research skills that would qualify me as an ideal candidate for the Clinical Research Nurse opening you advertised in *Nursing Today*.

I am a dedicated professional capable of working with physicians and nursing, laboratory, and professional specialty groups, and can offer more than fourteen years of responsible experience ranging from Staff Nurse and Charge Nurse to Clinical Research Nurse with a major teaching hospital.

I have a Bachelor of Science in Nursing, and my graduate studies have focused on epidemiology and international health. My experience encompasses sound knowledge of nursing quality assurance programs and in-service education programs. Throughout my career, I have worked both independently and as part of a team on studies involving psoriasis, cardiology, AIDS, sickle-cell anemia, amyloid, diabetes, and oncology.

Please contact me at the above address, or call (404) 555-5555 to arrange a mutually convenient time for a meeting. I am very interested in joining the nursing staff at Any Hospital and hope to speak with you soon.

Thank you for your consideration.

Sincerely,

Chris Smith, R.N., B.S.N

Enc. professional profile

■ Valuable research experience is highlighted in detail.

■ Introduction demonstrates candidate's suitability for advertised position.

RESPONSE TO A CLASSIFIED ADVERTISEMENT
(Conference Coordinator)

178 Green Street
Racine, WI 53406

December 22, 1996

Pat Cummings
Artistic Director
Any Deaf Theatre
1140 Main Street
De Forest, WI 53532

Dear Mr. Cummings:

The position of Conference Director advertised the January issue of *Deaf Today* is of great interest of me, and I have enclosed my professional profile for your review.

I am a deaf person who has had the opportunity to complete my undergraduate and graduate studies, and who has worked in responsible positions requiring strong leadership, planning, organizational, administrative, and communication skills. Throughout my career, I have worked with individuals and groups in diverse settings within public, private, artistic, and government sectors.

I am well versed in visual and performing arts as a student, performer, coordinator, instructor, and facilitator with concentration in providing services for, and instructing, the deaf community and the general public. I have the communication, public relations, and people skills to establish an annual conference for Any Deaf Theatre that will meet the criteria of excellence you are looking for in a lasting international artistic exchange. It is a challenging undertaking that I feel I am capable of achieving.

Should you need additional information, please contact me at (414) 555-5555 TTY.

I look forward to your return response.

Sincerely,

Chris Smith

Enc. professional profile

■ Letter immediately states candidate's purpose.

■ Candidate focuses on applying skills and experiences to advertised position.

RESPONSE TO A CLASSIFIED ADVERTISEMENT
(Contracted Typist)

178 Green Street
Baltimore, MD 21202
(301) 555-5555

February 14, 1996

Pat Cummings
Sales Manager
Any Corporation
1140 Main Street
Washington, DC 19180

Dear Ms. Cummings:

I am responding to your advertisement published in the *Washington Post* on February 13 concerning the position of Contracted Typist.

My qualifications for this position include a typing speed of 70 wpm on an IBM Selectric typewriter, and 90 wpm on a computer keyboard. In addition, I hold a Bachelor of Arts degree in English from Worcester State College with concentrations in writing and literary criticism.

I have a 386 machine with an HP laser printer II. I often rely on Microsoft Word for Windows for documentation and manuscript work, but remain flexible to any custom requirements. I use the integrated grammar and spell checker features of Word on all documents.

I would be glad to make myself available for an interview and typing test at your convenience. I look forward to learning more about Any Corporation.

With best regards,

Chris Smith

Enc. resume

■ Mentioning typing and word processing skills can be advantageous for administrative and office support positions.

■ Candidate's functional skills are applicable to advertised position.

RESPONSE TO A CLASSIFIED ADVERTISEMENT
(Cosmetologist)

178 Green Street
Auburn, WA 98071
(206) 555-5555

August 13, 1996

Pat Cummings
Owner
Any Boutique
1140 Main Street
Seattle, WA 98134

Dear Mr. Cummings:

Enclosed please find my resume. I am very interested in applying for the position of Cosmetologist that was advertised in the *Seattle Post Intelligencer* on August 13, and am confident that you will find my skills ideally applicable to your needs.

Thank you in advance for your anticipated consideration. I look forward to meeting with you to discuss this opportunity.

Sincerely,

Chris Smith

Enc. resume

■ Letter is short and to the point.

■ Enclosure line suggests candidate is a meticulous, detail-orientated professional.

RESPONSE TO A CLASSIFIED ADVERTISEMENT
(Customer Service Representative)

178 Green Street
Decorah, IA 51201
(319) 555-5555

September 6, 1996

Pat Cummings
Director of Public Relations
Any Corporation
1140 Main Street
Northampton, MA 01060

RE: Customer Service Support

Dear Ms. Cummings:

My interest in the above position has incited me to forward my resume as requested in your advertisement published in the *Boston Sunday Globe*.

During the past several years at Fortmiller, Inc., my experience has been concentrated in the areas of billing, credit, collection, and customer service. In my current position as Customer Service Supervisor, I maintain the efficiency and accuracy of complex billing systems. This position also requires generating detailed reports for management. My position has given me the opportunity to set policies and procedures, implement systems, and participate in staffing and training personnel. During my tenure, 55 percent of the entry-level staff I trained advanced to managerial positions within Fortmiller, Inc.

After reading your requirements for the position advertised, I am confident of my ability to provide you with the experience and quality of performance you expect.

After reviewing my qualifications, I would appreciate meeting with you for further discussion. I will call within the week to schedule an interview.

Yours sincerely,

Chris Smith

Enc. resume

■ Qualifications highlight candidate's leadership skills.　　■ Candidate details applicable work experience.

RESPONSE TO A CLASSIFIED ADVERTISEMENT
(Dental Hygienist)

178 Green Street
Deer Park, NY 11729
(516) 555-5555

March 3, 1996

Pat Cummings
Dentist
1140 Main Street
Lynbrook, NY 11563

Dear Mr. Cummings:

I would like to offer the attached confidential resume as an application for the Dental Hygienist position you advertised in the *Times-Union*.

I am confident that my training and experience could be effectively applied to the requirements of the position as described. If you would like any additional information, please do not hesitate to contact me. I look forward to meeting with you and further discussing the mutual benefit of our joining forces.

Thank you in advance for your consideration.

Sincerely,

Chris Smith

Enc. resume

■ Letter suggests discretion.

■ Closing invites addressee to inquire about additional information.

RESPONSE TO A CLASSIFIED ADVERTISEMENT
(Dentistry Department Manager)

178 Green Street
Gaithersburg, MD 20879

February 10, 1996

Pat Cummings
Chief Administrator
Any Hospital
1140 Main Street
Chapel Hill, NC 27514

RE: Manager—Department of Dentistry

Dear Ms. Cummings:

The position you advertised is of great interest to me, and I hope to convince you of my capability to cost-effectively execute the responsibilities of Dentistry Department Manager.

My experience with Johns Hopkins Medical School's Department of Ophthalmology, Maryland Eye & Ear Infirmary, and Blue Cross/Blue Shield has involved interfacing and dealing with all operations and administrative departments on matters pertaining to fiscal and business reporting. I have extensive experience with MIS and firsthand experience with sophisticated programs designed to accommodate and control the rapid and profitable growth of business.

My business management, staff training and supervision, and administrative experience are essential requirements for maintaining equitable controls for a highly complex business. I can provide cost-effective fiscal management to maintain and increase profitability. Through efficient tracking and control systems, budget planning, and administration, I can generate cost savings and greater profit margins.

Should you require additional information, I will be glad to meet with you for further discussion. I can be reached at (301) 555-5555. In the interim, I look forward to meeting with you and joining your management team in the near future.

Sincerely,

Chris Smith

Enc. resume

■ Letter highlights candidate's management skills.

■ Including telephone number is necessary in a cover letter.

RESPONSE TO A CLASSIFIED ADVERTISEMENT
(Director of Public Works)

178 Green Street
Liberty, SC 29657
(803) 555-5555

September 22, 1996

Pat Cummings
District Supervisor
Any Office
1140 Main Street
Charleston, SC 29403

Dear Mr. Cummings:

I am very interested in the position of Director of Public Works for the town of
Liberty as advertised in the September 20 edition of the *Post and Courier*.

During the past thirteen years, I have been actively involved in the management of
diverse projects which require the ability to work with engineering, architectural,
and construction professionals on public and private rehabilitation, restoration, and
construction programs. My experience ranges from concept to sign-off and the
supervision of in-house and field crews on both privately and city/federally funded
building and highway contracts.

I am an effective manager and budget administrator, and have the ability to work
in harmony with individuals and groups in a busy construction/public works
environment where concentration is on community services, safety, and the
environment. As a longtime resident in the town of Liberty, I believe I could
reflect personal, as well as the local interest in providing quality DPW services. I
am confident of my ability to direct an efficient, cost-effective, and productive
department.

Enclosed is my business profile for your consideration. I would like to learn more
about the position, and will call your office early next week to see if we can
schedule a meeting.

Thank you for your time.

Sincerely,

Chris Smith

Enc. business profile

■ Candidate matches his/her
qualifications with potential
employer's needs.

■ Four short paragraphs is the ideal
length for a cover letter.

RESPONSE TO A CLASSIFIED ADVERTISEMENT
(Editorial Assistant)

178 Green Street
Austin, TX 78746
(512) 555-5555

June 4, 1996

Pat Cummings
Vice-President
Any Corporation
1140 Main Street
Dallas, TX 75275

Dear Ms. Cummings:

I am very interested in the Editorial Assistant position listed recently in the *Dallas Morning News*, and am including my resume and a writing sample as an application. I am familiar with Any Corporation's publications, and would love the opportunity to contribute to your efforts.

My accomplishments include:

- Experience editing books and other materials for a wide variety of clients, including Reiling Press, Wilson Smith, and numerous corporate clients.
- Experience writing consumer materials, including chapters for fiction books published by Hollis Press, and a complete nonfiction book entitled *Easy Do It Resumes* (O'Leary Press).

Should you need additional information or writing samples, please feel free to contact me at the above-listed number. I look forward to joining the editorial team at Any Corporation, and will call your office next week to discuss this opportunity further.

Thank you.

Sincerely,

Chris Smith

Enc. resume
    writing samples

■ Publications are impressive and add weight to cover letter.

■ Job descriptions emphasize candidate's accomplishments.

RESPONSE TO A CLASSIFIED ADVERTISEMENT
(Events Planner)

178 Green Street
Tiverton, RI 02878
(401) 555-5555

August 21, 1996

Pat Cummings
Vice-President of Public Relations
Any Corporation
1140 Main Street
Chicago, IL 60605

Dear Mr. Cummings:

Please accept this letter as an application for the Events Planner position
advertised in the *Providence Journal* on August 20. My confidential resume is
enclosed for your review.

The position described is exactly the opportunity I am looking for. I am confident
my six years' experience in public relations, coupled with my drive and
enthusiasm, would enable me to make a significant contribution to your
organization.

I believe the most important qualification of an Events Planner is the ability to
plan well and soundly, and then to imbue a staff with the spirit of teamwork—in
other words, to provide leadership and effective administration. I would describe
myself as a well-organized, results-oriented, and effective problem-solver.

I welcome the opportunity to meet with you to further discuss my qualifications
and your needs. Thank you for your time and consideration.

Sincerely,

Chris Smith

Enc. resume

■ Beyond matching qualifications
with requirements, candidate
highlights personal attributes
applicable to advertised position.

■ Closing thanks addressee in
advance for attention.

RESPONSE TO A CLASSIFIED ADVERTISEMENT
(Features Reporter)

178 Green Street
Emmitsburg, MD 21727

July 20, 1996

Pat Cummings
Senior Reporter
Any Newspaper
1140 Main Street
Largo, MD 20772

Dear Ms. Cummings:

I am interested in the Features Reporter position advertised in the *Baltimore Sun*. As a recent graduate of Mount St. Mary's College with a degree in Journalism, I am eager to begin a long-term association with a newspaper as a reporter.

As detailed in the enclosed resume, I possess broad experience in various fields of journalism. My internship with the *Emmitsburg News* provided me the opportunity to sharpen my researching skills. My duties included field reporting, writing copy, and editing a variety of articles, all demanding strict deadlines. My skills in photography made me a greater asset to the *Emmitsburg News*, as I was able to photograph the subjects of stories as well. In addition, while completing my degree at Mount St. Mary's, I worked as Editor of the yearbook and Layout Editor of the student newspaper, where I became proficient in desktop publishing.

I currently have a flexible schedule and am available for an interview at almost any time, given advance notice. I can be reached at (301) 555-5555. I am very interested in reporting for *Any Newspaper* and hope to hear from you soon.

Sincerely,

Chris Smith

Enc. resume

■ Internship experience demonstrates candidate's familiarity with field of work.

■ For recent graduates, extracurricular activities demonstrate potential for productivity.

RESPONSE TO A CLASSIFIED ADVERTISEMENT
(Field Finance Manager)

178 Green Street
Richmond, VA 23220

January 17, 1996

Pat Cummings
Chief Financial Officer
Any Corporation
1140 Main Street
Washington, DC 20002

Dear Mr. Cummings:

I am inquiring about the Central Area Field Finance Manager position advertised in the *Richmond Times-Dispatch*.

Enclosed you will find my resume, which details the skills necessary to enhance the central area's performance:

- Experience advising *Fortune* 100 and small company senior management on strategy, planning, and budgeting.
- Strong accounting and finance academic preparation combined with significant work experience.
- Excellent working knowledge of microcomputer technology.

Finally, one item not on my resume is my desire to enter a high-growth industry with a leader. The Finance Manager position offers such an opportunity.

Please feel free to contact me at (804) 555-5555 if you have any questions and would like to meet.

Sincerely yours,

Chris Smith

Enc. resume

■ Bullets provide a clear and crisp presentation.

■ Letter outlines candidate's skills relevant to advertised position.

RESPONSE TO A CLASSIFIED ADVERTISEMENT
(Film Archivist)

178 Green Street
New Castle, DE 19270
(302) 555-5555

July 22, 1996

Pat Cummings
Curator
Any Library
1140 Main Street
Macon, GA 31201

RE: Film Archivist Position; *Moving Picture Pictorial*, July 19, 1996

Dear Ms. Cummings:

I am interested in your advertised position for a Film Archivist. My passion for film and my applicable skills make me confident that I am a qualified candidate.

Currently, I am a reporter for the *Vertov Film Journal*, a monthly entertainment magazine. In addition, I am capable of shooting, printing, and developing 35-mm, black-and-white film. During my last year at Brandeis, I researched, wrote, and edited a one-hundred page senior honors thesis on the filmmaker Sergei Eisenstein. I enjoyed that project immensely, and would enjoy researching film and film-related literature on a daily basis.

I am aware that your library's film archive is the largest in the South. I would welcome the opportunity to employ my talents at Any Library, and am willing to relocate if offered the position.

I have enclosed a resume and a few writing samples for you to look over at your convenience. Thank you for your time, and I hope to meet with you soon to discuss your Film Archivist position even further.

Sincerely,

Chris Smith

Enc. resume
    writing samples

■ Research projects illustrate candidate's initiative.

■ Willingness to relocate can be advantageous.

RESPONSE TO A CLASSIFIED ADVERTISEMENT
(Fundraiser)

178 Green Street
Roswell, NM 88202

June 2, 1996

Pat Cummings
Director
Any Organization
1140 Main Street
Alamogordo, NM 88311

Dear Mr. Cummings:

I am writing in response to your advertisement for a fundraiser that appears in this month's *Not-for-Profit Now!* Your organization strikes me as particularly dynamic, and I know that my energy, enthusiasm, and skills can only complement the success of your fiscal campaigns.

After graduating from the University of New Mexico last June, I have been working in the University's development office at the Office of Public Programs. UNM is in its second year of a $450 million capital campaign—$25 million of which was achieved this fall in a single record-breaking donation. My role in this stimulating and exciting time at the University has been as the Campaign Registration Coordinator. This position has afforded me many valuable experiences, not the least of which has been working for the University's expert fundraisers. Observant to detail and acutely aware of my surroundings, I have had the opportunity to become appreciative of the techniques of my colleagues, responsive to the interests of a variety of personalities, and proactive in the fulfillment of our goals. My job demands efficiency, precision, and the ability to juggle several different projects simultaneously. I feel confident that I can apply my skills in your organization.

Capable and eager, I am seeking this challenge. I have enclosed my resume for your consideration. I look forward to speaking with you soon about my qualifications, and can be reached easily at (505) 555-5555.

Sincerely,

Chris Smith

Enc. resume

■ Letter focuses on filling employer's needs, not the job candidate's.

■ Discussion of experience clearly spells out candidate's area of expertise.

RESPONSE TO A CLASSIFIED ADVERTISEMENT
(Gemologist)

178 Green Street
Gainseville, FL 36608
(904) 555-5555

June 2, 1996

Pat Cummings
Vice-President
Any Institute
1140 Main Street
Tampa, FL 33611

Dear Ms. Cummings:

I was very excited to read about the opening for a Gemologist in the latest edition of your company newsletter. I would like to submit my credentials as an application for this opportunity.

I became interested in the import/export of precious gems several years ago while living in Nepal. Upon my return to the United States, I enrolled in what my research revealed to be the best gemology school, the Gemologist Institute of America, in Santa Monica, California. This year I graduated with honors, and hold the title of Graduate Gemologist.

The enclosed resume summarizes my background, most of which has an emphasis in public relations, sales, promotions, and dealing with people of all socioeconomic levels and cultures. I am presently searching for an opportunity, with an institute such as yours, which could benefit from my training, skills, and knowledge in the technical and business facets of gemology.

After you have reviewed my qualifications, I would appreciate interviewing with you for this position. I am very interested in the opportunity that it provides and am confident that my training and experience fit your requirements. Please note that I plan to follow up with a call in a few days.

Sincerely,

Chris Smith

Enc. resume

- Educational credentials strengthen cover letter.

- Closing refers addressee to telephone number in return address.

RESPONSE TO A CLASSIFIED ADVERTISEMENT
(Home Economist/Coordinator)

178 Green Street
Reno, NV 89520
(702) 555-5555

July 25, 1996

Pat Cummings
Director, Home Economics Program
Any University
1140 Main Street
Seattle, WA 98109

Dear Mr. Cummings:

My interest in the position of Home Economist/Coordinator described in your advertisement in the *Seattle Times* has prompted me to forward the attached resume for your evaluation.

In addition to earning a B.S. degree in Home Economics and Nutrition Education, I have completed coursework in psychology and learning development, and have undergone supplemental training at the professional level with each employer since graduation, including a teaching hospital.

I possess excellent verbal, written, and interpersonal skills. In addition, I hold extensive experience with the development and training-related duties of seminars in my areas of expertise, and relate easily to all age groups and socioeconomic levels. As an alumnus of the University of Washington at Seattle and a native of the state of Washington, I am well acquainted with the overall family/business environment in which I would be working.

I will be in Washington on Friday, August 5. I would like to arrange to meet with you at this time to convince you of my ability to successfully fill your position. I will call your office on July 27 to schedule an interview time.

Thank you very much for your consideration.

Sincerely,

Chris Smith

Enc. resume

■ Continuing education indicates candidate's ongoing commitment to his/her field.

■ Closing provides specific time frame to allow for meeting.

RESPONSE TO A CLASSIFIED ADVERTISEMENT
(Hospital Administrator)

178 Green Street
Lapeer, MI 48446
(313) 555-5555

June 17, 1996

Pat Cummings
District Vice-President
Any Health Resource Corporation
1140 Main Street
Flint, MI 48502

RE: Hospital Administrator

Dear Ms. Cummings:

After reading your advertisement in the *Flint Journal*, I believe that Keller Memorial Hospital is in need of an Administrator who can provide direction, as well as strong marketing and financial expertise, to develop and implement its purpose.

During my sixteen years as President/Treasurer of a multibranch, multistate prosthetics, orthodontics, DME business, I directed all phases of operations from the construction of headquarter and manufacturing facilities to the sales and marketing of custom and durable medical products. Also, I have a strong background in the preparation of business plans and strategies, financial and budget analysis, financial package design, and forecasts and projections. All of my motivation has been directed toward new business development and expanding services in the health care field.

In addition, I am a strong organizer, enthusiastic speaker, capable leader, and team player who can interface effectively with medical professionals as well as support staff. In the role of Hospital Director, I am confident that I can provide you with the energy and experience to achieve results, and would welcome the opportunity to reiterate this in a personal interview. I will contact your office next Monday to schedule a mutually covenient time to meet.

Thank you for your time.

Sincerely,

Chris Smith

Enc. resume

■ Introduction demonstrates candidate's suitability for advertised position.

■ Setting desired position apart from body of letter may be advantageous when responding to classified advertisement.

RESPONSE TO A CLASSIFIED ADVERTISEMENT
(Hotel Manager)

178 Green Street
Traverse City, MI 49684

January 23, 1996

Pat Cummings
District Manager
Any Corporation
1140 Main Street
Marquette, MI 49855

Dear Mr. Cummings:

Enclosed is my resume, which I submit as a candidate for the Hotel Manager position as advertised in the *Detroit Free Press* on January 23.

My experience in the hospitality industry is broadly based, and my accomplishments reflect a proven ability to perform in diverse and varied functions. My positions have ranged from Front Desk Clerk and Director of Sales and Marketing, to my current position as Assistant General Manager of a prestigious three-thousand-room hotel. In this capacity I am responsible for all operation aspects of the rooms division, including front office, housekeeping, maintenance, reservations, quality control, and communications. I am also a member of the executive committee involved in all budgetary and policy decision-making.

I have been involved in hospitality management for ten years, and while my present position is satisfying, the position of Hotel Manager you offer seems to provide the ideal next step, and an opportunity for a long-term association with a new organization.

I would greatly appreciate the opportunity to discuss your requirements, and how I might fulfill them. Please telephone me at your convenience. During the day, I can be reached at (616) 555-5555.

Thank you for your consideration.

Sincerely,

Chris Smith

Enc. resume

■ Discussion of experience
indicates a series of promotions.

■ Candidate includes all relevant
experience to advertised position.

RESPONSE TO A CLASSIFIED ADVERTISEMENT
(International Buyer)

178 Green Street
Knoke, IA 50553
(515) 555-5555

February 3, 1996

Pat Cummings
Senior Marketing Manager
Any Corporation
1140 Main Street
Chicago, IL 60605

Dear Ms. Cummings:

In response to your advertisement in the February 1 edition of the *Chicago Sun-Times* for an International Buyer, I would like to submit my application for your consideration.

As you can see, my qualifications match those you seek:

YOU REQUIRE:
- A college degree
- Fluency in Italian and French
- Office experience
- Typing skills
- Willingness to travel

I OFFER:
- A Bachelor's degree in English from Long Island University
- Fluency in Italian, German, and French
- Experience as a receptionist at a busy accounting firm
- Accurate typing at 60 wpm
- A willingness to travel

I feel that I am well qualified for this position and can make a lasting contribution to Any Corporation. My salary requirement is negotiable.

I would welcome the opportunity for a personal interview with you at your convenience.

Sincerely,

Chris Smith

Enc. resume

■ Format is organized and visually appealing.

■ Discussion details how candidate's qualifications will benefit potential employer.

RESPONSE TO A CLASSIFIED ADVERTISEMENT
(Legal Assistant)

178 Green Street
Shoshoni, WY 82649
(307) 555-5555

September 18, 1996

Pat Cummings
Partner
Any Corporation
1140 Main Street
Chicago, IL 60605

Dear Mr. Cummings:

I am writing in response to your advertisement in the September 17th edition of
the *New York Times*. Having recently graduated from New England School of
Law, it is my intention to relocate to Chicago. I have enclosed my resume for your
consideration.

My work experience and my scholastic endeavors have thoroughly prepared me
for employment in a firm that specializes in various segments of law. This fall and
past summer, I have been interning for a small general practice firm where I am
entrusted with a great deal of responsibility. I write appellate briefs, I write
memoranda in corporate, contract, and criminal law, and I draft complaints and
answers. I also actively participate in attorney-client conferences by questioning
clients and by describing how the law affects the clients' suits.

I would appreciate the opportunity to meet with you and discuss how my
qualifications could be guided to meet your needs.

Thank you for your time and consideration. I look forward meeting with you at
your convenience.

With best regards,

Chris Smith, Esq.

Enc. resume

- Internship experience demonstrates candidate's familiarity with field of work.
- Response letter immediately states candidate's purpose for writing.

RESPONSE TO A CLASSIFIED ADVERTISEMENT
(Librarian)

178 Green Street
Stanford, CA 94305
(415) 555-5555

January 24, 1996

Pat Cummings
Head Librarian
Any Library
1140 Main Street
Havre, MT 59501

Dear Ms. Cummings:

I was very excited to discover the availability of the Librarian position with Any Library. The job description as printed in the *Billings Gazette* suggests an "on-your-feet-and-running"-styled position, which would be a welcome extension of my present work.

My experience at the Stanford Law School for the past two years has focused mostly on editorial, research, and administrative work with book manuscripts, journals, and dissertations. I am confident this experience qualifies me for the position.

With that in mind, I enclose my resume and appreciate your consideration of me as a serious candidate. I am moving to Montana permanently next month, but would be happy to meet with you earlier for a personal interview.

Sincerely,

Chris Smith

Enc. resume

■ Candidate clearly expresses eagerness to work for specific employer.

■ Direct quote suggests candidate is a meticulous, detail-oriented professional.

RESPONSE TO A CLASSIFIED ADVERTISEMENT
(Loan Officer)

178 Green Street
Owensboro, KY 42302

March 2, 1996

Pat Cummings
Branch Manager
Any Bank
1140 Main Street
Lexington, KY 40506

RE: Loan Officer Position

Dear Mr. Cummings:

In response to last Friday's advertisement in the *Lexington Herald-Leader*, I have
enclosed my resume for your review. As you can see, my qualifications are an
ideal match for your requirements.

You require:
- Over five years' experience.
- Skill in personnel and customer service relations.
- Extensive lending knowledge.
- A willingness to travel.

I offer:
- Nine years of rapidly progressive and responsible experience with a
  service-oriented commercial bank.
- Five years of full responsibility for the management of branch banking
  operations, training and directing, and coordinating activities of personnel,
  and establishing and implementing relationship banking programs for
  quality customer service and satisfaction.
- Skill in implementing institution policies, procedures, and practices
  concerning lending and new business development, and granting or
  extending lines of credit and commercial, real estate, and consumer loans.
- A willingness to travel.

I would welcome the opportunity of a personal interview to discuss the details of the position available and my capability to achieve mutual goals. I am well qualified to handle the position, and confident I will make a valuable contribution to your staff. Please contact me at the above address or by phone at (502) 555-5555.

I look forward to hearing from you.

Sincerely,

Chris Smith

Enc. resume

■ Unique format demonstrates candidate's ability to meet advertised job requirements.

■ Closing encourages reader to respond to letter.

RESPONSE TO A CLASSIFIED ADVERTISEMENT
(Masonry Supply Manager)

178 Green Street
Waterbury, CT 06708

December 5, 1996

Pat Cummings
General Manager
Any Corporation
1140 Main Street
Hartford, CT 06115

Dear Ms. Cummings:

My interest in the position of Masonry Supply Manager (*Hartford Courant*, November 30) has prompted me to forward my resume for your review and consideration.

During the past ten years, my experience has been concentrated in the masonry and plastering products supply industry with a building materials firm. During my six years as General Manager, I took an old line business, which had undergone several years of poor management, and reversed the trend. I upgraded the firm's image and customer and vendor relations, which subsequently increased the dollar volume and bottom line profits by 300 percent.

I am presently looking for a position where my experience will make a positive contribution to the start-up or continuing profitable operation of a business in which I am so well experienced.

I will contact you in a few days to arrange a meeting for further discussion. In the interim, should you require additional information, I may be reached at (203) 555-5555 between 9:00 A.M. and 5:00 P.M.

Sincerely,

Chris Smith

Enc. resume

■ Letter cites advertisement's specific publication and date.

■ Use of concrete examples highlights candidate's achievements.

RESPONSE TO A CLASSIFIED ADVERTISEMENT
(Meeting Planner)

178 Green Street
Rohnert Park, CA 94928
(707) 555-5555

May 11, 1996

Pat Cummings
Vice-President, Marketing
Any Corporation
1140 Main Street
San Francisco, CA 94132

RE: Meeting Planner Position

Dear Mr. Cummings:

After reading your advertisement in the *San Francisco Chronicle*, I believe my qualifications match your requirements for a Meeting Planner.

During the past seven years, I have held positions requiring communications, sales, marketing, and supervisory skills in people-oriented, retailing, media, and educational environments. I am currently seeking a career opportunity offering a new scope of responsibility and more permanent challenge requiring creative skills as well as follow-through capability as an individual or member of a production team.

I am a quick study and have good presentation and communications training. I pride myself in the fact that I can readily take direction, and provide organization, creative input, and an enthusiastic approach to the various segments of a position.

I believe I am the right candidate for the position of Meeting Planner and would like the opportunity to discuss your requirements and my ability to handle the responsibilities of the position offered. I will call your office next Monday to schedule an interview at your convenience.

I appreciate your time and consideration.

Sincerely,

Chris Smith

Enc. resume

■ Letter outlines candidate's skills relevant to advertised position.

■ Powerful adjectives, when used sparingly, ensure maximum impact.

RESPONSE TO A CLASSIFIED ADVERTISEMENT
(Multimedia Specialist)

178 Green Street
Sparkill, NY 10976
(914) 555-5555

April 18, 1996

Pat Cummings
Director, Human Resources
Any Corporation
1140 Main Street
Staten Island, NY 10301

Dear Ms. Cummings:

This is in reply to your advertisement for a Multimedia Specialist published in the April 16 edition of the *New York Daily News*. In addition to a strong interest in catching the multimedia wave, I was attracted to the inviting tone of your advertisement. I would love a chance to meet and talk with you about the opportunity.

Toward this end, I have composed the following comparison demonstrating how my background and experience directly qualify me for the requirements listed for the position.

Your requirements:
- Lots of experience working in and consulting to small businesses.
- Enjoy using computers (but don't necessarily have any programming experience).
- Responsible for working with business writers, editors, and programmers to help design software packages for small businesses.

My qualifications:
- Was considered the "guru" of the small business market during my six years at Lotus.
- Generated over 50 percent of my consulting income in the past year from small business clients.
- Confess to a rather strong attachment to computers, especially considering that I've made my livelihood as a result of their existence for the past thirteen years.
- Walked in their shoes. Conceived of and authored an OS/2 *Tips and Techniques* software training tool for IBM.

- Led Lotus' entry into the small business market segment through managing product development and the launch of the 1-2-3 Small Business Kit and the Lotus spreadsheet for DeskMate. By designing innovative marketing programs leveraging the strengths of Tandy and small business administration, I enhanced product visibility that eventually led to an increase in sales by 75 percent.

I look forward to hearing from you, and for the chance to "get in on the fun."

Sincerely,

Chris Smith

Enc. resume

■ Letter responds to specific requirements outlined in classified advertisement.

■ Candidate conveys a large amount of information in quick and easy-to-read format.

RESPONSE TO A CLASSIFIED ADVERTISEMENT
(Newspaper Intern)

178 Green Street
Charlotsville, VA 22906

April 7, 1996

Pat Cummings
Managing Editor
Any Newspaper
1140 Main Street
Lexington, VA 24450

Dear Mr. Cummings:

I enclose my resume in response to your listing in the University of Virginia's career services office for a internship position with your newspaper. I am currently a junior majoring in English at UVA, and am seeking valuable career experience for the months of June through mid-September. I am hoping to use this summer to explore possible opportunities within the field of newspaper publishing.

The position you outline is one I feel I could enhance with my writing, editing, and expressive skills gained as an English major, as well as my past work experience, which has involved a great deal of organization, discipline, and responsibility. My active leadership and service roles have also helped me develop strong interpersonal and communication skills which I feel would make me a worthy addition to your staff.

I would greatly appreciate the opportunity to discuss with you how I might best meet your needs. I will call your office next week to confirm receipt of my resume and inquire about the publicized opening. In the interim, if you have any questions, please do not hesitate to call me at (804) 555-5555.

Thank you for your consideration in this matter.

Sincerely yours,

Chris Smith

Enc. resume

- Personal interests and activities are relevant to candidate's field of interest.
- Letter clarifies candidate's career goals.

RESPONSE TO A CLASSIFIED ADVERTISEMENT
(Occupational Health Manager)

178 Green Street
Des Plaines, IL 60016
(708) 555-5555

July 26, 1996

Pat Cummings
Vice-President, Managerial
Any Corporation
1140 Main Street
Indianapolis, IN 46206

RE: TQR Manager Position

Dear Ms. Cummings:

My interest in the position of Occupational Health Manager recently advertised in
the *Indianapolis Star* has prompted me to forward my resume for your
consideration.

In addition to my experience as a certified occupational health nurse and hands-on
clinical expertise, I have twenty-one years of experience in positions which
involved autonomous responsibility for the development and implementation of
occupational health programs. All of these positions required sound knowledge of
OSHA and general occupational health issues in critical work areas.

I received several commendations for my dedication and professionalism, and
continually received recognition for my communication skills and leadership
excellence. Based on my qualifications, I believe I am the right person to oversee
the delivery of occupational health services for one or more of your clients.

The enclosed resume is a brief summary of my qualifications. I would be delighted
to meet with you in a personal interview and will call your office during the week
of August 5.

Sincerely,

Chris Smith, R.N.

Enc. resume

■ Response letter emphasizes
candidate's supervisory skills.

■ After name, candidate includes
professional title.

RESPONSE TO A CLASSIFIED ADVERTISEMENT
(Office Receptionist)

178 Green Street
Gastonia, NC 28054
(704) 555-5555

January 16, 1996

Pat Cummings
Personnel Supervisor
Any Corporation
1140 Main Street
Mt. Olive, NC 28465

Dear Mr. Cummings:

I am interested in applying for the Office Receptionist position as advertised in the
Herald Sun, dated January 16. Attached please find my resume.

My areas of expertise lie in administration, organization, documentation,
communications, and cost control. I am a detail-oriented individual and enjoy
customer/client interaction. Additionally, I believe that an organization's client
relationships are a tangible asset in a world where individualized service and
assistance is rapidly declining. My administrative skills include a 70 wpm typing
speed and proficiency on multiple word processing programs and spreadsheet
applications.

I look forward to hearing from you and learning more about Any Corporation.

Sincerely,

Chris Smith

Enc. resume

■ Experience reinforces candidate's
suitability for advertised position.

■ Including a telephone number is
essential in a cover letter.

RESPONSE TO A CLASSIFIED ADVERTISEMENT
(Park Maintenance Supervisor)

178 Green Street
Zanesville, OH 43701
(614) 555-5555

August 28, 1996

Pat Cummings
Chairperson
Any Reservation
1140 Main Street
Youngstown, OH 44501

RE: Park Maintenance

Dear Ms. Cummings:

Please accept the enclosed resume as my expressed interest in applying for the Park Maintenance position you advertised in the August 26 edition of the *Vindicator*. For the past twelve years, I have held a senior-level position as Fire Chief of the Zanesville Fire Department.

Although my position is secure, it is strictly administrative and does not allow me to physically participate, as I have in the past, in actual fire fighting or other hands-on activities that provide the outdoor work environment I most enjoy. For some time, I have realized that I must make a change, and the position described in your advertisement is what I have been looking for.

I have worked on a family farm, attended a degree program on agriculture, and by choice always worked full-time or part-time with tree and excavation services. I am thoroughly familiar with the operation, maintenance, and repair of equipment, and with safety practices for its operation; I also have the necessary background to train and supervise work crews using this equipment. Because my prime interest is job satisfaction, the salary is secondary and negotiable.

I feel confident that I can provide Any Reservation with reliability, dedication, and quality work performance that will maintain the forested properties in the condition parks should be kept and enjoyed.

Since the department is not aware of my interest in making a change, your confidence is appreciated. I look forward to your return response.

Yours sincerely,

Chris Smith

Enc. resume

■ Letter focuses on filling employer's needs, not the job candidate's.

■ Closing informs addressee of need for confidentiality.

RESPONSE TO A CLASSIFIED ADVERTISEMENT
(Photographer/Writer)

178 Green Street
Poughkeepsie, NY 12601

July 22, 1996

Pat Cummings
Human Resources Director
Any Corporation
1140 Main Street
Bellingham, WA 98225

Dear Mr. Cummings:

I am responding to the ad placed in the July 18 edition of the *Seattle Times* for the position of Photographer/Writer.

I am an accomplished photographer with over ten years of experience in the industry. My career has provided me with the opportunity to work in the areas of commercial and industrial photography, portraiture, and wedding photography. I hold a Bachelor of Arts degree in English from Clark College where relevant coursework included Feature Writing, Photojournalism, and News Reporting.

I have attended seminars and workshops with the Fred Jones Workshop and the Winona School of Professional Photography. My photos have appeared in the Winona course catalog, BBI Printing Company's catalog, and numerous Smithco publications (including annual reports and newsletters).

My published writings include *A Shutterbug's Notes* and *Picture Your Pet*.

I would welcome the opportunity to discuss with you how my qualifications may suit your company's needs. Please contact me at the above address or by phone at (601) 555-5555. Thank you.

Sincerely,

Chris Smith

Enc. resume

- Candidate succinctly outlines his/her relevant qualifications.
- Applicable coursework, workshops, and seminars are highlighted.

RESPONSE TO A CLASSIFIED ADVERTISEMENT
(Political Staffer)

178 Green Street
Bristol, RI 02809
(401) 555-5555

January 25, 1996

Pat Cummings
Director
Any Organization
1140 Main Street
Providence, RI 02908

Dear Ms. Cummings:

I am responding to the Political Staffer position advertised in the January 24 edition of the *Providence Evening Bulletin*.

Currently, I am employed as an Administrative Assistant at the State House in Providence. My primary responsibilities include writing press releases, researching and drafting legislation, and consistent constituent contact. I have also worked with various committees and legislators regarding an array of legislative issues.

I hold a Bachelor of Arts degree from Boston University in Political Science with a concentration in Public Policy. In addition to my coursework at BU, I worked as an intern at the Lieutenant Governor's office during the spring of 1994 and actively worked for several political and social causes on campus and in the Boston area. I also organized and managed my own successful campaign for Secretary of Student Affairs.

I am eager to continue my political career in the position of Staffer for your organization. I have the commitment, energy, and drive necessary to contribute successfully to your cause. I will call your office on January 29 to schedule an interview time that is convenient for you.

Thank you for your consideration.

Sincerely,

Chris Smith

Enc. resume

■ Educational credentials relate specifically to advertised position.

■ Activities highlight candidate's involvement in local community.

RESPONSE TO A CLASSIFIED ADVERTISEMENT
(Preschool Director)

178 Green Street
St. Paul, MN 55105

July 10, 1996

Pat Cummings
Principal
Any High School
1140 Main Street
Minneapolis, MN 55404

RE: Preschool Director Position

Dear Mr. Cummings:

As a Speech/Language Clinician with extensive experience in the management and administration of programs dealing with special needs in education, I feel I have the qualifications necessary to succeed in the position as advertised in the *Star Tribune.*

During the past eleven years, my experience with a professional, private agency has been concentrated in the area of special needs programs for multiple school districts. Prior to that, my work as a Speech Language Clinician involved the development and implementation of programs directed toward special education for preschoolers through twelfth grade in a public school system.

Although my positions were diverse and my achievements provided professional satisfaction, I am interested in making a new association with a large, highly recognized institution such as Any High School. As Part-Time Preschool Director, I hope to utilize my broad-based experience in special education to make a meaningful contribution to your professional management staff.

The enclosed resume summarizes my background and experience. I would appreciate the opportunity to meet with you to further discuss my qualifications and how I can best contribute to your needs. Please contact me at the above address or by phone at (612) 555-5555.

I look forward to hearing from you.

Yours sincerely,

Chris Smith

Enc. resume

■ Response letter immediately introduces candidate's qualifications.

■ Candidate explains how extensive experience will benefit potential employer.

RESPONSE TO A CLASSIFIED ADVERTISEMENT
(Product Developer)

178 Green Street
Bismarck, ND 58501
(701) 555-5555

February 15, 1996

Pat Cummings
Chief Executive Officer
Any Technology
1140 Main Street
Bismarck, ND 58501

Dear Ms. Cummings:

I read with much excitement in your company newsletter the announcement of openings within your new products development department.

Please note that I have more than ten years of experience in manufacturing R&D, management of new product development, and existing product redevelopment/upgrade. I am especially experienced with complex composite materials, precision metal castings, and PC board industries. In addition, I have extensive experience both as teacher and lecturer at several well-known universities. This expertise is supported by a Ph.D. in Materials Science/Engineering.

I am eager to join the Any Technology team, as its reputation for innovation is unparalleled. I will call to schedule an interview so that we may discuss further my qualifications and your requirements. Thank you for your consideration.

Sincerely,

Chris Smith

Enc. resume

■ Advanced degrees add weight to cover letter.

■ Closing reiterates candidate's interest in specific corporation.

RESPONSE TO A CLASSIFIED ADVERTISEMENT
(Production Assistant)

178 Green Street
Birmingham, AL 35294
(205) 555-5555

October 2, 1996

Pat Cummings
Vice-President, Production
Any Corporation
1146 Main Street
Mobile, AL 36630

RE: Production Assistant Position

Dear Mr. Cummings:

Your recent advertisement in the *Mobile Register* interests me, as my experience matches your requirements.

You require:	*I offer:*
• IBM word processing	• Microsoft Word, WordPerfect experience
• Production experience	• Two years' experience as a Production Assistant with Formins Inc.
• A Bachelor's degree	• A BS in Mass Communications

I would appreciate the opportunity to discuss how I might contribute to your organization. I will call your office the week of October 10th to schedule an interview at your convenience. In the meantime, I may be reached at the above listed daytime phone number or in the evenings at (205) 555-5555.

Thank you for your consideration.

Sincerely,

Chris Smith

Enc. resume

■ Format is neat and professional.　　■ Including an evening telephone number is optional in a cover letter.

RESPONSE TO A CLASSIFIED ADVERTISEMENT
(Production Controller)

178 Green Street
Pittsburgh, PA 15217
(412) 555-5555

February 23, 1996

Pat Cummings
Hiring Manager
Any Corporation
1140 Main Street
Boston, MA 02215

RE: Production Controller

Dear Ms. Cummings:

After seven years of progressively responsible experience in production, electro-mechanical assembly, soldering, testing, total quality management, and shipping and receiving a precision manufacturing operation, I feel I have all the qualifications you require for the above advertised position.

During the past several years, my responsibilities as Group Leader necessitated that I provide a harmonious work atmosphere. While accomplishing this objective, I developed training procedures which allowed for cross-training, multiethnic, multicultural, production personnel to work at ten assembly stations. This assured that all stations could be covered despite employee absences. In addition, I implemented TQM, which resulted in a 40 percent increase in productivity, a 20 percent decrease in production costs, and a flurry of letters from satisfied clients.

I am aware of Any Corporation's innovative approach to TQM, which has been used as an example across the country. I desire the opportunity to apply manufacturing know-how to the smooth running of your production operations.

Thank you for reviewing my credentials. I will contact you to arrange an interview.

Yours sincerely,

Chris Smith

Enc. resume

■ Percentages accentuate candidate's achievements.

■ Candidate immediately expresses suitability for desired position.

RESPONSE TO A CLASSIFIED ADVERTISEMENT
(Program Coordinator)

178 Green Street
Holland, MI 49423
(616) 555-5555

September 30, 1996

Pat Cummings
Language Coordinator
Any Institute
1140 Main Street
Detroit, MI 48226

Dear Mr. Cummings:

I discovered your advertisement for a Program Coordinator, English as a Second
Language, with your translation and interpreting service in the *Detroit Free Press*.
I was very much intrigued and am enclosing my resume detailing my relevant
experience.

I feel I am particularly qualified for this job as a result of my double language
major in college as well as my current enrollment in two-language proficiency
certificate programs. I am a person who deeply believes in the importance of
language enrichment. I would like the chance to work for an organization that
reflects both my interests and my personal commitment.

Having grown up in a bilingual (Spanish/English-speaking) environment and
having studied abroad in both Spain and Mexico, I am well aware of the demands
and technical challenges involved in the translation business. Language is forever
evolving and new expression and technology breed new linguistic mutations daily.
To meet these challenges and maintain my skills, I work on my languages weekly,
both by continuing to take language classes and tutoring children in the
fundamentals.

Given the opportunity, I am confident that my skills and language experience
could make an immediate and long-term contribution to Any Institute. I would be
delighted to discuss my qualifications with you. I will call your office on October
7 to schedule a convenient interview time.

Sincerely,

Chris Smith

Enc. resume

■ Foreign language skills and
international exposure strengthen
applicant's candidacy.

■ Position applied for is clearly and
immediately defined.

RESPONSE TO A CLASSIFIED ADVERTISEMENT
(Project Manager)

178 Green Street
Charleston, SC 29411
(803) 555-5555

April 10, 1996

Pat Cummings
Director of Human Resources
Any Corporation
1140 Main Street
Charleston, SC 29411

Dear Ms. Cummings:

In response to your ad for Project Manager in the April 9 edition of the *Post and Courier*, I have enclosed my resume for your review and consideration.

With over twenty years of construction experience, I am familiar with project management in the role of owner's representative as well as general contractor/manager. I have managed projects regionally and nationally.

I will contact you the week of April 17 so that we may schedule an interview. I look forward to discussing my credentials and the requirements of the position with you.

Sincerely,

Chris Smith

Enc. resume

■ Letter highlights candidate's management skills.

■ Letter is brief and concise.

RESPONSE TO A CLASSIFIED ADVERTISEMENT
(Public Relations Associate)

178 Green Street
Keuka Park, NY 14478
(315) 555-5555

May 2, 1996

Pat Cummings
Vice-President
Any Firm
1140 Main Street
Riverdale, NJ 10471

Dear Mr. Cummings:

In response to your advertisement in the *New York Times* for the Public Relations Associate position, I would like to touch on particular aspects of my background that should be of interest to you.

Between 1989 and 1993, I supervised (as a civilian employee) the internal formation and public relations programs for the U.S. Army in Frankfurt, Germany. As Director of Information Services, I was responsible for writing and publishing internal publications, brochures, and other communications. I also edited a community newspaper and magazine during this time.

For two years prior to that association, I edited a variety of military publications, both newspapers and magazines, while serving as a member of the uniformed services in Germany. During this period, I wrote news, sports, and feature articles as well as press releases. I conducted media events, prepared slide presentations, gave briefings, and designed other internal and external promotional materials in support of the 7th Infantry Division and its 30,000 American soldiers and family members in four German communities.

In 1993, I returned to the United States and completed work for my Master of Arts degree in Communications from Rutgers University. Prior to my relocation, I managed an annual budget of $500,000 while supervising a staff of eight in the Connecticut gaming industry. I also wrote promotional articles for the casino in the local newspaper and am adept at PageMaker, Microsoft Word, and Ventura desktop publishing programs.

I look forward to discussing my background and experience in detail with you and would be glad to make myself available for an interview at your convenience.

Sincerely yours,

Chris Smith

Enc. resume

- Including a military record can be advantageous if it relates to candidate's job objective.

- Specifically citing number of personnel supervised draws attention to candidate's leadership abilities.

RESPONSE TO A CLASSIFIED ADVERTISEMENT
(Publicist)

178 Green Street
East Point, GA 30344
(404) 555-5555

February 4, 1996

Pat Cummings
Publicity Director
Any Corporation
1140 Main Street
Rome, GA 30162

Dear Ms. Cummings:

I am responding to your advertisement in the *Atlanta Constitution* for a Publicist.

I am confident that I have the skills and experience necessary to successfully meet the requirements of this position. As an Advertising and Promotions Assistant for a major newspaper, I have acquired strong interpersonal and communication skills. In addition, I have extensive experience with a number of computer systems and applications.

As the newest member of your publicity department, I would prove to be a diligent, organized, and enthusiastic employee. Could we meet for further discussion? I would be available at your convenience.

I look forward to your response.

Sincerely,

Chris Smith

Enc. resume

■ Candidate expresses willingness to meet at addressee's convenience in closing.

■ Candidate immediately specifies position being applied for.

RESPONSE TO A CLASSIFIED ADVERTISEMENT
(Publisher's Assistant)

178 Green Street
Topeka, KS 66621
(913) 555-5555

January 18, 1996

Pat Cummings
Vice-President of Editorial
Any Corporation
1140 Main Street
Topeka, KS 66621

Dear Mr. Cummings:

I am writing in response to your advertisement in the *Topeka Capital-Journal* for the Publisher's Assistant position. Please consider me an applicant for the position.

I believe you will find that my training and varied experience are well suited for this position. My background as an administrative assistant, magazine production assistant, and teacher demonstrate my capacity to handle the challenges of providing superior executive support.

As a current temporary assignment worker with Alltemps in Topeka, I have become highly computer literate in both Macintosh and IBM environments and accompanying software programs. I am organized and accurate, master new information rapidly, communicate effectively, and work well with other people.

Thank you for reviewing my credentials. I will call in a week to schedule a convenient time to discuss my qualifications and your expectations.

Sincerely,

Chris Smith

Enc. resume

■ Temporary experience is relevant to full-time employment.

■ Candidate's functional skills are applicable to advertised position.

RESPONSE TO A CLASSIFIED ADVERTISEMENT
(Purchasing Agent)

178 Green Street
Gorve Village, IL 60007
(708) 555-5555
FAX (708) 444-4444

February 4, 1996

Employment Manager
Any Corporation
1140 Main Street
Chicago, IL 60628

RE: Purchasing Agent

Dear Ms. Cummings:

Please accept this letter and resume as an initial application for the position you advertised in the January 18 edition of the *Macon Telegraph*. I am a self-motivated individual who can work well with people, grasp and expand on new ideas, tackle and follow through on difficult projects, and achieve or exceed objectives.

Please note that I have six years of experience ranging from Purchasing Clerk to Senior Buyer for multisite operations with purchases in excess of $1.5 million. I have been a key contributor to the successful setup and startup of new branch locations, from bare wall facility to fully trained and operating activity. In addition, my experience has encompassed sales support and telemarketing.

I have a proven track record because I am strongly motivated, well organized, and have excellent communication skills. I am confident of my ability to make an immediate as well as long-term contribution to Any Corporation, and feel that a personal interview would give us the opportunity to expand upon your requirements and my ability to meet them.

I appreciate your consideration of my application and look forward to your reply.

Sincerely,

Chris Smith

Enc. resume

■ Candidate matches his/her qualifications with potential employer's needs.

■ Including a FAX number is optional in a cover letter.

RESPONSE TO A CLASSIFIED ADVERTISEMENT
(Real Estate Sales Associate)

178 Green Street
Milwaukee, WI 53201
(414) 555-5555

December 20, 1996

Pat Cummings
Vice-President
Any Properties
1140 Main Street
Milwaukee, WI 53201

RE: Advertisement in *Real Estate Weekly*, December 20, 1996

Dear Mr. Cummings:

I am writing to apply for the above-listed position. I am interested in contributing my real estate expertise to Any Properties.

I offer nearly twenty years of intensive experience involving the most sophisticated aspects of commercial and residential real estate sales and leasing, as well as associated areas of real estate development, property management, and rehabilitation. In addition to a current brokers' license, I am very well grounded in real estate and business law.

I am considered a highly organized team player, with excellent verbal and written communications skills, an eye for detail, and the necessary persistence to conceive, package, and bring the big deals home.

My resume is a quick summary of my background and professional experience, but I feel that during the course of a personal interview my potential to contribute to Any Properties could be more effectively demonstrated. I will call to establish a mutually convenient time for such a meeting.

Thank you for your consideration.

Sincerely,

Chris Smith

Enc. resume

■ Setting desired position apart from body of letter may be advantageous when responding to classified advertisement.

■ Candidate includes licensure relevant to his/her field.

RESPONSE TO A CLASSIFIED ADVERTISEMENT
(Regional Manager)

178 Green Street
Dubuque, IA 52001

August 7, 1996

Pat Cummings
Management Supervisor
Any Corporation
1140 Main Street
Peosta, IA 52068

Dear Ms. Cummings:

Please accept this inquiry as my expressed interest in the Regional Manager position advertised in the August issue of *Automotive Monthly*.

During the past twenty-two years, I have developed a successful track record as a professional with internationally recognized expertise in the automotive industries. In the last twelve years, I have specialized in customer satisfaction program development and strategic implementation consulting.

My extensive management experience has encompassed the design and evaluation of corporate marketing strategies and involved the evaluation of policies, projects, and new products. This experience is supported by a B.A. in Economics, an M.A. in Economics, M.B.A. coursework, a D.Sc., and a D.E.S. in Applied Mathematics.

Although my present position provides interesting diversity and challenge, I feel that it is time to move on to other opportunities. The enclosed professional profile provides only a portion of my qualifications and activities which I will be glad to expand on during a personal meeting. I will call your office on Wednesday, August 14, to schedule a mutually convenient meeting time.

Thank you for your consideration.

Sincerely,

Chris Smith

Enc. professional profile

- Educational credentials accentuate candidate's qualifications.

- Candidate quantifies extensive experience.

RESPONSE TO A CLASSIFIED ADVERTISEMENT
(Researcher)

178 Green Street
Washington, DC 20057
(202) 555-5555

October 31, 1996

Pat Cummings
Human Resources Director
Any Newspaper
1140 Main Street
Chicago, IL 60605

Dear Mr. Cummings:

I am writing in response to the Researcher position advertised in the *Washington Post* on October 30. Please allow me to outline my skills as they apply to your stated requirements:

Writing Experience: I have authored or coauthored five books on sports and communications. In addition, I have been a reporter for both magazines and newspapers for many years. I have written over 3,500 articles for publication, on topics ranging from crime and sports to medicine and humor. I know how to conceive of and research topics, and I am comfortable writing on almost any subject and in a range of styles. I am confident I would have no trouble matching the established style of your book series.

Editing Experience: I have copyedited a number of books on business topics and worked as an editor for several newspapers. I am capable of doing either minor polishing or major rewriting and, more importantly, of being able to tell which job is needed. In addition, I taught English Composition and Writing for the Print Media at the high school level for five years.

I have enclosed a resume as well as a brief sample of my writing for your review. I look forward to meeting with you to discuss further how I could contribute to your organization.

Sincerely,

Chris Smith

Enc. resume
writing samples

■ Categorizing qualifications adds strength to cover letter.

■ Unique format demonstrates candidate's ability to meet advertised job requirements.

RESPONSE TO A CLASSIFIED ADVERTISEMENT
(Restaurant Manager Trainee)

178 Green Street
Grand Junction, CO 81502
(303) 555-5555

November 15, 1996

Pat Cummings
Manager
Any Restaurant
1140 Main Street
Denver Post, CO 80202

RE: Restaurant Manager Trainee

Dear Ms. Cummings:

Please accept the enclosed resume as application for your position advertised in
the November 14 edition of the *Denver Post*.

During the past seven years, I have held positions of responsibility in banquet/
special event catering, function management, and restaurant food service operations.

Currently, I am seeking a new association with a firm that can benefit from my
experience in the above areas. I have additional experience in front desk operation,
possess good organizational, leadership, training, and supervisory skills, and can
provide quality service and performance in a high-volume setting. As my resume
indicates, the vast diversity of food service settings I have been associated with
has made me extensively experienced in the management of virtually any type of
food, beverage, and kitchen staff.

I have continually heard and read many favorable reviews of Any Restaurant, and
I have always enjoyed my own dining experiences there. I would love to join your
management team after completing the requisite training program. I will call you
next Monday to arrange a mutually convenient time to discuss this opportunity
further.

Sincerely,

Chris Smith

Enc. resume

- Unrelated work experience is
  omitted from response letter.
- Closing emphasizes candidate's
  enthusiasm for desired position.

RESPONSE TO A CLASSIFIED ADVERTISEMENT
(Sales Representative)

178 Green Street
Northridge, CA 91324
(818) 555-5555

April 17, 1996

Ms. Pat Cummings
Vice-President
Any Corporation
1140 Main Street
Pittsburgh, PA 15217

Dear Mr. Cummings:

Please accept the enclosed resume as an expressed interest in contributing relevant experience to the position of Sales Representative, as advertised in the *Pittsburgh Post-Gazette*, on Wednesday, April 11.

I have accumulated several years of experience in the development of sales and marketing strategies. I have been involved in a number of diverse employment situations, including a self-owned business, in which I successfully utilized various sales techniques, including cold calling, telemarketing, and prospecting. In my first two years at FloSoft, I increased our client base by 25 percent. While at the Brian Agency, I was part of a sales team that generated a record-breaking $10 million in one year. In addition, I have held numerous positions where I supervised and developed personnel and assisted in the facilitation of daily operations.

I would welcome the opportunity to meet with you and discuss ways in which my capabilities could be directed to suit your needs. I await your call to arrange a mutually convenient time to meet.

I look forward to talking with you in the near future. Thank you for your time and consideration.

With best regards,

Chris Smith

Enc. resume

■ Dollar amounts quantify candidate's accomplishments.

■ Introduction immediately refers to publication where advertisement appeared.

RESPONSE TO A CLASSIFIED ADVERTISEMENT
(Senior HVAC Technician)

178 Green Street
New Martinsville, WV 26155
(304) 555-5555

November 12, 1996

Pat Cummings
Human Resources Director
Any Corporation
1140 Main Street
Charlestown, WV 25301

Dear Ms. Cummings:

At the request of Donald Lee of your department, I am enclosing my resume in answer to the advertisement in last Friday's *Charleston Gazette* for an experienced Senior HVAC Technician.

I possess nine years of experience in after-warranty maintenance, preventive maintenance programs, and complete overhaul of major systems within a multibuilding, mixed-use industrial complex. I have also completed extensive and continuous education and training on the latest and most cost-efficient energy systems and control.

Presently, I am seeking a new association with an institution such as Any Corporation where I can apply my technical as well as supervisory skills to provide quality, cost-efficient, energy control system maintenance at a time when energy prices are at an all-time high.

I would welcome the opportunity to discuss your requirements and my ability to handle the responsibilities of the position offered. Could we meet for a personal interview? I can make myself readily available whenever you are free.

Thank you for your time, Ms. Cummings.

Sincerely,

Chris Smith

Enc. resume

■ Basis for referral is immediately established.

■ Candidate thanks addressee for time extended.

RESPONSE TO A CLASSIFIED ADVERTISEMENT
(Site Location Supervisor)

178 Green Street
Smithfield, RI 02917

April 16, 1996

Pat Cummings
General Manager, Properties
Any Corporation
1140 Main Street
Bridgeville, PA 15017

RE: Executive Position, Site Location and Store Build-Outs

Dear Mr. Cummings:

I am confident that I am the person you seek in your advertisement in the April 15 edition of the *Providence Evening Bulletin*. My interest is in joining a firm which has a need for a representative capable of working effectively with clients in real estate development, property management, and finance. Because of a broad and diverse background, I am well qualified to provide consulting and/or management services to clients with problems involving planning, financing, budgeting, scheduling, and monitoring any phase of development-related activity.

During the past fifteen years, my experience as a developer, general manager, owner, and manager of residential, commercial, and industrial projects has been extensive. In conjunction with these projects, I was actively involved in investment analysis, whole loans and structured transactions, and financial control to assure quality completion within schedules and budgets.

I relate well to individuals and groups at all levels of responsibility and can fulfill management responsibilities while expediting project completions from inception to final inspection.

Although my resume is enclosed, I would be able to provide you with additional pertinent information as to my capabilities and goals during a personal interview. I am free to relocate and/or travel and the compensation package is negotiable. I can be reached at the above address or by phone at (401) 555-5555.

Sincerely,

Chris Smith

Enc. resume

■ Experience reinforces candidate's professional objective.

■ Candidate emphasizes how past business experience is relevant.

RESPONSE TO A CLASSIFIED ADVERTISEMENT
(Social Worker)

178 Green Street
Northridge, CA 91324
(818) 555-5555

July 19, 1996

Pat Cummings
Director
Any Agency
1140 Main Street
Northridge, CA 91324

Dear Ms. Cummings:

In response to your advertisement in the summer edition of the *Social Justice Journal*, I would like to offer my services to fill the vacancy in the Social Worker position. I am confident you will find my experience and abilities qualify me for the position.

I possess extensive diverse and applicable experience. As stated in my resume, I received a Bachelor's degree in Dance Therapy, an interdisciplinary major, which involved extensive research into child psychology as well as artistic ability. While in college, I worked with children in a volunteer program called P.A.L.S, in which we visited and recreated with children in housing projects. I also visited a day-care program to study the psychology behind children's drawings for my senior research project. In addition, in high school, I worked with mentally disturbed adults.

As you can see, my background corresponds to your requirements. I look forward to hearing from you to discuss this job further.

Sincerely,

Chris Smith

Enc. resume

- ■ Volunteer experience gives candidate a competitive edge.
- ■ Research projects illustrate candidate's initiative.

RESPONSE TO A CLASSIFIED ADVERTISEMENT
(State Administrator)

178 Green Street
Riverside, CA 92521
(909) 555-5555

December 23, 1996

Pat Cummings
President, New England Offices
Any Organization
1140 Main Street
Sacramento, CA 95821

Dear Mr. Cummings:

In response to your advertisement in the December 20 edition of the *Sacramento Bee*, please find my resume enclosed for your review. I am very interested in securing the position of State Administrator available at Any Organization.

During the past twelve years, I have held diverse and progressively responsible positions in development for nonprofit service organizations, universities, and educational institutions. These responsibilities have ranged from Secretary to Director of Development.

Throughout this period, I have been heavily involved in development strategies, annual fund campaigns, marketing and mailing programs, and media and public relations. Although these positions have been challenging and broad in scope, I feel that my expertise may be utilized to a better advantage by your organization.

I hope that, after reviewing my qualifications, you will consider me as the right candidate for State Administrator. I am confident of my abilities, and would like to schedule an interview to reiterate my desire for the position. I will call you on December 27 to follow up my inquiry.

I appreciate your time and look forward to speaking with you.

Sincerely,

Chris Smith

Enc. resume

■ Since company name and information is provided in advertisement, candidate promises to follow up inquiry.

■ Candidate focuses on relevant functional skills.

RESPONSE TO A CLASSIFIED ADVERTISEMENT
(Store Manager)

178 Green Street
New Haven, CT 06520
(203) 555-5555

December 22, 1996

Pat Cummings
District Supervisor
Any Corporation
1140 Main Street
Jacksonville, FL 32231

Dear Ms. Cummings:

In response to your advertisement for a Store Manager in the December 15 edition of the Sarasota *Herald-Tribune*, I am forwarding my resume. As detailed below, my experience qualifies me for the position.

You require:
* Managerial experience
* Superior written and verbal skills
* Budget management abilities

I offer:
* Five years as senior manager in a chain bookstore with an annual volume in excess of $2 million. Ability to manage inventory, personnel, cash flow.
* Accreditation as a high school teacher. Recognition for "Where We're At," a lighthearted historical essay.
* At University Towers, decreased outstanding rents by $5,000. Reorganized Sturtevant's retail promotions, effecting a 50 percent budget reduction.

May we discuss how I may contribute to your organization? I am available at your convenience to discuss employment opportunities, and the possibility of relocation.

Thank you for reviewing my credentials. I look forward to our initial conversation.

Sincerely,

Chris Smith

Enc. resume

■ Candidate focuses on applying skills and experiences to advertised position.

■ Format is organized and visually appealing.

RESPONSE TO A CLASSIFIED ADVERTISEMENT
(Systems Trainer)

178 Green Street
Natchitoches, LA 71497
(318) 555-5555

July 16, 1996

Pat Cummings
Director
Any Corporation
1140 Main Street
Lafayette, LA 70504

Dear Mr. Cummings:

In response to your advertisement in the July 13 edition of the *Times*, I would like to apply for the position of Systems Trainer.

I am a skilled professional with extensive experience in the management of in-house and client training services on state-of-the-art systems using technical and business applications. Although my current position has been challenging and provides a real sense of achievement, I feel it is time for a change to a firm such as Any Corporation where I can use my skills to establish meaningful changes in system automation and train personnel to a high level of performance.

In addition to a Bachelor of Science degree in Education and postgraduate study in computer science and business, I offer nine years of project and senior management experience with concentration in training, documentation, and related companywide services for business and technical environments. I have hands-on experience with many software and hardware systems, and believe that I can initiate and implement cost-effective, efficient breakthroughs in systems and training as I have for my previous employer.

I am confident in my ability to handle the responsibilities of the position offered. Could we meet in a personal interview?

I look forward to your reply.

Sincerely,

Chris Smith

Enc. resume

■ Closing is straightforward and concise.

■ Job descriptions indicate how candidate contributed to his/her previous employers.

RESPONSE TO A CLASSIFIED ADVERTISEMENT
(Technical Writer)

178 Green Street
Santa Fe, NM 87501

July 22, 1996

Pat Cummings
Publicity Director
Any Tech
1140 Main Street
Santa Fe, NE 87501

Dear Ms. Cummings:

I am applying for the Technical Writer position advertised in July's *Engineering World*. My relevant experience is diverse, and establishes me as a first-class candidate for this opportunity.

My writing experience is extensive. I am currently employed as a Technical Writer at Computer Systems International. My past work experience includes newspaper and freelance writing. At Computer Systems, I document software for use by manufacturers on IBM mainframes. We release three documentation sets: user guides, references, and batch operations and sample reports.

Since graduating from the University of Maine with a Journalism/English degree, my editorial experience has been diverse and rewarding. I edited medical manuscripts for medical and scientific publications and Henderson Medical Center. Specific duties included editing text for content, style considerations, grammar, and spelling. I also verified resources, coordinated artwork, and acted as liaison between physicians and journal editors.

At the *Albuquerque Journal*, as a sports editor and general assignment/ photographer, I wrote sports and news articles and features. I also took and processed photographs and designed pages. At MediaCorps, as a staff writer, I prepared press packages on new products.

I am available for an interview scheduled at your convenience. I may be reached at (505) 555-5555 (days) and (505) 444-4444 (evenings). Thank you for your consideration.

Sincerely,

Chris Smith

Enc. resume

■ Introduction is brief and attention-grabbing.

■ Educational credentials relate specifically to advertised position.

RESPONSE TO A CLASSIFIED ADVERTISEMENT
(Telemarketer)

178 Green Street
Omaha, NE 68182
(402) 555-5555

January 22, 1996

Pat Cummings
Director of Marketing and Sales
Any Corporation
1140 Main Street
Lincoln, NE 68522

Dear Mr. Cummings:

I am responding to your advertisement in search of a telemarketing professional in the *Lincoln Journal* dated January 16.

The enclosed resume provides details of my solid career experience in marketing and sales. My accomplishments include:

- Managing and directing sales of a national publication to business decision-makers and chief executive officers of major financial, educational and municipal leaders which resulted in $175,000 sales in a four-month period.
- Creating and implementing marketing strategy of a family-owned retail establishment which produced substantial increase in sales.
- Establishing a marketing and public relations plan for a consulting firm which increased client base and significantly enhanced public recognition of firm.
- Writing, editing, directing, and producing public service television program which involved timely legal and medical issues.

I would be pleased to discuss this matter with you in a personal interview and look forward to hearing from you.

Sincerely,

Chris Smith

Enc. resume

■ Letter uses bullets to highlight candidate's achievements related to advertised position.

■ Response letter immediately states candidate's purpose for writing.

RESPONSE TO A CLASSIFIED ADVERTISEMENT
(Television Camera Operator)

178 Green Street
Pineville, LA 71359
(318) 555-5555

January 18, 1996

Pat Cummings
Production Manager
Any Television Station
1140 Main Street
New Orleans, LA 70018

Dear Ms. Cummings:

I aspire to find a challenging position where I am able to apply my technical and production talents. When I read your job description for a Television Camera Operator in the Sunday *Times-Picayune*, I felt that my background and skills would be a wonderful match for your requirements.

During the past three years, I have worked extensively as a Production Assistant and Technical Operator in a television studio involving all aspects of video production. I also have written, directed, produced, and edited three short 8 mm films and a music video which was shot using ENG equipment. These projects allowed me to sharpen many skills, such as conceptualization, camera work, and editing. In addition, I have received a Bachelor of Science degree and gained additional experience in video and camera operation from Ellis Technical Training School.

Once given the opportunity to demonstrate my talents, I am sure that I can prove to be a worthwhile addition to your station. Also, I am confident of my ability to quickly excel through a training program and soon begin taping. I look forward to the opportunity for an interview and to meet with you in person.

Sincerely,

Chris Smith

Enc. resume

- Candidate's practical experience outweighs his/her education.
- Response letter immediately introduces candidate's qualifications.

RESPONSE TO A CLASSIFIED ADVERTISEMENT
(Translator)

178 Green Street
Lawrenceville, GA 30246
(404) 555-5555

June 2, 1996

Pat Cummings
Head Translator
Any Organization
1140 Main Street
Atlanta, GA 30318

Dear Mr. Cummings:

I am writing in response to your May 30th advertisement in the *Atlanta Constitution* for a Translator. I was immediately intrigued by this position and would like to be considered in your search.

I am convinced that my interest, combined with my experience, could be well utilized by your organization. While completing my Bachelor of Science degree at Emory University, I worked as a Translating Assistant in the translation center on campus. My duties included translating documents from both Spanish and Russian into English and vice versa, verbally communicating with international contacts, and entering and editing articles and poetry for publication. It should be noted that several of the articles were in foreign languages I do not speak, which required very strong attention to detail in their translation.

While at Emory, I spent a semester studying abroad in St. Petersburg, Russia. As a personal tutor, I developed lessons for English instruction to foreign students. This unique opportunity, as well as my extensive travel throughout Latin America, allowed me to sharpen my verbal and written Russian and Spanish translation skills.

I believe my experience and knowledge would successfully be applied to the Translator position you are seeking to fill. I would like to speak with you further in a personal interview and will call your office to schedule a convenient time. Thank you for your time and I look forward to meeting with you.

Sincerely,

Chris Smith

Enc. resume

■ Foreign language skills strengthen candidate's qualifications.

■ College activities are related to candidate's field of study and career objective.

RESPONSE TO A CLASSIFIED ADVERTISEMENT
(Travel Agent)

178 Green Street
New Britain, CT 06050
(203) 555-5555

January 29, 1996

Pat Cummings
Owner
Any Travel Agency
1140 Main Street
New London, CT 06320

Dear Ms. Cummings:

I am responding to your advertisement in the *Wichita Eagle* for the position of
Travel Agent.

As my enclosed resume indicates, I possess eleven years of extensive experience
in the travel and tourism fields. As sole owner of a tourism-related business for
four years, I oversaw and advised thirty host homes and inns operating in the New
England area. I was independently responsible for maintaining accurate business
records, purchasing supplies, and writing and editing all public relations materials,
contracts, and policy guidelines. I enjoy writing and promoting New England as a
premier business and leisure destination, and would welcome the opportunity to
broaden my local attention to include the rest of the nation.

In addition, my association with the Greater Connecticut Convention and Visitor's
Bureau and the Southern Connecticut Bureau, as well as the Connecticut Chamber
of Commerce, has considerably heightened my awareness of visitor markets and
related disposable income. I believe my knowledge of current visitor trends
coupled with my affinity for customer travel make me a qualified candidate for a
position as a Travel Agent.

Thank you in advance for your generous consideration. I may be reached at my
home phone number indicated above should you desire to contact me. I would be
happy to make myself available for a personal interview at your convenience.

Sincerely,

Chris Smith

Enc. resume

■ Job-related affiliations
demonstrate candidate's active
participation in his/her field.

■ Candidate expresses knowledge
in his/her field of interest.

RESPONSE TO A CLASSIFIED ADVERTISEMENT
(Writing Instructor)

178 Green Street
Richmond, VA 23219
(804) 555-5555

June 1, 1996

Pat Cummings
Dean
Any College
1140 Main Street
Winston-Salem, NC 27108

Dear Mr. Cummings:

Please consider this letter and the enclosed resume as an application for the position of Writing Instructor as advertised in the *Richmond Times-Dispatch* last Wednesday.

I have been a college-level teacher of writing for the past eleven years and offer strong writing, editing, and proofreading skills. I am also a writer; my published works include short stories, essays, and poems. Last February, a one-act play of mine was produced in New York City. I also have experience ghostwriting, editing for the *Chapel Hill Review*, and publicity writing for a Raleigh rock group.

I am confident that the above-listed experience distinguishes me as a qualified candidate for your opening. I would be delighted to discuss further how my abilities match your requirements.

I have enclosed a writing sample and can provide letters of recommendation if needed.

Thanks for your attention to this matter.

Sincerely,

Chris Smith

Enc. resume
    writing sample

■ Enclosure line refers to all attached materials.

■ Qualifications are geared to candidate's field of interest.

RESPONSE TO A CLASSIFIED ADVERTISEMENT
(Yacht Salesperson)

178 Green Street
San Francisco, CA 94132
(415) 555-5555

June 6, 1996

Pat Cummings
Vice-President, Sales
Any Corporation
1140 Main Street
Modesto, CA 95354

Dear Ms. Cummings:

If you are looking for an energetic, dedicated representative for the position in yacht sales you advertised in the *Modesto Bee*, I believe we have good reason to meet.

In addition to a Bachelor of Arts degree in Business Administration and Marketing, I have several years of successful experience in advertising, promoting, and selling high-priced properties to clients in the upper income bracket. My experience and extensive travel as a co-host at international and domestic conferences, attended by government and business leaders, required refined communication skills and the ability to effectively negotiate with high-level decision-makers.

I would like to utilize these skills within Any Corporation to penetrate markets and increase sales of big-ticket items such as yachts. I am willing to travel, and believe that I will, through my persistent efforts, meet, and even exceed, mutual sales objectives.

Enclosed please find my resume. I will follow up this inquiry with a phone call in several days. I am very interested in learning more about the position and how my qualifications might suit you.

Sincerely,

Chris Smith

Enc. resume

■ Willingness to travel can be advantageous.

■ Educational credentials accentuate candidate's qualifications.

RESPONSE TO A CLASSIFIED ADVERTISEMENT
(Youth Center Director)

178 Green Street
Tuscaloosa, AL 35401
(205) 555-5555

August 20, 1996

Pat Cummings
Regional Director
Any Youth Center
1140 Main Street
Palo Alto, CA 94203

Dear Mr. Cummings:

Please accept the enclosed resume for the Executive Director position at Any
Center as advertised in the *Los Angeles Times*. I am excited to learn about this
position and the opportunity to work with a progressive youth services organization.

As my resume indicates, during the past two years I have been researching and
developing a new youth center in the Tuscaloosa County area. Thus far, I have
developed programs serving over fifteen hundred individuals and families, with a
budget size almost doubling in one year. As I have learned, starting a youth center
from scratch is a process that involves a great deal of planning on all levels. Much
of my experience includes grant and proposal writing, public relations, and board
and committee development. Also, community and corporate presentations are
part of my monthly schedule.

My present responsibilities and past experience have thoroughly prepared me for a
branch executive position. As Director of Any Center, I would make an immediate
contribution to your staff through my ability to effectively manage your staff and
create positive customer relations. I am eager to accept new challenges, and look
forward to meeting with you regarding this position.

I appreciate your time and consideration.

Sincerely,

Chris Smith

Enc. resume

■ Letter immediately refers
addressee to attached resume.

■ Candidate clearly indicates type of
position desired.

11
Response to a "Blind" Advertisement

"Blind" advertisements do not list employer information, and generally direct inquiries to a post office box rather than a company's address. Since you're not provided with a company name in a blind ad, your cover letter should sharply define your knowledge of the industry, position (if mentioned), and how your qualifications specifically match up to the stated requirements. In other words, tailor your letter to any information given. For example, consider a blind ad that reads:

Large-size law firm in need of Paralegal with experience in legal research, writing briefs, and office administration.

You need to target everything in your response: what you know of the operations of large-size firms; why you want to be and remain a Paralegal; how much experience you have in legal research and writing; and exactly what office skills you have. Avoid long-winded passages that don't follow these guidelines. Keep it brief and to the point. Without knowing your readers, you've caught their attention. They're more likely to invite you for an interview, and suddenly you're one step closer to getting the job.

RESPONSE TO A "BLIND" ADVERTISEMENT
(Administrator: Parks and Recreation Department)

178 Green Street
Jaffrey, NH 03452
(603) 555-5555

April 16, 1996

Personnel Manager
P.O. Box 7777
Hanover, NH 03755

Dear Personnel Manager:

The April 13 edition of the *Union Leader* ran an advertisement for a Parks and Recreation Department Administrator. I am very interested in making a significant contribution to convention planning, special event planning, and/or recreation products and services.

As my resume indicates, I offer twelve years of solid experience ranging from Waterfront Director to my most recent position as Program Administrator for all recreational aspects of a municipal park and recreation department. Currently, I am seeking a new association with an organization that can benefit from my management and administrative expertise. I welcome the opportunity for a meeting.

Thank you for your consideration.

Sincerely,

Chris Smith

Enc. resume

■ Letter is brief and concise.

■ Candidate matches his/her qualifications with potential employer's needs.

RESPONSE TO A "BLIND" ADVERTISEMENT
(Applications Programmer)

178 Green Street
Harrisburg, PA 17101

February 20, 1996

P.O. Box 7777
Harrisburg, PA 17101

RE: Applications Programmer

To whom it may concern:

If you have a need for a competent Programmer Analyst with expertise in application development, maintenance, and enhancement of programs in purchasing, inventory control, contracts management, and related logistics applications, then we have good reason to meet.

During the past thirteen years, I have handled projects for Agtech and CompWare that require the ability to work effectively with large systems as well as PC-based software environments. My experience with the maintenance, development, and enhancement of programs is extensive and has required interaction with all departments and users to provide guidance and assistance in developing programs for procurement and logistic applications.

Although my present position has provided diversity and challenge, I am ready for a change and would like to join an organization in the public or private sector which has a need for my capability to cost-effectively handle the position of Programmer Analyst.

The enclosed professional profile outlines my experience. I would like to meet for an interview, during which I can find out more about your company and will expand on the mutual benefits of my joining your ranks.

Since my present employer is not aware of my intent to make a change, I would appreciate your handling this inquiry in the strictest confidence. Should you require additional information prior to our meeting, please contact me at the above address or by phone at (717) 555-5555. I look forward to your return response.

Yours sincerely,

Chris Smith

Enc. professional profile

■ Letter outlines candidate's skills relevant to advertised position.

■ Qualifications highlight candidate's problem-solving ability.

RESPONSE TO A "BLIND" ADVERTISEMENT
(Assistant Personnel Officer)

178 Green Street
Vienna, VA 22211

June 1, 1996

Human Resources Director
P.O. Box 7777
Arlington, VA 22203

Dear Human Resources Director:

I am writing to express my interest in the Assistant Personnel Officer position as advertised in the May 30 edition of the *Washington Post*.

As the enclosed resume indicates, I offer extensive experience including my most recent position as Assistant Staff Manager at Virginia General Hospital. In this capacity I recruited and trained administrative and clerical staffs, ancillary and works department staffs, and professional and technical staffs. I also evaluated personnel, conducted disciplinary and grievance interviews, signed employees to contracts, and advised staff on conditions of employment, entitlements, and maternity leave.

Should my qualifications be of interest to you, please contact me at the above address or by phone at (703) 555-5555. I look forward to hearing from you.

Sincerely,

Chris Smith

Enc. resume

■ Candidate's most relevant work experience is prioritized.

■ Qualifications call attention to candidate's relevant supervisory and administrative experience.

RESPONSE TO A "BLIND" ADVERTISEMENT
(Business Consultant)

178 Green Street
Dedham, MA 02026
(617) 555-5555
E-Mail: CSMITH@world.qqq.bac

March 29, 1996

Human Resources Director
P.O. Box 7777
Cincinnati, OH 45221

Dear Human Resources Director:

I am responding to your advertisement for a Business Consultant in today's *Wall Street Journal*; it is likely that my consulting and executive experience with small businesses well-matches the requirements for the position.

In 1984, while General Manager of Kimcorp, I developed an extension to the company's core production services business: a fast-turnaround, low-cost (and high-margin) circuit prototyping service. In addition, I conceived of the functional specifications of a software package that would help designers do board layout on their PC's. Since then I have kept my hands on computers wherever they have helped me in my business or consulting activities.

Enclosed is a copy of my resume. I look forward to speaking with you in more detail about this opportunity.

Sincerely,

Chris Smith

Enc. resume

■ Technical language is acceptable when it relates to candidate's field.

■ Including an e-mail address may be advantageous for certain fields of work.

RESPONSE TO A "BLIND" ADVERTISEMENT
(Case Manager)

178 Green Street
Golden, CO 80301
(303) 555-5555

May 27, 1996

Hiring Coordinator
P.O. Box 7777
Aurora, CO 80014

Dear Hiring Coordinator:

Please accept this letter and my accompanying resume as expressed interest in the
Case Manager position advertised in the May 1996 issue of *Sociology Today*.

With a successful record of diverse social work experience, an eager desire to
learn, and the determination to get the job done, I am confident that you will profit
from my assistance. Most recently, I served as Case Manager for Dylan High
School where I worked closely with at-risk students, coordinated outreach and
referral services, supervised staff, and assisted community-based agencies and
educational institutions in all activities involving students. In addition, my
experience is supported by a Bachelor of Science degree in Social Work.

I would welcome the opportunity to discuss the position in detail. I can be reached
between 5 p.m. and 10 p.m., Monday through Friday, at the above phone number.
I look forward to your reply.

Sincerely,

Chris Smith

Enc. resume

■ Closing cites specific times
candidate may be reached.

■ Candidate includes all relevant
experience to advertised position.

RESPONSE TO A "BLIND" ADVERTISEMENT
(Catering Manager)

178 Green Street
Mobile, AL 36608

October 13, 1996

P.O. Box 7777
Gainesville, GA 30503

RE: Catering Manager

Dear Sir/Madam:

I write in response to your advertisement in the *Southern States Service Weekly*. Currently, I am seeking a new association with a firm than can benefit from my ten years in the food service industry.

I have held positions of responsibility in banquet/special event catering, function management, and restaurant food service operations. I have additional experience in front desk operation, and I possess good organizational, leadership, training, and supervisory skills. I can also provide quality service and performance in a high-volume setting, and manage food, beverage, and kitchen staff with ease.

The enclosed resume summarizes my experience. I would like the chance to expand on my qualifications in a personal interview. I am anxious to learn more about your firm and the available position, and to show you how I can meet your requirements.

Please contact me at the above address or at (205) 555-5555 so that we may schedule a meeting time. I thank you for your time.

Sincerely,

Chris Smith

Enc. resume

■ Candidate quantifies extensive experience.

■ Setting desired position apart from body of letter may be advantageous when responding to a "blind" advertisement.

RESPONSE TO A "BLIND" ADVERTISEMENT
(Chief Executive Officer)

178 Green Street
Madison, WI 53706
(608) 555-5555

July 24, 1996

P.O. Box 7777
River Falls, WI 54022

RE: Chief Executive Officer position

Dear Sir or Madam:

Selecting the right CEO for a $100 million U.S.-based operation can be a grueling process. I would like to take the stress out of the process by suggesting that you review my qualifications and the experience I can bring to your company.

As Corporate Vice-President of Sales, with an established record for the development of approximately $100 million in sales, my responsibilities have covered the gamut of successful strategies and techniques for growth and profitability. My involvement in sales, marketing, staff development, and production interface has been extensive, and my ability to organize and manage is well documented in goals I've achieved with my present and past employers.

My resume is enclosed. If it is bottom-line results you are looking for, then we have good reason to meet for further discussion and mutual gain. Should you require additional information prior to our meeting, please do not hesitate to contact me.

I look forward to your return response.

Sincerely,

Chris Smith

Enc. resume

- ■ Introduction captures addressee's attention.
- ■ Experience reinforces candidate's suitability for advertised position.

RESPONSE TO A "BLIND" ADVERTISEMENT
(Editorial/Computer Production Manager)

178 Green Street
Beloit, WI 53511
(608) 555-5555

August 8, 1996

Hiring Director
P.O. Box 7777
South Milwaukee, WI 53172

Dear Hiring Director:

I am interested in the Editorial/Computer Production Manager position that you advertised in the *Milwaukee Journal*. Let me briefly match your needs as I understand them to my background.

Your requirements:
- Proofreading, researching, and writing skills.
- Knowledge of PC-oriented desktop publishing.
- Knowledge of computer on-line programs.

My relevant skills:
- Proficiency in proofreading and copyediting attained during seven years with a typesetting company. Completed freelance project in keying and copyediting for an IMIS Research reference book.
- Computerized a pre-PC typesetting system. Set up a WordPerfect-based newsletter system and completed initial work for a PageMaker-based hardware/software setup. Familiar with typesetting and pay layout issues both from pre-PC and PC eras.
- Utilized PC communications for over ten years. Independently set up an E-Mail system using CompuServe. Expanded knowledge of on-line systems as a library and information sciences student.

I hope you agree that my qualifications suit this position ideally. May we schedule a personal interview?

I look forward to hearing from you.

Sincerely,

Chris Smith

Enc. resume

- Computer skills relate specifically to requirements outlined in advertisement.

- Format is organized and visually appealing.

RESPONSE TO A "BLIND" ADVERTISEMENT
(Executive Sous Chef)

178 Green Street
Austin, TX 78704
(512) 555-5555

July 7, 1996

P.O. Box 7777
Roanoke, VA 24001

RE: Executive Sous Chef

Dear Sir or Madam:

I am enclosing a copy of my resume for your review and hope it will convince you
that I am the right choice for the position of Executive Sous Chef for your facility.

My experience in the restaurant industry goes back to my high school days and has
taken me through all phases of the culinary arts in progressively responsible
positions. During the past fifteen years, I have had the opportunity to work with
Leisuretyme Properties. In my present position as Sous Chef at the Naturne Hotel
in Austin, I have the responsibility for both the brasserie and Charles Fisheries
which generate food revenues of $6 million, and have direct supervision of a staff
of thirty.

My experience with Leisuretyme included extensive work with banquet
preparation and special themes for up to 2,500 guests in a facility generating $19
million in banquet business. Because of my ability to organize, train, and work
effectively with personnel in quality, high-volume restaurants, I was able to
maintain a low-turnover, conscientious, highly productive work force in an
industry notorious for personnel problems.

Based on my qualifications, I feel confident that I can handle the responsibilities
of Executive Sous Chef and maintain high-quality food services. In addition, I am
willing to relocate given a suitable opportunity.

Please contact me so that we may discuss how I may contribute my expertise to
your organization. I look forward to our initial conversation.

Sincerely,

Chris Smith

Enc. resume

■ Letter incorporates industry
knowledge into discussion of
qualifications.

■ Response letter emphasizes
candidate's supervisory skills.

RESPONSE TO A "BLIND" ADVERTISEMENT
(Field Finance Manager)

178 Green Street
Presque Island, ME 04769
(207) 555-5555

February 6, 1996

Professional Staffing
P.O. Box 7777
Bangor, ME 04401

RE: Field Finance Manager

Dear Professional Staffing:

Please accept this letter and enclosed resume as an application for your opening advertised in the *Bangor Daily News*.

As a 1993 graduate of the University of Maine's Graduate School of Business, I have over six years of business and financial analysis experience. This includes two years of domestic and international travel as an Internal Auditor for Manyfoods, Inc., two years of credit analysis at Millbury, and a treasury internship as Envirlab. Since my graduation, I have been working as a Business Analyst in the areas of banking, real estate, and restaurant management.

I have been recognized for my creative spirit and ability to identify implementable solutions to current business problems. The following highlights some of my achievements:

- Participated in the due diligence and/or postacquisition reviews of five acquisitions.
- Planned, coordinated, and/or participated in the compliance and productivity audits of forty-one independent business units.
- Participated in the fraud review of a major business unit.
- Researched, developed, and planned a cash collection reorganization that, when implemented, will save $120,000 per year.

Based on my job experience and educational qualifications, I am confident I can make an immediate contribution to your firm. I would appreciate the opportunity to further discuss my credentials with you in person. Thank you.

Sincerely,

Chris Smith

Enc. resume

■ Bulleted statements highlight candidate's on-the-job achievements.

■ Candidate emphasizes how past business experience is relevant.

222

RESPONSE TO A "BLIND" ADVERTISEMENT
(Labor Relations Specialist)

178 Green Street
Worcester, MA 01610

April 8, 1996

Personnel Representative
P.O. Box 7777
Lowell, MA 01852

Dear Personnel Representative:

I am very interested in the Labor Relations Specialist position that appeared in the April 5 edition of the *Worcester Telegram & Gazette*. Enclosed is a copy of my resume for your review.

I offer over fifteen years of human resource and labor relations experience which includes the following positions: Labor/Management Relations Analyst, Field Representative, and Legislative Assistant. I am fluent in Spanish, willing to travel, and anxious to put my skills to work for your organization.

Please call me at (508) 555-5555 with any further questions. I look forward to hearing from you.

Sincerely,

Chris Smith

Enc. resume

■ Letter cites advertisement's specific publication and date.

■ Telephone number included in closing is omitted in return address.

RESPONSE TO A "BLIND" ADVERTISEMENT
(Legal Associate)

178 Green Street
Alfred, NY 14802
(607) 555-5555

October 28, 1996

P.O. Box 7777
Conway, SC 29526

RE: Legal Associate

Dear Sir/Madam:

In addition to a Juris Doctor degree, I recently received a Master of Law in Banks and Banking Law Studies with a concentration in International Law. I am looking for the opportunity to join the legal staff of a bank or corporation where I can put my experience in general legal practice and recent graduate degree to practical use and further develop my legal capabilities.

My expertise is in the supervision of associate and support legal staff in all phases of research, document preparation, and coordination as required for all legal issues. I am well organized, accurate, and conscientious, interface well with individuals and groups, and feel confident that I can be a contributing asset to your firm.

I am most anxious to become a part of your firm and would appreciate meeting with you at your convenience. The enclosed resume is a brief summary of my academic accomplishments and work experience.

I look forward to your response.

Sincerely,

Chris Smith

Enc. resume

■ Educational credentials relate specifically to advertised position.

■ Closing expresses candidate's interest in furthering candidacy through an interview.

RESPONSE TO A "BLIND" ADVERTISEMENT
(Librarian)

178 Green Street
Quincy, MA 02171

July 22, 1996

Personnel Director
P.O. Box 7777
Amherst, MA 01003

RE: Librarian-July 21, 1996

Dear Personnel Director:

In response to the July 21 advertisement in the *Boston Sunday Globe*, I have enclosed my resume for your review.

In addition to an M.L.S. degree and ALA accreditation, I have twelve years' experience as a Bibliographer, Acquisitions, Special Collections and Reference Librarian with concentration in history and additional experience in philosophy and religion. In these positions, I provide general and specialized reference services, develop and manage collections, perform faculty liaison work, and conduct bibliographic instruction sessions at undergraduate and graduate levels. I am also experienced in assisting and training others in the use of electronic resources including CD-ROM, as well as other networked information resources for research.

Although my present position provides a challenging and rewarding atmosphere, I am interested in making a change where I can contribute my knowledge and experience in an academic setting. I have the ability to undertake a broad scope of responsibility and work effectively with a diverse population of students, faculty, and staff.

I am anxious to learn more about this position. Should you require additional information, please contact me at the above address or by phone at (617) 555-5555. I look forward to your response.

Sincerely,

Chris Smith

Enc. resume

- ■ Professional accreditation enhances candidate's qualifications.

- ■ Unrelated work experience is omitted from response letter.

RESPONSE TO A "BLIND" ADVERTISEMENT
(Major Account Manager)

178 Green Street
Shreveport, LA 71101

November 14, 1996

Personnel Director
P.O. Box 7777
New Orleans, LA 70140

RE: Major Account Manager

Dear Personnel Director:

During the past fifteen years, I have progressively advanced from positions ranging from Applications Maintenance Programmer to Regional Account Manager to my current position as National Account Manager. In this capacity, I am responsible for selling large computer systems to support from 30 to 250 users with an internationally recognized computer corporation.

Although these positions have been fast-paced and challenging, I feel that my expertise can be more effectively utilized to provide high visibility for increased sales through working with upper management decision-makers on the development of pre- and post-sales support programs. I am certain I can capture your share of the high-performance market. I am a high-energy, aggressive individual who enjoys a challenge and is willing to accept responsibility. As a member of your management staff, I am confident that I can make the same outstanding contribution to your firm as I have to my present employer.

The enclosed resume summarizes my background and experience in the above areas. Should you require additional information, please feel free to contact me at the above address or by phone at (318) 555-5555. I welcome your acknowledgment and look forward to a meeting at your earliest convenience.

Yours sincerely,

Chris Smith

Enc. resume

■ Letter illustrates continual career progression.

■ Beyond matching qualifications with requirements, candidate highlights personal attributes applicable to advertised position.

RESPONSE TO A "BLIND" ADVERTISEMENT
(Manufacturing Test Technician)

178 Green Street
Glendive, MT 59330

June 5, 1996

Human Resources Director
P.O. Box 7777
Billings, MT 59107

RE: Manufacturing Test Technician

Dear Human Resources Director:

I am writing this letter with the expressed intent of applying for your position advertised in the June 3 edition of the *Billings Gazette*. It is my interest to join your engineering staff in an area where I can utilize my academic as well as practical experience on new product applications and engineering development.

I offer six years of experience, with three as a Test Technician on top-quality, electronic audio systems and as a member of a technical academic team working on a 3,000-line computer program designed to debug software. Additionally, I have supervisory and sales responsibility in a retail setting.

I have directed my career, through study and work, toward a full-time profession in engineering and I feel that my education and diversity of environments and responsibility enable me to make a positive and immediate contribution to your organization.

I would like to arrange a personal interview to further expand upon your requirements and my ability to meet them. I can be reached at the above address or between the hours of 9:00 a.m. and 4 p.m. at (406) 555-5555.

I look forward to meeting you.

Sincerely,

Chris Smith

Enc. resume

- Introduction immediately refers to publication where advertisement appeared.
- Candidate invites addressee to respond to inquiry since specific employer is unknown.

RESPONSE TO A "BLIND" ADVERTISEMENT
(Marketing Analyst)

178 Green Street
Beachwood, OH 44122

January 2, 1996

Department of Human Resources
P.O. Box 7777
Dayton, OH 45402

RE: Marketing Analyst

Dear Sir or Madam:

I am writing to request your consideration of my application for the position advertised in today's *Dayton Daily News*.

Please note that in addition to a Bachelor of Science degree in Marketing, I have three years of responsible experience ranging from Merchandise Analyst to Senior Analyst with a rapid-growth, nationwide apparel retailer. I am responsible for recruiting, screening, and providing job overview and subsequent personnel training in retailing/distribution. Working with reports generated by a national computer network, I perform in-depth analyses of sales results and inventory levels with a view toward providing the ideal merchandise mix and qualities to targeted markets.

In addition, I have experience working in private clubs, membership operations, banking, and television. I have excellent communication and interpersonal skills, work well under pressure as either an individual contributor or as a team player, and relate easily to all management levels in the performance of responsibilities.

It would be my pleasure to outline my potential for making a significant contribution to your corporation in an interview. I can be reached at the above address or by phone at (216) 555-5555.

I hope to hear from you soon.

Sincerely,

Chris Smith

Enc. resume

- Response letter immediately states candidate's purpose for writing.
- Letter avoids abbreviations and slang.

RESPONSE TO A "BLIND" ADVERTISEMENT
(Medical Assistant)

178 Green Street
Lawton, OK 73505

February 10, 1996

P.O. Box 7777
Plateville, WI 53818

RE: Medical Assistant

Dear Sir or Madam:

My interest in the position of Medical Assistant that you advertised in *Health Support Monthly* has prompted me to forward my resume for your review and consideration.

In addition to ten years of experience as a Home Health Aide, In-patient Claim Representative, and, since 1996, Medical Assistant with Smith Rehabilitation Hospital, I have good knowledge of medical terminology, procedure codes, and medical office systems including related computerized applications. I have an Associate degree in Sociology, was graduated as a medical assistant, and am currently a candidate for an Associate degree in Nursing.

My career objective is to develop further my medical and support skills in areas that will give me the opportunity to participate in the administration of quality health care. I would welcome the opportunity to discuss whether my abilities and goals suit your requirements and expectations. Please contact me at the above address or at (405) 555-5555 during the daytime to schedule an interview.

Thank you.

Yours sincerely,

Chris Smith

Enc. resume

- Candidate immediately refers to advertised position.
- Discussion of experience is very specific.

RESPONSE TO A "BLIND" ADVERTISEMENT
(Nurse's Aide)

178 Green Street
Cleveland, OH 44143

November 26, 1996

Hiring Coordinator
P.O. Box 7777
Dayton, OH 45463

RE: Nurse's Aide Position

Dear Hiring Coordinator:

In response to the advertisement in the November 12 edition of the *Dayton Daily News,* please accept the enclosed resume as my initial application.

I am CPR-certified and possess a strong clinical background. The classes I attend as part of Ohio State University's Nursing program allow me the formal training necessary for the position. With my experience and education, I am confident that I would be a valuable asset to the nursing staff.

I would appreciate the opportunity to meet with you to further discuss the position offered. I can be reached at the above address or at (216) 555-5555.

I look forward to your reply.

Sincerely,

Chris Smith

Enc. resume

■ Professional certification and strong educational background add strength to cover letter.

■ Letter uses short sentences and common words.

RESPONSE TO A "BLIND" ADVERTISEMENT
(Operations Manager)

178 Green Street
Siloam Springs, AR 72761

April 2, 1996

Personnel Director
P.O. Box 7777
Little Rock, AR 77203

RE: Operations Manager

Dear Personnel Director:

In response to last Friday's advertisement in the *Arkansas Democrat-Gazette*, I am enclosing my resume for your consideration.

During the past seven years, I have gained progressively responsible experience in areas of sales/marketing, technical, and product management, as well as new product introduction/market development, warehousing, and distribution.

My positions have ranged from Sales/Marketing Representative to Product Manager. I have been fully responsible for start-up, marketing, and promotion of new technology for a manufacturer of architectural and industrial coatings and finishes, sold worldwide. Also, I hold a Bachelor's of Arts degree in Economics and I have completed advanced professional and technical study in architecture, protective architectural/industrial coating, and finishes.

Although my positions have been challenging and fast-paced, at this point in my career I am seeking a new, long-term association where my expertise, creativity, and motivation can be more fully utilized. I have a proven track record and I feel that a personal meeting would give us an opportunity to expand on our mutual objectives.

I can be reached at the above address or by phone at (501) 555-5555. Thank you for your consideration and response. I look forward to hearing from you.

Sincerely,

Chris Smith

Enc. resume

- Candidate uses closing to suggest possibility of interview.
- One page is standard length for cover letters.

RESPONSE TO A "BLIND" ADVERTISEMENT
(Optical Manufacturer)

178 Green Street
Baltimore, MD 21201

July 23, 1996

Senior Manufacturing Manager
P.O. Box 7777
Bethesda, MD 21211

Dear Senior Manufacturing Manager:

My interest in the Optical Manufacturer position advertised in the July 20 edition
of the *Baltimore Sun* has prompted me to submit the enclosed resume for your
review. During the past fifteen years, my experience has ranged from Lamination
Technician to Production and Manufacturing Manager in the optical industry. I
offer excellent skills in technical sales and marketing support, production and
product management, manufacturing management, communications and
presentations, and trade show coordination.

Although my positions have been diverse and challenging, I am currently seeking
a new position that will offer the opportunity to contribute to the growth and
profitability of a company with a diverse product line in industrial, commercial, or
military markets.

I will be glad to furnish you with additional information pertaining to my
qualifications. Please feel free to contact me at the above address or by calling
(301) 555-5555.

Sincerely,

Chris Smith

Enc. resume

- Introduction demonstrates
  candidate's suitability for
  advertised position.

- Closing is straightforward and
  concise.

RESPONSE TO A "BLIND" ADVERTISEMENT
(Payroll Supervisor)

178 Green Street
Big Stone Gap, VA 24219
(703) 555-5555

June 6, 1996

Human Resources Associate
P.O. Box 7777
Richmond, VA 23219

RE: Payroll Supervisor

Good morning!

As an experienced Payroll Administrator, I am confident that I am the qualified candidate you are searching for as listed in the June 5 edition of the *Richmond Times-Dispatch*.

Please note that in addition to a Bachelor of Arts degree in Economics, my background encompasses ten years of progressively responsible and sophisticated hands-on experience ranging from Marketing Research Assistant and Union Benefits Coordinator, to Human Resources Administrator, to my present position as Payroll Administrator. In this capacity, I focus on the day-to-day details of my financial operations and training in important organizational and operational areas of a company's general business operation.

I am well organized, detail-oriented, and committed to servicing your corporation in an efficient and productive way. I am very eager to learn more about the responsibilities of the position and how I can begin to make a contribution to your overall success.

Sincerely,

Chris Smith

Enc. resume

■ Letter focuses on filling employer's needs, not the job candidate's.

■ Powerful adjectives, when used sparingly, ensure maximum impact.

RESPONSE TO A "BLIND" ADVERTISEMENT
(Pharmaceutical Administrator)

178 Green Street
Rock Springs, WY 82902

September 6, 1996

Human Resources Representative
P.O. Box 7777
Casper, WY 82604

RE: Pharmaceutical Administrator

Dear Human Resources Representative:

I recently spotted your advertisement in the September 4 edition of the *Casper Star Tribune*. I am very interested in seeking an association with an established organization as a Pharmaceutical Administrator and have enclosed my resume for your perusal.

I have a Master's degree in Hospital Pharmacy Administration and two related bachelor degrees. In addition, for the past fifteen years I have had progressively responsible experience ranging from Staff Pharmacist to Supervisor of a three-hundred-bed community hospital. I am well versed in medical terminology, have good communication and presentation skills, and I work effectively with physicians, clinical staffs, and hospital administration.

Based on my extensive experience in pharmaceuticals, combined with my energy and enthusiasm for a career in the health care field, I believe I am well qualified for this position.

Please contact me at the above address, or call (307) 555-5555 to arrange a mutually convenient time for a meeting, during which we may further discuss your current or anticipated needs and my ability to fill the position.

Thank you for your time.

Yours sincerely,

Chris Smith

Enc. resume

■ Candidate's highest educational achievement is shown before other less significant degrees.

■ Response letter emphasizes candidate's supervisory skills.

RESPONSE TO A "BLIND" ADVERTISEMENT
(Production/Materials Control Manager)

178 Green Street
Fairfield, CT 06430

July 21, 1996

P.O. Box 7777
Danbury, CT 06813

RE: Production/Materials Control Manager

Dear Sir or Madam:

Production/materials control management is my forte, and I am looking for a new opportunity where I can put these skills to work for a company interested, as I am, in profitable growth and mutual gain for the long term. Please accept the enclosed resume as my expressed interest in applying for the position you advertised in the July 19 edition of the *North Jersey Herald and News*.

I am considered by my associates to be a dynamic, persistent achiever with a composite background of technical, sales, management, and training experience. During the past twenty years my positions have ranged from Production Control Manager to Vice-President of Operations and President with world-leading manufacturers of cutting tools, industrial process controls, and electronics. My expertise encompasses selection, training, and development of competent team leaders and support personnel, with hands-on experience in the design and installation of materials.

I would be happy to meet with you to discuss, in detail, your requirements and my ability to handle the responsibilities of the position offered. I am very interested in learning more about your corporation and am confident I can provide you with effective and profitable management.

Should you require additional information prior to our meeting, please contact me at the above address or by phone at (203) 555-5555.

Yours sincerely,

Chris Smith

Enc. resume

■ Introductory sentence draws attention.

■ Closing emphasizes candidate's enthusiasm for desired position.

RESPONSE TO A "BLIND" ADVERTISEMENT
(Sales Manager)

178 Green Street
Girdletree, MD 21829
(301) 555-5555

October 13, 1996

P.O. Box 7777
Chicago, IL 60605

RE: Sales Manager position

Dear Sir or Madam:

The position for Sales Manager advertised in the *Chicago Tribune* on October 12 intrigues me. I believe you will find me well qualified.

I am an innovative achiever. I feel that in a growth industry like cable television, there is a need for a representative who can meet and beat the competition. I feel that I have all the necessary ingredients to contribute to the success of Any Corporation and, if necessary, I am willing to take a step backward as long as there is potential for forward momentum. All I need is a starting point.

The enclosed confidential resume summarizes my proven track record as the Vice-President of Sales for a $2 million operation. I have strong communications skills and the ability to prepare and make presentations to decision-makers on all levels.

I feel that a personal meeting would give us the opportunity to discuss your short- and long-term objectives and my ability to direct your organization toward successfully achieving those goals.

Thank you for your attention to this matter. I look forward to speaking with you.

Sincerely yours,

Chris Smith

Enc. resume

■ Letter suggests discretion.

■ Setting desired position apart from body of letter may be advantageous when responding to a "blind" advertisement.

RESPONSE TO A "BLIND" ADVERTISEMENT
(Staff Photographer)

178 Green Street
Tyler, TX 75799

July 20, 1996

Department of Human Resources
P.O. Box 7777
San Antonio, TX 78297

RE: Staff Photographer

To whom it may concern:

I am responding to your July 18 advertisement in the *San Antonio Express* for a photographer.

As you will be able to see from my resume, I have a Bachelor of Fine Arts degree in Photography from the University of Texas. My extensive photography experience includes several years of printing and processing with a variety of black-and-white materials, and custom and production printing of color negatives. In addition, I am familiar with 35 mm, 2-1/4, and 4 x 5 equipment. I also have experience teaching photography in a bachelor's program.

I would very much like to arrange an opportunity to meet with you and review my portfolio. I am confident that I can convince you of my skill as a photographer, as well as my dedication to producing a product of highest quality.

I can be reached at the above address or by phone during the evening at (903) 555-5555. Thank you for your consideration of my application.

Sincerely,

Chris Smith

Enc. resume

- Stating that a portfolio is available on request is beneficial for certain positions.

- Candidate invites addressee to respond to inquiry since specific employer is unknown.

RESPONSE TO A "BLIND" ADVERTISEMENT
(Teacher)

178 Green Street
Newport, RI 02840

May 14, 1996

Search Committee
P.O. Box 7777
Providence, RI 02908

RE: Sixth Grade Teaching Position

Dear Search Committee:

I have enclosed my resume in response to your advertisement in the May edition of *Education in New England.*

During the past several years, I have been preparing myself for a position as a teacher in an established school system, where I can apply my teaching, training, and administrative experience to manage and motivate a classroom of students toward higher education.

As a Student Teacher with the Easton Public School System, I successfully taught literature, public speaking, and creative writing at the secondary level. I received my Bachelor's degree and certification in Elementary Education in 1994 from Stonehill College in Easton, Massachusetts. Also, I have acted as a Substitute Teacher in several school districts over a four-year period and have designed, organized, and taught my own summer course for gifted children in the town of Newport for the past two years.

Currently, I am seeking an opportunity with a system that offers continued professional development and the opportunity for advancement in the field of education. I would welcome a personal interview to discuss in detail my ability to handle the teaching position and my compatibility with the rest of your staff.

In the interim, should you require additional information, please contact me at the above address or by phone at (401) 555-5555.

Yours sincerely,

Chris Smith

Enc. resume

■ Temporary experience is relevant to full-time employment.

■ Candidate immediately refers to advertised position.

RESPONSE TO A "BLIND" ADVERTISEMENT
(Technical Sales Associate)

178 Green Street
Valdosta, GA 31698
(912) 555-5555

January 24, 1996

Sales Director
P.O. Box 7777
Macon, GA 31201

RE: Technical Sales Associate position

Dear Sales Director:

I have more than sixteen years of diverse product development, sales and marketing, and technical support experience for a leading worldwide computer company. You will note from my enclosed resume that my background runs parallel to the demands outlined in the January 23 edition of the *Macon Telegraph*.

Accustomed to multimillion-dollar marketing and product development responsibilities, I am now postured for a new position in technical sales offering me broader opportunities. I can bring dynamic leadership, technical support acumen, and decisive marketing skills to your firm. To illustrate, I have been responsible for conceptualizing and developing software/hardware and marketing techniques, possess solid problem-solving skills, and am known for my proven ability to motivate others.

As you can see, my qualifications closely match your requirements. I am looking forward to a personal meeting with you to discuss this opportunity. Please call to arrange a time for us to get together. Salary requirements are open to discussion.

I look forward to your reply.

Sincerely,

Chris Smith

Enc. resume

■ Separating major accomplishments from body provides emphasis.

■ Candidate focuses on applying skills and experiences to advertised position.

RESPONSE TO A "BLIND" ADVERTISEMENT
(Typist)

178 Green Street
Toledo, OH 43660

April 11, 1996

P.O. Box 7777
Toledo, OH 43660

Dear Personnel Manager:

I am interested in the part-time position of At-Home Typist for which you advertised in the February 13 edition of the *Toledo Blade*.

My typing speed is 50 wpm. I am, at present, a part-time student at Ohio State University. I am confident your company can utilize my time and qualifications. Please consider the enclosed resume as an application.

I have an IBM compatible PC with an Intel 486DX microprocessor. I also have the Microsoft Word software package. I am anxious to put this equipment, in addition to my typing skills, to work for your organization.

When would it be a convenient time for an interview? Please call me at (419) 555-5555.

Sincerely,

Chris Smith

Enc. resume

■ Mentioning typing and word processing skills can be advantageous for administrative and office support positions.

■ Response letter immediately introduces candidate's qualifications.

RESPONSE TO A "BLIND" ADVERTISEMENT
(Underwriter)

178 Green Street
Klamath Falls, OR 97601

July 9, 1996

P.O. Box 7777
Anchorage, AK 99514

RE: Underwriter position

Dear Sir or Madam:

I am writing with an expressed interest in applying for your advertised position in Sunday's edition of the *Anchorage Daily News*. I am a highly experienced professional underwriter with a successful track record in the development of new business, the management of highly productive and diversified underwriting activities, and the support of sales and marketing operations.

I have a record of outstanding success as a Security Underwriter in establishing and maintaining profitable relationships with accounts and agents throughout the Pacific Northwest. In my current position, I have developed marketing and client contacts from a start-up base to $1.7 million in gross premiums.

I am eager to continue my successful track record with a new associate that is in need of an aggressive, dedicated professional. I would like to learn more about your corporation and how I can begin to make a substantial and long-term contribution to your success. I would be glad to travel to Anchorage for a personal interview at your convenience.

Please contact me at the above address or at (503) 555-5555 if I can be of further assistance. I hope to hear from you soon.

Yours sincerely,

Chris Smith

Enc. resume

- Background summary accentuates candidate's acquired professional skills and impressive track record.
- Willingness to travel can be advantageous.

RESPONSE TO A "BLIND" ADVERTISEMENT
(Writer/Researcher)

178 Green Street
Pompano Beach, FL 33063
(305) 555-5555

December 27, 1996

Personnel Manager
P.O. Box 7777
Tampa, FL 32714

Dear Personnel Manager:

    I feel I have the experience and ability to fill the Writer/Researcher position advertised on December 26 in the *Tampa Tribune.*

    Writing Experience: I have written or co-written five books on business management and communications. In addition, I have been a reporter for magazines and newspapers for many years. I have written over 3,000 articles for publication, on topics ranging from crime to sports to medicine to humor. I know how to conceive of and research topics, and I am comfortable writing on almost any subject and in a range of styles. I would have no trouble matching the established style of your book series.

    Editing Experience: I have edited a number of books on business topics and worked as an editor on several newspapers. I am capable of doing either minor polishing or major rewriting, and more importantly, of being able to tell which is needed. In addition, I taught English Composition and Communications at the college level for three years. My grammar and editing skills are, I believe, exceptional.

    Publications Management Experience: Before moving to the Florida area, I was the Publications Coordinator for an international business consulting firm and had ultimate responsibility for the production of more than twenty books a year. I have also had responsibility for the production of several daily newspapers and magazines. In each of these positions, I supervised writers, managed the copyediting operation, and oversaw all production activities. I am very comfortable working with tight deadlines—in over fifteen years, I missed less than 1 percent of my deadlines.

    Because of my background, I feel I am the ideal candidate for your position. I have enclosed a resume as well as a brief sample of my writing. I look forward to meeting with you to further discuss how I could work with your organization.

Sincerely,

Chris Smith

Enc. resume
    writing sample

■ Categorizing qualifications adds strength to cover letter.

■ Summary of experience highlights candidate's achievements.

12
"Cold" Letter to a Potential Employer

With a "cold" cover letter you can directly contact potential employers without a referral or previous correspondence. Job-seekers most commonly use this type of letter to advertise their availability to hiring managers or personnel departments. Presumably, after researching your field, you will have devised a list of the top employers you would like to work for, and gathered basic company information for each. A cold letter should incorporate company knowledge with a discussion of relevant qualifications. When writing a cold letter keep in mind you are not applying for a specific position. State your skills and accomplishments but let the employer decide how you may best suit his or her needs.

"COLD" LETTER TO A POTENTIAL EMPLOYER
(Accountant)

178 Green Street
Chester, PA 19013
(215) 555-5555

November 19, 1996

Pat Cummings
Hiring Manager
Any Corporation
1140 Main Street
Philadelphia, PA 19130

Dear Ms. Cummings:

During the past seven years, my experience has ranged from Fixed Asset Accountant/Financial Management Trainee to Senior Cost Accountant of a $250 million processing operation.

Currently, I am seeking a long-term career opportunity and association with a well-seasoned manufacturer or high-tech firm that has a need for an accountant with a good knowledge of and experience in cost accounting, general accounting, and finance.

The enclosed resume outlines my background in the above areas. Throughout my experience, I have been aware of, and continually impressed by, the diverse services offered by Any Corporation. Needless to say, I am eager to join a team such as yours.

I look forward to the opportunity to meet in a personal interview. I will call you November 29 to arrange a convenient time.

Yours sincerely,

Chris Smith

Enc. resume

- Closing specifies that candidate will follow up inquiry.

- Career objective gives focus without limiting candidate's opportunities.

"COLD" LETTER TO A POTENTIAL EMPLOYER
(Accounts Receivable Clerk)

178 Green Street
Philadelphia, PA 19134

December 2, 1996

Pat Cummings
Manager, Accounts Receivable
Any Corporation
1140 Main Street
Macungie, PA 18062

Dear Mr. Cummings:

I would like to express my interest in applying my relevant experience and background to a position in the accounts receivable department at Any Corporation.

In addition to an Associate's degree in Administration, I possess four years of bookkeeping and general office experience. While at Independence Bank, I performed word processing and data entry involving trust fund information, daily sales records, payroll expenses, and invoices. As an Academic Records Assistant at Drexel University, I was responsible for the maintenance and input of thousands of alumni records. I can type 65 wpm, and am proficient in most major computer programs and spreadsheet applications. Of additional interest, I have a fluent command of the Spanish language, both oral and written, and have a reading knowledge of Italian.

The record-keeping nature of my past experience has given me a facility for detail, much patience, and the ability to keep accurate records, all of which I am confident can be successfully applied to an Accounts Receivable position with Any Corporation.

My resume is enclosed for your inspection. Should you have any questions or wish to schedule an interview, please do not hesitate to call me at (215) 555-5555. I look forward to hearing from you soon.

Sincerely,

Chris Smith

Enc. resume

- Unrelated work experience is omitted.
- Mentioning typing and word processing skills can be advantageous for administrative and office support positions.

"COLD" LETTER TO A POTENTIAL EMPLOYER
(Administrative Assistant)

178 Green Street
Delaware City, DE 19706
(302) 555-5555

January 18, 1996

Pat Cummings
Director, Human Resources
Any Corporation
1140 Main Street
New Castle, DE 19720

Dear Ms. Cummings:

I am interested in applying for an Administrative Assistant position with Any
Corporation. I graduated in May 1993 with an Associate degree in Computer
Information Systems from the University of Delaware.

I have worked in the university's main computer room for two years, and I have
developed advanced skills in a large number of software packages on both IBM
and Macintosh systems, including WordPerfect and Word for Windows 6.0. More
recently, I worked as a receptionist for four months with Cammarata Designs, Inc.,
where I gained exposure to all facets of administrative work: typing 60 wpm,
phone contact, customer relations. With my educational background, proven
academic success, and desire to learn and excel, I am confident I can make a
significant contribution to your staff.

My enclosed resume provides additional information about my education and
experience. I will be glad to make myself available for an interview at your earliest
convenience to discuss how my qualifications would be consistent with your
needs. Thank you for your time and consideration.

Sincerely,

Chris Smith

Enc. resume

■ Letter immediately states
candidate's purpose.

■ Valuable computer skills are
highlighted.

"COLD" LETTER TO A POTENTIAL EMPLOYER
(Administrative Director)

178 Green Street
Sarasota, FL 34236

August 20, 1996

Pat Cummings
Controller
Any Corporation
1140 Main Street
Bangor, ME 04401

Dear Mr. Cummings:

My desire to locate a challenging growth opportunity in a fast-paced business environment has prompted me to forward the attached resume for your evaluation.

Please note that in addition to my formal education, I have eight years of hands-on management experience working in large-scale distribution, shipping and receiving, warehouse, and department store environments, involving up to 50,000 line items.

My primary focus is in areas of distribution, warehousing, and general operations management. My experience, however, also encompasses all aspects of personnel management as well as purchasing, inventory control, security and safety, merchandising, MIS, and quality management.

Please contact me at the above address or call (813) 555-5555, so that we may arrange a mutually convenient interview.

Thank you for your consideration.

Sincerely,

Chris Smith

Enc. resume

■ Candidate's practical experience outweighs his/her education.

■ Closing is brief and to the point.

"COLD" LETTER TO A POTENTIAL EMPLOYER
(Advertising Executive)

178 Green Street
Minster, OH 45865

June 3, 1996

Pat Cummings
Senior Art Director
Any Advertising Agency
1140 Main Street
Dayton, OH 45401

Dear Ms. Cummings:

I am not a stranger to hard work, long hours, and tight schedules. To achieve mutual objectives, I am open to training, travel, and new assignments, and will provide dedication and quality performance.

During the past seven years, my experience has been concentrated in directing and coordinating the design, illustration, and concept development of promotional and direct mail marketing pieces for an established advertising agency. I have completed advanced coursework in commercial art and specialized technology.

Although my position is diversified and provides me with challenge and decision-making responsibilities in a creative and highly competitive industry, I feel it is time for a change. I am interested in joining a company, such as Any Advertising Agency, where I can apply my education and experience to develop new skills which will lead to my advancement within your art department.

I have enclosed a resume and project sample. I would welcome the opportunity to present a portfolio of my work and discuss my qualifications in greater detail.

To arrange an interview, please contact me at the above address or by phone at (419) 555-5555 days or (419) 555-4444 evenings.

I look forward to your return response.

Sincerely,

Chris Smith

Enc. resume
  sample

■ Introductory sentence draws attention.

■ Enclosure lines refer to all attached materials.

"COLD" LETTER TO A POTENTIAL EMPLOYER
(Advertising Sales Associate)

178 Green Street
Decatur, GA 30032
(404) 555-5555

August 26, 1996

Pat Cummings
Personnel Director
Any Corporation
1140 Main Street
Augusta, GA 30901

Dear Mr. Cummings:

Given both my sales experience and my objective of a career in the fast-paced advertising industry, I would like to explore options within Sales at Any Corporation.

I have been involved in sales/customer service with a major U.S. carrier for four years, in which time I gained the exposure and valuable work experience necessary for success. I have learned the art, as well as the importance of, creating a strong rapport with clients and demonstrating outstanding customer service for successful sales. I have also learned unique approaches to problem-solving and how to deal with rejection with renewed optimism and good humor. In addition, I possess exceptional written, communication, and organizational skills. I am proficient in Microsoft Word for Windows and can type effectively at 65 wpm.

I look forward to expanding my career in sales and advertising with Any Corporation. I would certainly appreciate the opportunity to discuss how I can apply my skills and knowledge to benefit your company. I would like to schedule an interview at your convenience, and will call you next week to do so. Thank you.

Sincerely,

Chris Smith

Enc. resume

■ Letter focuses on acquired skills relevant to field of interest.

■ Closing suggests a meeting to follow letter.

"COLD" LETTER TO A POTENTIAL EMPLOYER
(Alumni Relations Coordinator)

178 Green Street
Kirkwood, MO 63122
(314) 555-5555

August 18, 1996

Pat Cummings
Director, Alumni Relations
Any University
1140 Main Street
St. Louis, MO 63141

Dear Ms. Cummings:

In my experience with alumni relations, I have been continually impressed by Any University's outstanding record of annual alumni contributions. Should you be in need of an addition to your staff, I would appreciate your consideration of my qualifications.

Please note that during the past ten years I have held diverse and progressively responsible positions in alumni relations at both university and private secondary school levels. During this period, I have been heavily involved in strategies, annual fund campaigns, marketing/mailing programs, and media/public relations. Although these positions have been challenging and broad in scope, I feel that my expertise would be more advantageous to your organization. I have been, and am confident I will continue to be, successful in achieving both short- and long-range objectives.

The enclosed, up-to-date resume details my background in these areas. Would it be possible to schedule a personal interview? I would be happy to make myself available at your convenience.

I look forward to your response.

Sincerely,

Chris Smith

Enc. resume

■ Phrasing request in question form is a strong closing.

■ One page is standard length for cover letters.

"COLD" LETTER TO A POTENTIAL EMPLOYER
(Architectual Engineer)

178 Green Street
Little Rock, AR 77203

March 9, 1996

Pat Cummings
Chief Engineer
Any Corporation
1140 Main Street
Tucson, AZ 85714

Dear Mr. Cummings:

Please accept this letter as an application for a position within your company. I have enclosed a resume for your consideration and review, but would like to draw your attention to several points.

I hold a Bachelor's degree in Architectural Engineering and possess six years of professional experience in increasingly responsible positions in the engineering, architectural, and construction fields. In my most recent position as Project Manager, I have been able to utilize my background in coordinating the structural, mechanical, electrical, and civil disciplines on several different projects.

My specific achievements include conceiving and supervising the construction of a fifty-acre industrial park and helping to reorganize Jiffy Contractors. In addition, the Army Corps of Engineers regularly relies on me for private consultations.

I believe that my qualifications would make me a valuable asset to your firm and look forward to a personal interview at your earliest convenience. Please contact me at the above address or by phone at (501) 555-5555.

Thank you very much for your time and consideration.

Sincerely yours,

Chris Smith

Enc. resume

■ Discussion of experience clearly spells out candidate's area of expertise.

■ Telephone number included in closing is omitted in return address.

"COLD" LETTER TO A POTENTIAL EMPLOYER
(Art Director)

178 Green Street
Schamburg, IL 60191
(708) 555-5555

March 3, 1996

Pat Cummings
Executive Director
Any Performing Arts Foundation
1140 Main Street
Chicago, IL 60632

Dear Ms. Cummings:

As a studio owner, manager, choreographer, performer, and producer, I feel I have much to offer in support of performing arts.

In addition to my successful experience, I have been actively involved in public relations and promotional activities. Such work requires the ability to communicate and work effectively with talented professionals as well as patrons of the arts. I am most effective in the capacity of planner, coordinator, manager, and representative in a creative environment and feel confident that I can contribute to the efforts of a performing arts foundation.

I have enclosed a professional profile for consideration regarding any suitable openings. Perhaps we could meet for a personal interview? I would love to share with you my experiences and dedication to the performing arts.

Sincerely,

Chris Smith

Enc. professional profile

■ Experience reinforces candidate's professional objective.

■ Candidate immediately introduces qualifications.

"COLD" LETTER TO A POTENTIAL EMPLOYER
(Arts Administrator)

178 Green Street
Arlington, VA 22203
(703) 555-5555

June 26, 1996

Pat Cummings
Director
Any Gallery
1140 Main Street
Vienna, VA 22108

Dear Mr. Cummings:

Last weekend I attended the opening of your newest exhibition, "Forming Meaning," and I especially appreciated your commitment to the local art scene. I am currently searching for an opportunity with a reputable gallery, and would be very interested in contributing my skills to your staff.

Please note that in addition to my broad formal education in areas related specifically to art and art education, I hold a Masters of Education degree in Administration. I also possess valuable experience in diverse aspects of museum operations, including exhibition and display, media presentation, proposal writing, and associated details of estimation and cost accounting.

I would like to arrange a mutually convenient time for an interview during which we could further discuss your current or anticipated needs.

Thank you for your consideration.

Sincerely,

Chris Smith

Enc. resume

■ Letter highlights candidate's acquired professional and educational training.

■ Closing thanks addressee in advance for attention.

"COLD" LETTER TO A POTENTIAL EMPLOYER
(Associate Editor)

178 Green Street
Needham, MA 02192
(617) 555-5555

June 18, 1996

Pat Cummings
Human Resources Director
Any Publishing Company
1140 Main Street
New York, NY 10128

Dear Ms. Cummings:

I have four years of publishing experience, including two years of scholarly journal experience in social science, physical science, and engineering which I would like to put to work at Any Publishing Company.

Specifically, I am seeking a position as an Associate Editor, Project Editor, or the equivalent in new book or journal development and administration. Originally from Long Island, I am planning to relocate to the New York area later this summer. Please consider the following highlights from my career:

- Developed a new book series in sociology through all phases of publication: from author contract negation to the creation of a series marketing plan.

- Acquired *Earth Day Every Day*, which was nominated for the Fortmiller Foundation's Prize and is already an "academic best-seller."

- Participated in a dynamic engineering program which included the launch of three new journals: *Physical Science*, *Micro Journal*, and the *Journal of Alternative Energy*.

In addition to a strong background in English literature and the social sciences at the University of Notre Dame, my training has included courses relevant to a position in medical publishing: Anatomy, Physiology, Medical Terminology, Nursing Procedures, Biology, and Radiographic Physics.

I will be in New York from July 20 to 30, during which time I would appreciate the opportunity to meet with you. Thank you for your consideration, and I look forward to speaking with you soon.

Sincerely,

Chris Smith

Enc. resume

■ Courses listed are related to candidate's field of interest.

■ Closing provides specific time frame to allow for meeting.

"COLD" LETTER TO A POTENTIAL EMPLOYER
(Audio-Visual Specialist)

178 Green Street
Proctorsville, VT 05153
(802) 555-5555

July 7, 1996

Pat Cummings
Personnel Manager
Any Corporation
1140 Main Street
Chicago, IL 60605

Dear Mr. Cummings:

In the interest of investigating career opportunities with your company, I am enclosing my resume for your consideration and review.

As you will note, I have fifteen years of educational and media experience. I am proficient in the operation of a wide variety of photographic, video, and audio equipment. I am regularly responsible for processing, duplicating, and setting up slide presentations, as well as synchronized slide and audio presentations.

I believe that my qualifications would make me an outstanding asset to your organization. I would very much appreciate the opportunity to personally interview with you at your convenience to further discuss my abilities and the needs of Any Corporation.

I look forward to hearing from you soon.

Sincerely,

Chris Smith

Enc. resume

■ Letter is easy and quick to read, and only relevant details are included.

■ Candidate expresses willingness to meet at addressee's convenience in closing.

"COLD" LETTER TO A POTENTIAL EMPLOYER
(Automated Systems Specialist)

178 Green Street
Toledo, OH 43660
(419) 555-5555

January 8, 1996

Pat Cummings
Vice-President
Any Corporation
1140 Main Street
Beachwood, OH 44122

Dear Ms. Cummings:

During the past thirteen years, I have had comprehensive experience in the design, development, sale, and operation of automated equipment designed for the food processing industry.

Currently, I am seeking a new association with a firm that can benefit from my experience in the above areas. I have a unique combination of skills: technical sales, application engineering, and technical liaison between engineering and production to test, debug, and refine automated food processing systems. In addition, I have experience as a Production Foreman and Supervisor responsible for postproduction with a company producing a wide variety of power tools distributed through the Midwest.

I am very interested in speaking with you about current opportunities with Any Corporation. I will call your office on Monday, January 15 to schedule a convenient interview time.

Thank you for your consideration.

Sincerely,

Chris Smith

Enc. resume

■ Letter cites specific date phone contact will be made.

■ Candidate does not limit available opportunities by stating specific position desired.

"COLD" LETTER TO A POTENTIAL EMPLOYER
(Aviation Specialist)

178 Green Street
Hunt Valley, MD 21031
(712) 555-5555

January 20, 1996

Pat Cummings
Senior Operations Manager
Any Airline
1140 Main Street
Baltimore, MD 21226

Dear Mr. Cummings:

I am very interested in locating a challenging position in an aviation-related operation, and have admired the fast-growing quality reputation Any Airline has gained in the national arena.

I possess nine years of diverse full-time and part-time experience within the airline industry, ranging from Ground Crew and Operations Agent to my current position as Senior Operations Dispatcher for a highly personalized, worldwide courier service. This experience is supplemented by a Bachelor of Science degree in Aviation Science/Aviation Management, and comprehensive advanced training courses in these areas.

My enclosed resume provides a good summary of the experience and training I feel can be put to effective use for your company. For this reason, I would like to arrange a personal meeting so that my immediate and long-term potential can be more fully expanded upon. I am happy to make myself available at your convenience.

I look forward to hearing from you.

Sincerely,

Chris Smith

Enc. resume

- Introduction states candidate's desire to join specific organization.
- Only relevant educational training is included.

"COLD" LETTER TO A POTENTIAL EMPLOYER
(Banking/Finance Professional)

178 Green Street
Barry Creek, CA 95916

July 7, 1996

Pat Cummings
Chief Hiring Officer
Any Corporation
1140 Main Street
Bakersfield, CA 93301

Dear Ms. Cummings:

I am writing to bring to your attention my years of experience in banking and finance, which include successful performance in such areas as fiduciary trust and real estate administration, investment management, and personal financial planning.

The enclosed resume summarizes my background. Please note that in addition to formal education in Business Administration and graduate study in Banking, I have more than twenty years of progressively responsible experience in positions ranging from Senior Trust Officer and Controller to my most recent involvement as Registered Investment Consultant.

Currently, I am seeking a challenging opportunity in which to apply this extensive background and experience, in a permanent, part-time situation.

I am currently available for an interview and will be glad to meet with you to further discuss additional details of my background and the mutual advantages of my joining your organization. In the interim, should your require additional information, please feel free to contact me by phone at (213) 555-5555 or (213)444-4444, or at the above address.

Thank you for your consideration. I look forward to speaking with you.

Sincerely,

Chris Smith

Enc. resume

■ Letter illustrates continual career progression.

■ Candidate indicates type of employment desired.

"COLD" LETTER TO A POTENTIAL EMPLOYER
(Business Consultant)

178 Green Street
Medford, WI 54451
(715) 555-5555 (days)
(715) 444-4444 (evenings)

September 12, 1996

Pat Cummings
Chairperson of the Board
Any Corporation
1140 Main Street
Schofield, WI 54476

Dear Mr. Cummings:

In the past several months, I have been studying operations at Any Corporation. By reading your annual report, company profile, and write-ups in several trade publications, I have been able to keep a close eye on both your costs and profits. If you agree that Any Corporation could benefit from an efficient, time-saving plan to cut production dollars, I would like to present my qualifications to you.

I am a skilled business consultant with over seventeen years' experience concentrated in the advertising field. I believe I can be of assistance to your organization. For your evaluation, I have prepared the attached business proposal which contains a detailed summary of a series of events and observations concerning trends in Any Corporation's operations that could be easily reversed.

I may be reached at either one of the above-listed numbers for a telephone conference, or to establish a mutually convenient time for a personal meeting. At such time, I would been pleased to demonstrate how I might be able to assist in correcting and/or eliminating many of the challenges touched upon in the attached proposal.

Thank you for your consideration.

Sincerely,

Chris Smith

Enc. business proposal

■ Introduction expresses candidate's knowledge of firm.

■ Discussion details how candidate's qualifications will benefit potential employer.

"COLD" LETTER TO A POTENTIAL EMPLOYER
(Buyer)

178 Green Street
El Cajon, CA 92020
(619) 555-5555

May 12, 1996

Pat Cummings
Personnel Coordinator
Any Corporation
1140 Main Street
Santa Ana, CA 97201

Dear Ms. Cummings:

If you are in need of a creative, innovative, professional buyer to add excitement to your inventories while generating bottom-line profits, then we have good reason to meet for further discussion.

During the past sixteen years I have had the opportunity to work in positions ranging from Merchandise Planner to Head Buyer at the headquarters level in major off-price retail chains. I have enjoyed rapid advancement and experienced the challenge of coordinating new concepts, introducing change associated with upscale fashion, and generating substantial increases in sales and profits.

Currently, I am looking for a new association with a growing chain that will benefit from my experience in identifying fashion trends, developing resources, and negotiating big buys for off-price retail operations. I am interested in a professional opportunity to utilize my market and product knowledge, and am anxious to achieve the same results for your chain as I have for my current employer.

Since my present employer is unaware of my search, your confidence is appreciated. I look foward to your response.

Sincerely,

Chris Smith

Enc. employment profile

■ Experiences are tailored to employer's needs.

■ Closing informs addressee of need for confidentiality.

"COLD" LETTER TO A POTENTIAL EMPLOYER
(Campaign Manager)

178 Green Street
Omaha, NE 68102
(402) 555-5555

December 23, 1996

Pat Cummings
Lieutenant Governor
Any State
1140 Main Street
Omaha, NE 68102

Dear Mr. Cummings:

During the past fourteen years, I have had diverse and progressively responsible
experience in development for nonprofit service organizations, universities, and
educational institutions. These responsibilities have ranged from Secretary to the
Director of Development.

During this period, I have been heavily involved in development strategies, annual
fund-raising campaigns, marketing and mailing programs, and media and public
relations. Although these positions have been exciting, I now feel that my
expertise would be put to better use in a new environment, namely for Any State.

I would appreciate the opportunity to discuss with you the contribution I can make
to the state administration. I will call your office the week of January 10 to
schedule a mutually convenient time to meet.

Thank you for your consideration.

Sincerely,

Chris Smith

Enc. resume

■ Closing indicates specific date
when candidate will follow up
inquiry.

■ Language is straightforward and
understandable.

"COLD" LETTER TO A POTENTIAL EMPLOYER
(Chef)

178 Green Street
Clarksville, TN 37044
(615) 555-5555

April 15, 1996

Pat Cummings
Manager
Any Hotel
1140 Main Street
Lexington, KY 40508

Dear Ms. Cummings:

During the past six years my positions have ranged from Sous Chef to Executive
Chef of a restaurant continually rated in the top one hundred restaurants and
institutions nationwide. My earlier experiences include associations with country
clubs, hotels, resorts, and four-star restaurants where I held a variety of positions
including, Waiter, Line Cook, and Saute Chef.

Because of my ability to organize, train, and work effectively with personnel in
quality, high-volume restaurants, I was able to maintain a conscientious, highly
productive work force. I have expertise in coordinating activities and directing the
indoctrination and training of chefs and other kitchen staff to ensure an efficient
and profitable food service.

In addition to being an honors graduate of the Culinary Institute of America, I
have received several national and regional awards for my creative culinary skills.

The enclosed resume is a brief summary of my qualifications. I would welcome
the chance to discuss the culinary opportunities offered at Any Hotel, and will call
during the week of May 1 to schedule a meeting.

Thank you for your consideration.

Yours sincerely,

Chris Smith

Enc. resume

- Impressive credentials and awards further enhance candidate's qualifications.

- Candidate's most relevant work experience is prioritized.

"COLD" LETTER TO A POTENTIAL EMPLOYER
(Civil Engineer)

178 Green Street
Providence, RI 02903

October 10, 1996

Pat Cummings
Hiring Director
Any Firm
1140 Main Street
New Britain, CT 06050

Dear Mr. Cummings:

I am interested in joining Any Firm's team, specifically the civil engineering division. I have ten years of progressively responsible experience acquired during roadway, civil, site, hazardous waste, and waterfront projects. This is supported by a Bachelor of Science degree in Forest Resource Management, Certification in Surveying Technology, completion of the Fundamentals in Surveying Examination, and hazardous site activities study.

Presently, I am investigating new, broader opportunities where my technical and supervisory skills can be effectively utilized.

If relocation is necessary, then I am ready to make that commitment. I am confident of my ability to make a positive and immediate contribution to your firm and would welcome the opportunity to personally discuss your current or anticipated staffing requirements during a one-on-one or phone interview.

I can be reached at the above address or by phone at (401) 555-5555. I await your reply.

Sincerely,

Chris Smith

Enc. resume

- Professional certification and strong educational background add strength to cover letter.

- Willingness to relocate can be advantageous.

"COLD" LETTER TO A POTENTIAL EMPLOYER
(Clinical Psychologist)

178 Green Street
Athens, GA 30607

March 14, 1996

Pat Cummings
Chair, Board of Directors
Any Hospital
1140 Main Street
Atlanta, GA 30354

Dear Ms. Cummings:

The enclosed professional profile is a summary of my academic and clinical experience in private practice, mental health clinics, and HMO's.

My experience as a Clinical Psychologist, Clinical Social Worker, and Research Psychologist spans more than twenty-five years working in clinical, academic, industrial, and community settings where I have treated individuals, couples, groups, and families. I have the professional qualifications and clinical skills to provide the quality psychotherapeutic and counseling services you require of all your health care providers. I am a board-certified Diplomat in Social Work, full member of AGPA and NEGP, and listed in the National Register for Health Service Providers in Psychology.

If you require additional information, please feel free to contact me at (404) 555-5555. I hope to hear from you shortly.

Sincerely,

Chris Smith

Enc. professional profile

■ Job-related affiliations demonstrate candidate's active participation in his/her field.

■ Closing invites addressee to inquire about additional information.

"COLD" LETTER TO A POTENTIAL EMPLOYER
(Clinical Researcher)

178 Green Street
Pueblo, CO 81001

November 7, 1996

Pat Cummings
Product Development Supervisor
Any Corporation
1140 Main Street
Gunnison, CO 81231

Dear Mr. Cummings:

I am interested in a challenging position requiring product management, product development, and clinical research/nursing skills. Any Corporation's research facility has earned a reputation as the most technologically advanced in the field and, for this reason, I am eager to join your staff.

My expertise covers the management of product development from clinical research for FDA approval to commercial marketability. I offer thirteen years of professional clinical experience with major teaching and trauma hospitals as a Staff RN and Therapeutic Apheresis Nurse Specialist. My most recent three years have been spent as Project Manager of Clinical Services and Product Manager with a firm specializing in clinical research and product development, concentrating in applications for autolymphocyte therapy (ALT).

I have excellent communication, computer, and writing skills and am well qualified to assume responsibility for clinical, regulatory, and related functions.

I am anxious to discuss how I might contribute to your organization. Please contact me at the above address, or call (719) 555-5555 to arrange a mutually convenient time for a meeting. Thank you for your consideration.

Sincerely,

Chris Smith, R.N.

Enc. resume

■ Specific company information illustrates candidate's commitment to his/her field.

■ Relevant work experience is emphasized while other positions are omitted.

"COLD" LETTER TO A POTENTIAL EMPLOYER
(Clinical Service Administrator)

178 Green Street
Orono, ME 04473
(207) 555-5555

February 21, 1996

Pat Cummings
Senior Administrator
Any Corporation
1140 Main Street
Portland, ME 04101

Dear Ms. Cummings:

If you are in need of a take-charge professional skilled in clinical service administration as well as quality assurance, utilization review, and risk management, then we have good reason to meet for further discussion.

In addition to a Master of Science degree in Business Administration, I offer thirteen years of progressively responsible, comprehensive experience including five years in my current position as Director of Service Administration at the medical teaching facility of the University of Maine. In this capacity, I developed a competent quality assurance support staff, and provided overall leadership and management for a department which supports and generates input to clinical chiefs in highly technical areas.

The enclosed resume summarizes my qualifications. I would appreciate the opportunity to interview and discuss in greater detail the mutual benefits of my joining your management team. I will call you on February 28 to schedule a convenient time.

Yours sincerely,

Chris Smith

Enc. resume

■ Closing suggests a meeting to follow letter.

■ Enclosure line suggests candidate is a meticulous, detail-oriented professional.

"COLD" LETTER TO A POTENTIAL EMPLOYER
(Communications Consultant)

178 Green Street
Wayne, NE 68787

November 11, 1996

Pat Cummings
Program Director
Any Corporation
1140 Main Street
Schenectady, NY 12308

Dear Mr. Cummings:

It is my interest in a consulting position with a communications company offering potential for advancement that has prompted me to forward my resume for your review and evaluation.

In addition to a Bachelor of Arts degree in Political Science/Communications, I have three years of concentrated experience with customer contact and service. My positions have ranged from Data Processing Analyst to Brokerage Service Representative to my most current position as New Business Representative. I have good organizational, communication, and interpersonal skills which I am confident could be effectively utilized in a firm such as yours.

If you have room for a highly motivated achiever in your firm, then we have good reason to meet. I feel strongly that my qualifications can be more fully demonstrated during a personal interview. I am able to travel to Schenectady at your convenience for a discussion. I can be reached at the above address or by phone at (402) 555-5555.

Thank you for your consideration and response.

Sincerely,

Chris Smith

Enc. resume

■ Letter avoids abbreviations and slang.

■ Letter tailors experience and skills to position applied for.

"COLD" LETTER TO A POTENTIAL EMPLOYER
(Computer Applications Programmer)

178 Green Street
Phoenix, AZ 85004
(602) 555-5555

April 15, 1996

Pat Cummings
Vice-President, Human Resources
Any Corporation
1140 Main Street
Anchorage, AK 99514

Dear Ms. Cummings:

I am seeking a position that requires not only technical expertise but decision-making skills to provide support and direction to a growing organization. Any Corporation's innovative MoneyManage software has placed your firm at the forefront of financial application developers. I am anxious to join your programming team. Based on my qualifications, I am confident of my ability to provide you with the technical/business planning and follow-through necessary to develop a concept into a marketable, profitable, and competitive product.

During the past fifteen years, my technical and management experience has ranged from Programmer specializing in communications software to Senior Manager of Data Base Management Products and Systems Performance. In all areas, I have played a key role in the development of products in a volatile environment of changing technology, and, as a result, was the recipient of *Financial Quarterly*'s "Product Manager of the Year" Award.

The enclosed resume summarizes my background and experience in the above areas. Please review my qualifications and contact me so that we can discuss your requirements and mutual objectives. Thank you for your consideration.

Sincerely,

Chris Smith

Enc. resume

■ Awards draw attention to candidate's significant accomplishments.

■ Candidate clearly expresses eagerness to work for specific employer.

"COLD" LETTER TO A POTENTIAL EMPLOYER
(Computer Programmer)

178 Green Street
Bunkie, LA 71322
(318) 555-5555

December 5, 1996

Pat Cummings
Hiring Director
Any Corporation
1140 Main Street
Chicago, IL 60605

Dear Mr. Cummings:

I am an experienced Computer Programmer ready, willing, and able to join Any Corporation.

I offer extensive knowledge of five computer languages and strong management, sales, and sales support experience. As a Computer Specialist, I was responsible for the management of a center handling the complete line of Honeywell computers and peripherals for home and commercial use. In addition to a Bachelor of Science degree in Business Administration, I will receive a certificate in Programming next May.

I feel confident that, given the opportunity, I can make an immediate contribution to Any Corporation. I would appreciate the opportunity to meet with you to discuss your requirements. I will call your office on Thursday, December 12, to schedule an appointment. Thank you for your consideration.

Sincerely,

Chris Smith

Enc. resume

■ First paragraph is short and hard-hitting.

■ Including telephone number is necessary in a cover letter.

"COLD" LETTER TO A POTENTIAL EMPLOYER
(Computer Software Designer)

178 Green Street
Decorah, IA 52101
(319) 555-5555

February 12, 1996

Pat Cummings
Personnel Director
Any Corporation
1140 Main Street
Cedar Rapids, IA 52402

Dear Ms. Cummings:

As a graduate student completing a Master of Science degree in Computer Science in March of this year, a challenging application software or system-oriented position interests me very much.

I believe that my two years' experience as a Data Base Designer, as well as my six months' experience as an Intern at Puttnee Bowles, gives me the necessary capabilities to successfully handle the responsibilities of a Computer Software Designer. I have considerable experience with DBMS packages such as Oracle, Ingres, DB2, Foxpro, and OS/2 Data Manager.

My academic training has provided valuable experience with C and many languages in the Unix/Windows environment. My education has exposed me to extensive programming assignments, wherein I could work individually or as part of a team. With competency in Unix, C, SAS, Pascal, and a variety of other programming languages, I am comfortable in SUNOS, DOS, and VAX operating systems. I have effectively used a variety of graphics, spreadsheet, data base, desktop publishing, word processing, and telecommunication applications.

I have a high degree of initiative, have the ability to communicate effectively, and grasp new concepts quickly. Further, I believe that my analytical skills and experience would positively contribute to the design department of your organization.

I would appreciate the opportunity to discuss my qualifications in a personal interview. I will call your office next Monday to follow up on my inquiry. I look forward to learning more about the software design projects at Any Corporation.

Sincerely,

Chris Smith

Enc. resume

- Technical language is acceptable when it relates to candidate's field.

- Internship experience is valuable for candidates with little job experience, particularly if it corresponds to the position sought.

"COLD" LETTER TO A POTENTIAL EMPLOYER
(Consulting/Management Specialist)

178 Green Street
Franklin Park, IL 60131

June 28, 1996

Pat Cummings
Operations Manager
Any Company
1140 Main Street
Skokie, IL 60076

Dear Mr. Cummings:

Is Any Company currently in need of a hardworking and intelligent
Consultant/Management Specialist with over ten years of experience? If so, then
please consider the following qualifications.

During the past eight years, I have been actively involved in the development and
administration of health and welfare funds, defined contribution plans, and
developed, designed, and implemented medical practice systems. This proficiency
has been applied to both union and company requirements. My professional
background is supported by a Master of Business Administration, Employee
Benefits Specialist Certification, and current candidacy for a Master of Science in
Computer Information Systems.

If I possess what you are looking for, please call me at (708) 555-5555. I eagerly
await your reply.

Sincerely,

Chris Smith

Enc. resume

■ Introducing letter with a question
draws attention to candidate.

■ Educational credentials
strengthen cover letter.

"COLD" LETTER TO A POTENTIAL EMPLOYER
(Controller)

178 Green Street
Sioux Falls, SD 57102

July 22, 1996

Pat Cummings
Hiring Officer
Any Corporation
1140 Main Street
Richmond, VA 23219

Dear Ms. Cummings:

During the past eight years I have held numerous progressively responsible
positions in the areas of general accounting, business, office management, and
project management.

Currently I am seeking a new association with a company where I can apply my
experience and skills toward both company and personal goals.

I consider myself to be a well-organized, self-motivated, productive individual. I
am open to additional training and am looking for a position that offers
advancement based on ability to perform.

The enclosed resume summarizes my background and experience. I am available
at your earliest convenience to discuss my qualifications with you during a
personal interview. I can be reached at the above address or by phone at (605)
555-5555.

Thank you in advance for your response.

Sincerely,

Chris Smith

Enc. resume

■ Discussion of experience
indicates a series of promotions.

■ Discussion of personal qualities
reiterates candidate's ability to
contribute to potential employer.

"COLD" LETTER TO A POTENTIAL EMPLOYER
(Country Club Manager)

178 Green Street
West Palm Beach, FL 33405
(407) 555-5555

April 13, 1996

Pat Cummings
Owner
Any Country Club
1140 Main Street
Sarasota, FL 34236

Dear Mr. Cummings:

I am writing to inquire about available management positions at Any Country Club. I have been an active member since 1985, and my familiarity with the club and its members would make me an excellent candidate for your consideration.

I am presently employed in a position that has presented challenges and personal satisfaction for a job well done. However, I feel that my education, training, and experience has prepared me for a broader scope of responsibility, and for this reason I am seeking a change.

I would like to associate with a quality facility in the hospitality industry that maintains high standards for services offered to guests or members. Based on my education and experience history, I can play a key role in achieving our mutual goals for success and profit by providing cost-effective management.

The enclosed resume summarizes my qualifications. I would welcome the opportunity to discuss my ability to meet your expectations for the position offered. Please contact me to schedule a mutually convenient time for an interview.

Thank you. I look forward to talking with you.

Sincerely,

Chris Smith

Enc. resume

■ Letter focuses on the needs of the employer, not the job candidate.

■ Type of position desired is clearly stated.

"COLD" LETTER TO A POTENTIAL EMPLOYER
(Editorial Assistant)

178 Green Street
New York, NY 10020
(212) 555-5555

March 13, 1996

Pat Cummings
Personnel Director
Any Corporation
1140 Main Street
Chicago, IL 60605

Dear Ms. Cummings:

I would like to inquire about upcoming entry-level editorial openings with Any Corporation.

I am presently a senior in good standing at New York University, due to graduate in May of this year. I am pursuing a Bachelor of Arts degree with a major in Journalism and a minor in both Economics and English Literature. I am proficient in both WordPerfect and Microsoft Word for Windows, and am familiar with both IBM and Macintosh operating systems. I am presently working as a Research Intern for the economics division of Tradewinds Publishing in Newark.

Enclosed you will find a copy of my resume. Letters of recommendation from employers and professors, as well as writing samples, will gladly be provided upon request. I will contact you next week about the possibility of arranging a meeting at your convenience.

I look forward to speaking with you.

Sincerely,

Chris Smith

Enc. resume

■ Relevant internship bolsters otherwise limited work experience.

■ Computer skills listed are related to candidate's field of interest.

"COLD" LETTER TO A POTENTIAL EMPLOYER
(Electrician)

178 Green Street
Lawrence, KS 66409

September 14, 1996

Pat Cummings
Staff Coordinator
Any Corporation
1140 Main Street
Topeka, KS 66607

Dear Mr. Cummings:

I am currently investigating availabilities in electrical operations, and would like to submit my qualifications for your review.

Although I am a newly licensed Journeyman Electrician, I have nine years of experience, five as an Apprentice and four as a Journeyman, handling all kinds of electrical installations while working with electrical contractors and as a subcontractor. I am capable of working independently or as a member of a team and feel confident in my ability to handle multiple responsibilities and provide quality performance in any assignment I undertake.

The enclosed resume is a brief summary of my experience. However, I would appreciate the opportunity to further discuss my qualifications. I will contact your division next Wednesday to schedule a meeting. Should you require additional information, please contact me at the above address or by phone at (913) 555-5555.

I am very interested in joining Any Corporation and look forward to your return reply.

Yours sincerely,

Chris Smith

Enc. resume

■ Candidate includes licensure relevant to his/her field.

■ Closing informs addressee that resume is enclosed.

"COLD" LETTER TO A POTENTIAL EMPLOYER
(Electromechanical Drafter)

178 Green Street
New Castle, DE 19720
(302) 555-5555

November 20, 1996

Pat Cummings
Chief Engineer
Any Corporation
1140 Main Street
Easton, PA 18044

Dear Ms. Cummings:

As a recent graduate with an Associate degree in Electromechanical Drafting, with concentration in Electromechanical Technology, my goal is to join a firm where I can apply my skills in a drafting environment.

Since 1991, I have held responsible part-time positions as a Marine Technician and a Mason Tender while earning my degree. I am able to handle assignments individually or as a team member. I am computer literate, am people-oriented, have good communication skills, and relate well to all levels of authority. Now I am seeking an opportunity for personal development and advancement based on the quality of my technical performance.

My resume is a good summary of my education, background, and experience, but I strongly feel that during the course of a personal interview my potential for making a significant contribution to your firm can be more fully demonstrated.

Should you require additional information, please contact me at the above address or phone number. I look forward to your return response.

Yours sincerely,

Chris Smith

Enc. resume

- Part-time work experience during school indicates candidate's strong work ethic.
- Closing refers addressee to telephone number in return address.

"COLD" LETTER TO A POTENTIAL EMPLOYER
(Elementary School Teacher)

178 Green Street
Lubbock, TX 79408
(806) 555-5555

July 7, 1996

Pat Cummings, Ph.D.
Superintendent
Any Public School
1140 Main Street
Chickasha, OK 73023

Dear Dr. Cummings:

My interest in contributing to the enhancement of elementary education within the Any Public School System has prompted my forwarding the enclosed resume for your review and consideration.

Currently, as an Elementary School Teacher responsible for thirty second-grade students, I am actively involved in the development and implementation of reading, writing, and math programs which effectively motivate accomplishment through both individual and group projects. My professional training and experience began with the Rockford Public School System as a Student Teacher at the Roosevelt Elementary School and as a Substitute Teacher within the system. I completed a Bachelor of Arts degree in Elementary Education in May 1987.

Additionally, I have been instrumental in instituting and selecting educational software for a new IBM computer system as well as instructing the teaching staff on its use. Presently, I am formulating a proposal to initiate the establishment of a high-ability learning program.

I am confident of my ability to stimulate and motivate children toward personal growth and achievement. I would welcome the opportunity to meet with you to discuss your current staffing requirements. In the interim, if any additional information is required, please contact me at the above address or phone number.

Sincerely,

Chris Smith

Enc. resume

- Computer skills listed are related to candidate's field of interest.
- Candidate tailors letter to his/her field of interest.

"COLD" LETTER TO A POTENTIAL EMPLOYER
(Engineer)

178 Green Street
Sacramento, CA 95852

July 20, 1996

Pat Cummings
Project Manager
Any Corporation
1140 Main Street
Modesto, CA 95354

Dear Mr. Cummings:

Are you in need of a highly qualified Engineer to successfully complete diverse construction projects? If so, I would like to offer my application for your review.

In addition to a Bachelor of Science degree with a concentration in Civil Engineering, I hold two Associates degrees in related subjects, as well as ten years of part-time and full-time employment holding responsible positions in construction. My knowledge includes construction of schools, parking areas, museums, medical facilities, office buildings, and other structures. I am experienced in supervision, engineering layout, construction coordination, purchasing, and many aspects related to the organization and business of construction.

After reviewing my resume, if you have a place in your organization for an experienced professional who works only to a standard of excellence, please contact me at the above address, or call (916) 555-5555. I would like to arrange a personal interview, during which we could further discuss my ambition and potential for service while in your employment.

Thank you for your consideration.

Sincerely,

Chris Smith

Enc. resume

- Discussion of experience is very specific.
- Closing encourages reader to respond to letter.

"COLD" LETTER TO A POTENTIAL EMPLOYER
(Engineering Instructor)

178 Green Street
Macon, GA 31201
(912) 555-5555

August 20, 1996

Pat Cummings
Headmaster
Any School
1140 Main Street
Evansville, IN 47713

Dear Ms. Cummings:

If you are in need of an Engineering Instructor to teach accredited classroom courses or conduct in-house seminars and training courses for students, then we have good reason to meet for further discussion.

I have extensive experience in teaching courses on proposal writing, pricing, component design, and equipment operation and control. My practical expertise is in electromechanical design and the analysis of mechanical systems. In addition, I offer five years' experience teaching engineering.

My experience as an Engineer, Principal Engineer Manager, Author, and Technical Writer is extensive. I am skilled in preparing and presenting complex technical reports to corporate clients and/or company management in support of contracts or proposed new developments. Currently, I am interested in joining an educational system where I can impart my engineering knowledge, experience, and writing skills to students in an academic or vocational environment, preferably on a per diem or course assignment basis. I have an excellent grasp of highly sophisticated systems and instrumentation, and I can provide your students with essential technical knowledge and support.

I would appreciate the opportunity to discuss my qualifications. I will call the school next week to schedule an interview. Thank you for your time.

Sincerely,

Chris Smith

Enc. professional profile

■ Four short paragraphs is the ideal length for a cover letter.

■ Letter focuses on acquired skills relevant to field of interest.

"COLD" LETTER TO A POTENTIAL EMPLOYER
(Esthetician)

178 Green Street
Hartford, CT 06115

April 2, 1996

Pat Cummings
Vice-President, Personnel
Any Corporation
1140 Main Street
New Haven, CT 06511

Dear Mr. Cummings:

Currently I am seeking a new association with the international sales/marketing division of Any Corporation. I offer professional expertise in opening new markets, salon/spa start-ups, introducing beauty products and services, and training.

I am a Licensed Esthetician who, during the past ten years, has held positions in France and the United States as Director of Education with a French manufacturer of beauty products sold to select European spas and Skin Care Director with an exclusive beauty spa.

In addition, I am a multilingualist fluent in Native French and German. I feel confident that I could make a valuable contribution toward increasing your product name visibility and market share in this global economy.

I would appreciate the opportunity to discuss your requirements for penetrating international markets. Should you require additional information, please contact me at the above address or by phone at (203) 555-5555.

I look forward to your return response.

Sincerely,

Chris Smith

Enc. resume

- International work experience adds weight to candidate's qualifications.

- Candidate immediately expresses suitability for desired position.

"COLD" LETTER TO A POTENTIAL EMPLOYER
(Executive Secretary)

178 Green Street
Allentown, PA 18105

August 5, 1996

Pat Cummings
Human Resources Manager
Any Corporation
1140 Main Street
Philadelphia, PA 19130

Dear Ms. Cummings:

If you are in need of an Executive Secretary who can double as an Administrative Assistant and handle the day-to-day details necessary to keep an operation running smoothly, then we have good reason to meet.

During the past seven years, I have provided administrative support to senior-level officers and account executives in a domestic and international sales/marketing environment. Although this position has been interesting, I am presently considering a position change with a company offering greater responsibility and growth potential than is evident with my present employer.

So that I can be considered for a position with your firm, I am enclosing a copy of my professional profile for your review. I would appreciate the opportunity to discuss my past achievements, and ways in which I can excel in a future position with Any Corporation.

Thank you for reviewing my credentials. I can be reached at the above address or by phone between 9:00 a.m. and 1:00 p.m. at (215) 555-5555.

Sincerely,

Chris Smith

Enc. professional profile

■ Candidate expresses best time of day to be reached in closing.

■ Letter is short and to the point.

"COLD" LETTER TO A POTENTIAL EMPLOYER
(Facilities Specialist)

178 Green Street
Riverside, CA 92502
(714) 555-5555

December 28, 1996

Pat Cummings
Human Resources Manager
Any Corporation
1140 Main Street
Fresno, CA 93786

Dear Mr. Cummings:

I am interested in exploring the opportunity of joining your company as a Facilities Specialist, or in a related role. The enclosed resume provides you with information concerning my background and abilities.

For over seven years, I have been employed in the commercial interior design field. During this time, I have progressed from Draftsperson to Project Manager. I have successfully designed and implemented a variety of new systems and procedures during my tenure, and have been recognized for having effected considerable increased revenues and measurable cost savings.

I admire Any Corporation's position on the cutting edge of design and I am anxious to join your firm. I would appreciate the opportunity for a personal interview, at your convenience, to discuss how my skills and abilities would be assets to your organization. If you desire further information at this time, I am happy to supply whatever you need.

Thank you again for your time. I will call the week of January 17 to schedule a mutually convenient meeting time.

Sincerely,

Chris Smith

Enc. resume

■ In closing, candidate specifically requests interview.

■ Letter incorporates company knowledge into discussion of qualifications.

"COLD" LETTER TO A POTENTIAL EMPLOYER
(Field Coordinator)

178 Green Street
Greenville, SC 29601
(803) 555-5555

July 10, 1996

Pat Cummings
Chief Executive Director
Any Campaign
1140 Main Street
Clinton, SC 29325

Dear Ms. Cummings:

Are you searching for a dynamic Field Coordinator or Campaign Manager for your upcoming campaign?

During the past two years, my graduate education at the University of Southern Carolina has been geared toward, and my experience concentrated in, areas dealing with government issues and the political campaign arena. I have worked as a Campaign Manager, Field Coordinator, Volunteer Organizer, and Fundraiser.

My motivation has always been toward a professional career in politics where I can play a key role in getting qualified candidates elected who can make a significant difference in the effectiveness of the offices they represent. As the enclosed resume reflects, my experience has been with local, state, and federal level campaigns. I feel confident that I have the skills required to make your constituents aware of the importance of voting your candidate into office.

I will call your office on Wednesday, July 17, to assure receipt of my letter and to schedule an interview. Thank you for your consideration. I am eager to join your team!

Sincerely,

Chris Smith

Enc. resume

■ Letter clarifies candidate's career goals.

■ Closing reiterates candidate's interest in position.

"COLD" LETTER TO A POTENTIAL EMPLOYER
(Financial Associate)

178 Green Street
Eugene, OR 97401
(503) 555-5555

October 17, 1996

Pat Cummings
Human Resources Director
Any Corporation
1140 Main Street
Portland, OR 97201

Dear Mr. Cummings:

I am a new graduate with a Bachelor of Arts degree in Political Science who can offer your firm dedication, skill, and a willingness to learn your industry while aspiring to performance-based advancement.

My interest is in business, investments, and finance. In keeping with this interest, I have developed a strong work ethic which is evidenced by the fact that I have maintained a part-time job during my four years of college. This included operating my own successful small business and working in other positions and internships. I function equally well working independently or as a member of a team, and feel confident that given the opportunity I can make a positive difference as a member of your firm.

The enclosed resume summarizes my experience. I am eager to meet for an interview during which I can fully express my capacity and desire to contribute to Any Corporation. I will call your office the week of October 24 to schedule a discussion.

Thank you for your time and consideration. I look forward to speaking with you in the near future.

Sincerely,

Chris Smith

Enc. resume

■ Part-time work experience during school indicates candidate's strong work ethic.

■ Letter expresses commitment to field of interest.

"COLD" LETTER TO A POTENTIAL EMPLOYER
(Financial Consultant)

178 Green Street
Clinton, MS 39058

May 8, 1996

Pat Cummings
Manager, Accounts Receivable
Any Corporation
1140 Main Street
Florence, MS 39073

Dear Ms. Cummings:

As a Credit and Collections Consultant, I have been instrumental in substantially improving accounts receivable management, cash flow control, and the reduction of bad debt risk for a rapidly growing, high-tech company.

Because of my performance during the past twelve years as Staff Accountant, Credit Analyst, Credit and Collection Manager, and Consultant, I was continually retained by new management during several acquisitions, mergers, and consolidations. I have held positions that have provided me with increasingly responsible experience and challenge. However, due to the planned move of my function to Canadian headquarters, I am currently investigating new consulting opportunities with companies that can benefit from my expertise as a Credit and Collection Specialist to improve their cash position.

Despite a damaged economy, I am confident of my ability to set up and manage credit and collection systems, procedures and controls, and employee training programs that will have the same positive results as experienced by my current employer.

The enclosed profile is a summary of my experience. I would appreciate the chance to discuss your credit/collection problems and my ability to come up with solutions without alienating your customer base. I will call your office on May 14 to arrange a convenient interview time.

Should you require additional information prior to our meeting, please contact me at the above address or by phone at (601) 555-5555.

I look forward to your return response.

Sincerely,

Chris Smith

Enc. professional profile

- Job descriptions emphasize candidate's accomplishments.

- Candidate emphasizes how past business experience can benefit potential employer.

"COLD" LETTER TO A POTENTIAL EMPLOYER
(Financial Planner)

178 Green Street
Gardenia, ND 58739

April 15, 1996

Pat Cummings
Personnel Manager
Any Corporation
1140 Main Street
Chicago, IL 60605

Dear Mr. Cummings:

Having had the opportunity to meet with Deborah Sturgis and the rest of the staff at the Fargo office, I am very much interested in starting my career in finance at Any Corporation.

I am planning a permanent relocation to the Chicago area in the late summer. I am submitting my resume for consideration for admittance into your Financial Planner Training Program.

Please note that I am currently completing my senior year at North Dakota University and will receive my Bachelor of Science degree with a major in Accounting and a concentration in Computer Programming this May. Throughout school, and during full-time and part-time employment, I have continued to strengthen my focus in these areas. In addition, I have excellent problem-solving skills and feel that, given the opportunity, I would be an immediate as well as a long-term asset to your firm.

My resume is a good summary but I feel strongly that it is during a personal interview that my potential to be of service to your organization would be more fully demonstrated. I plan to be in the Chicago area the week of May 1 and would welcome the opportunity to meet with you. I will follow up with a phone call on April 25 to arrange such a meeting. In the interim I can be reached at the above address or by telephone at (701) 555-5555.

Thank you for your time and consideration.

Sincerely,

Chris Smith

Enc. resume

■ Candidate immediately introduces purpose for writing.

■ Candidate indicates time frame for follow-up contact.

"COLD" LETTER TO A POTENTIAL EMPLOYER
(Flight Attendant)

178 Green Street
Helena, MT 59601
(406) 555-5555

January 3, 1996

Pat Cummings
Attendant Supervisor
Any Airline
1140 Main Street
Phoenix, AZ 85023

Dear Ms. Cummings:

I am an ambitious, career-oriented, energetic individual with a keen interest in becoming associated with and contributing to the growth of Any Airline in the capacity of a Flight Attendant.

I possess six years of diverse business experience in both the retail and hospitality industries. I understand that excellent customer/public relations and support, along with strong communication skills, are requirements for maintaining efficient airline operations and a strong public image.

I feel confident that, given the opportunity, I can make an immediate contribution to the flight system at Any Airline. I would appreciate the chance to personally meet to discuss your requirements and my ability to meet them.

I look forward to meeting with you.

Yours sincerely,

Chris Smith

Enc. resume

■ Discussion of personal qualities reiterates candidate's ability to contribute to potential employer.

■ Closing reiterates candidate's interest in specific corporation.

"COLD" LETTER TO A POTENTIAL EMPLOYER
(Foreperson/Ironworker)

178 Green Street
Spartanburg, SC 29304

August 4, 1996

Pat Cummings
Personnel Manager
Any Corporation
1140 Main Street
Sioux City, IA 51102

Dear Mr. Cummings:

During the past ten years, my career has grown steadily. I began with the position of Journeyman Ironworker/Foreman Ironworker with the Local #10, and have progressed to Senior Project Manager constructing commercial and industrial steel buildings in the United States and Canada.

I am an effective negotiator skilled in dealing with subcontractors, vendors, and suppliers, and in the coordination and scheduling of manpower, equipment, and materials to meet deliveries, time schedules, and budgets. I am well qualified to assume responsibilities for projects from pre-job site inspections to final completion.

I would welcome the chance to personally discuss my capabilities and your anticipated requirements. Please contact me at the above address or by phone at (803) 555-5555 to arrange for a mutually convenient time for such a meeting.

Thank you for your consideration and early response.

Sincerely,

Chris Smith

Enc. resume

- Letter focuses on candidate's past job experience while incorporating functional qualifications.
- Candidate expresses knowledge in his/her field of interest.

"COLD" LETTER TO A POTENTIAL EMPLOYER
(Fundraiser)

178 Green Street
Rollins College, FL 32789
(407) 555-5555

June 1, 1996

Pat Cummings
Staff Coordinator
Any Organization
1140 Main Street
Orlando, FL 32809

Dear Ms. Cummings:

I am a committed, creative, and industrious professional eager to use my skills in a challenging fund-raising position, and am very interested in learning more about the opportunities available at Any Organization.

My experience in nonprofit development, public relations, and especially fund-raising, would be a strong asset to your organization. I have spent over three years as the Development and Public Relations Assistant at the Women's Educational Society. My experience has encompassed preparing grant proposals, compiling program books for fund-raising events, writing correspondences for the executive director, contributing to the quarterly newsletter, and generating donation acknowledgments. I am involved with the production of two yearly appeals, and publish the employee newsletter. In addition, as a member of the Executive Committee for my alumni class at Rollins College, I produce a quarterly newsletter with news from over fifteen hundred classmates.

I am Macintosh and IBM literate, and am familiar with many word processing programs. I taught myself desktop publishing on the Macintosh in order to produce my alumni newsletter. In addition, I am solely responsible for the fundraising data base program in my office. This includes updating and maintaining donor records, generating daily income reports and financial analyses, and training staff and volunteers in data entry procedures.

I have enclosed a resume, as well as copy of my employee newsletter and a program book to serve as writing samples. Please contact me if you need further information. Thank you.

Sincerely,

Chris Smith

Enc. resume
    writing samples

■ Candidate's most recent position is outlined in detail.

■ Letter emphasizes achievements, and does not simply list job responsibilities.

"COLD" LETTER TO A POTENTIAL EMPLOYER
(Graphic Artist)

178 Green Street
Bridgeville, PA 15017
(412) 555-5555

September 20, 1996

Pat Cummings
Director of Human Resources
Any Corporation
1140 Main Street
New York, NY 10108

Dear Mr. Cummings:

I am extremely interested in putting my graphics expertise to work for Any
Corporation. Your great successes in the past year, including your six-figure
accounts with Kitters Cola and the Mooburger Company, impressed all of us in the
advertising business. I want to get in on the fun and excitement! Enclosed is a
copy of my resume.

I operate from my own computerized studio where I design with the latest graphic-
related hardware and software. I offer extensive experience in:

- Designing marketing literature with QuarkXpress, Aldus Freehand, and
  Photoshop.

- Preparing complicated files on the Macintosh as final mechanicals, for
  direct export to the printing company.

- Communicating and working directly with clients, supervisors, and
  department heads.

- Estimating jobs firsthand and working directly with vendors.

- Directing graphic art departments and supervising projects.

Do my credentials sound suitable for a position at Any Corporation? I would be
more than happy to meet with you and show you a portfolio of my work at your
convenience. I will call your office next week to schedule an interview. Thank you
for your consideration.

Sincerely,

Chris Smith

Enc. resume

- Bulleted statements highlight candidate's on-the-job achievements.

- Letter reveals candidate's continued research in his/her field of interest.

"COLD" LETTER TO A POTENTIAL EMPLOYER
(Head Nurse)

178 Green Street
Woodland Hills, CA 91367
(818) 555-5555

May 29, 1996

Pat Cummings
Director of Nursing
Any Facility
1140 Main Street
Long Beach, CA 90844

Dear Ms. Cummings:

Last week, I read an article in the *Press Telegram* that praised Any Facility's excellent staff and patient services among area health care centers. I am looking for a nursing opportunity in the Long Beach area, and this piece confirmed my desire to join your esteemed organization.

I offer more than twelve years of experience ranging from Nursing Assistant and Charge Nurse to Nursing Supervisor for a 120-bed, multilevel nursing facility catering to patients afflicted with Alzheimer's, renal disease, and other geriatric conditions. My experience encompasses diverse areas of health care supervision, including patient assessment and staff development, as well as the coordination of other resident care services including physical therapy, dietary, housekeeping, pharmacy, and social services.

I am interested in joining the staff at Any Facility. I would welcome the opportunity to arrange a mutually convenient time in which we could further discuss your current or anticipated needs in terms of my qualifications.

Thank you for your consideration.

Sincerely,

Chris Smith

Enc. resume

■ Letter outlines series of promotions.

■ Letter emphasizes candidate's strong work history.

"COLD" LETTER TO A POTENTIAL EMPLOYER
(Health Services Coordinator)

178 Green Street
Providence, RI 02903

January 8, 1996

Pat Cummings
Controller
Any Corporation
1140 Main Street
Providence, RI 02903

Dear Mr. Cummings:

During the past fifteen years I have been involved in administration and management in the health care field.

Currently I am seeking a senior-level position in home/health care services in a public health hospital or hospital-based home care agency, where I can apply my expertise in the planning and administration of service delivery systems.

In addition to a Master of Science degree in Community Health Nursing, I have extensive experience ranging from home care program planning, and to all areas of proposal writing and funding requests to budget administration and third-party payments.

The enclosed resume summarizes, in part, my background and experience in the above areas. I would appreciate the opportunity to meet with you to discuss your professional requirements and my ability to direct an organization, such as yours, dedicated to quality health care systems and services.

I feel confident, based on my strong academic and professional credentials, that I can create an effective professional environment. If you require additional information, please feel free to contact me at the above address, or by phone at (401) 555-5555.

Thank you for your consideration.

Yours sincerely,

Chris Smith

Enc. resume

■ Closing reiterates candidate's qualifications for position.

■ Unrelated work experience is omitted.

"COLD" LETTER TO A POTENTIAL EMPLOYER
(Human Resources Professional)

178 Green Street
Grenvil, NE 68941
(402) 555-5555

October 19, 1996

Pat Cummings
Staff Coordinator
Any Corporation
1140 Main Street
St. Louis, MI 63130

Dear Ms. Cummings:

I am writing regarding opportunities your firm may have for experienced human
resources professionals.

I have a solid track record as a Human Resources Generalist working in a fast-
paced environment with a reputable professional services firm in the Omaha area.
I have successfully provided staff planning, recruiting, and employee relations
support for several of the firm's key high-technology practices, which provide
systems engineering and management consulting services. In addition, I have more
than six years of solid accomplishment as a Management Analyst, Systems
Analyst, and Environmental Management Consultant providing technical and
management services to both government and commercial clients.

I am now seeking new and challenging responsibilities in an organization that
would benefit from my background and specific mix of skills. I am willing to
relocate and/or travel for the right opportunity.

Perhaps we could meet soon to discuss available openings at Any Corporation?
Thank you for your time and consideration.

Sincerely,

Chris Smith

Enc. resume

- Letter stresses candidate's extensive experience and significant accomplishments.
- Candidate uses closing to suggest possibility of interview.

"COLD" LETTER TO A POTENTIAL EMPLOYER
(Human Services Coordinator)

178 Green Street
Washington, DC 20024

November 6, 1996

Pat Cummings
Director
Any Agency
1140 Main Street
Washington DC 20005

Dear Mr. Cummings:

During the past ten years, my experience has been concentrated as an Area Office
Manager and Child Advocate Coordinator in the coordination and management of
human services information and resources for multicultural, multilingual
populations in the Washington, D.C. area.

Currently, I am seeking a new association with an agency, in the public or private
sector, which has a need for a qualified professional. I can offer broad experience
working with, and coordinating the efforts of, public, private, and charitable
resources, educational systems, and providers of human services to community
residents or company employees.

I am especially interested in the field of human services as I am dedicated to the
quality of life and learning for the less fortunate. I possess strong organizational,
communication, and teaching skills, as well as the ability to work well under
stressful or crisis situations.

The responsibilities of the position you advertised sound like an ideal match for
my experience and commitment. I would be glad to make myself available for an
interview at your convenience to discuss this further. Should you require
additional information prior to our meeting, please contact me at the above address
or by phone at (202) 555-5555. I plan to make a follow-up call within a few days.

I look forward to speaking with you.

Yours sincerely,

Chris Smith

Enc. resume

■ Dedication to candidate's field of
interest is emphasized.

■ Related work experience is
accentuated.

"COLD" LETTER TO A POTENTIAL EMPLOYER
(Insurance Salesperson)

178 Green Street
Lubbock, TX 79408
(806) 555-5555

July 16, 1996

Pat Cummings
Sales Director
Any Insurance Company
1140 Main Street
Houston, TX 77027

Dear Ms. Cummings:

Currently, I am seeking a new association within the insurance industry where I can apply my combined experience with the sales and knowledge of insurance products and services. I am interested in a home office staff or sales position where there is opportunity for increased responsibility and compensation based on personal performance.

During the past thirteen years, I have built a successful career in the insurance agency, first as a Sales Representative with Unlimited Trust Insurance and then for ten years with Lubbock Mutual Life Insurance. In both positions I established myself as a consistent top producer selling a broad scope of insurance and investment products to businesses and professionals.

I have enclosed a resume for your perusal. I am anxious to discuss in greater detail my credentials for contributing to the profitability and increased customer satisfaction of your firm. Please contact me so that we may explore the possibility of a mutually beneficial association. Thank you.

Sincerely,

Chris Smith

Enc. resume

■ Job descriptions indicate how candidate contributed to his/her previous employers.

■ Letter immediately states candidate's purpose.

"COLD" LETTER TO A POTENTIAL EMPLOYER
(Interior Designer)

178 Green Street
Lindsay, NE 68644
(402) 555-5555

May 18, 1996

Pat Cummings
Senior Interior Designer
Any Design Company
1140 Main Street
Lincoln, NE 68521

Dear Mr. Cummings:

I am an energetic, creative, career-oriented individual with a genuine interest in pursuing a professional career in the area of interior design. For this reason, I am forwarding my resume for your consideration.

Please note that in addition to a Bachelor of Arts degree in Interior Design/Visual Arts, I have more than seven years of part-time and full-time experience encompassing the sale and follow-through of complete design concept for both commercial and residential clientele.

Throughout my experience, I have kept myself updated on trends and major players in the industry. I am familiar with your work at Any Design Company and would be honored to join your talented team. Could we meet for further discussion? I would love to show you my portfolio and convince you of my abilities.

I look forward to hearing from you.

Sincerely,

Chris Smith

Enc. resume

■ Stating that a portfolio is available on request is beneficial for certain positions.

■ Closing reiterates candidate's knowledge of organization.

"COLD" LETTER TO A POTENTIAL EMPLOYER
(International Sales Associate)

178 Green Street
Los Angeles, CA 90066
(213) 555-5555

April 1, 1996

Pat Cummings
Controller
Any Corporation
1140 Main Street
Boston, MA 02215

Dear Ms. Cummings:

During the past fifteen years I have played a key role in the development of international markets for the sale of capital and laboratory equipment, systems, and services. Currently, I am seeking a new association with a firm that can benefit from my expertise in the development of profitable overseas markets. Any Corporation's commitment to developing overseas accounts makes me eager to join your international team.

Throughout my career in foreign service and international sales, I have developed and currently maintain excellent personal, business, and government contacts with key product movers in pharmaceuticals, cosmetics, and chemical manufacturing; food processors; scientific laboratories; and health institutions worldwide.

My peers and associates consider me to be a goal setter and achiever, and I am confident I can produce the same beneficial results in the development of international markets for your products as I have for my present employer. If you can use an executive who is thoroughly familiar with international market development and sales, I would like to discuss my qualifications with you during a personal interview. I will be glad to expand on my experience. I will call your office next week to schedule a mutually convenient meeting time.

Sincerely,

Chris Smith

Enc. resume

■ International work experience adds weight to candidate's qualifications.

■ Letter clarifies candidate's career goals.

"COLD" LETTER TO A POTENTIAL EMPLOYER
(Jewelry Designer)

178 Green Street
Fresno, CA 93786
(209) 555-5555

August 15, 1996

Pat Cummings
Creative Director
Any Corporation
1140 Main Street
Los Angeles, CA 90053

Dear Mr. Cummings:

Of all the fine jewelry designs being produced today, in my estimation yours is singularly the best. I would like to put my talent as a Jewelry Designer to work for Any Corporation.

I have devoted the past seven years developing and refining my design skills while maximizing my technical knowledge. In addition to producing my own designs, I currently work as a model maker for Gemmz, Inc., a Fresno jewelry maker. During this time, I have made significant contributions to the company:

- Three of my designs were featured as part of Gemmz's flagship line at the 1995 International Jewelry Bazaar.
- Developed a buffing method in our Fresno production facility which is being implemented nationwide.
- Earned a fine arts degree in jewelry design.
- Won several design awards.

I would like to discuss some of the options available at Any Corporation and the possibility of my designing jewelry for you. I will call on September 1 to arrange an interview.

Thank you for your consideration.

Sincerely,

Chris Smith

Enc. resume

- Bullets provide a clear and crisp presentation.
- Career objective is supported by awards and accomplishments.

"COLD" LETTER TO A POTENTIAL EMPLOYER
(Jewelry Sales/Buyer)

178 Green Street
Neptune, NJ 07754
(415) 555-5555

July 18, 1996

Pat Cummings
General Manager
Any Store
1140 Main Street
Cherry Hill, NJ 08002

Dear Ms. Cummings:

I am a recent graduate of the Gemological Institute of America with a year of successful sales/buying experience of precious metals, gems, and antique jewelry.

Currently, I am looking for a new association with a major jewelry store where I can apply my sales and customer relations skills to continue my proven track record of increasing profit and market share. During my year at Monahan Jewelers, I was responsible for increasing company sales by 10 percent while creating a substantially larger customer base.

The enclosed resume summarizes my experience. I am very much interested in Any Store because of your top-notch reputation in the field. I am confident of my ability to represent you in an ethical and professional manner, and look forward to hearing from you soon.

Yours sincerely,

Chris Smith

Enc. resume

■ Closing reiterates candidate's interest in specific corporation.

■ Letter focuses attention on candidate's major skills and accomplishments.

"COLD" LETTER TO A POTENTIAL EMPLOYER
(Landscape Designer)

178 Green Street
Puyallip, WA 98374
(206) 555-5555

July 6, 1996

Pat Cummings
Manager
Any Corporation
1140 Main Street
Seattle, WA 98109

Dear Mr. Cummings:

During the past twenty-five years, my education, training, and experience have been concentrated as an Arborist and Landscape Designer; for nineteen of those years I have been with a tree and landscape company. Although my projects were diverse and offered me the opportunity to work with clients on creative project design and maintenance, I would like a change.

I am interested in concentrating my experience and education with a distinguished corporate complex such as Any Corporation which has a need for an experienced, dependable professional skilled in creative planning and maintenance. In addition to my experience, I am a certified Arborist and have a Bachelor of Science in Environmental Design from the University of Washington in Seattle. Based on my qualifications, I feel confident that I can bring both technical skill and stability to the position.

The enclosed resume is a summary of my experience. I look forward to the opportunity to discuss, in detail, your requirements and my ability to perform the responsibilities of the position.

Should you require any additional information, please contact me at the above address or by phone. I look forward to your return response.

Yours sincerely,

Chris Smith

Enc. resume

■ Candidate refers to attached resume in closing.

■ Qualifications are geared to candidate's field of interest.

"COLD" LETTER TO A POTENTIAL EMPLOYER
(Lawyer)

178 Green Street
Glendale Heights, IL 60139
(708) 555-5555

February 26, 1996

Pat Cummings
Hiring Coordinator
Any Law Firm
1140 Main Street
Chicago, IL 60606

Dear Ms. Cummings:

I am a 1994 graduate of Chicago-Kent College of Law interested in a position as an Associate with Any Law Firm. I am particularly interested in the firm's real estate, corporate, finance, and litigation departments.

As my enclosed resume indicates, upon graduation I accepted a job with the Chicago-based law firm Glavin and Joyce. As a first year associate, I worked in the firm's litigation, real estate, finance, and corporate departments. In May of 1995, I accepted a position with the Brussels-based international consulting firm Brunkhorst and Associates. On their behalf, I act as a consultant and advisor on American law as it relates to the offshore funding of U.S. commercial real estate.

Although I enjoy my present position, I would very much like to become associated with an up-and-coming firm such as yours so that I can continue my development as a lawyer. My association with a well-established, full-service law firm would also enable me to better service Brunkhorst and Associates and its clients.

If my qualifications are of interest to you, I would like to visit your offices for an interview. I will contact you Monday, March 4, to discuss available opportunities. Thank you for your attention and I look forward to speaking with you.

Sincerely,

Chris Smith

Enc. resume

■ Candidate tailors letter to his/her field of interest.

■ Including a telephone number is essential in a cover letter.

"COLD" LETTER TO A POTENTIAL EMPLOYER
(Legal Assistant)

178 Green Street
Kankakee, IL 60901
(815) 555-5555

April 16, 1996

Pat Cummings
Director of Human Resources
Any Law Firm
1140 Main Street
Chicago, IL 60611

Dear Mr. Cummings:

During the course of my research into area law firms, I found that Any Law Firm was continually ranked as one of the leading organizations in the greater Chicago area. For this reason, I would like to submit my resume for your consideration.

In addition to a Comprehensive Certificate in Paralegal Studies and a Bachelor of Science degree in Business Administration, I offer your firm over five years' experience as a Consumer Mediator with the Attorney General's office. In addition, I possess more than seven years of comprehensive business experience working and negotiating with senior-level management and decision-makers associated with *Fortune* 500 consumer products manufacturers and key account retailers. I am fully trained in all aspects of office maintenance, including Microsoft Word, Word for Windows, and WordPerfect word processing programs. I maintain a typing speed of 75 wpm.

My positions have been challenging and provided me with continual growth and success, but I made the decision to change my career direction. Instead of accepting a headquarters position, I opted to complete a program in paralegal studies and work toward making a meaningful contribution through legal avenues.

My first interest is in applying my legal studies to further my development and advancement in the profession. I am flexible, adaptable, a good writer and communicator, as well as a fast study. I feel confident that with minimal supervision, I am ready to provide paralegal support service to your staff in any area of law.

I am eager to continue my career in legal assistance with Any Law Firm, and would like to arrange for a meeting at your convenience. I will phone your office on April 26 to discuss this further.

I look forward to speaking with you.

Yours sincerely,

Chris Smith

Enc. resume

■ Closing expresses enthusiasm for follow-up phone contact.

■ Interest in new field is emphasized.

"COLD" LETTER TO A POTENTIAL EMPLOYER
(Legal Associate)

178 Green Street
New York, NY 10128

July 10, 1996

Pat Cummings
Hiring Officer
Any Law Firm
1140 Main Street
Syracuse, NY 13221

Dear Ms. Cummings:

I am enclosing a copy of my resume for your review. Please consider me for an associate position with Any Law Firm.

During the past several years, my efforts have been concentrated in law-related positions while completing my requirements for a Juris Doctor degree from Yale Law School. These positions gave me the opportunity to gain firsthand experience in those areas of the legal profession dealing with real estate, corporate finance, and litigation, which required legal drafting and research skills. As a result of my studies, I was admitted to the Connecticut Bar in December 1995.

I would like the opportunity to meet with you for further discussion. I am very interested in joining your firm and would look forward to an interview at your earliest convenience. I can be reached at the above address or by phone between 6 p.m. and 10 p.m. at (212) 555-5555.

Sincerely,

Chris Smith

Enc. resume

■ Impressive educational background strengthens cover letter.

■ Closing cites specific times candidate may be reached.

"COLD" LETTER TO A POTENTIAL EMPLOYER
(Librarian)

178 Green Street
Boston, MA 02215

December 28, 1996

Pat Cummings
Director, Personnel
Any Library
1140 Main Street
Cambridge, MA 02138

Dear Mr. Cummings:

I am an experienced researcher who has worked extensively with archival records and secondary sources. Currently, I am seeking an opportunity to apply my acquired research skills to a full-time position as a Librarian.

My training has emphasized the importance of precise organization and the thoughtful use of evidence to make clear historical arguments, and my work in the Library of Congress, the Boston Public Library, and the Hauptstaatarchiv Stuttgart has shown me the usefulness of these skills in an actual research environment. As a Librarian and as a Consultant at Boston University, I have gained valuable experience supervising staff members, working directly with students and professors, and choosing and instructing departments on new reference procedures. I have also achieved expertise in the following areas: WordPerfect, automated library reference networks, copying, and filing.

I would welcome the opportunity to work at Any Library. I have enjoyed my time at Boston University, yet am eager to put my skills to work in a nonacademic environment.

Enclosed please find a copy of my resume, which summarizes my qualifications. I will be glad to furnish any additional information that you desire, and you may reach me at (617) 555-5555 to discuss opportunities. I look forward to speaking with you.

Thank you very much for your consideration.

Sincerely,

Chris Smith

Enc. resume

■ Letter tailors experience and skills to position applied for.

■ Type of position desired is clearly stated.

"COLD" LETTER TO A POTENTIAL EMPLOYER
(Manufacturer)

178 Green Street
Little Compton, RI 02837
(401) 555-5555

August 27, 1996

Pat Cummings
Personnel Manager
Any Corporation
1140 Main Street
Chicago, IL 60605

Dear Ms. Cummings:

During the past fourteen years, my experience has been in all phases of custom casework and millwork manufacturing. Currently, I am investigating new opportunities in the Chicago area where my family and I are planning permanent relocation.

The enclosed resume summarizes my background and experience in the above areas. I am highly motivated, profit-oriented, and recognized for my ability to direct a manufacturing function and produce quality goods within cost-budget and time schedules.

I am very much interested in joining your organization, and am currently available for interviews. I will call you on Wednesday, September 4, to confirm that you received my resume and answer any questions you might have.

Sincerely,

Chris Smith

Enc. resume

■ Letter is short and to the point.

■ Closing indicates specific date when candidate will follow up inquiry.

"COLD" LETTER TO A POTENTIAL EMPLOYER
(Marketing Director)

178 Green Street
Ada, OK 74820
(405) 555-5555

January 2, 1996

Pat Cummings
Director of Recruiting
Any Corporation
1140 Main Street
Sandy Springs, SC 29677

Dear Mr. Cummings:

It takes a seasoned marketing professional to provide the leadership, motivation, and strategies to introduce new products, develop profitable territories, and direct a productive and profitable organization in marketing. I have the experience and skills to build a sound customer base for your firm and feel we have good reason to meet.

I offer extensive marketing experience including twenty years as Director of Marketing for a multimillion-dollar sportswear manufacturer. This position required the successful establishment of new markets and major contacts regionally and nationally. During my time in that position, I was able to secure thirteen long-term contracts with national retail chains.

Currently, I am seeking a new association with a company that can benefit from my expertise. I would welcome the opportunity for a personal interview that would allow me to further expand on my background and help us determine the mutual benefits joining your firm would imply.

I will call you the week of January 22 to arrange a mutually convenient meeting time. Thank you for your consideration.

Yours sincerely,

Chris Smith

Enc. resume

■ Candidate immediately expresses suitability for desired position.

■ Summary of experience highlights candidate's achievements.

"COLD" LETTER TO A POTENTIAL EMPLOYER
(Marketing/Development Executive)

178 Green Street
Troy, MI 48098
(313) 555-5555

June 14, 1996

Pat Cummings
Staff Manager
Any Corporation
1140 Main Street
Grand Rapids, MI 49503

Dear Ms. Cummings:

During twenty years of employment with major corporations such as Peters and Miller, B.K. Murphy Company, and Bennett Trade Company, I played a key role in marketing as well as the development and introduction of new product lines at national and regional levels.

Currently, I am seeking a new position in which I can utilize my marketing expertise to provide planning and support to a chief executive officer or general manager with marketing responsibility.

The enclosed business profile summarizes my experience in the development, marketing, and sale of food and nonfood products for domestic, overseas, and military markets. I am very much interested in your company and its products and welcome the opportunity to meet with you at your convenience. In the interim, should you require additional information, please do not hesitate to contact me.

Sincerely,

Chris Smith

Enc. business profile

■ Letter indicates how candidate contributed to his/her previous employers.

■ Letter relies on action verbs rather than passive verbs for emphasis.

"COLD" LETTER TO A POTENTIAL EMPLOYER
(Marketing Intern)

178 Green Street
Augusta, GA 30901
(706) 555-5555

July 21, 1996

Pat Cummings
Personnel Director
Any Corporation
1140 Main Street
Detroit, MI 48226

Dear Mr. Cummings:

My interest in a marketing internship with your reputable firm has prompted me to forward my resume for your review.

As a fourth-year student and candidate for a Bachelor of Arts degree in Marketing, I am looking for an opportunity to develop my skills in marketing and product management. In return, I offer academic marketing experience, superb written and verbal skills, and a keen desire to learn the ins and outs of the marketing business.

I will call your office the week of July 28 to schedule an interview. Thank you for your consideration, and I look forward to speaking with you.

Yours sincerely,

Chris Smith

Enc. resume

- Letter emphasizes valuable skills.
- Powerful adjectives, when used sparingly, ensure maximum impact.

"COLD" LETTER TO A POTENTIAL EMPLOYER
(Massage Therapist)

178 Green Street
Houston, TX 77091
(713) 555-5555

July 5, 1996

Pat Cummings
Massage Therapist
Any Clinic
1140 Main Street
Dallas, TX 75738

Dear Ms. Cummings:

I am a graduate of the Morgan School of Massage Therapy and a Licensed Therapist with experience in several innovative methods of massage therapy. I am confident that Any Clinic continues to believe in and encourage the therapeutic advantages of massage therapy, since becoming the first organization in Dallas to institute these practices. For this reason, I would like to submit my credentials for consideration in reference to any job availability for a Massage Therapist.

With twelve years of experience, I have the specialized professional training and practical skills to evaluate and provide clients with the treatment that will best address problems relating to cure, rehabilitation, or general health maintenance. I am dedicated to applying these acquired skills and feel confident that I can provide Any Clinic with the ethical, professional services you would expect from a Licensed Massage Therapist.

The enclosed resume briefly summarizes my experiences. I would be glad to meet with you at your convenience. I look forward to hearing from you.

Sincerely,

Chris Smith

Enc. resume

- Including professional accreditation and licensure may be advantageous for certain kinds of work.

- Specific company information illustrates candidate's commitment to his/her field.

"COLD" LETTER TO A POTENTIAL EMPLOYER
(Mechanical Engineer)

178 Green Street
Laconia, NH 03102
(603) 555-5555

January 6, 1996

Pat Cummings
Recruitment Officer
Any Corporation
1140 Main Street
Newark, NJ 07101

Dear Mr. Cummings:

For more than twenty years, I have been actively involved in precision machining work encompassing the development of working prototypes, specialty machine building/design, and precision tool/die production for high-speed equipment.

My work is diverse and challenging, and it requires talent and technical skill to evaluate needs and solve complex problems. While I have been challenged by my previous experiences, I would like to join a professional group where I can concentrate my skills on the design and development of prototypes and models that are part of projects on the leading edge of discovery.

I have hands-on experience with the use, maintenance, and programming of all types of mechanical and hydraulic equipment used in precision machining, and can provide you with the quality work necessary for your purposes.

Should you have any questions, please contact me at the above address or by phone. I plan to make a follow-up call on January 14.

I look forward to your return response.

Yours sincerely,

Chris Smith

Enc. resume

■ Discussion of experience clearly spells out candidate's area of expertise.

■ Qualifications highlight candidate's problem-solving ability.

"COLD" LETTER TO A POTENTIAL EMPLOYER
(Multimedia Manager)

178 Green Street
Cinnaminson, NJ 08077
(609) 555-5555

November 1, 1996

Pat Cummings
Hiring Director
Any Corporation
1140 Main Street
Chicago, IL 60605

Dear Ms. Cummings:

As a member of the Newark Computer Society, I am very interested in Any Corporation's growth and innovation in the field of multimedia technology. I am currently conducting a job search in the Chicago area, and would like to apply for a position within your management structure.

During the past fourteen years, my experience has ranged from Senior Auditor with Keane & Co. Peripherals to my current position as Vice-President/Controller of a $90 million, multiplant CD-ROM manufacturing operation. I believe that my expertise and entrepreneurial insight can be utilized to the advantage of a growing enterprise with a need for effective and efficient financial management and cost control.

If your company can use a profit-oriented and financially astute executive, I would like to discuss my qualifications with you during a personal interview. Thank you for your time and consideration.

Sincerely,

Chris Smith

Enc. resume

■ Discussion details how candidate's qualifications will benefit potential employer.

■ Candidate clearly expresses eagerness to work for specific employer.

"COLD" LETTER TO A POTENTIAL EMPLOYER
(Mutual Funds Broker)

178 Green Street
Honolulu, HI 96813
(808) 555-5555

April 14, 1996

Pat Cummings
Controller
Any Corporation
1140 Main Street
Chicago, IL 60611

Dear Mr. Cummings:

I am writing to inquire about employment opportunities within your organization, which, according to *Money Managers' Report*, is the fastest-growing mutual funds broker in the country.

I have been involved in the areas of sales and business for the past twenty years. On "Black Monday" I solidified a $1 million lease in the largest mall in the West, and then consummated the agreement during one of the worst economic scares since the Depression of the 1930's. I am the only private broker to raise construction money from Warga Property Investors, the top-grossing real estate trust in the world.

I am a highly motivated and principled professional who knows that her energy level, expertise, and commitment to success will produce results. I would be interested in meeting with you to discuss your current or anticipated needs in terms of my qualifications and career objectives. I will contact your office in the coming weeks to schedule an interview.

Thank you for your consideration.

Sincerely,

Chris Smith

Enc. resume

■ Introduction expresses candidate's knowledge of firm.

■ Use of concrete examples highlights candidate's achievements.

"COLD" LETTER TO A POTENTIAL EMPLOYER
(Nurse)

178 Green Street
New York, NY 10128

September 9, 1996

Pat Cummings
Nursing Director
Any Hospital
1140 Main Street
Pittsburgh, PA 15217

Dear Ms. Cummings:

I am eager to continue my professional nursing career in a midsize metropolitan hospital, and am especially interested in your organization's widely respected Disease Task Force Unit. Please consider the enclosed resume as application for suitable positions at Any Hospital.

Please note that in addition to fourteen years of experience ranging from Staff Nurse (ER) to Head Nurse/Supervisor (orthopedics/OR), I have extensive, ongoing responsibilities in areas of staff selection and training, purchasing/vendor negotiations, budget responsibilities, and committee and task force implementation and involvement.

I am presently planning to relocate permanently to Pennsylvania, and I am seeking serious interviews for the near future. I would welcome the opportunity to put my experience to work for Any Hospital, and I feel confident that I can make an immediate and valuable contribution to your facility.

In the interim, I can be reached at the above address or by phone at (212) 555-5555. I look forward to hearing from you soon.

Sincerely,

Chris Smith

Enc. resume

■ Experience reinforces candidate's professional objective.

■ Career objective gives focus without limiting candidate's opportunities.

"COLD" LETTER TO A POTENTIAL EMPLOYER
(Nurse: Anesthesia)

178 Green Street
Trenton, NJ 08618
(609) 555-5555

April 3, 1996

Pat Cummings
Human Resources Coordinator
Any Hospital
1140 Main Street
Trenton, NJ 08618

Dear Dr. Cummings:

As a recent graduate of the New Jersey Medical Center School of Nurse
Anesthesia, I am anxious to explore the possibility of a position within your
anesthesia department.

In addition to technical academic course work and extensive exposure to the
administration of anesthetics during all surgical specialties, I have six years of
professional experience in med/surg and SICU nursing. I established and maintain
an excellent record for dedication, quality of direct patient care, and clinical
interface with multidiscipline health care systems.

I offer a strong work ethic comprised of flexibility, reliability, and stamina. I
consider myself a professional dedicated to providing patients with the highest
quality of health care throughout the treatment and recovery processes.

I will call you within the week to schedule a mutually convenient time to meet.
Thank you for your time.

Sincerely,

Chris Smith

Enc. resume

■ Only relevant educational training
is included.

■ Closing specifies that candidate
will follow up inquiry.

"COLD" LETTER TO A POTENTIAL EMPLOYER
(Office Manager)

178 Green Street
Kingsport, TN 37660

January 11, 1996

Pat Cummings
Director of Human Resources
Any Corporation
1140 Main Street
Yukon, MO 65589

Dear Mr. Cummings:

My interest in associating with an established firm such as Any Corporation has prompted me to forward my resume, which briefly summarizes my experience in office and department management.

As Office/Department Manager, I was responsible for directing and coordinating the activities of accounting and support personnel in a $10 million manufacturing operation. I concurrently managed the cutting room and handled the purchasing of approximately $5 million in raw materials, supplies, and capital equipment used in manufacturing, sales, and distribution of branded and private label products through mass merchandisers.

This position required entrepreneurial skills and the capability to "wear many hats" in a small, active manufacturing operation. During my six years at Kimco, the company increased profits and was able to expand its staff by 15 percent.

I would appreciate the opportunity to discuss, on a one-on-one basis, openings within your company. I can be reached at the above address or by phone at (615) 555-5555. If I do not receive a response, I will call within a few days to arrange a mutually convenient meeting time.

Sincerely,

Chris Smith

Enc. resume

■ Candidate's most recent position is outlined in detail.

■ Dollar amounts quantify candidate's accomplishments.

"COLD" LETTER TO A POTENTIAL EMPLOYER
(Operations Executive)

178 Green Street
Alexandria, LA 71301
(703) 555-5555

March 17, 1996

Pat Cummings
Hiring Manager
Any Corporation
1140 Main Street
Birmingham, AL 35229

Dear Ms. Cummings:

If you are in need of an aggressive, highly motivated Operations Executive, then we have good reason to meet.

During the past twelve years, I have held progressively responsible positions ranging from Field Representative to General Manager of a $10 million multibranch operation. Currently, I am seeking an opportunity to apply this experience to foster the growth and profits of your company through greater market penetration and increased sales volume.

The enclosed resume summarizes my background and experience. I am very interested in joining the operations team at Any Corporation and feel that I can produce the same beneficial results for your firm as I have for prior employers. I would consider a personal discussion to be mutually advantageous. I am open to relocation and/or travel, and the compensation package is negotiable.

I will call your office on March 26 to follow up on my inquiry. Thank you for your time and consideration.

Sincerely,

Chris Smith

Enc. resume

■ Closing thanks addressee in advance for attention.

■ Introductory sentence draws attention.

"COLD" LETTER TO A POTENTIAL EMPLOYER
(Operations Manager)

178 Green Street
Santa Ana, CA 97201
(714) 555-5555

April 10, 1996

Pat Cummings
Staff Director
Any Corporation
1140 Main Street
St. Petersburg, FL 35701

Dear Mr. Cummings:

I am presently searching for a position at the decision-making level in areas of
customer service/sales support. I read about Any Corporation's recent expansion
in this month's *Investing Now,* and am interested in exploring employment
opportunities at your firm.

Please note that my fifteen years of broad-based management experience
encompasses a full range of customer service functions. Most recently my talents
were put to use as Customer Service Manager for a well-established and growing
computer service company providing computer systems, time-sharing business
application programs, software packages, and associated support services
internationally. My intensive experience in sophisticated aspects of customer
support management includes on-site training of customer staff and management
in diverse computer business and manufacturing applications, and associated sales
support activities. I am willing to relocate for the right opportunity.

I would like to arrange a mutually convenient time for a meeting, during which we
may further discuss your current or anticipated needs. I will call your office next
week to schedule an interview.

Thank you for your consideration.

Sincerely,

Chris Smith

Enc. resume

■ Letter emphasizes candidate's
strong work history.

■ Relevant work experience is
emphasized while other positions
are omitted.

"COLD" LETTER TO A POTENTIAL EMPLOYER
(Pharmacy Director)

178 Green Street
Santa Clara, CA 95053

June 22, 1996

Pat Cummings
Director, Health Care Services
Any Corporation
1140 Main Street
Colorado Springs, CO 80903

Dear Ms. Cummings:

As Assistant Director of Pharmacy with a high-volume, forty-store chain, I have
the management and sales expertise to deal with multidiscipline health care
professionals necessary to fill a position within the management structure of your
organization.

In addition to holding a Bachelor of Science in Pharmacy, I am a Registered
Pharmacist with eight years of progressively responsible experience encompassing
general management and in-house and field sales experience in a rapid growth
environment.

I am well versed in regulations controlling therapeutic drug treatment, have sound
knowledge of medical terminology, work well in an independent setting or team
effort, and enjoy the clinical and nonclinical but professional aspects of services
involving health care products or services. Based on my experience and
professional qualifications, I consider myself to be well qualified to handle the
responsibilities of a management position.

I hope to hear from you to schedule a personal interview at your convenience. I
can be reached at the above address or at (408) 555-5555 from 9:00 a.m. to 5:00
p.m. weekdays or at (408) 555-4444 on weekends. I am willing to relocate for the
right compensation package.

Sincerely,

Chris Smith

Enc. resume

■ Candidate immediately introduces his/her qualifications.

■ Experiences are tailored to employer's needs.

"COLD" LETTER TO A POTENTIAL EMPLOYER
(Plant Manager)

178 Green Street
Little Rock, AR 72204
(501) 555-5555

July 7, 1996

Pat Cummings
Personnel Manager
Any Corporation
1140 Main Street
Chicago, IL 60605

Dear Mr. Cummings:

Are you looking for a competent plant manager who will effectively handle all aspects involved in the smooth operation of your organization? If so, I would like to present my attached, confidential resume for your consideration.

Please note that, in addition to more than five years of vocational training and hands-on experience with automated, semiautomated, and mechanical plant equipment and systems, I have also been involved in purchasing and negotiations. Although presently employed in a responsible position, I feel that an association with your firm may offer better growth potential than I can foresee with my present employer.

Thank you for your consideration. I look forward to hearing from you.

Sincerely,

Chris Smith

Enc. resume

■ Letter is easy and quick to read, and only relevant details are included.

■ Letter suggests discretion.

"COLD" LETTER TO A POTENTIAL EMPLOYER
(Printer)

178 Green Street
Athens, GA 30601
(404) 555-5555

May 29, 1996

Pat Cummings
Manager, Production Department
Any Corporation
1140 Main Street
Atlanta, GA 30340

Dear Ms. Cummings:

My interest in a position in printing or related areas of graphic arts prompts me to forward my resume for your review.

During the past six years, I have been employed with a major insurance company where I rapidly advanced from an entry-level position to Operator of a Xerox 9900 printing system. This experience, combined with my formal education in graphic arts, college-level courses in business administration, and experience in various areas of retail business operations, has equipped me with a sound background. I am confident of my ability to make a creative and productive contribution as a member of your publication and training department.

I will be spending a week, from July 27 to August 3, in your area prior to permanent relocation. I hope to meet during my visit, and would like to hear from you to set a convenient time and date for an interview. At that time, we will have the opportunity to discuss your requirements and my ability to handle the responsibilities of a position at Any Corporation.

I look forward to your return response.

Sincerely,

Chris Smith

Enc. resume

■ Closing provides specific time frame to allow for meeting.

■ Candidate expresses knowledge in his/her field of interest.

"COLD" LETTER TO A POTENTIAL EMPLOYER
(Production Manager)

178 Green Street
Tampa, FL 33620
(813) 555-5555

January 13, 1996

Pat Cummings
Vice-President, Operations
Any Corporation
1140 Main Street
Babson Park, FL 33827

Dear Mr. Cummings:

If you are in need of an experienced manager skilled in production planning, scheduling, and control for a quality production operation, then we have good reason to meet.

During the past seven years, I have held progressively responsible positions, leading to Senior Production Control/Personal Computer Planner in a multiple product line operation. This association has offered me the opportunity for personal development, while contributing to the company's rapid growth.

My complex and diverse assignments requires that I troubleshoot, investigate, and resolve problems by developing solutions that are cost-efficient, increase production, and improve quality during high-volume production.

Although my position is secure, I feel it is time for a change to a position that offers greater responsibility, as well as the authority to make decisions in the best interest of the company.

My achievements in the past attest to my ability to contribute to a winning team. I am anxious to discuss how I may continue to uphold my personal standards of excellence while a part of Any Corporation. For this reason, I will call to schedule a mutually convenient interview time.

I look forward to speaking with you.

Yours sincerely,

Chris Smith

Enc. employment profile

- One page is standard length for cover letters.

- Unrelated work experience is omitted.

"COLD" LETTER TO A POTENTIAL EMPLOYER
(Project Manager)

178 Green Street
Deer Park, NY 11729

March 19, 1996

Pat Cummings
Recruitment Manager
Any Corporation
1140 Main Street
New York, NY 10022

Dear Ms. Cummings:

During the past eight years, I have been actively involved as a Mechanical
Engineer and Project Manager with companies specializing in commercial
building and highway bridge reconstruction as well as full turnkey nuclear and
fossil fuel plant construction.

Presently, I am phasing out of a general management position, and looking to
make a new association with a firm where I can apply my combined technical,
management, and administrative skills to achieve cost-effective and profitable
competition of heavy construction or engineering projects.

The enclosed resume summarizes my background and experience in the above
areas. I am presently available for an interview and would like to arrange a time at
your convenience.

I can be reached at the above address or by phone at (516) 555-5555. I am
sincerely interested in position possibilities offered by your firm, and plan to make
a follow-up call within a few days.

Sincerely,

Chris Smith

Enc. resume

■ Candidate does not limit available
opportunities by stating specific
position desired.

■ Letter avoids abbreviations and
slang.

"COLD" LETTER TO A POTENTIAL EMPLOYER
(Property Manager)

178 Green Street
Mill Valley, CA 94941
(415) 555-5555

May 19, 1996

Pat Cummings
Personnel Director
Any Corporation
1140 Main Street
Fresno, CA 93786

Dear Mr. Cummings:

I am writing to investigate opportunities in which I could apply my skills to
property management and real estate investments with your company's holdings.

As you will note, I have more than fifteen years' experience in general property
management, including both residential and commercial properties. During the
past five years, I have managed an absentee-owner property management company
which has grown from 400 to 750 units while maintaining a vacancy rate below 5
percent. I offer a thorough knowledge of all aspects of property management, from
locating, negotiating, and acquiring property through leasing, maintenance, and
financial management.

I strongly believe my qualifications would prove to be an asset to Any
Corporation. I would greatly appreciate the opportunity to present my skills in a
personal interview.

Thank you for your time and consideration.

Sincerely,

Chris Smith

Enc. resume

■ Letter focuses attention on
candidate's major skills and
accomplishments.

■ Enclosure line suggests candidate
is a meticulous, detail-orientated
professional.

"COLD" LETTER TO A POTENTIAL EMPLOYER
(Public Relations Assistant)

178 Green Street
Wheatland, ND 58079
(701) 555-5555

September 10, 1996

Pat Cummings
Vice-President, Human Resources
Zepf, Costigan, and Nardizzi
1140 Main Street
Los Angeles, CA 90053

Dear Ms. Cummings:

Please accept the enclosed copy of my resume as a preliminary application for a position with Zepf, Costigan, and Nardizzi.

In addition to my degree in Journalism and Public Relations, I have four years of experience working with a modeling/talent agency and a modeling school. In both the teaching and model recruitment/placement environments, I have worked with key accounts in areas where image building and high visibility for client services or products was the ultimate objective. These activities also included selection and placement of models for union and nonunion television commercials. I have the skills to coordinate creative programs and innovative functions involving clients and the general public, and feel confident that I could successfully apply my experience to a position in your firm.

I will be in the Los Angeles area at the end of the month and will call your office during the week of September 24. I look forward to talking with you.

Sincerely,

Chris Smith

Enc. resume

- Discussion of experience is very specific.
- Letter emphasizes valuable skills.

"COLD" LETTER TO A POTENTIAL EMPLOYER
(Quality Control Specialist)

178 Green Street
San Bernardino, CA 92403

May 27, 1996

Pat Cummings
Director, Personnel
Any Corporation
1140 Main Street
Burbank, CA 91510

Dear Mr. Cummings:

During the past twelve years, my experience has been concentrated in quality assurance and quality control in the coated paper and plastics industry.

I have remained with the company through several acquisitions and staff reductions and in each case, have advanced to positions of broader responsibility. However, I feel it is time for a change. I would like to join a firm that has a need for someone like myself, skilled in the development of preventive maintenance programs that improve productivity, material handling procedures, and inventory availability.

I am thoroughly experienced with quality control methods and environmental regulations involving material waste processing and disposal, and I am fully qualified to supervise and coordinate a full range of quality control/assurance activities in a high-volume, custom product manufacturing or processing operation.

The enclosed resume is a summary of my background and experience. If you are in need of additional information, please contact me at the above address or by phone at (714) 555-5555.

I am very interested in opportunities with Any Corporation and look forward to hearing from you.

Sincerely,

Chris Smith

Enc. resume

■ Telephone number included in closing is omitted in return address.

■ Letter focuses on candidate's past job experience while incorporating functional qualifications.

"COLD" LETTER TO A POTENTIAL EMPLOYER
(Real Estate Banker)

178 Green Street
Sunnyvale, CA 94088
(408) 555-5555

August 3, 1996

Pat Cummings
Associate Director
Any Bank
1140 Main Street
Newtown Square, PA 19093

Dear Ms. Cummings:

I am interested in exploring opportunities within the real estate
investment/mortgage lending department of Any Bank. Should you be in need of
someone with my qualifications, I would be eager to lend assistance to your
organization.

In addition to a Bachelor of Science degree in Management with a major in
Finance and a real estate salesperson's license, I have diverse experience in
positions that have required strong communication and interpersonal skills in
dealing with associates, customers, and personnel. My current position as Portfolio
Administrator/Fund Accountant is diverse and detailed; however, I am interested
in applying my financial background to areas involving new business development
and account administration.

I am confident that my skills and abilities could benefit Any Bank. I would
appreciate the opportunity to talk with you regarding suitable opportunities within
your organization.

Sincerely,

Chris Smith

Enc. resume

■ Including professional
  accreditation and licensure may
  be advantageous for certain kinds
  of work.

■ Letter immediately refers
  addressee to attached resume.

"COLD" LETTER TO A POTENTIAL EMPLOYER
(Repair Technician)

178 Green Street
Sioux Falls, SD 57105
(605) 555-5555

January 29, 1996

Pat Cummings
Repair Maintenance Operator
Any Corporation
1140 Main Street
Salt Lake City, UT 84111

Dear Mr. Cummings:

Please accept the enclosed resume as an expressed interest in exploring employment opportunities available in the repair and maintenance division of Any Corporation.

I have acquired training and extensive experience in the installation and repair of various heating, electrical, and power systems for commercial, industrial, and residential properties. My employment has required that I develop proficiency in the fabrication of plumbing systems and in the coordination of repair service for equipment malfunctions. In various management capabilities, I have facilitated all administrative and fiscal operations for service companies and managed personnel. I possess exceptional communication, leadership, and troubleshooting skills. In response to an increasingly multicultural industry, I possess a fluency in Portuguese and conversational abilities in Spanish and French. I feel that my accomplishments have prepared me to assume the responsibilities demanded at Any Corporation.

I would welcome the opportunity to meet with you and discuss ways in which my capabilities could be guided to suit your needs. Please consider the enclosed and direct your response to the above address or telephone number. I will follow up this correspondence with a phone call early next week.

I look forward to speaking with you in the near future. Thank you for your time.

With best regards,

Chris Smith

Enc. resume

■ Foreign language skills strengthen candidate's qualifications.

■ Closing refers addressee to telephone number in return address.

"COLD" LETTER TO A POTENTIAL EMPLOYER
(Research Assistant)

178 Green Street
Manchester, NH 03104
(603) 555-5555

July 31, 1996

Pat Cummings
Human Resources Director
Any Bank
1140 Main Street
Chicago, IL 60605

Dear Ms. Cummings:

Having majored in Mathematics at Rice University, where I also worked as a
Research Assistant, I am confident that I would make a successful addition to your
economics research department.

In addition to my strong background in mathematics, I offer significant business
experience, having worked in a data processing firm, a bookstore, and a restaurant.
I am sure that my courses in statistics and computer programming would prove
particularly useful in an entry-level position.

I am attracted to Any Bank by your recent rapid growth and the superior
reputation of your economic research department. After studying different
commercial banks, I have concluded that Any Bank will be in a strong competitive
position to benefit from upcoming changes in the industry, such as the phasing out
of Regulation X.

I would like to interview with you at your earliest convenience.

Sincerely,

Chris Smith

Enc. resume

■ Closing reiterates candidate's
company knowledge.

■ Letter includes course work that
corresponds to position desired.

"COLD" LETTER TO A POTENTIAL EMPLOYER
(Retail Sales Manager)

178 Green Street
Fairfax, VA 22030

April 11, 1996

Pat Cummings
Retail Sales Director
Any Corporation
1140 Main Street
Charleston, WV 25301

Dear Mr. Cummings:

During the past twenty years, I have played a key role in the development of new markets and increased profitability for the sales of women's and junior apparel to large department stores and mass merchandisers.

Currently, I am seeking a new association with a company that can benefit from my expertise as a highly productive, dynamic, profit-oriented manager with a proven record of achievement in sales and sales management. Additionally, I have a consistent record for achieving sales goals, expanding market share, reducing costs, and increasing profits.

The enclosed resume summarizes my background and experience. If Any Corporation can use an executive who is qualified to assume responsibility for the profitable direction of expanding or diversifying market strategy, I would like to discuss my qualifications with you during a personal interview.

I look forward to an opportunity to produce the same beneficial results for your corporation as I have for previous employers. I can be reached at the above address or by phone at (703) 555-5555.

Thank you for your consideration.

Yours sincerely,

Chris Smith

Enc. resume

■ Dynamic action verbs give letter impact.

■ Background summary accentuates candidate's acquired professional skills and impressive track record.

"COLD" LETTER TO A POTENTIAL EMPLOYER
(Retail Salesperson)

178 Green Street
Cherry Fork, OH 95618
(513) 555-5555

July 21, 1996

Pat Cummings
Hiring Manager
Any Corporation
1140 Main Street
Cincinnati, OH 45202

Dear Ms. Cummings:

During the past three years as a Sales Representative with Fits Like a Glove, Inc., I have successfully sold to and serviced retail accounts throughout the midwestern states. In this capacity, I established a record for the development of new business and solid client relationships which have generated additional business and referrals. As principal owner, I managed all areas of independent department store operations specializing in family ready-to-wear accessories, athletic wear, and athletic footwear and equipment.

Currently I am looking for a new opportunity where I can utilize my sales, merchandising, management, and communications skills to contribute to the efficiency and bottom-line results of a firm providing quality products and service to a diverse consumer population or dealer network.

Among retailers, Any Corporation's name emerges as the industry leader with respect to aggressive sales techniques. I feel that I can be a valuable part in such an environment.

I will call your office to schedule an interview. Thank you for your consideration and I look forward to speaking with you.

Sincerely,

Chris Smith

Enc. resume

- Summary of experience highlights candidate's achievements.
- Closing reiterates candidate's knowledge of organization.

"COLD" LETTER TO A POTENTIAL EMPLOYER
(Sales Executive)

178 Green Street
Beetown, WI 53802

June 6, 1996

Pat Cummings
Staff Coordinator
Any Corporation
1140 Main Street
Milwaukee, WI 53201

Dear Mr. Cummings:

Your firm has been brought to my attention as one that can provide the challenge, diversification, and stability I am looking for in a company.

For over fifteen years, I have held progressively more responsible jobs selling industrial and agricultural chemicals, pharmaceuticals, and related products with a multinational manufacturer and distributor. I am an effective time and territory manager, have sound knowledge of sales techniques and strategies, and have been successful in new business and marketing development in each position held.

The enclosed resume summarizes my background and experience. I am interested in permanent relocation to your area, but I am willing to travel.

I am highly productive, profit oriented, and cost conscious, and can contribute much to increasing your share of the market. I feel that a meeting, at your convenience, could be mutually beneficial. I can be reached at the above address or by phone at (414) 555-5555.

Yours sincerely,

Chris Smith

Enc. resume

■ Willingness to travel can be advantageous.

■ Candidate details applicable work experience.

"COLD" LETTER TO A POTENTIAL EMPLOYER
(School Administrator: Secondary Level)

178 Green Street
Hartford, CT 06120
(203) 555-5555

July 14, 1996

Pat Cummings
Superintendent
Any Public School
1140 Main Street
Bridgeport, CT 06604

Dear Dr. Cummings:

During the past twelve years as Principal of Murray Central High School,
I have had the opportunity to provide leadership in a multiracial, multilingual
urban high school during a complex, volatile era. Please accept the enclosed
resume as an application for an administrative position with Any Public School.

My positions with the Murray School System have been challenging and
have provided a setting where I was able to develop a variety of new programs and
implement existing programs to create a winning tradition of academic excellence.
My purpose was to motivate students toward educational improvement, higher
education, improved self-image, and job preparedness.

In my years with this secondary school, I have achieved the goals I projected
for the school, students, parents, and business and residential community. Now, I
am ready for a change to a school system where I can once again provide the
leadership to uphold and strengthen educational standards and achieve desired
objectives. With my background, experience, proven leadership skills, and
dedication to quality education, I am well qualified and prepared to make the same
commitment to Any Public School.

The enclosed profile is a summary of my experience. I look forward to the
opportunity to discuss, in further detail, my educational philosophy, my ability to
fill your requirements, and why I am qualified for an administrative position at
Any Public School. I look forward to your response.

Yours sincerely,

Chris Smith

Enc. profile

■ Qualifications are geared to candidate's field of interest.

■ Letter indicates how candidate contributed to his/her previous employers.

"COLD" LETTER TO A POTENTIAL EMPLOYER
(Security Specialist)

178 Green Street
Ranier, OR 97048
(503) 555-5555

May 31, 1996

Pat Cummings
Personnel Manager
Any Corporation
1140 Main Street
Chicago, IL 60605

Dear Mr. Cummings:

Are you currently seeking a Security Specialist to maintain or upgrade the security of your organization? If so, I would like to apply for the position.

During the past twenty years, I have gained experience and education encompassing all aspects of law enforcement, and security procedures and implementation.

I feel confident that I can make an immediate contribution to Any Corporation, and I believe that a personal conversation would be to our mutual advantage. I will call your office on Tuesday, June 11, to schedule an appointment at your convenience.

Thank you for your attention. I look forward to speaking with you.

Sincerely,

Chris Smith

Enc. resume

■ Introducing letter with a question draws attention to candidate.

■ Closing is brief and to the point.

"COLD" LETTER TO A POTENTIAL EMPLOYER
(Social Worker: Counseling)

178 Green Street
Fort Worth, TX 76114
(817) 555-5555

March 17, 1996

Pat Cummings
Director, Mental Health Services
Any Center
1140 Main Street
Dallas, TX 75206

Dear Ms. Cummings:

My involvement with a number of local counseling centers has given me the opportunity to become familiar with Any Center's work. My observations of your facility and its staff has confirmed my desire to join your organization in a counseling or group leader capacity.

For the past fifteen years, my experience has ranged from Mental Health Aide to Peer Counselor and Group Leader working with alcoholics, drug abusers, and the mentally/emotionally disabled. I am a candidate for a Master's degree in Counseling/Psychology, and am well trained in alcohol/substance abuse counseling, and the provision of related health care services to individuals and/or groups at all age levels.

I am very interested in joining your staff. I will call your office next week to schedule an interview at your convenience.

Yours sincerely,

Chris Smith

Enc. resume

■ Letter highlights candidate's acquired professional and educational training.

■ Unrelated work experience is omitted.

"COLD" LETTER TO A POTENTIAL EMPLOYER
(Social Worker: Geriatrics)

178 Green Street
Great Falls, MT 59403
(406) 555-5555

July 3, 1996

Pat Cummings
Director, Human Services
Any Corporation
1140 Main Street
Billings, MT 59107

Dear Mr. Cummings:

My interest in continuing my professional career as a clinical social worker in the geriatric area of human services has prompted me to forward my resume for your consideration.

In addition to graduate work, licenses, and registration in the field of social work, I have nine years of professional experience ranging from Psychiatric Caseworker to Clinical/Research Social Worker at Worthy Hospital. Recently, I conducted research and coauthored a publication on geriatrics, an undertaking that has focused my interest on the problems of aging and the older adult population.

I would appreciate meeting with you for further discussion after you review my qualifications. In the interim, please feel free to contact me if you have any questions.

I look forward to learning more about Any Corporation.

Sincerely yours,

Chris Smith

Enc. resume

■ Publication is impressive and adds weight to cover letter.

■ Closing invites addressee to inquire about additional information.

"COLD" LETTER TO A POTENTIAL EMPLOYER
(Social Worker: Medical)

178 Green Street
Geneseo, NY 14454
(716) 555-5555

April 2, 1996

Pat Cummings
Outreach Director
Any Hospital
1140 Main Street
Oneonta, NY 13820

Dear Ms. Cummings:

I am a newly Licensed Medical Social Worker investigating new opportunities in which to apply my education and experience. I am capable of working independently or as a member of a team, and I feel confident in my ability to handle the responsibilities of the position and provide quality performance in any assignment I undertake.

In addition, I offer excellent administrative and clinical experience and am anxious to put my skills to work for Any Hospital.

I look forward to your immediate reply.

Sincerely,

Chris Smith

Enc. resume

- ■ Candidate includes licensure relevant to his/her field.
- ■ Language is straightforward and understandable.

"COLD" LETTER TO A POTENTIAL EMPLOYER
(Telemarketer)

178 Green Street
Juneau, AK 99801
(907) 555-5555

February 23, 1996

Pat Cummings
Director, Marketing
Any Corporation
1140 Main Street
Anchorage, AK 99514

Dear Mr. Cummings:

I am a highly-motivated individual with a proven sales record who is interested in securing a challenging telemarketing position. I have enclosed my resume for your consideration.

During the past ten years, I have been employed as a Telemarketer selling sophisticated products or services to hospitals, institutions, and medical professionals, as well as filtration systems to end-users. During this time, I have successfully increased company sales by 40 percent and have established an impressive customer base. I possess extensive telephone and interpersonal skills, and am proficient with all aspects of office operations, including dBase and Lotus 1-2-3 computer applications.

I feel confident that my experience can be successfully applied to a telemarketing position at Any Corporation. I will call your office next week to discuss this matter further.

Yours sincerely,

Chris Smith

Enc. resume

■ Letter emphasizes achievements, and does not simply list job responsibilities.

■ Letter immediately refers addressee to attached resume.

"COLD" LETTER TO A POTENTIAL EMPLOYER
(Television Production Assistant)

178 Green Street
Hito, HI 96720
(606) 555-5555

June 24, 1996

Pat Cummings
Production Director
Any Television Station
1140 Main Street
Honolulu, HI 96822

Dear Ms. Cummings:

I am very interested in launching a career in the broadcast communications industry, and have enclosed my resume for any entry-level, production positions available at Any Television Station.

This May I graduated from the University of Hawaii-Hito with a Bachelor of Arts degree in Communications. Throughout my education, I have taken relevant broadcast communication courses dealing with production, writing, and research. Also, I was actively involved in the university newspaper. My duties entailed researching events and local talent, conducting interviews, and writing articles for the entertainment section of the paper.

Last summer, I worked as an intern for WBZT-TV's "Island Beat." I was given the opportunity there to coproduce a local talk show which required exceptional organizational and interpersonal skills. I preinterviewed and scheduled guests for the show, handled financial and transportation details, and researched show topics. I also networked resource organizations to locate potential guests and panel members. I believe that with my working knowledge of the broadcast and television industries, combined with my ability to adapt quickly to new situations and activities, I would make a valuable contribution to your station.

I would like to meet to further discuss possible availabilities at Any Television Station and present my qualifications in greater detail. I will be in the Honolulu area the week of July 1, and would appreciate an interview at your convenience.

I look forward to hearing from you.

Sincerely,

Chris Smith

Enc. resume

■ Personal interests and activities are relevant to candidate's field of interest.

■ Internships strengthen candidate's short work history.

"COLD" LETTER TO A POTENTIAL EMPLOYER
(Textile Specialist)

178 Green Street
Bloomington, IN 47405
(812) 555-5555

April 23, 1996

Pat Cummings
Vice-President, Human Resources
Any Corporation
1140 Main Street
Chicago, IL 60601

Dear Mr. Cummings:

During my successful career in textiles, I have advanced to positions of Director of Wool Procurement of an international corporation and Senior Vice-President of a national profit trading center. These responsible positions have provided me with the administrative and management expertise to contribute to the efficiency, growth, and profitability of Any Corporation.

I possess extensive experience in trading, sourcing, purchasing, new market and business development, import/export, and profit center management. Although my current position has been challenging and rewarding, my decision to relocate permanently to Chicago makes it necessary for me to seek new opportunities with a company, such as yours, that can utilize the full scope of my experience to achieve mutual objectives.

I have enclosed a resume for your perusal. As of May 1, I will be residing in Chicago and will be available for an interview at your convenience. I will make a follow-up phone call next Monday to schedule a meeting time.

Sincerely,

Chris Smith

Enc. resume

■ Candidate emphasizes how past business experience can benefit potential employer.

■ Letter cites specific date phone contact will be made.

"COLD" LETTER TO A POTENTIAL EMPLOYER
(Underwriter)

178 Green Street
Syracuse, NY 13221

April 10, 1996

Pat Cummings
Senior Claims Adjuster
Any Corporation
1140 Main Street
New York, NY 10010

Dear Ms. Cummings:

Currently, I am seeking a new association with an underwriter or a corporate
liability insurance department where there is a need for expertise in claims
settlement.

During the past ten years, my experience in the liability insurance field has ranged
from Transcriber to Senior Field Claims Representative. My skills range from
fact-finding analysis to negotiating settlements, demanding strong training and
management skills.

The enclosed resume summarizes my background in the above areas. I am very
much interested in Any Corporation and would be glad to furnish you with
additional information during a personal interview. I can be reached at the above
address or by phone at (315) 555-5555.

Thank you for your consideration.

Sincerely yours,

Chris Smith

Enc. resume

■ First paragraph is short and hard-hitting.

■ Including telephone number is necessary in a cover letter.

"COLD" LETTER TO A POTENTIAL EMPLOYER
(Upper-Level Manager: Accounting)

178 Green Street
Giants Pass, OR 97526
(503) 555-5555

October 21, 1996

Pat Cummings
Controller
Any Corporation
1140 Main Street
Boston, MA 02101

Dear Mr. Cummings:

In the interest of investigating career opportunities with Any Corporation, I am enclosing my resume for your review.

During the past fourteen years, my experience has ranged from Senior Auditor with Hans Anderson and Company, Public Accountants, to Controller, to my current position as Vice-President of a $50 million multiplant manufacturing operation.

The positions have been fast-paced, challenging, broad in scope, and have required strong financial and strategic planning capability. I am a C.P.A. and have the ability to recognize, troubleshoot, and resolve financial and administrative problems. I feel that my experience and entreprenurial insight can be utilized to the advantage of a growing enterprise with a need for effective and efficient financial management and cost control. My proven record of achievement has led to rapid promotions.

If your company can use a profit-oriented and financially astute executive, I would like to discuss my qualifications with you during a personal interview. I can be reached at my home or office, at which time I will be glad to provide you with additional information.

Thank you for your time and consideration.

Sincerely,

Chris Smith

Enc. resume

■ Discussion of experience indicates a series of promotions.

■ Background summary accentuates candidate's acquired professional skills and impressive track record.

"COLD" LETTER TO A POTENTIAL EMPLOYER
(Veterinarian)

178 Green Street
Nanticoke, PA 18634
(717) 555-5555

September 17, 1996

Pat Cummings, D.V.M.
Head Veterinarian
Any Animal Hospital
1140 Main Street
Easton, PA 18042

Dear Dr. Cummings:

I am a graduate of the Wiley College School of Veterinary Medicine where I received my D.V.M. degree in 1995. I am interested in pursuing a career in which I can apply my academic and practical skills.

In addition to a graduate degree and two undergraduate degrees, I offer research and clinical experience obtained through three separate externships which involved studying dairy herds in Switzerland, orangutans in Borneo, and domestic work elephants in India.

As a Medical Engineer for Lorri Electric and a Medical Assistant for a general practitioner, I was exposed to clinical procedures and gained hands-on experience in the installation of and servicing of computerized diagnostic equipment. As a Behavioral Specialist, I worked with clients and families in a psychiatric setting. Based on these experiences and my dedication to the veterinary profession, I believe that I am well suited for this position.

I am eager to offer my skills and experience to Any Animal Hospital. I will contact your office to arrange a time when we may discuss mutually beneficial opportunities.

Sincerely,

Chris Smith, D.V.M.

Enc. resume

■ Educational credentials strengthen cover letter.

■ Internships strengthen candidate's short work history.

"COLD" LETTER TO A POTENTIAL EMPLOYER
(Visual Media Production Assistant)

178 Green Street
San Francisco, CA 94111
(415) 555-5555

October 16, 1996

Pat Cummings
Media Coordinator
Any Corporation
1140 Main Street
Santa Ana, CA 92701

Dear Mr. Cummings:

I am a recent graduate from the University of Southern California seeking opportunities in the photographic and visual media fields. I feel my experiences could provide a significant contribution to your corporation. Some of my accomplishments include:

- Direction and supervision of computer-aided graphic design and manual pasteup procedures for the *College Companion*, the largest college newspaper in California.

- Proficiency in page layout, both manual and electronic; photographic imaging; and computerized scanning procedures.

- Conceiving and producing cover layouts for *The Week Gone By*.

- Hands-on training in electronic still photography, computer graphics, lithography, and illustration.

I am confident that the skills I have acquired both in the classroom and through hands-on experience make me an ideal candidate for a position in visual media production. I would like to meet with you to discuss my qualifications further and will call next week to schedule an interview.

Thank you for your time and consideration.

Yours sincerely,

Chris Smith

Enc. resume

- Bulleting draws attention to major accomplishments.
- College activities are related to candidate's field of study and career objective.

13
Letter to an Employment Agency

 When searching for a job, many candidates rely on the help of employment agencies. These agencies offer services to a wide range of job-seekers, primarily for clerical or support staff positions. Letters addressed to employment agencies should focus on who you are, what type of position you are looking for and in what specific industry, and some of your strongest skills related to that field. In order for the agency to place you in an appropriate position, you should mention personal preferences, including geographic and salary requirements. Conclude your letter with a statement specifically stating how you can be reached, or when you will follow up on your letter.

LETTER TO AN EMPLOYMENT AGENCY
(Accounting Manager)

178 Green Street
Hazelwood, MO 63042
(606) 555-5555

July 18, 1996

Pat Cummings
Director
Any Employment Agency
1140 Main Street
Bridgeton, MO 63042

Dear Ms. Cummings:

The enclosed resume outlines my diverse experience in accounting and finance management. I am in search of an appropriate opportunity in the greater Missouri area.

The following are some of the strengths and capabilities that I can bring to a position:

- Solid understanding of financial statement preparation and review.

- Proficiency at budget preparation and various written analysis.

- Proven ability to organize department goals to meet overall corporate goals.

- Competency in terms of resource management, including people and systems.

- Strong leadership qualities including upgrading and motivating staff resources.

I would welcome the opportunity to meet with you to discuss my background and credentials. Thank you for your time and consideration.

Sincerely,

Chris Smith

Enc. resume

- Bullets inform agency contact of candidate's qualifications.
- Candidate informs agency of geographical preference.

LETTER TO AN EMPLOYMENT AGENCY
(Administrative Assistant)

178 Green Street
Madison, WI 53706

July 17, 1996

Pat Cummings
Representative
Any Employment Agency
1140 Main Street
Milwaukee, WI 53201

Dear Mr. Cummings:

I am searching for an administrative position in the real estate, international finance, or import/export industry. Such a position seems to fit very well with my education and achievements, as well as my career interests.

As a B.A. graduate of the University of Wisconsin's School of Business, I have been thoroughly educated in all aspects of the business environment. In addition, I am a very motivated and ambitious person. While pursuing my academic studies, I was accepted into and participated in the University Study Abroad Program in Tokyo, Japan.

I am interested in pursuing a full-time, entry-level position which would allow me to utilize my computer, administrative, and finance skills, as well as my interests in real estate and travel. I would be willing to relocate, given a salary range of $20,000 to $28,000.

I would appreciate consideration for any suitable opportunities. You can contact me between 8:00 a.m. and 6:00 p.m. weekdays at (608) 555-5555.

Thank you for your consideration.

Sincerely,

Chris Smith

Enc. resume

- Foreign language skills and international exposure, in exchange programs and/or internships, are valuable assets in today's global market.

- When writing to an employment agency, including compensation requirements is optional.

LETTER TO AN EMPLOYMENT AGENCY
(Advertising/Graphic Design Assistant)

178 Green Street
Topeka, KS 66612

April 18, 1996

Pat Cummings
Director
Any Employment Agency
1140 Main Street
St. Paul, MN 55401

Dear Ms. Cummings:

I am writing with the hope that one of your clients in the field of Advertising/
Graphic Design is in need of an entry-level assistant.

I possess strong verbal and written communication skills and pay close attention to
detail, while maintaining a flair for creativity. I feel that I am a well-disciplined,
highly-motivated person with a strong desire to succeed in Advertising/Graphic
Design. To support my enthusiasm, I possess excellent IBM and Macintosh
computer skills and a typing speed of 55 wpm.

Thank you in advance for reviewing the enclosed resume. I would be happy to
further discuss my experience and qualifications with you in person. Please feel
free to contact me at (913) 555-5555 if I can be of further assistance. Once again,
thank you for your consideration.

Sincerely,

Chris Smith

Enc. resume

- Including computer skills may be advantageous for certain fields of work.
- Candidate informs agency contact only of experiences and skills related to his/her field of interest.

LETTER TO AN EMPLOYMENT AGENCY
(Bookkeeper)

178 Green Street
Kunia, HI 96759

July 17, 1996

Pat Cummings
Partner
Any Employment Agency
1140 Main Street
Honolulu, HI 96813

Dear Mr. Cummings:

If one of your clients is in need of a highly motivated Bookkeeper who can handle the day-to-day details necessary to continue a smooth operation, I would appreciate your consideration of my enclosed resume.

During the past nine years, I have gained diverse experience in accounting, bookkeeping, administration, office maintenance, and customer service within the manufacturing, distribution, property management, retail, and automotive services industries. I have sound knowledge of credit policies and collection procedures to control accounts receivable and loss reduction while retaining good customer relations and business.

Although my preference is to stay on the Pacific Coast, I would consider relocation based upon salary, benefits, and future opportunity for growth. My present salary is $28,000.

I am most interested in the opportunities available with your client base and hope to hear from you to arrange a meeting. I can be reached at the above address or by phone at (808) 555-5555.

Sincerely,

Chris Smith

Enc. resume

- Candidate includes all relocation information.
- Candidate includes only applicable skills.

LETTER TO AN EMPLOYMENT AGENCY
(Chemist)

178 Green Street
Tacoma, WA 98405
(206) 555-5555

April 16, 1996

Pat Cummings
Chief Researcher
Any Corporation
1140 Main Street
Wichita, KS 67202

Dear Ms. Cummings:

Thank you for the time you extended to me during our recent conversation. I have enclosed a current resume for your review with reference to one of your client firms.

For the past eight years, my experience has been as a Teacher of Secondary and College-level Chemistry. During the past year, I was one of two educators chosen for the first Henderson Fellowship, where I had the opportunity to apply my education, training, and experience in chemistry and physical science to industry.

It was such an exciting and challenging experience that I am presently investigating new opportunities where I can transfer my technical and teaching skills to a permanent assignment in the corporate arena.

Again, allow me to reiterate my willingness to relocate should an attractive opportunity present itself. I look forward to speaking with you.

Sincerely,

Chris Smith

Enc. resume

■ Candidate thanks addressee for time extended.

■ Awards draw attention to candidate's significant accomplishments.

LETTER TO AN EMPLOYMENT AGENCY
(Claims Processor)

178 Green Street
Tarrytown, NY 10591

December 4, 1996

Pat Cummings
Employment Specialist
Any Employment Agency
1140 Main Street
Bronx, NY 10474

Dear Mr. Cummings:

My interest in securing a position of Claims Processor with one of your client companies has prompted me to forward my resume for your review.

In addition to six years of experience as Home Health Aide, In-patient Claim Representative, and, since 1992, Medical Assistant with Marifield Rehabilitation Hospital, I have sound knowledge of medical terminology, procedure codes, and medical office systems including related computerized applications. I possess an Associate degree in Sociology, graduated as Medical Assistant, and am currently a candidate for an Associate degree in Nursing.

My career objective is to further develop my medical and support skills in areas that will give me the opportunity to contribute to the quality and efficiency of health care. My salary is negotiable, depending on the opportunity.

Should you require additional information, please contact me at the above address or by phone at (914) 555-5555. I can be available for a meeting at your convenience.

Thank you for your consideration.

Sincerely,

Chris Smith

Enc. resume

- Candidate informs agency contact of career goals.
- Candidate informs agency contact of relevant educational training.

LETTER TO AN EMPLOYMENT AGENCY
(Computer Operations Supervisor)

178 Green Street
Sinking Spring, PA 19608
(215) 555-5555

July 14, 1996

Pat Cummings
Associate
Any Employment Agency
1140 Main Street
Lancaster, PA 17605

Dear Ms. Cummings:

During the past several years, I have gained broad-based experience in data communications, telecommunications, and personnel supervision with major information resource corporations. Presently, I am looking for a new association with a firm where I can combine my computer science and supervisory skills.

Should you be aware of any suitable opportunities, please contact me. I look forward to hearing from you.

Sincerely,

Chris Smith

Enc. resume

■ Candidate does not restrict job opportunities.

■ Candidate invites employment contact to respond to inquiry.

LETTER TO AN EMPLOYMENT AGENCY
(Cook)

178 Green Street
Sioux Falls, SD 57117
(605) 555-5555

April 5, 1996

Pat Cummings
Director
Any Employment Agency
1140 Main Street
Dayton, OH 45402

Dear Mr. Cummings:

I will be moving to the Dayton area next month, and would like to submit my qualifications for any suitable opportunities available through your agency.

I am an accomplished cook with experience in a wide variety of food service institutions, including restaurants, catering services, and banquet functions. My areas of expertise include all aspects of food preparation, from ordering ingredients to presentation.

As you can see from my enclosed resume, I most recently worked as a Rounds Cook at the McGuiness Inn. In addition to cooking to order, I performed several supervisory duties, such as scheduling shifts, providing inventory control, and troubleshooting problems.

I will be visiting Dayton to secure housing arrangements during the week of April 15. I would be available to meet with you or a client within this time frame. In the interim, I will call your office next week to see if I can provide you with any additional information.

Thank you in advance for your consideration.

Sincerely,

Chris Smith

Enc. resume

■ Writing to an employment agency may only be applicable for certain service-oriented and/or support positions.

■ Closing provides specific time frame to allow for meeting.

LETTER TO AN EMPLOYMENT AGENCY
(Cosmetologist)

178 Green Street
Arlington, TX 76015

March 4, 1996

Pat Cummings
Associate
Any Employment Agency
1140 Main Street
Fort Worth, TX 76110

Dear Ms. Cummings:

Please accept the enclosed resume as my expressed interest in obtaining your job search assistance.

For the past twenty years, I have been employed in the field of cosmetology, in positions ranging from Hairdresser and Instructor to Owner/Operator of my own salon. I possess a valid cosmetology license and have completed several courses in related subjects. I am thoroughly trained in:

- Instruction of all levels of cosmetology theory and practical applications.
- Store promotions and customer relations.
- Hairdressing, permanents, and hair coloring.
- Manicuring, skin care, and facials.

I am currently investigating opportunities where I can apply these skills in either a training school or salon setting. I would greatly appreciate any assistance you could provide in identifying area employers who might be looking for a professional with my qualifications.

My resume is enclosed. Please feel free to contact me at (817) 555-5555. Thank you.

Sincerely,

Chris Smith

Enc. resume

■ Bullets make cover letter easy to read.

■ Candidate includes training pertinent to his/her field of interest.

LETTER TO AN EMPLOYMENT AGENCY
(Dental Assistant)

178 Green Street
Lafayette, IN 47902
(317) 555-5555

May 3, 1996

Pat Cummings
Associate
Any Employment Agency
1140 Main Street
Indianapolis, IN 46225

Dear Mr. Cummings:

I am a trained Dental Assistant with several years of both clinical and administrative experience. Currently, I am conducting a job search in this area and have heard about your agency's placement record through several acquaintances. Please allow me to familiarize you with my qualifications in an effort to secure your assistance:

- Over six years of experience as a Dental Assistant, contributing to direct patient care and patient relations.

- Honor graduate as a Dental Assistant from National Education Center.

- Sound knowledge of medical terminology and clinical procedures.

- Certified in first aid, cardiopulmonary resuscitation, electrocardiography.

- Additional experience as Receptionist/Secretary with an executive search/management consulting firm, a financial management company, and realty firms.

I would like to find a full-time position in the greater Indianapolis vicinity that would allow me to extensively utilize these skills. My compensation requirement is in the mid- to low-twenties.

If your agency could provide me with any assistance in securing such a position, I would appreciate hearing from you. Also, please contact me if you require any additional information.

I look forward to working with you to find gainful employment.

Sincerely,

Chris Smith

Enc. resume

- Introduction indicates candidate's familiarity with specific agency.
- Professional certification and strong educational background add strength to cover letter.

LETTER TO AN EMPLOYMENT AGENCY
(Director of Operations)

178 Green Street
Dallas, TX 75240

July 26, 1996

Pat Cummings
Director
Any Employment Agency
1140 Main Street
Houston, TX 77251

Dear Ms. Cummings:

If one of your client companies is in need of a person who can handle the day-to-day details necessary to continue a smooth operation, then we have good reason to meet.

During the past twelve years my experience has ranged from Credit and Collection Manager with a high-tech company to Service Coordinator with a manufacturer of sophisticated medical systems. In these capacities, I provided detailed administrative support to senior-level managers, field service engineers, and other department personnel.

I am currently contemplating a change and would like to be considered for a position with a progressive management team. I have expertise in complex manual and computer generated reports, work well independently or as a member of a team, and have extensive troubleshooting, problem-solving, customer service, interpersonal, and communication skills.

Should my qualifications meet the needs of a client, I would be happy to learn of the opportunity. Please note, I am available for immediate, full-time work. I can be reached at (214) 555-5555.

I hope to hear from you soon.

Sincerely,

Chris Smith

Enc. resume

- Candidate informs agency of his/her date of availability.
- First paragraph is short and hard-hitting.

LETTER TO AN EMPLOYMENT AGENCY
(Director of Pharmacy)

178 Green Street
Weston, WV 26452
(304) 555-5555

June 22, 1996

Pat Cummings
Director
Any Employment Agency
1140 Main Street
Clarksburg, WV 26302

Dear Mr. Cummings:

I am a Registered Pharmacist with eight years of progressively responsible experience encompassing general management, in-house, and field sales experience in the pharmaceuticals industry. I would like to request your assistance as a professional employment agency, should one of your clients have a need for a Director of Pharmacy.

I am well versed in regulations controlling therapeutic drug treatment, have sound knowledge of medical terminology, and enjoy the clinical and nonclinical but professional aspects of services involving health care products or services. I am currently seeking a management position supervising either several chain locations or a large in-house staff. I am willing to relocate and/or travel to find the right position. My present salary is $40,000.

I look forward to hearing from you, should my qualifications prove to be a match.

Sincerely,

Chris Smith

Enc. resume

■ Candidate immediately informs employment agency of job objective.

■ Candidate informs agency contact of all relevant information, including travel availability and salary requirements.

LETTER TO AN EMPLOYMENT AGENCY
(Executive Assistant)

178 Green Street
Mobile, AL 36625
(203) 555-5555

July 18, 1996

Pat Cummings
Associate
Any Employment Agency
1140 Main Street
Birmingham, AL 25202

Dear Ms. Cummings:

I am an experienced Executive/Administrative Assistant seeking appropriate
career opportunities in the corporate arena.

In addition to five years of staff experience at Bradstreet and Associates, I have
worked for three years as an Executive Assistant to the President and Executive
Vice-President of a software development company. In that capacity, my
responsibilities included a variety of assignments, both independent and with team
projects, writing and typing executive correspondence, and other administrative
activities. My word processing and spreadsheet expertise includes Microsoft Word
for Windows, Lotus 1-2-3, and Excel, and my technical background enables me to
quickly develop expertise in other such software. I am a very organized, detail-
oriented individual who enjoys staff projects and produces high quality work. My
resume is enclosed.

Should your client needs and my experience prove to be a good match, I would
welcome an opportunity to meet with you.

Sincerely,

Chris Smith

Enc. resume

■ Introductory sentence specifies
position desired.

■ Including computer skills may be
advantageous for certain fields of
work.

LETTER TO AN EMPLOYMENT AGENCY
(Hotel Administrator)

178 Green Street
Murfreesboro, TN 37133

April 2, 1996

Pat Cummings
Manager
Any Employment Agency
1140 Main Street
Nashville, TN 37214

Dear Mr. Cummings:

I would like to request your assistance. I am searching for an avenue to contribute my developed customer relations and administrative skills to a challenging position in a hotel. My qualifications include:

* Well developed interpersonal skills, having dealt with a diversity of clients, professionals, and staff members.
* Detail- and goal-orientated approach to work.
* Ability to function well in high-stress atmosphere.
* Knowledge both EECO and APTEC computers systems.

As my enclosed resume reveals, I have direct experience as a Hotel Clerk in two large capacity institutions. Additionally, my work as a Secretary has provided me with knowledge of basic clerical duties and customer relations.

Please contact me at (615) 555-5555 if you feel that my qualifications match the needs of one of your clients. I would be happy to meet with you for further discussion, should you need any additional information.

I appreciate your consideration of my request.

Sincerely,

Chris Smith

Enc. resume

■ Candidate suggests informational meeting with agency.

■ Bullets inform agency contact of candidate's qualifications.

LETTER TO AN EMPLOYMENT AGENCY
(Housekeeper)

178 Green Street
Melrose Park, IL 60160

March 27, 1996

Pat Cummings
Associate
Any Employment Agency
1140 Main Street
Twin Falls, ID 83303

Dear Ms. Cummings:

My interest in securing a position in housekeeping or related support activities has prompted me to forward my resume for your review.

During the past seven years, my experience has been concentrated in housekeeping and related nonclinical services with a quality professional nursing home operation. I enjoy working with people in a professional or resort environment and feel confident that I can make a contribution to the quality image an institution would like to uphold as a member of its housekeeping staff.

I will be spending a week, from April 27 to May 3, with family in your area prior to permanent relocation. I would welcome the opportunity to meet with you or one of your clients at that time.

If I can provide you with additional information, please contact me at the above address or by phone at (312) 555-5555.

Thank you for your consideration.

Sincerely,

Chris Smith

Enc. resume

- Candidate describes work environment preferences.
- Candidate invites employment contact to respond to inquiry.

LETTER TO AN EMPLOYMENT AGENCY
(Insurance Account Manager)

178 Green Street
Las Cruces, NM 88003

October 7, 1996

Pat Cummings
President
Any Employment Agency
1140 Main Street
Albuquerque, NM 87103

Dear Mr. Cummings:

As per your request during our recent conversation, I am enclosing my business profile for your review and for submission to one of your client firms.

My experience as an Account Manager and Office Manager has provided me with expertise in all facets of insurance agency operation. Once oriented to the policies of a new firm, I have the knowledge and skill to assume responsibility for either of the above positions.

Any assistance you can provide in arranging interviews with prospective employers will be much appreciated. Should you require additional information prior to our meeting, please contact me at the above address or call me at (505) 555-5555.

Sincerely,

Chris Smith

Enc. business profile

- Letters to employment agencies are generally brief and to the point.

- Candidate requests agency's assistance in scheduling interviews.

LETTER TO AN EMPLOYMENT AGENCY
(Insurance Underwriter)

178 Green Street
Falndreau, SD 57028

March 4, 1996

Pat Cummings
Director
Any Corporation
1140 Main Street
Chicago, IL 60605

Dear Ms. Cummings:

During the past ten years, my experience has been in the liability insurance field in positions ranging from Transcriber to Senior Field Claims Representative. Currently, I am seeking a new association with an underwriter or a corporate liability insurance department where there is a need for expertise in claims settlement, from fact-finding analysis to negotiation.

I am hoping that among your many clients there may be one or two who are looking for someone who is knowledgeable in the area of corporate liability insurance; if so, I would like to explore the opportunity. I may be reached at (605) 555-5555 during regular business hours or at (605) 555-4444 evenings.

I look forward to hearing from you.

Sincerely,

Chris Smith

Enc. resume

■ Including a business number is optional in a cover letter.

■ Letters to employment agencies are generally brief and to the point.

LETTER TO AN EMPLOYMENT AGENCY
(Legal Administrator)

178 Green Street
Jacksonville, FL 32203

August 7, 1996

Pat Cummings
Partner
Any Employment Agency
1140 Main Street
Tallahassee, FL 32302

Dear Mr. Cummings:

I would like to be considered for a court or legal-related administrative position with any appropriate clients you may service. I have recently relocated to the Florida area from Washington, D.C., and am seeking employment which would utilize my leadership, education, and experience.

In Washington, I was the Office Manager for a respected court reporting firm. All of my primary job responsibilities required organization, attention to detail, writing, and significant computer skills. I have extensive experience working on multiple projects and meeting deadlines in a team-oriented environment. As a result, I have developed strong time management and interpersonal skills.

I have enclosed my resume for your review. Should you need additional information, please do not hesitate to contact me at (904) 555-5555. I look forward to hearing from you. Thank you for your time.

Sincerely,

Chris Smith

Enc. resume

- Candidate immediately informs employment agency of job objective.
- Letter focuses on acquired skills rather than detailing past employers.

LETTER TO AN EMPLOYMENT AGENCY
(Medical Assistant)

178 Green Street
Cedar City, UT 84720

July 3, 1996

Pat Cummings
Director
Any Employment Agency
1140 Main Street
Smithfield, UT 84335

Dear Ms. Cummings:

Your agency has been recommended to me for job placement within the health care field. I am a trained Medical Assistant searching for a new association with a firm in the Southwest.

Prior to working with professional service firms and a manufacturing company, I spent four years as a Medical Receptionist. My continued interest in, and dedication to, the health care field recently prompted me to pursue additional study at Salt Lake Community College. I have enclosed my resume which further outlines my background.

After you have reviewed my qualifications, I would appreciate hearing from you with reference to available Medical Assistant positions where I can, perhaps, also apply my business experience. I am looking for an opportunity in the $20,000 to $30,000 range. If I can be of any further assistance, please contact me at the above address or by phone at (801) 555-5555.

Sincerely,

Chris Smith

Enc. resume

■ Introduction indicates candidate's familiarity with specific agency.

■ Continuing education demonstrates candidate's dedication to his/her field.

LETTER TO AN EMPLOYMENT AGENCY
(Office Manager)

178 Green Street
La France, SC 29656
(803) 555-5555

March 30, 1996

Pat Cummings
Associate
Any Employment Agency
1140 Main Street
Spartanburg, SC 29304

Dear Mr. Cummings:

Finding the right person for the job is often difficult, costly, and at times disappointing. However, if one of your clients is in need of a reliable, competent, and well-organized individual for their office management staff, I have the qualifications and dedication for the position.

During the past ten years, I have held progressively responsible positions in office management with manufacturing, distribution, export, and service companies. Recently, I made a permanent relocation to La France, and am interested in joining a company in the South Carolina area that can benefit from my experience.

I have broad experience with manual and automated accounting/administrative systems, customer service, personnel supervision, event/meeting planning, credit and collection, and executive support. I function best in a diverse, busy environment and have established a reputation for being organized and capable of coordinating and handling multiple assignments cost-effectively and to schedule.

The enclosed business profile summarizes my qualifications. Should you know of any suitable opportunities, I would appreciate your consideration.

I look forward to hearing from you.

Sincerely,

Chris Smith

Enc. business profile

■ Introduction captures addressee's attention.

■ Candidate describes work environment preferences.

LETTER TO AN EMPLOYMENT AGENCY
(Operations Manager)

178 Green Street
Phoenix, AZ 85012
(602) 555-5555

January 15, 1996

Pat Cummings
Director
Any Employment Agency
1140 Main Street
Keyport, WA 98101

Dear Ms. Cummings:

I am relocating to your area next month. Your agency's name comes highly recommended as a superior job placement service and, for this reason, I am enclosing my resume for your review.

I am interested in locating a challenging position in which to consolidate experience and utilize chemical, electro-mechanical, and mechanical skills. I would be a good match for a progressive, technically oriented company seeking conscientious, intelligent support in the areas of research, manufacturing, or production.

Please note that in fifteen years I have occupied progressively responsible and sophisticated positions with RHG Corporation which included Automated Manufacturing Machine Operator, Research and Development Assistant, and Senior Laboratory Technician. I am highly skilled in all trades and have more than six years of experience in the management and supervision of fleet maintenance operations for cars and trucks. I have additional training in accounting, real estate, supervision, and management and I am considered an expert in automotive and general mechanics.

Do you know of any available or anticipated openings that match my qualifications? If so, I can be reached at the address and telephone number above until February 1.

I appreciate your time.

Sincerely,

Chris Smith

Enc. resume

■ Qualifications call attention to candidate's relevant supervisory and administrative experience.

■ Candidate does not restrict job opportunities.

LETTER TO AN EMPLOYMENT AGENCY
(Property Manager)

178 Green Street
Salamanca, NY 14779
(716) 555-5555

May 13, 1996

Pat Cummings
Director
Any Corporation
1140 Main Street
Chicago, IL 60605

Dear Mr. Cummings:

In July of this year I will be permanently relocating to the Chicago area. I am forwarding the attached resume for your evaluation because of my desire to contribute my comprehensive experience in real estate/property management to a locally based company.

I have two years of direct experience involving all aspects in the management of 275 apartments and four commercial units in three buildings. My responsibilities include a range of activities, from advertising and promotion of apartments to competitive analysis of rate structures.

My experience also includes contractor negotiations, liaison with government and service agencies, personnel relations, financial management, and other functions basic to the effective management of complex properties.

If you know of any company with a current need for a bright, outgoing property manager with an orientation to sales, please do not hesitate to contact me.

Thank you for your consideration.

Sincerely,

Chris Smith

Enc. resume

■ Candidate includes only applicable skills.

■ Closing encourages reader to respond to letter.

LETTER TO AN EMPLOYMENT AGENCY
(Purchasing Agent)

178 Green Street
Walla Walla, WA 99362
(509) 555-5555

December 4, 1996

Pat Cummings
Manager
Any Employment Agency
1140 Main Street
Yakima, WA 98909

Dear Ms. Cummings:

I am an experienced professional interested in pursuing my purchasing career
within a progressive and challenging environment. Glen Guapo, an associate of
mine referred me to your agency, noting your excellent placement record for those
with similar qualifications.

During the past five years, I have held progressively responsible positions ranging
from Purchasing Secretary to Regional Distribution Supervisor and Purchasing
Agent in the high-tech manufacturing and retail industry. I have been actively
involved in vendor evaluation, vendor lead-time, and customer delivery
scheduling, sourcing, negotiating, and monitoring, and have followed through on
purchases from sampling to accounts payable.

Although these positions have been fast-paced, challenging, and broad in scope, I
feel that my expertise in purchasing can be utilized to better advantage by one of
your client companies. I am confident that my diverse background has given me
the flexibility to undertake varied and expanding responsibilities in these areas,
and I am open to travel to secure the right opportunity. Salary requirement:
$28,000 to $35,000.

Please do not hesitate to contact me if you need any additional information. I
would be happy to come in and speak with you or a potential employer. Thank you
for your time.

Sincerely,

Chris Smith

Enc. resume

■ Candidate informs agency contact
of all relevant information,
including travel availability and
salary requirements.

■ Candidate immediately names
referral.

LETTER TO AN EMPLOYMENT AGENCY
(Quality Control Specialist)

178 Green Street
South Bend, IN 46619

July 23, 1996

Pat Cummings
Director
Any Employment Agency
1140 Main Street
Memphis, TN 38109

Dear Mr. Cummings:

My interest in locating a position in quality control/quality assurance with a firm in the Memphis area has prompted me to forward this up-to-date resume for your review. I am planning permanent relocation to Tennessee in September and I would appreciate any assistance in finding a suitable employer.

My background includes a Bachelor of Science degree in Biology and Associate degrees in Math and Science. I also have seventeen months of solid, hands-on experience as a Quality Control Analyst with a manufacturer of instrumentation for environmental analysis. My knowledge in these areas includes all current inspection systems, procedures, and equipment used to maintain standards to critical tolerance. I am certain of my ability to make an immediate, long-term contribution to my employer.

Please contact me at the above address or by phone at (219) 555-5555 if you know of any quality control vacancies or related positions. I look forward to hearing from you in the near future.

Sincerely,

Chris Smith

Enc. resume

■ Impressive educational experience and qualifications help compensate for candidate's short employment history.

■ Introductory sentence specifies position desired.

LETTER TO AN EMPLOYMENT AGENCY
(Retail Manager)

178 Green Street
Landover, MD 20785
(410) 555-5555

June 16, 1996

Pat Cummings
Director
Any Employment Agency
1140 Main Street
Grand Rapids, MI 49506

Dear Ms. Cummings:

In a month I plan to permanently relocate to the Detroit area. I am forwarding the
attached resume for your consideration due to my desire to contribute my
experience in retail management to a nationally recognized grocery chain.

During the past eighteen months I have advanced to Shift Manager with Any
Natural Foods Market. Working with natural foods is both a vocation and an
avocation for me. I have the ability to work with employees and customers to
establish high visibility and a quality image for the market, and also, stress the
benefits of natural foods to health and fitness. I am service-oriented and feel
confident that I can implement and maintain the quality standards of employee
performance expected of a first-rate management team.

After you have had a chance to review my qualifications, I would appreciate a
meeting to discuss market manager positions.

Sincerely,

Chris Smith

Enc. resume

■ Candidate suggests informational
meeting with agency.

■ Letter expresses commitment to
field of interest.

LETTER TO AN EMPLOYMENT AGENCY
(Sales/Customer Service Representative)

178 Green Street
Trenton, NJ 08619
(609) 555-5555

November 4, 1996

Pat Cummings
Employment Representative
Any Employment Agency
1140 Main Street
Linwood, NJ 08221

Dear Mr. Cummings:

I am writing to inquire if your agency might be able to assist me in my search for a position in either sales or customer service.

As you can see from my enclosed resume, I have over seven years' experience in positions ranging from Sales Assistant, Claims Investigator, and Bank Teller. Some of my applicable skills include:

- Act as liaison between customers, staff, and management.

- Investigating and resolving customer requests and problems.

- Tracking and expediting sales orders; ascertaining order accuracy.

- Processing a wide range of financial transactions; maintaining accuracy and balance.

- IBM and Macintosh word processing, Lotus 1-2-3.

I would be interested to discuss any employment opportunities you feel would be applicable to my skills. Please note that I am willing to travel, and negotiate a salary in the $25,000 to 35,000 range. Do not hesitate to contact me if you need any additional information.

I will follow up this inquiry with a phone call next week.

Sincerely,

Chris Smith

Enc. resume

■ Letter focuses on functional skills applicable to potential employer.

■ When writing to an employment agency, including compensation requirements is optional.

LETTER TO AN EMPLOYMENT AGENCY
(Secretary)

178 Green Street
Clinton, MS 39060

January 18, 1996

Pat Cummings
Staff Associate
Any Employment Agency
1140 Main Street
St. Louis, MO 63122

Dear Ms. Cummings:

Enclosed please find my resume for your review regarding potential employment with your client community. I would be interested in a secretarial position where I could utilize my administrative and secretarial skills.

As my resume outlines in more detail, I have earned an Associate degree in the Secretarial Program at Macomb Community College. In addition, my current tenure at Gaudet and Growney has afforded me the opportunity to further develop competent organizational and analytical skills. In the everyday operations of the department, the general merchandise manager relies on me to organize meetings and coordinate all communications to our ten-store chain. These responsibilities have enabled me to expand my general office skills.

Although my employment at Gaudet and Growney has been a positive experience, I am seeking a position that will offer more advancement opportunity.

As you will notice from my resume, I possess excellent secretarial and administrative skills. I have nine years of administrative experience working both in the merchandising department and in the executive offices of my current employer. I am also knowledgeable in a variety of software programs. My compensation requirements are in the $25,000 to $35,000 range, and I would be willing to relocate.

I would welcome the opportunity to speak with you regarding my qualifications. I can be reached at (601) 555-5555, ext. 226 (days) or (601) 555-4444 (evenings).

Thank you for your consideration.

Sincerely,

Chris Smith

Enc. resume

■ Writing to an employment agency may only be applicable for certain service-oriented and/or support positions.

■ Candidate informs agency contact only of experiences and skills related to his/her field of interest.

LETTER TO AN EMPLOYMENT AGENCY
(Security Guard)

178 Green Street
Minden, NV 89423

May 4, 1996

Pat Cummings
Director
Any Employment Agency
1140 Main Street
Las Vegas, NV 89125

Dear Mr. Cummings:

I understand that your agency provides job placement services in the greater Las Vegas area. Having recently moved to the area, I would greatly appreciate your assistance in securing a position.

For the past eight years, I have worked in the security industry as a Guard. My interest in this field developed from a position with the Willow Mead Art Museum, in Wyoming. As a Security Guard at the museum, my duties included patrol, surveillance, and control of facilities and areas. I also maintained reports, records, and documents as required by administration.

For the past three years as a bank Security Guard, I was responsible for ensuring safety and security of customers, bank employees, and bank assets. My compensation for that position was in the high $20,000 range.

I look forward to finding a similar position through your agency. I can begin working immediately. Please contact me to schedule interviews at (702) 555-5555.

Sincerely,

Chris Smith

Enc. resume

■ Candidate requests agency's assistance in scheduling interviews.

■ Candidate informs agency of his/her date of availability.

LETTER TO AN EMPLOYMENT AGENCY
(Stenographer)

178 Green Street
Troutdale, OR 97060
(503) 555-5555

January 3, 1996

Pat Cummings
Representative
Any Employment Agency
1140 Main Street
Portland, OR 97208

Dear Ms. Cummings:

Recently, a friend of mine, Sean Wilson, recommended your agency to assist me
in my job search. I understand you successfully found Sean a clerical position last
month. I am searching for a challenging position as a Stenographer, to which I
could apply the following qualifications:

- Strong shorthand and speed writing skills at 120 wpm.

- Excel at Gregg Simplified and Diamond Jubilee methods; proficient with
  the Pitman method.

- Expertise in the transcription, editing, and interpreting of stenographic
  characters into clear, concise, and precise English.

- Typing skills that include word processing at 80 wpm and typewriter
  production at 70 wpm.

My experience is supplemented by an Associate degree in Secretarial Sciences and
a certificate of accomplishment from the Executive Secretarial Program at
Katherine Gibbs secretarial school.

I would prefer to stay in the greater Portland area, and would ask for a salary
starting between $20,000 and $24,000. If you could provide me with any
assistance in this regard, I would be greatly appreciative.

I look forward to hearing from you.

Sincerely,

Chris Smith

Enc. resume

- Candidate informs agency of
  geographical preference.

- Candidate informs agency contact
  of relevant educational training.

LETTER TO AN EMPLOYMENT AGENCY
(Wait Person)

178 Green Street
Reston, VA 22091
(703) 555-5555

December 19, 1996

Pat Cummings
Representative
Any Employment Agency
1140 Main Street
Vienna, VA 22180

Dear Mr. Cummings:

I am searching for a challenging position in the fast-food industry in which work experience and a commitment to excellence will have valuable application.

Currently, I am working as a Server/Bartender for a 250-capacity restaurant in Reston, VA. In addition to my serving duties, I am responsible for register control, assistant shift supervision, and conflict resolution. I work well in both relaxed or fast-paced, high-pressure environments.

I would like to continue my career in food service upon my relocation to your area next month. If you should be aware of any available opportunities, I would appreciate your assistance. Until January 1, I can be reached at (215) 555-5555. After that date, I will be residing at the above address and telephone number.

Thank you for your time. I will be in contact soon to confirm that you have received this inquiry and attached resume.

Sincerely,

Chris Smith

Enc. resume

■ Candidate includes all relocation information.

■ Candidate describes work environment preferences.

14
Letter to an Executive Search Firm

Although executive search firms actively recruit candidates for client companies, don't let this discourage you from writing. A well-crafted cover letter can alert an otherwise unknowing recruiter of your availability. Remember, this is your chance to shine. Highlight your most impressive accomplishments and attributes and briefly summarize all relevant experience. If you have certain preferences, such as geographical location, travel, and salary, mention them in your cover letter. Generally, if executive search firms are interested, they'll call you, so keep your closing succinct.

LETTER TO AN EXECUTIVE SEARCH FIRM
(Buyer)

178 Green Street
Charleston, WV 25322
(304) 555-5555

March 7, 1996

Pat Cummings
Executive Recruiter
Any Company
1140 Main Street
Huntington, WV 25755

Dear Ms. Cummings:

I am a creative, innovative buyer who can add excitement to your client companies' inventories while generating bottom-line profits.

During the past eighteen years, I have had the opportunity to work in positions ranging from Merchandise Planner to Head Buyer at the headquarters level of major off-price retail chains. I have enjoyed rapid advancement and experienced the challenge of coordinating new concepts and introducing change associated with upscale fashion and trends. Recently, my efforts generated a 75 percent increase in sales and profits.

Currently, I am looking for a new association with a growing chain that will benefit from my experience and successes in identifying fashion trends, developing resources, and negotiating big buys for off-price retail operations. The professional opportunity I am looking for will utilize my market and product knowledge and ingenuity to achieve the same results for your clients as I have for my current employer.

I am interested in positions with a salary range from $75,000 to $90,000 and will relocate for the right opportunity.

Since my current employer is unaware of my current search, your confidence is appreciated.

Sincerely,

Chris Smith

Enc. resume

■ Compensation requirements are often included in executive search letters.

■ Candidate informs recruiter of need for confidentiality.

LETTER TO AN EXECUTIVE SEARCH FIRM
(Chief Executive Officer)

178 Green Street
Irmo, SC 29063

October 25, 1996

Pat Cummings
Executive Recruiter
Any Corporation
1140 Main Street
Chicago, IL 60605

Dear Mr. Cummings:

During the past twenty years, I have gained experience ranging from National Sales Manager/Director of Marketing to CEO of a $25-million athletic shoe manufacturer. I have earned the reputation for being a highly skilled senior-level manager in the areas of manufacturing, new business start-up and management, company reorganization and expansion, and design and development, at both regional and national levels.

Although my positions have been challenging and fast-paced, at this point in my career I am seeking new opportunities in an advisory capacity, which may ultimately lead to an equity position. I am looking for an environment where my expertise, creativity, and motivation can be fully utilized toward upgrading and/or expanding new or existing businesses. My salary requirement is $80,000 to $100,000.

If you would like any additional information, please do not hesitate to call me at (803) 555-5555. I am best reached weekdays between 8:00 a.m. and 1:00 p.m.

I look forward to your response.

Sincerely,

Chris Smith

Enc. resume

- Executive search letters are especially effective for top-level professionals.
- Candidate focuses on responsibilities of most recent position.

LETTER TO AN EXECUTIVE SEARCH FIRM
(Commercial Transportation Specialist)

178 Green Street
New Castle, DE 19720
(302) 555-5555

January 7, 1996

Pat Cummings
Superintendent
Any Shipping Company
1140 Main Street
Wilmington, DE 19850

Dear Ms. Cummings:

My interest in an executive position with a major maritime shipper, such as one of
your client companies, has prompted me to forward my resume for your review
and consideration.

During the past eight years, I have had concentrated management experience in
marine transportation with the United States Military Sealift Command. A major
portion of my responsibilities involved navigation in heavily traveled areas, as
well as the supervision and training of anywhere from one hundred to two hundred
personnel during watch.

Although my present assignments are challenging, I am ready for a change to
commercial marine transportation and I feel that I can offer one of your client
companies a great deal of relevant experience and commitment.

Please do not hesitate to contact me should you know of a suitable match for my
skills. I am willing to travel for the right opportunity.

I look forward to speaking with you.

Sincerely,

Chris Smith

Enc. professional profile

■ Specifically sighting number of
personnel supervised draws
attention to candidate's
leadership abilities.

■ Candidate details how past
military experience will benefit
potential employer.

LETTER TO AN EXECUTIVE SEARCH FIRM
(Corporate President)

178 Green Street
Redmond, WA 98052
(206) 555-5555

December 24, 1996

Pat Cummings
Executive Recruiter
1140 Main Street
Seattle, WA 98103

Dear Mr. Cummings:

I have enclosed a business profile and request your consideration for any current or anticipated search assignments.

During the past twenty years, I have had the opportunity to apply innovative, leadership, and profit-making skills in positions ranging from President of a successful start-up business developed to $7 million in annual sales, to Vice-President, Product Management/Business Development, with a $750 million rapid growth computer resale company.

My skill in undertaking new challenges, ability to implement change, and expertise in developing compatible, professional teams during the transition phases of acquisitions, mergers, and consolidations enables me to provide stability and profitability to growth situations. Presently, I am looking for a position change where I have the responsibility for making meaningful decisions and the authority to implement plans to achieve corporate objectives.

My desire is to find an exciting, growth-oriented position. Thus, I would be willing to relocate to secure a salary in the $100,000 range.

Please contact me should my qualifications be of interest to one of your client firms. Thank you for your consideration.

Sincerely,

Chris Smith

Enc. business profile

■ Executive search letters provide detailed information regarding candidate's impressive track record.

■ Candidate immediately and concisely informs recruiter of his/her qualifications.

LETTER TO AN EXECUTIVE SEARCH FIRM
(Director of Administration)

178 Green Street
York, PA 17405

January 13, 1996

Pat Cummings
Executive Recruiter
1140 Main Street
Philadelphia, PA 19130

Dear Ms. Cummings:

Although my present position as Director of Administration has been a most responsible and rewarding experience, personal and family obligations have influenced my decision to return to the Pennsylvania area. For this reason, I am contacting you, in confidence, for assistance in my job search.

During the past fourteen years, my positions as Operations Manager and Director of Administration, with both large and small firms, have given me the hands-on experience and expertise to do a fine job for one of your client companies.

I have enclosed a business profile that briefly outlines my background and experience. I would be happy to meet with you so that you can evaluate and match my skills with the needs of one of your clients. My prime requirements for a position are job satisfaction, good growth potential, a compatible environment, and compensation within the $75,000 to $90,000 range.

I plan to be in your area from February 5 to 16, and hope to meet with you at that time. In the interim, should you require additional information, please contact me at the above address or by phone at (717) 555-5555.

Sincerely,

Chris Smith

Enc. business profile

■ Explaining reason for job search is optional.　　■ Benefits to potential employer are emphasized.

LETTER TO AN EXECUTIVE SEARCH FIRM
(Director of Information Services)

178 Green Street
Idaho Falls, ID 83415
(208) 555-5555

August 15, 1996

Pat Cummings
Executive Recruiter
1140 Main Street
Boise, ID 83706

Dear Mr. Cummings:

During our meeting at the Minority Professional Recruiting Center on July 22, we had a chance to discuss opportunities with your client firms that are of great interest to me.

Although my position with McDavid Associates provides a professional and interesting environment, I feel it is time for a change. I am currently seeking a challenging environment where I can apply my combined technical knowledge, experience, and ability to create and implement innovative concepts for greater information systems efficiency. I can offer:

- Thirteen years of experience with MIS corporate information systems.
- Experience in the operation and supervision of administrative functions of several UNIX systems using UNIX System V (release 3.0) operating software.
- Skill in communicating with domestic/international networks/mainframes and network system support.
- Capability to work as a team member, team leader, and/or independent contributor, working off-site via modem and data network, to assist users in sales, finance, manufacturing, and production.
- Ability to generate positive results in company's information systems and networks by streamlining systems and improving personnel/user training and performance.

I have enclosed a resume and would appreciate meeting with you to discuss my qualifications. Relocation is not a problem and my compensation requirements are in the low $70,000 range.

Thank you for your consideration.

Yours sincerely,

Chris Smith

Enc. resume

■ Separating major accomplishments from body draws attention.

■ Avoid technical jargon unless it is specific to candidate's field.

LETTER TO AN EXECUTIVE SEARCH FIRM
(Engineering Administrator)

178 Green Street
Lansdale, PA 19446

November 4, 1996

Pat Cummings
Executive Recruiter
Any Firm
1140 Main Street
Philadelphia, PA 19114

Dear Ms. Cummings:

I am currently exploring administrative opportunities in the engineering field.
Enclosed is my resume for your consideration.

Please note that my seventeen years of practical experience have involved working
on major commercial and industrial projects in the Middle East as a Construction
Engineer, Construction Manager, and Planning and Systems Engineer. This
experience is supported by a multilingual capability, a Bachelor of Science degree
in Civil Engineering, a Master of Science degree in Engineering Administration
with concentration in Construction Management, and broad experience with
computers.

I look forward to discussing with you my potential to contribute to your clients'
needs. If you will please contact me at the above address or by phone at (215) 555-
5555, I would like to establish a mutually convenient time for a personal
interview. My salary has ranged from $75,000 to its most current $95,000 and I
am open to opportunities that offer similar compensation.

Thank you for your attention.

Sincerely,

Chris Smith

Enc. resume

- Letters to executive search firms are best utilized by a candidate with extensive experience in his/her field of interest.

- Executive search letters generally allow recruiter to respond to candidate's inquiry.

LETTER TO AN EXECUTIVE SEARCH FIRM
(Executive Administrator)

178 Green Street
Columbia, SC 29202

December 15, 1996

Pat Cummings
Director
Any Executive Search Firm
1140 Main Street
Spartanburg, SC 29304

Dear Mr. Cummings:

If one of your client firms is in need of an innovative executive with broad experience in product management, business development, and high-tech products service operations, then we have good reason to meet for further discussion.

I am an aggressive professional who enjoys challenge and is willing to accept the responsibility for capturing my corporate share of targeted and strategic markets. As a leader or member of a professional national and/or international marketing staff, I am confident that I can make the same outstanding contribution to your client firm as I have to my present employer.

During the past seventeen years, I have progressively advanced from positions ranging from Senior Sales Representative, Strategic Account Manager, and Marketing Manager to my most current position as Strategic Alliance Marketing and Business Development Manager with an internationally recognized computer company.

Although these positions have been fast-paced and challenging, I feel that my expertise in selling concepts and working with vendors worldwide on the development and execution of joint marketing ventures can be effectively utilized to provide high visibility and develop new applications for increased sales. Please note, I am willing to relocate for the right opportunity.

The enclosed resume summarizes my background and experience in the above areas. Should you require additional information, please feel free to contact me at the above address or by phone at (803) 555-5555. I would welcome your acknowledgment and look forward to a meeting at your earliest convenience.

Sincerely,

Chris Smith

Enc. resume

■ Candidate details all relevant experience.

■ Candidate informs recruiter of willingness to travel and/or relocate.

LETTER TO AN EXECUTIVE SEARCH FIRM
(Financial Administrator)

178 Green Street
Albany, GA 31708

November 15, 1996

Pat Cummings
Senior Consultant
Any Search Firm
1140 Main Street
Jacksonville, FL 32207

Dear Ms. Cummings:

Should one of your clients find themselves in need of a business professional with expertise in strategic planning, domestic and international finance, marketing, and general management, I ask that you consider my enclosed executive profile.

My expertise derives from thirteen years of experience in profit-center management, investment banking, and asset management for Fortune 100 and 500 companies, institutions, and individual investors with diverse holdings in ranges of $1 to $500 million. I have sound knowledge of the implementation of mergers/acquisitions, developmental strategies, and business plans for major corporate and independent investors in the United States and abroad.

My decision to permanently relocate to the greater Florida area now makes it necessary for me to look into new opportunities. I am interested in joining the management staff of an established financial corporation. My current annual compensation is $80,000.

I am innovative, well organized, skilled in working with decision-makers, and capable of directing a well disciplined management organization that can accept the challenge of bringing business plans into functioning profit modes.

Should you be aware of a suitable opportunity, please contact me at the above address or business phone at (912) 555-5555. I appreciate your consideration.

Yours sincerely,

Chris Smith

Enc. executive profile

■ Summary of experience accentuates candidate's acquired professional skills and impressive track record.

■ Including a business number is optional in a cover letter.

LETTER TO AN EXECUTIVE SEARCH FIRM
(Labor Relations Specialist)

178 Green Street
Kalamazoo, MI 49006

June 15, 1996

Pat Cummings
Executive Recruiter
1140 Main Street
Chicago, IL 60605

Dear Mr. Cummings:

My experience encompasses over ten years of decision-making responsibility for human resource development, manpower planning, and labor law and relations, affecting hundreds of employees in the public and private sectors. In addition to the training and supervision of sizable staffs, I have been involved in collective bargaining for management, wage and salary administration, employee benefits, safety and training, and making and enforcing labor law considerations.

I am currently interested in a firm that offers stability, growth, and profits. I am willing to relocate if offered a challenging assignment. My salary requirement is $45,000 to $55,000.

I have enclosed my resume for your review. If I may provide you with additional information, please call me at (616) 555-5555. I look forward to discussing my qualifications with you in more detail.

Sincerely,

Chris Smith

Enc. resume

■ Candidate highlights areas of expertise.

■ Experiences are tailored to employer's needs.

LETTER TO AN EXECUTIVE SEARCH FIRM
(Lawyer: International Law)

178 Green Street
New Hope, MN 55428
(612) 555-5555

March 24, 1996

Pat Cummings
Executive Recruiter
1140 Main Street
Minneapolis, MN 55426

Dear Ms. Cummings:

I feel that you, as an executive in a search company, might be effective in matching me with the legal staff of one of your client firms.

In addition to a Juris Doctor degree, I recently received a Master of Laws in Banking Law Studies with a concentration in International Law. My expertise is in the supervision of associate and support legal staff in research, document preparation, and coordination as required for all legal issues. I am well organized, accurate, and conscientious, interface well with individuals and groups, and feel confident that I can be a contributing asset to one of your client firms.

I have enclosed a professional profile of my academic accomplishments and work experience. My last compensation was $90,000, although I feel my value has substantially increased since attaining my recent degree. Should you wish to discuss my qualifications further, I can be reached at my office at (612) 555-4444, extension 22.

I look forward to working together.

Sincerely,

Chris Smith

Enc. professional profile

■ Advanced degrees add weight to cover letter.

■ Benefits to potential employer are emphasized.

LETTER TO AN EXECUTIVE SEARCH FIRM
(Management Consultant)

178 Green Street
Gusher, VT 84030
(802) 555-5555

April 1, 1996

Pat Cummings
Executive Recruiter
Any Corporation
1140 Main Street
Chicago, IL 60605

Dear Mr. Cummings:

I have played a key role in designing, implementing, reorganizing, and managing a variety of functions—including operations, manufacturing, materials, engineering, and quality assurance—for nationally and internationally recognized corporations.

Currently, I am seeking a position with a company that can benefit from my twenty years of progressively responsible management experience in the above areas. My expertise is diverse and includes:

- Five years as Director of Operations for a $60 million manufacturer.

- More than six years as Materials Manager with a multiplant, multiwarehouse, $10 million manufacturer of industrial rubber products.

- Over nine years as Manufacturing Coordinator with a toy manufacturer, with responsibilities related to the physical set-up of new or expansion of existing manufacturing and support facilities; manpower planning; industrial union relations; and capital equipment investment and materials purchases.

I have enclosed my resume for your review. Should you be conducting a search for someone with my background at the present time or in the near future, I would greatly appreciate your consideration. I would be happy to discuss my background in greater detail with you, on the phone or in person. Thank you for your time.

Yours sincerely,

Chris Smith

Enc. resume

- Candidate highlights areas of expertise.

- Separating major accomplishments from body draws attention.

LETTER TO AN EXECUTIVE SEARCH FIRM
(Operations Manager)

178 Green Street
Minnetonka, MN 55343
(612) 555-5555

March 23, 1996

Pat Cummings
President
Any Search Firm
1140 Main Street
Minneapolis, MN 55408

Dear Ms. Cummings:

Based on my diverse background and experience with high-end, mid-range, and low-end hardware, software, and network products designed for many industries, I feel confident that I can make a valuable contribution toward new product planning, market development, and expansion for a firm within your client base.

My extensive experience over the last seventeen years has required the ability not only to develop and market packaged and customized software for many industries in domestic and international markets, but also to provide the support products for end-users at all levels. Because of this diversity, I am easily able to transfer my skills to marketing other products.

In addition to a strong marketing and sales background, I have also established a record for setting up, staffing, and managing top-producing, profitable district offices.

The enclosed profile is a brief summary of my qualifications. Should you be aware of an advanced marketing and development position within the $70,000 to $80,000 range, please consider my qualifications.

Thank you in advance for your attention to this matter.

Sincerely,

Chris Smith

Enc. professional profile

- Letters to executive search firms are best utilized by a candidate with extensive experience in his/her field of interest.

- Letter focuses attention on candidate's major skills and accomplishments.

LETTER TO AN EXECUTIVE SEARCH FIRM
(Plant Manager)

178 Green Street
Madison Heights, MI 48071
(313) 555-5555

July 18, 1996

Pat Cummings
President
Any Search Firm
1140 Main Street
Detroit, MI 48239

Dear Mr. Cummings:

During the past ten years, I have held positions ranging from Production Supervisor to Plant/Operations Manager with a $16 million manufacturer and importer of electrical products. Presently, I am seeking a new association with a firm, where I, as a seasoned manager, can contribute to its cost-effective, quality operation and profitability in keeping with management objectives.

In my current position as Plant Manager, I restructured and developed a stable work force and environment. Under my direction, the company has benefited from the efficient performance of a supervisory staff and support personnel in all phases of plant operations including production, purchasing, inventory control, warehousing, distribution, and maintenance of a 325,000-plus-square-foot facility.

The enclosed resume summarizes my background and experience in the above areas. Based on my skills in dealing with employees, vendors, and management, I would welcome the opportunity to apply my proven track record to one of your client firms as I have for my present and prior employers. Relocation is not a problem and my compensation requirements are in the $60,000 to $70,000 range.

If you need additional information, I can be reached at the above address or phone.

Thank you for your consideration.

Sincerely,

Chris Smith

Enc. resume

- Candidate immediately highlights substantial accomplishments that would interest industry professional.

- Letter indicates how candidate contributed to his/her previous employers.

LETTER TO AN EXECUTIVE SEARCH FIRM
(President/CEO)

178 Green Street
Warwick, RI 02886
(401) 555-5555

August 3, 1996

Pat Cummings
Personal Consultant
Any Search Firm
1140 Main Street
Pawtucket, RI 02860

Dear Ms. Cummings:

In the course of your search assignments, you might have a need for an experienced President/CEO with expertise in all phases of real estate development and construction.

During the past twenty years as a Developer of large real estate complexes and President of a major real estate development group, I managed large projects, from site acquisition and master planning through approvals. I have successfully marketed award-winning residential and commercial mixed-usage developments representing $185 million in sales. Currently, I am involved in negotiating site acquisitions, and planning, coordinating, and managing large real estate development/construction projects for both foreign and domestic investors with interests throughout the Northeast.

My positions require strong administrative, management, financial, and interpersonal skills, as well as the capability to negotiate effectively and successfully with financial institutions, regulatory agencies, development professionals, and contractors. Presently, I am looking for a new association with a firm where my expertise can be used to achieve mutual objectives for growth and profit.

My preference is to remain in my present regional location, with which I am most familiar. My current salary is in the low six figures. After you have reviewed my qualifications, I can arrange to meet with you at your convenience.

Thank you for your attention to this matter.

Sincerely,

Chris Smith

Enc. professional profile

- Candidate informs recruiter of acceptable relocation areas.

- Letter stresses candidate's extensive experience and significant accomplishments.

LETTER TO AN EXECUTIVE SEARCH FIRM
(Senior Accountant)

178 Green Street
Concord, NH 03302
(603) 555-5555

July 20, 1996

Pat Cummings
Executive Recruiter
1140 Main Street
New York, NY 10022

Dear Mr. Cummings:

I believe that the varied accounting, finance, and general management experience I have gained over the course of my career will be of significant interest to you in your current or anticipated client searches.

As a seasoned, certified Accountant, I have successfully managed general ledger, cash accounting, accounts payable, employee disbursements, and fixed asset operations. As a Manufacturing Plant Controller, I managed the accounting activities and the general administrative functions of a $35 million manufacturing plant. I have:

- Prepared, analyzed, and presented P&L, balance sheet, departmental expense, manufacturing variance, and other operating reports.

- Prepared, $2 million annual departmental operating budgets, analyzed results, initiated required operational improvements, and prepared forecasts.

- Developed annual strategic and operational improvements which resulted in a 15 percent increase in efficiency.

- Oversaw human resources, purchasing, payroll, and other plant administrative functions.

- Maintained quality accounting operations by implementing internal controls testing programs.

I have also managed the interface between my group and the data center running my applications, directed the MIS professionals that supported my applications, directed the MIS professionals that supported my systems, and managed the enhancement projects that steadily improved day-to-day operations. I am also operational with spreadsheet and word processing applications on IBM and Macintosh systems.

My resume is enclosed. While my prime interest is securing a position on the East Coast, I am willing to relocation for the right opportunity and compensation ($80,000 to $95,000).

Thank you for your consideration.

Sincerely,

Chris Smith

Enc. resume

■ Candidate quantifies accomplishments with dollar figures and percentages.

■ Candidate focuses on responsibilities of most recent position.

LETTER TO AN EXECUTIVE SEARCH FIRM
(Senior Business Analyst)

178 Green Street
Blacksburg, VA 24061
(703) 555-5555

April 7, 1996

Pat Cummings
Executive Recruiter
1140 Main Street
Manassas, VA 22110

Dear Ms. Cummings:

During the past twenty years, I have played a significant role in financial systems development as well as accounting, financial planning, and audit management dealing with international and domestic markets.

Although I am presently employed as Senior Business Analyst, with a $150 million division of Medfort Corporation, I feel it is time for a change. I am currently seeking a new association with a company that can benefit from my expertise in:

- Accounting systems design and installation;

- Account department organization and management;

- Financial planning management (domestic and international marketing); and

- Financial project design and management.

I am an effective developer of strategic financial and accounting systems with special skill as a problem-solver and professional group manager. While my preference is to stay within the Mid-Atlantic region, I would consider relocation should the right position present itself. My salary requirements are in the $70,000 to $85,000 range.

I look forward to hearing from you, should a suitable match for my qualifications be available.

Sincerely yours,

Chris Smith

Enc. resume

- Candidate informs recruiter of acceptable relocation areas.

- Candidate immediately and concisely informs recruiter of his/her qualifications.

LETTER TO AN EXECUTIVE SEARCH FIRM
(Vice-President of Banking)

178 Green Street
Atlanta, GA 30303
(404) 555-5555

December 21, 1996

Pat Cummings
President
Any Search Firm
1140 Main Street
Atlanta, GA 30340

Dear Mr. Cummings:

I am an accomplished Vice-President who can significantly contribute to the successful operations of one of your client banking institutions.

I possess extensive experience in multibranch operations, including the following areas:

- Successfully developing and personally marketing new products for small businesses.

- Rewriting and implementing branch system policies and procedures.

- Troubleshooting operations and establishing improved financial controls.

- Budget planning and controls, audits.

My compensation requirement is within the $75,000 to $85,000 range, and I would consider traveling a fair distance to a job location. I have enclosed a professional profile and would be happy to provide additional information if needed.

I look forward to hearing from you regarding placement possibilities.

Sincerely,

Chris Smith

Enc. professional profile

- Executive search letters generally allow recruiter to respond to candidate's inquiry.

- Discussion of experience is very specific.

LETTER TO AN EXECUTIVE SEARCH FIRM
(Vice-President of Nursing)

178 Green Street
Woonsocket, RI 02895
(401) 555-5555

April 15, 1996

Pat Cummings
Consultant
Any Search Firm
1140 Main Street
Warwick, RI 02893

Dear Ms. Cummings:

At a recent conference, I was made aware that your firm is in the process of making a search for the Vice-President of Nursing at Any Hospital.

During the past sixteen years, my experience has been with referral hospitals—eleven years as Assistant Director of Nursing, with Emory Hospital and five years in my current position as Vice-President, Nursing with Newman General Hospital. My experience working with private practice physicians and proven ability to establish a collegial and cooperative team effort between doctors and nurses, in both hospitals, has enabled me to successfully achieve the best in cost-effective, quality patient care.

My past and current positions have been challenging and provided me with the satisfaction of developing programs which made positive contributions to the professional and quality image of both hospitals and research projects. However, at this point in my career, the position of Vice-President of Nursing at Any Hospital particularly interests me. It will offer me a broader scope of responsibility and the opportunity to utilize my administrative experience and clinical background in a larger facility and in a setting with which I am thoroughly familiar.

The enclosed confidential profile summarizes my experience. I could be available at your convenience to discuss your client's requirements and my ability to handle the responsibilities of the position offered.

Thank you for your consideration of my application.

Sincerely,

Chris Smith

Enc. professional profile

■ Candidate informs recruiter of need for confidentiality.

■ Executive search letters provide detailed information regarding candidate's impressive track record.

LETTER TO AN EXECUTIVE SEARCH FIRM
(Vice-President of Sales)

178 Green Street
Houston, TX 77248
(713) 555-5555
(713) 444-4444 FAX

August 2, 1996

Pat Cummings
Recruiter
Any Search Firm
1140 Main Street
Hartford, CT 06102

Dear Mr. Cummings:

Currently, I am considering a move to the Northeast and am pursuing executive positions with profitable, aggressive retail corporations. Your firm has been recommended to me as one which services a wide client base in this area. In this regard, I would request your consideration of my qualifications.

As a corporate Vice-President of Sales with an established record for the development of approximately $215 million in sales, my responsibilities have covered the gamut of successful strategies and techniques for growth and profitability. My involvement in sales, marketing, staff development, and production interface has been extensive, and my ability to organize and manage is well documented in goals I have achieved with my present and prior employers. My salary requirements lie in the $200,000 to $250,000 range, plus bonuses.

The enclosed resume highlights my accomplishments. I would welcome the opportunity to discuss my qualifications further should a client wish to consider me for a position.

Thank you for your time.

Sincerely,

Chris Smith

Enc. resume

- Executive search letters are especially effective for top-level professionals.

- Candidate immediately highlights substantial accomplishments that would interest industry professional.

15
Networking Letter

For the most part, networking letters refer to a third-party industry contact to help garner the reader's attention and compel him or her to assist you in your job search. It is essential to achieve the right tone in your networking letters. Unless you are very familiar with a contact, you should word your correspondence in a businesslike manner. In other words, do not use your addressee's first name, or rely on an overly casual writing style. Likewise, if you have been in contact with this person recently, it could be very useful to remind him or her: "It was great seeing you at the Chicago Writers' Convention last month" or "It has been several months since we bumped into each other on that flight to London. How are you?"

Many networking letters are written to an addressee whom the candidate has not met, but has been referred to by a mutual acquaintance. In this case, immediately state the name of the person who referred you, such as "Jean Rawlins suggested I contact you." It is generally more effective to ask a contact with whom you are unfamiliar for assistance and names of people to contact, than it is to ask for a job. Chances are, if your letter is politely persuasive, people will be interested in talking with you.

NETWORKING LETTER
(Administrative Assistant)

178 Green Street
Durango, CO 81301

November 16, 1996

Pat Cummings
Attorney at Law
Any Firm
1140 Main Street
Pueblo, CO 81001

Dear Mr. Cummings:

Recently, Luke Gokey suggested I contact you concerning any assistance you might be able to provide with my job search. I am interested in joining an organization in a position that would utilize my legal, administrative, and managerial knowledge and experience. The enclosed resume will provide you with information concerning my background and abilities.

As indicated, my law-related background is extensive and varied. For twelve years, I have supervised records and staff activities within the Any County Registry of Deeds. Unfortunately, I have reached the plateau of responsibility level within the structure of this position, and am now seeking to continue in my career progression.

I am especially interested in a legal administrative position, preferably with a private firm or corporation. I am willing to relocate and/or travel and am not restrictive on starting salary.

Should you know of any related openings or contacts to whom I should pass my resume, please do not hesitate to call me at (303) 555-5555. Thank you for your time. I look forward to hearing from you in the near future.

Sincerely,

Chris Smith

Enc. resume

■ Candidate requests additional referrals from networking contact.

■ Candidate clearly indicates type of position desired.

NETWORKING LETTER
(Advertising Executive)

178 Green Street
Neptune, NJ 07754
(908) 555-5555

August 14, 1996

Pat Cummings
Communications Director
Any Agency
1140 Main Street
Hackensack, NJ 07601

Dear Ms. Cummings:

Please find attached my resume. I spoke with Jim Shaffer last week and he
suggested I send my credentials to you prior to meeting in person.

As we discussed, I have five-plus years of advanced press, governmental, and
business experience. My background provides a broad base of skills that allows
me to handle a variety of situations and responsibilities.

I look forward to meeting with you at your earliest possible convenience.

Sincerely,

Chris Smith

Enc. resume

■ Introduction refers to attached
resume.

■ Letter is easy and quick to read,
and only relevant details are
included.

NETWORKING LETTER
(Advisor)

178 Green Street
Burbank, CA 91501

January 18, 1996

Pat Cummings
Director
Any Corporation
1140 Main Street
Vernon, CA 90058

Dear Mr. Cummings:

At the suggestion of Walter Durrane, I am enclosing my resume for your
consideration pertaining to advising or related assignments with Any Corporation.

I have recently retired from a long and successful general medical practice.
However, as an active professional, I am interested in contributing my expertise as
a representative for a public agency such as the Fraud Control Unit at Any
Corporation. I have been actively involved as an Evaluator and Advisor for
insurance companies, attorneys, industrial and insured claims, and I would like to
transfer these skills in the continuation of my profession.

I look forward to meeting you to further discuss my ability to fulfill your
requirements. In the interim, I may be reached at the above address or by phone at
(818) 555-5555.

Sincerely,

Chris Smith

Enc. resume

■ Basis for referral is immediately
established.

■ Language is straightforward and
understandable.

NETWORKING LETTER
(Architectural Designer)

178 Green Street
Mount Laurel, NJ 08054

November 13, 1996

Pat Cummings
Principal Engineer
Any Corporation
1140 Main Street
Minneapolis, MN 55440

Dear Ms. Cummings:

During a recent discussion with Mackenzie Simon, a current member of your firm,
I expressed an interest in making a change and he suggested that I contact you
with reference to opportunities within your organization.

In conjunction with five years of experience as a Chief Engineer and ten years as
an Architectural/Environmental Designer, I hold a Bachelor's degree in
Architectural Design. This combination is ideally applicable to projects and
programs involving those areas of asbestos abatement, specifications writing, and
the monitoring of in-force contracts which I understand are all an integral part of
your business. My background in architectural design and construction as well as
engineering management, from design to production, would enable me to become
a valuable contributor to one or more areas of your firm.

My resume is enclosed. I am especially interested in working in areas to which
your firm is dedicated, and I would like to meet with you for further discussion.
My preference is to remain in the Northeast area; however, traveling is not a
problem. I can be reached at the above address or by phone at (609) 555-5555,
extension #234, between 8:30 a.m. and 5:00 p.m. EST.

Yours sincerely,

Chris Smith

Enc. resume

■ Candidate informs networking
   contact of all relevant information,
   including geographical preference.

■ Candidate focuses on relevant
   functional skills.

NETWORKING LETTER
(Assistant Hospital Administrator)

178 Green Street
Rapid City, SD 57007
(605) 555-5555

July 4, 1996

Pat Cummings
Hospital Administrator
Any Hospital
1140 Main Street
Rapid City, SD 57007

Dear Mr. Cummings:

Upon completion of my coursework this month, I will be searching for a full-time position in hospital administration. During the past year as a volunteer at your hospital, I have gained a great deal of personal satisfaction and continued interest in working at a facility caring for older citizens. I would like to call upon your experience in this field to assist me in any way possible as I begin my job search.

Although you may already be aware of my qualifications, I have enclosed my resume for your perusal. In addition to a Bachelor of Science degree in Business Administration, I can offer five years of part-time and full-time experience in office administration, accounting, computer operations, and credit/collections that can be beneficial to your organization. I am willing to work in an entry-level position allowing me to interface with professionals from whom I can learn and further develop my skills to handle greater responsibilities.

I would like to meet with you briefly when I come in to volunteer for the final time on July 17. Any organization/contact names or industry insight you could provide would greatly enhance my search efforts. I will call your office this Friday to arrange a time on the 17th that would be convenient for you.

Thank you for your time, Mr. Cummings.

Sincerely,

Chris Smith

Enc. resume

■ Reminds networking contact of common experience.

■ Letter clarifies candidate's career goals.

NETWORKING LETTER
(Auto Salesperson)

178 Green Street
Brooklyn, NY 11201
(718) 555-5555

December 2, 1996

Pat Cummings
Regional Manager
Any Corporation
1140 Main Street
Rochester, NY 14623

Dear Ms. Cummings:

During a recent visit to Rochester, my longtime friend Bill Atwood suggested your name as a valuable contact in the field of auto sales. I understand that your corporation has contracted Bill's agency several times to promote your regional dealerships. I would like to take this opportunity to ask for any assistance you might be able to provide with my job search.

Due to recent downsizing, I am seeking a new, long-term association with an aggressive, fast-paced dealership. During the past eight years, my positions have ranged from Salesperson to Sales Manager with a high-volume dealership. My expertise is in developing, training, motivating, and managing a top-producing sales team in a highly competitive market. I am an effective communicator with presentation skills designed to generate results when dealing with management, personnel, and the general public. I have established and continually maintained a record of achievement as Salesperson of the Month and Salesperson of the Year for generated sales and margin of profit.

Should your schedule permit, I will be visiting the Rochester area next week and would love to meet with you. Your insight into the market and the future of the industry, as well as any specific advice or contact names you could provide, would be very helpful. I will call your office next Monday to see if we can find a convenient time to meet.

Thank you for your consideration, Ms. Cummings, and I hope to speak with you soon.

Sincerely,

Chris Smith

Enc. resume

■ Explaining reason for job search is optional.

■ Job descriptions emphasize candidate's accomplishments.

NETWORKING LETTER
(Bank Manager)

178 Green Street
St. Louis, MO 63130

June 8, 1996

Pat Cummings
Vice-President, Operations
Any Bank
1140 Main Street
Omaha, NE 68124

Dear Mr. Cummings:

Jennifer Mills, a colleague of mine at United Bank in St. Louis, suggested your name as an authority in the Midwest banking industry. Jennifer mentioned meeting you on a visit to your Omaha office last month, and was impressed by both the reputation and successful operations of your branches. I am writing to ascertain any information you can provide regarding banking opportunities in the Nebraska area, where I will be relocating next month.

As my enclosed resume indicates, I am a skilled professional with over ten years of relevant experience. In addition to an MBA degree (Executive Program —five years field representative experience required), and a BA degree in Economics and Finance, I have more than eighteen years of comprehensive banking experience. My expertise includes all aspects of banking and finance, credit administration, and management, including commercial lending and development, real estate loans, and end-to-end joint venture management. My experience also encompasses a successful term as Chief Financial Officer for a Japanese-American joint venture, and a term as Vice-President, Bank of St. Louis.

I will be visiting the Omaha area next week to begin my job search. Would your schedule permit a few moments to speak with me at this time? I would greatly appreciate any information or guidance you could provide, and my calendar is very flexible. Please contact me at the above address, or call (314) 555-5555 (early morning or evenings). Thank you for your time.

Sincerely,

Chris Smith

Enc. resume

■ Candidate immediately names referral.

■ Letter stresses candidate's extensive experience and significant accomplishments.

NETWORKING LETTER
(Beverage Manager)

178 Green Street
Lexington, KY 40508
(606) 555-5555

April 10, 1996

Pat Cummings
Vice-President, Importing
Any Corporation
1140 Main Street
Philadelphia, PA 19130

Dear Ms. Cummings:

It was a pleasure skiing with you and Alex Park last month. Alex has been telling me for years how well we would get along, and it was a pleasure discovering that his instincts were correct. At that time, you urged me to forward a resume, so that you could inform me of suitable career opportunities at Any Corporation and other refreshment dealers.

During the past six years, I have been involved in customer service and operations management for a company that offers complete office beverage services to businesses and plants throughout the United States. One of my responsibilities has been testing, evaluating, introducing, and promoting gourmet coffees and beverages to discriminating coffee drinkers. In addition, I managed key accounts and was involved in training personnel in methods of beverage brewing that would assure quality results.

Although my position has been challenging, I feel it is time for me to make a change to the primary segment of the coffee industry, importing and roasting, which I feel can offer me broader responsibilities and opportunities. I would like to apply my combined knowledge and experience in the office coffee service business to operations or sales to institutional accounts and resellers such as office beverage services.

I am pleased to see that Any Corporation is expanding its beverage services to the Midwest. I am confident, due to my years of experience, that I could be a key player in such a growth environment. May we meet to discuss?

Sincerely,

Chris Smith

Enc. resume

■ Candidate reminds networking contact of last encounter.

■ Closing reiterates candidate's knowledge of organization.

NETWORKING LETTER
(Broadcast Manager)

178 Green Street
Menomonie, WI 53818

May 4, 1996

Pat Cummings
Deejay
Any Radio Station
1140 Main Street
Madison, WI 53715

Dear Mr. Cummings:

As you may recall, I am scheduled to graduate from the University of Wisconsin
this month. The internship I completed at your station last spring has definitely
confirmed my desire to seek a career in broadcasting, and I am writing to ask for
your assistance to reach this objective.

My desire is to participate in the management training program of a progressive
broadcaster, studio, or agency seeking a highly motivated achiever who sees
success in a ground-floor opportunity that offers enhanced potential for career
growth and advancement based upon outstanding performance. As I prepare to
graduate, I am attempting to gather contact names and information concerning
major players in the industry. I hope to schedule some informational interviews
while still in school to begin my job search.

Mr. Cummings, I recall from my time at the station that you are especially
knowledgeable about the industry as a member of the Wisconsin Broadcasters
Association. Any assistance you could provide in the way of referrals or general
advice would be greatly appreciated. Would it be possible to get together for lunch
one afternoon after your broadcast? If so, please contact me at (608) 555-5555 to
arrange a mutually convenient time to meet. Thank you for your time.

I hope to hear from you soon.

Sincerely,

Chris Smith

Enc. resume

■ Candidate briefly reintroduces
himself/herself to networking
contact in opening.

■ Candidate does not limit available
opportunities by stating specific
position desired.

NETWORKING LETTER
(Business Consultant)

178 Green Street
Price, UT 84501

February 21, 1996

Pat Cummings
Marketing Director
Any Catalog
1140 Main Street
Salt Lake City, UT 84130

Dear Ms. Cummings:

Congratulations! I recently read on the on-line network about the success of your new women's clothing catalog. You have certainly succeeded in broadening your market share while increasing your reputation and profit margin.

As you know, during the past twenty years, I set up and managed a unique mail-order collectible stamp business from product research and procurement to ultimate sale. Currently, I am looking for a new opportunity where I can utilize my advertising, market research, and sales and merchandising skills in flex-time, per diem, or project assignments. While I have thoroughly enjoyed running my own business, I am ready to slow down and focus my efforts on freelance or part-time work.

Ms. Cummings, I am writing to you as a colleague in the catalog business who is familiar with my experience. I would appreciate your assistance in referring me to any organization in need of a professional with my qualifications. I can offer a strong background in catalog development, media selection, and advertising design which has generated more than normal returns. In addition, I have expertise with complex customer data bases, inventory control systems, and forms design to simplify maintenance of mail-order, inventory, and international databases. I am capable of working effectively in a number of areas requiring creative, innovative thinking and have the ability to work independently or as a team member.

Enclosed please find several copies of my business profile. Should your organization have any openings, or should you know of a company in need, I would greatly appreciate your forwarding my materials to the appropriate contacts. Please don't hesitate to contact me at the above address or by phone at (801) 555-5555. Thank you.

Sincerely,

Chris Smith

Enc. business profiles

- ■ Candidate indicates type of employment desired.
- ■ Candidate familiarizes networking contact with relevant skills and experiences.

NETWORKING LETTER
(Business Manager)

178 Green Street
St. Joseph, MO 64507
(816) 555-5555

October 5, 1996

Pat Cummings
Executive Vice-President
Any Corporation
1140 Main Street
St. Peters, MO 63376

Dear Mr. Cummings:

Thank you for taking the time out of your schedule to speak with me yesterday. It is always a pleasure to speak with a friend of David's. As I mentioned on the phone, I am seeking a new association with a company that can benefit from my experience in the development, implementation, and management of manufacturing and business information systems and networks.

As you know, I have devoted the past sixteen years to senior-level positions and played a key role in designing and managing systems that provide support to all facets of corporate functioning and strategic decision-making on domestic or international levels. To better acquaint you with my expertise and record of success in modern, automated management, manufacturing, and business information systems and control methods, I am enclosing a summary of my qualifications and accomplishments.

If you are aware of a firm in need of a professional with my qualifications, I would appreciate you forwarding my business profile for their review and further discussion.

Should you or a receptive firm require additional information, please contact me at the above address or by phone during the daytime at (816) 555-4444. If there is any assistance I can provide you, Pat, please do not hesitate to let me know.

With best regards,

Chris Smith

Enc. business profile

■ Candidate thanks addressee for time extended.

■ Candidate requests that attached resume be forwarded.

NETWORKING LETTER
(Chief Financial Officer)

178 Green Street
El Paso, TX 79998
(915) 555-5555

June 25, 1996

Pat Cummings
President
Any Bank
1140 Main Street
Menomonie, WI 54751

Dear Ms. Cummings:

I am currently seeking a position as a Chief Financial Officer. Brad Peltser
suggested that I contact you in order to focus my job search. I am exploring the
Midwest as a site for relocation, and am anxious to learn more about the
Midwestern job market.

I have a record of outstanding success in the management of corporate financial
operations for fast-paced manufacturing companies and associated commercial
operations, in multilocation, multistate, and international environments.

My sixteen years of progressively responsible experience has encompassed
management of all aspects of the financial and treasury functions, in a range from
Cost Accounting Manager to Chief Financial Officer and Vice-President, Finance.
This experience has fully encompassed the successful management of corporate
real estate, human resources, and general operations areas. In addition to holding
an M.B.A. in Finance, and a B.A. in Accounting, I have been a Certified Public
Accountant since 1980.

May we meet? I am eager for your advice about the job market in the Midwest for
senior-level officers.

Thank you for your consideration.

Sincerely,

Chris Smith

Enc. resume

- ■ Candidate immediately specifies type of position sought.
- ■ Candidate quantifies extensive experience.

NETWORKING LETTER
(Commercial Real Estate Sales Executive)

178 Green Street
Honolulu, HI 96841

February 20, 1996

Pat Cummings
Staff Coordinator
Any Real Estate Company
1140 Main Street
San Francisco, CA 94111

Dear Mr. Cummings:

Are you in need of a well-organized, highly motivated, profit-oriented representative to market and sell acquired properties? Lee Yang, from your commercial sales division, felt that my qualifications would make me an excellent contribution to your staff.

During the past fifteen years, I have been actively involved in diverse industries with concentration on both residential and commercial properties. I have successfully managed and taken various businesses from foreclosed to profitable and salable properties. My ability to start up, set up, reorganize, and manage profitable business operations also applies to the management of major accounts or territories to increase market share.

Please find my resume enclosed. I would like to arrange a personal interview at your convenience. I am planning to relocate to your area, I am free to travel, and the compensation package is negotiable. Please contact me at the above address or by phone at (808) 555-5555.

I look forward to your return response.

Yours sincerely,

Chris Smith

Enc. resume

■ Introducing letter with a question draws attention to candidate.

■ Candidate notifies networking contact of travel availability and/or compensation requirements.

NETWORKING LETTER
(Community Relations Specialist)

178 Green Street
Winchester, VA 22601
(703) 555-5555

August 21, 1996

Pat Cummings
Director, Community Planning
Any Organization
1140 Main Street
Virginia Beach, 23456

Dear Ms. Cummings:

I am writing at the suggestion of Barbara Winters, a fellow member of the Community Outreach Organization in Winchester. I am currently in search of a long-term association with an organization in the field of community relations. Barbara mentioned her frequent working relationship with Any Organization, and felt your office may be in need of a skilled professional with my qualifications.

During the past fifteen years, my experience has been concentrated in areas of community relations and government affairs working in public, university, and private industry settings. I have extensive experience working with various populations and divergent groups, and have been actively involved and successful in troubleshooting and resolving problems during the planning and decision-making processes pertaining to issues impacting communities.

I possess strong presentation, communication, and interpersonal skills, and I have trained and managed support staffs into efficient and productive teams. Based on my qualifications, I feel confident of my ability to make a significant contribution to your organization.

Although my resume provides a good summary of my background and experience, I would like to arrange a mutually convenient meeting, during which we can further discuss any availabilities within Any Organization. Please contact me at the above address or phone, or by FAX at (703) 444-4444.

Thank you for your time.

Sincerely,

Chris Smith

Enc. resume

- Professional memberships show candidate's commitment to his/her field.

- Including a FAX number is optional in a cover letter.

NETWORKING LETTER
(Construction Engineer)

178 Green Street
Huntington, WV 25755

July 20, 1996

Pat Cummings
President
Any Construction Company
1140 Main Street
Montgomery, WV 25136

Dear Mr. Cummings:

Jeff Fallon of B&D Construction, forwarded me your company name as one who may be in need of an addition to your construction team. My desire is to find a challenging position in which to utilize my formal training and practical experience in the construction field.

In addition to a Bachelor of Science degree with concentration in Civil Engineering, I have two Associate degrees in related subjects, as well as eleven years of term and full-time employment holding responsible positions in construction. My knowledge includes construction of schools, parking structures, museums, medical facilities, office buildings, and other structures. I am experienced in supervision, engineering layout, construction coordination, purchasing, and many aspects related to the organization and business of construction.

After reviewing my resume, if you have a position in your organization for someone with training and experience who will work to a high standard of excellence, please contact me at the above address, or call (304) 555-5555. I would like to arrange a personal interview, during which we could further discuss my potential for service while in your employment.

Thank you for your consideration.

Sincerely,

Chris Smith

Enc. resume

■ Letter highlights candidate's acquired professional and educational training.

■ Networking letter establishes candidate's knowledge of his/her field.

NETWORKING LETTER
(Construction Manager)

178 Green Street
Newnan, GA 30264
(404) 555-5555

January 20, 1996

Pat Cummings
Project Manager
Any Construction Company
1140 Main Street
Macon, GA 31208

Dear Ms. Cummings:

It has been about two years since our last meeting, but I am sure you remember the work we completed together on the Independence Office Park in Macon. Since that time, I have continued my association with T & C Construction until cutbacks were instituted last week. Ms. Cummings, I would like to ask for your assistance as I begin my search for a new position.

Currently, I am seeking an association with a firm where I can utilize my knowledge and expertise in the area of project management, property management, field crew supervision, negotiations, purchasing, and construction office operation. I have supervised on-site crews on various commercial and residential projects, have good communication and negotiation skills, and work well with vendors, owners, management, office, and construction trades. I am a licensed Hydraulic Equipment Operator, hold a Class II license on heavy construction equipment, and have extensive experience in the operation of major, heavy construction, earth moving, and transportation equipment.

I wonder if we could get together at your convenience for a meeting. Any contact names or general advice you could provide would greatly assist me as I construct a job-hunting campaign. I would also very much like to get reacquainted and learn what has been going on at Any Construction over the last two years. I will call you soon to confirm a good time to meet.

Sincerely,

Chris Smith

Enc. resume

■ Letter solicits networking contact's advice rather than assistance with job placement.

■ Candidate includes licensure relevant to his/her field.

NETWORKING LETTER
(Consultant)

178 Green Street
St. Charles, MO 63302
(314) 555-5555

November 6, 1996

Pat Cummings
President
Any Corporation
1140 Main Street
Chesterfield, MO 63017

Dear Mr. Cummings:

I obtained your company name from my client, Fred Mosley, President of ISS, Incorporated. My expertise is in working with small, nonprofit health care and human services organizations, such as ISS, who have problems meeting their commitments because of budget constraints. As an experienced independent consultant, I implement cost-effective techniques to put in place the systems, programs, and controls necessary to generate the dollars to meet and exceed fund-raising goals.

During the past twenty years, I have played a key role in the management, planning, and successful execution of projects which require working with decision-makers, committees, volunteer groups, and community organizations on institutional/organizational development. I am qualified to handle such projects, from needs survey to achievement of projected funding objectives, and I am prepared to provide you, or any suitable corporation you are aware of, with this expertise on a per-assignment rather than full-time basis. Depending on your needs, my consulting fees will be quoted on a per-project or hourly basis.

If you are in the process of, or are planning, a campaign, please contact me so that we can arrange a meeting to discuss your requirements. I can be reached at the above address or phone, or by FAX at (314) 444-4444. I will be glad to provide you with a client list and documentation of my achievements at that time.

Sincerely,

Chris Smith

Enc. professional profile

■ First paragraph introduces candidate to networking contact.

■ Discussion details how candidate's qualifications will benefit potential employer.

NETWORKING LETTER
(Corporate Treasurer)

178 Green Street
Canyon, TX 79016
(806) 555-5555

June 4, 1996

Pat Cummings
Vice-President
Any Corporation
1140 Main Street
Cedar City, UT 84720

Dear Ms. Cummings:

At the suggestion of Tom Poudrier, I am submitting my resume for the Corporate
Treasurer position. I have followed your company's rapid growth during the past
two years, and read with much excitement your prediction for further expansion in
the trade journal *Real Estates*. I wish to be a part of this exciting atmosphere.

During the past thirteen years, I have compiled a record of success as Vice-
President/Treasurer of a multicorporate real estate development and management
company, and I have ten years of additional experience as Corporate Treasurer and
Controller with a nonprofit educational research firm and an electronic
manufacturer.

I am pursuing a new opportunity utilizing my financial and management expertise.
My interest is in working in a business or nonprofit environment where my
associates and I share the common goal of profitable growth and mutual gain.

After reviewing my qualifications, I would appreciate you contacting me for a
personal meeting. I can be reached at the above address, by phone, or a message
may be left at (806) 555-4444. I appreciate your consideration.

Sincerely,

Chris Smith

Enc. resume

■ Specific company information
illustrates candidate's commitment
to his/her field.

■ Candidate informs networking
contact of work experience in field
of interest.

NETWORKING LETTER
(Credit Officer)

178 Green Street
Baton Rouge, LA 70821
(504) 555-5555

May 25, 1996

Pat Cummings
Chief Loan Officer
Any Bank
1140 Main Street
LaPlace, LA 70069

Dear Mr. Cummings:

Pursuant to your recent conversation with my father, I am forwarding the attached resume for your evaluation. It is my desire to participate in a leading commercial credit training program as a first step in my commercial banking career. I understand that your loan officer development program is regarded as one of the finest in the industry.

Please note that in addition to receiving my recent Master of Business Administration degree in Finance and Management Policy with honors, I have a Bachelor of Arts degree in Economics and two years of progressively responsible experience working in diverse areas of operations and marketing support with McEllis Industries, Inc.

I would like to demonstrate my potential to succeed with your bank, working as an individual contributor or as a team member, to the achievement of mutual goals and objectives. For this reason, I welcome the opportunity to meet with you in order to further discuss your current or anticipated needs in terms of my qualifications and career objectives. I will contact your office on Wednesday, May 29 to schedule a convenient interview time.

Sincerely,

Chris Smith

Enc. resume

■ Basis for referral is immediately established.

■ Educational honors indicate candidate's potential to excel.

NETWORKING LETTER
(Customer Support Representative)

178 Green Street
Scranton, PA 18510

April 1, 1996

Pat Cummings
Customer Support Manager
Any Corporation
1140 Main Street
Greenburg, PA 15601

Dear Ms. Cummings:

I am a former college classmate of your son Dennis, and have, since graduation, worked as a Customer Support Representative for a manufacturer of high-volume copier and reprographic equipment. Although my position has been challenging and fast-paced, at this point in my career, I am seeking a new, long-term association where my expertise and motivation can be more fully utilized.

I had lunch with Dennis last week while on a business trip to Pittsburgh, and he suggested that you might have an availability within the customer support department of your corporation. I have enclosed my resume as an expressed interest in applying for such an opening.

During the past three years, I have gained progressively responsible experience in providing sales support and training to new hires and end-users of major commercial, institutional, industrial, and government accounts on a national level. I am an effective representative and support individual with the ability to provide liaison between sales, service, customers, and corporate personnel.

I would love to meet with you to further outline my experiences and how I could contribute successfully to your firm. Please contact me when you have a free moment to schedule an interview. I can be reached at the above address or by phone at (717) 555-5555. I look forward to hearing from you.

Sincerely,

Chris Smith

Enc. resume

■ Networking letter may allow for personal discussion.

■ Letter emphasizes valuable skills.

NETWORKING LETTER
(Director of College Development)

178 Green Street
Pittsburgh, PA 15217
(412) 555-5555

June 8, 1996

Pat Cummings
Alumni Development Director
Any University
1140 Main Street
New Haven, CT 06520

Dear Mr. Cummings:

I am glad we had the opportunity to meet at the Educational Development Symposium. I thoroughly enjoyed exchanging ideas about the interplay between the academic and the financial worlds. Your development ideas have enriched the scope of my knowledge and I hope our discussion benefited you as well. As you suggested, I have enclosed a resume to remind you of my background.

In addition to a Master of Education in Administration and Supervision and Bachelor of Arts degree in Business Administration, I offer ten years of experience in positions ranging from Assistant Director of Alumni and Parent Relations with a four-year college, to my most recent position as Director of the Annual Fund with a college preparatory school.

My experience includes a full range of management responsibilities including full knowledge of the institutional advancement field, public/client relations, development/fund-raising, special event planning, marketing/sales, and promotion/advertising.

I am interested in exploring opportunities at other colleges. If you know of any such opportunities, or have colleagues who may be aware of developmental opportunities at other universities, I would appreciate it if you could provide this information.

I hope to speak with you again soon.

Sincerely,

Chris Smith

Enc. resume

■ Candidate reminds networking contact of last encounter.

■ Educational credentials accentuate candidate's qualifications.

NETWORKING LETTER
(Director of Information Services)

178 Green Street
Bellingham, WA 98226
(206) 555-5555

November 19, 1996

Pat Cummings
Director of Informational Services
Any Municipality
1140 Main Street
Bellingham, WA 98226

Dear Ms. Cummings:

After so many years of working in your department, it is with mixed emotions that I greet your departure. While I will regret your absence, I congratulate you on your retirement and the successful conclusion of your years of service.

At your retirement celebration, you informed me that you recommended me to the search committee as your replacement. I would be honored to act in this position, and thank you for your recommendation. As you suggested, I here remind you of my career history.

During the past fourteen years, I have held positions as Manager of Systems Planning and Development, Principal Systems Analyst, and Manager of Computer Operations with Any Municipality. In this capacity, my responsibilities have included directing the operations of a data processing center serving numerous departments within the city hall complex. In keeping with the numerous changes in municipal systems and procedures, my work in data processing has been increasingly complex and required extensive program development, system analysis, troubleshooting and problem-solving, employee training, and supervision in computer operations.

Allow me to reiterate my interest to contribute my energy and skills to Any Municipality. I am confident that, given this opportunity, I can uphold your standard of service which, as a result of your efforts, the city has come to expect.

Thank you for your kind consideration.

Sincerely,

Chris Smith

Enc. resume

■ Candidate familiarizes networking contact with relevant skills and experiences.

■ Candidate chronicles career progression within firm.

NETWORKING LETTER
(Driver)

178 Green Street
Cookeville, TN 38505
(901) 555-5555

June 21, 1996

Pat Cummings
Shipping Services Manager
Any Corporation
1140 Main Street
Florence, MS 39703

Dear Mr. Cummings:

Last week I spoke with Brooke Breyfogle, who encouraged me to contact you. My desire to drive for Any Corporation has prompted me to forward the attached resume for your evaluation.

Please note that in addition to six years as a Package Car Driver for United States Shipping, I received intensive training in Diesel Mechanics while a member of the U.S. Marine Corps. I also managed a Marine auto hobby shop where I learned basic auto mechanics. In my current job. I have gained valuable insight into the task of working effectively while on a tight schedule, maintaining good customer relations, and interfacing regularly with employees and management.

I will contact your office on Monday to establish a mutually convenient time for a meeting, during which we may more fully discuss your current or anticipated driver needs in terms of my qualifications.

Thank you for your time and consideration.

Sincerely,

Chris Smith

Enc. resume

■ Candidate details how past military experience will benefit potential employer.

■ In closing, candidate specifically requests interview.

NETWORKING LETTER
(Editor)

178 Green Street
Arlington, VA 22207
(703) 555-5555

December 9, 1996

Pat Cummings
Vice-President, Editorial
Any Corporation
1140 Main Street
Wise, VA 24293

Dear Ms. Cummings:

John Curran suggested that I write you. He spoke very highly of your creative,
market-sensitive approach to publishing and your tremendous success in
publicizing your books. He also said that you might have plans to expand your
editorial team. If so, I thought that my qualifications might interest you.

I have seven years' experience as a Nonfiction Editor. For the past two years, I
have acquired books for McDoogle's Professional Book Group. There, I worked
with authors on books that address the wide range of challenges facing today's
managers and small business owners—from cash management to business
security. I also acquired books on personal business topics such as Margaret
Miller's *Loving Your Job* for the career/self-help market. A January 1997 release,
Miller's book already has received a strong response from book clubs (20,000
copy advance order) and an enthusiastic endorsement from Michael Morin.

Earlier in my career, I acquired books on health, fitness, recreation, and other
nonfiction topics for Stevens & Dunn. Although designed for the academic
environment, these books had strong crossover appeal to the trade market. Also, I
have procured many author contacts and book ideas I would like to pursue.

I would love to meet with you and find out more about Any Corporation's
publishing program as well as possible ways we might work together. I will call
you within a week to see if we can schedule an appointment soon. Thank you.

Sincerely,

Chris Smith

Enc. resume

■ Relevant work experience is
emphasized while other positions
are omitted.

■ Candidate informs networking
contact of his/her commitment to
field of interest.

NETWORKING LETTER
(Electrical Engineer)

178 Green Street
Mt. Pleasant, MI 48859

July 18, 1996

Pat Cummings
Director, Products and Services
Any Corporation
1140 Main Street
Kalamazoo, MI 49007

Dear Mr. Cummings:

Thank you for taking the time to speak with me on the phone yesterday. I saw your nephew Brenden last night and sent your regards as you requested. Brenden hopes to see you soon, and confirms that he is, indeed, working hard to graduate.

As I mentioned on the phone, I am a candidate for a Bachelor of Science degree in Electrical Engineering, anticipating graduation in May 1996. I have enclosed my resume per your request. Ideally, I would like to find a position in which I could contribute to a firm's technical products and services through my combined academic and practical experience.

I certainly do not expect that you will be able to provide me with a position, Mr. Cummings, but I would greatly appreciate any leads or contact names you may know of in the field. Additionally, would it be possible to meet? I would love to get your insight into the industry, as well as hear any advice you could provide for my search. Please contact me at the above address or by phone at (517) 555-5555 to arrange a mutually convenient time to get together.

I appreciate your time.

Sincerely,

Chris Smith

Enc. resume

■ Letter appeals to networking contact's knowledge of industry.

■ Career objective gives focus without limiting candidate's opportunities.

NETWORKING LETTER
(Elementary Teacher)

178 Green Street
Medford, MA 02155
(617) 555-5555

July 18, 1996

Pat Cummings
President
Any Teachers' Association
1140 Main Street
Everett, MA 02149

Dear Ms. Cummings:

Hello! I hope that you are enjoying your new position at the Union. We certainly miss you at Medford Elementary. Many of the students still ask when you are returning, and the teacher's room has been so quiet without you. When are you coming back to visit us?

Pat, I am also writing on a business-related subject. Since the town lost its override appeal this month, I have found myself out of a job. I was hoping that, as Association President, you might know of a school system in need of an education veteran.

I am seeking a position that involves teaching and motivating children toward academic success and self-improvement, possibly where I can utilize my certification and six years' experience in special needs. I am especially interested in a professional environment that caters to the development and well-being of children either in an educational or child-care setting.

If you could refer me to any leads you might be aware of, I would be grateful. I've enclosed my resume to assist you in the brainstorming process. I'll call you early next week to talk further.

Thank you for taking the time to assist me. I look forward to catching up soon!

With best regards,

Chris Smith

Enc. resume

- Familiarity with networking contact allows for personalized writing style.
- Dedication to candidate's field of interest is emphasized.

NETWORKING LETTER
(Environmental Services Director)

178 Green Street
Provo, UT 84602
(801) 555-5555

November 22, 1996

Pat Cummings
Director
Any Corporation
1140 Main Street
Washington, PA 15301

Dear Mr. Cummings:

My desire to locate a position in the management of large-scale environmental services or related operations with an institution offering enhanced potential for career growth and development has prompted me to forward the attached resume for your evaluation. Mindy LeMouge suggested that you may be aware of such a position.

Please note that in addition to an Associate degree in Public Environmental Health, and intensive additional professional-level training in this area, I possess eighteen years of progressively responsible experience in the management of environmental services operations for commercial and institutional employers.

My experience encompasses all aspects of departmental management, including the development of policies and procedures, personnel hiring, training, supervision and evaluation, scheduling, customer and vendor negotiations and relations, cost estimation, budget development and management purchasing, payroll, management reporting, inventory control, scheduling, and wage and salary negotiation.

I would appreciate a chance to meet, in which we could discuss the environmental industry. Frankly, I would appreciate any advice you, with your expertise, could offer me regarding my current job search. I will call your office to schedule a mutually convenient time for such a meeting.

Sincerely,

Chris Smith

Enc. resume

■ Type of position desired is clearly stated.

■ Letter highlights candidate's management skills.

NETWORKING LETTER
(Executive Nonprofit Director)

178 Green Street
Sedalia, MO 65301
(816) 555-5555

April 21, 1996

Pat Cummings
Chairperson
Any Foundation
1140 Main Street
Odessa, TX 79762

Dear Ms. Cummings:

Dean Wareham recently informed me of the open position of Executive Director of Any Foundation. Mr. Wareham suggested that I contact you directly before entering the general applicant pool.

During the past fifteen years, I have established a record of achievement in leadership positions with a nationally renowned, nonprofit organization. My positions as Development, Public Relations, and Telecommunications Director required the capability to handle multimillion dollar budgets and development drives. In addition, I was responsible for all areas of public relations and marketing for multiple projects, the most recent being a $95 million retirement community which required extensive contact with the legal profession.

My expertise, as outlined in my resume, meets all the requirements essential to the position of Executive Director of Any Foundation, including monitoring responsibility, long- and short-term planning, and the implementation of policies and procedures for a well-run organization. Based on my qualifications, I feel that I can provide management and administrative expertise for positive direction and quality membership services.

I look forward to hearing from you.

Thank you for your time.

Sincerely,

Chris Smith

Enc. resume

■ Candidate immediately names referral.

■ Closing reiterates candidate's qualifications for position.

NETWORKING LETTER
(Field Service Manager)

178 Green Street
Belleville, MI 48112

August 20, 1996

Pat Cummings
Human Resources Manager
Any Cancer Institute
1140 Main Street
Boston, MA 02118

Dear Mr. Cummings:

During a recent conversation with Dr. Elizabeth Bradley, a specialist in children's leukemia, I mentioned my interest in the human resources division of Any Cancer Institute, specifically for the Field Service Manager position advertised.

Dr. Bradley has firsthand knowledge of my organizational and management skills, as well as my comprehensive training and experience dealing with the day-to-day management of care control for children. She recommended that I contact you directly, to make you aware of my interest in the position and my conviction that I am capable of handling the position to achieve the goals of Any Cancer Institute.

Although I have forwarded an application to your director of human resources, I am enclosing a copy of my resume for your review. I am planning to relocate permanently to the Boston area and hope to do so as an employee of your facility. Any assistance you can provide is appreciated.

Should you require additional information, please contact me at the above address or by phone at (313) 555-5555 or (313) 555-4444.

Yours sincerely,

Chris Smith

Enc. professional profile

- Introduction states candidate's desire to join specific organization.
- Candidate informs networking contact of mutual acquaintance.

NETWORKING LETTER
(Finance Assistant)

178 Green Street
Zephyr Cove, NV 89448
(702) 555-5555

March 30, 1996

Pat Cummings
Senior Loan Administrator
Any Corporation
1140 Main Street
Chicago, IL 60605

Dear Ms. Cummings:

I truly enjoyed our conversation last week at the Racquet Ball Club. I hope you relish the remainder of your stay in Las Vegas.

As you may recall, I will be graduating from the University of Las Vegas in May with a degree in Finance. For the past three months, I have been interning at Marshall Howard Company. I have learned the auditing and payment coordination aspects of the business in-depth, gaining praise for my motivation, professionalism, and willingness to take on new tasks.

Currently, I am looking for an entry-level finance position with a dynamic company. I would greatly appreciate any assistance you could provide. Enclosed is my resume and a letter of recommendation for your review.

Thank you in advance for your help. It is greatly appreciated!

Sincerely,

Chris Smith

Enc. resume
　　　letter of recommendation

- Internship experience is valuable for candidates with little job experience, particularly if it corresponds to the position sought.

- Candidate thanks networking contact in advance for his/her assistance.

NETWORKING LETTER
(Finance Executive)

278 Green Street
Maryville, MO 64468
(816) 555-5555

May 14, 1996

Pat Cummings
Executive Vice-President
Any Corporation
1140 Main Street
Fulton, MO 65251

Dear Mr. Cummings:

I received your name as a key figure in the Missouri banking industry from a mutual friend, Rebecca Meader. I understand that Rebecca is a fellow member of the Fulton Country Club and has often accompanied you on the golf course. She generously offered your services as a contact for my job-search campaign.

For the past fifteen years, I have acted as a top producer in new business development, consumer leading, system implementation, personnel management and training, customer service, and financial counseling. Although my positions have been challenging, at this point in my career, I am exploring new opportunities in which to apply this extensive background and experience in banking and finance.

Please note that in addition to formal education and a degree in Business Administration, I have undertaken advanced study in financial counseling, mortgage banking, and the quality processing. My qualifications have been earned through multiple branch management with a $140 million credit union in the greater St. Louis area, as well as through extensive customer support and technical coordination experience providing support and training to select client personnel on an IBM-automated ordering system.

I would greatly appreciate your consideration of my enclosed resume for any suitable availabilities at Any Corporation, and would welcome the opportunity to speak with you in a personal meeting. Please feel free to contact me at the above address or phone, or by FAX at (816) 555-4444. Thank you for your consideration, Mr. Cummings.

I look forward to hearing from you.

Sincerely,

Chris Smith

Enc. resume

■ Candidate informs networking contact of work experience in field of interest.

■ Including a FAX number is optional in a cover letter.

NETWORKING LETTER
(Finance Manager)

178 Green Street
Downers Grove, IL 60515
(708) 555-5555

January 25, 1996

Pat Cummings
Human Resource Director
Any Bank
1140 Main Street
New York, NY 10128

Dear Ms. Cummings:

John Monroe, of First Avenue Bank, informed me that you might be expanding
your staffing needs. Based on my comprehensive experience in the field of
finance, I can offer your firm a broad range of management and administrative
skills in banking.

During the past twenty-five years, I have played a key role in the trust banking
industry in positions ranging from Tax Officer to my current position as Chief
Trust Officer. Because of my ability to adapt strategies to changing conditions, I
was able to apply innovative approaches that increased productivity, accuracy, and
profits. As a result, customer service, corporate visibility and image, and customer
base were substantially improved.

I am confident I could contribute my expertise to the continued success of Any
Bank, and would welcome the chance to discuss career opportunities. I will call
your office to schedule an interview.

Thank you for your time.

Sincerely,

Chris Smith

Enc. resume

■ Candidate immediately introduces
qualifications.

■ Candidate immediately introduces
purpose for writing.

NETWORKING LETTER
(Genetic Research Technician)

178 Green Street
Baton Rouge, LA 70821
(504) 555-5555

March 17, 1996

Pat Cummings
Director
Any Center
1140 Main Street
Lake Charles, LA 70602

Dear Mr. Cummings:

I am a good friend of Anne Connelly, who I understand is a colleague of yours at
Any Center. Anne thought that, as an experienced veteran of biomedical research,
you would be able to offer some valuable assistance with my job search.

I am currently searching for a challenging position as a Genetic Research
Technician. In addition to a Bachelor's degree in Biology with a concentration in
Genetics, which I received in 1993, I have hands-on laboratory experience as a lab
assistant conducting studies for neuropsychology. I have researched and written
class papers on germ line therapy, genetic technology, legal aspects of genetics,
and genetics testing in the workplace. I am a highly motivated, career-oriented
individual who would like to contribute to an established facility by combining
both my academic and practical experience, as outlined in the enclosed resume.

Would it be possible to meet? I would like to briefly solicit your advice and,
possibly, gather any further names to contact in the field. I will call your office on
Friday to confirm a time.

Thank you for your consideration.

Sincerely yours,

Chris Smith

Enc. resume

- Letter appeals to networking contact's knowledge of industry.
- Valuable research experience is highlighted in detail.

NETWORKING LETTER
(Golf Instructor)

178 Green Street
Albuquerque, NM 87190
(505) 555-5555

February 14, 1996

Pat Cummings
Director
Any Golf Club
1140 Main Street
Las Cruces, NM 88003

Dear Ms. Cummings:

As a result of a recent referral from Mr. David Stefan regarding an entry-level
instructing opening with Any Golf Club, I am submitting my resume for your
review.

I possess eight years of education, training, coaching, and playing experience. My
involvement with the game of golf began in high school and, since then, my skill
level and affection for the sport have increased. Currently, I am seeking a career
opportunity where I can offer my education and experience to make a positive
contribution by maintaining high standards and a professional image within a club
environment.

I am very interested in this opening. Could I perhaps schedule a personal interview
with you at your convenience? I will contact your offices Monday, February 19 to
discuss an appropriate meeting time.

Sincerely,

Chris Smith

Enc. resume

■ Candidate informs networking
contact of his/her commitment to
field of interest.

■ Phrasing request in question form
is a strong closing.

NETWORKING LETTER
(Human Resources Manager)

178 Green Street
Rockford, IL 61108
(815) 555-5555

July 7, 1996

Pat Cummings
Division Manager
Any Corporation
1140 Main Street
Kankakee, IL 60901

Dear Mr. Cummings:

It was a real pleasure talking to you during the S.H.R.M. Conference & Exposition in St. Louis. I found our discussion both interesting and very informative.

As I mentioned, I am currently in search of a new career opportunity in human resources management and would appreciate your assistance. My most recent assignments include the following:

- More than three years directing the human resources activities, systems, procedures, and programs for Yurof Supplies, Inc.
- Creating from scratch a full personnel administration system for Buttrick Tool & Die Co.
- Three years as Industrial Relations Manager for the Cancellare Group, supervising a department of eleven employees.

I do not expect that you would know of a suitable opening for me at this time. However, I would value any ideas or suggestions you may have which could help direct my job search.

The enclosed resume details my professional experience and some of my accomplishments. Should you hear of anything, or simply have a suggestion for me, please give me a call.

Thank you very much for your time and consideration. I hope to talk to you again soon.

Sincerely,

Chris Smith

Enc. resume

■ Bullets in networking letter draw attention to candidate's accomplishments.

■ Candidate immediately thanks addressee for pleasurable meeting.

NETWORKING LETTER
(Insurance Manager)

178 Green Street
Wayne, NE 68787

October 7, 1996

Pat Cummings
Underwriter
Any Insurance Agency
1140 Main Street
York, NE 68467

Dear Ms. Cummings:

It was very nice speaking with you yesterday and learning about the changes
taking place at Any Insurance Agency. Per your request, I am enclosing my
business profile for your review.

My experience as an underwriter, account manager, and office manager have
provided me with expertise in all facets of insurance agency operation. Once
oriented to the policies of a new firm, I feel I have the knowledge and skill to
assume responsibility for any of the above, or related, positions.

Any assistance you can provide in my search for a position would be much
appreciated. Should you require additional information, please contact me at the
above address or call me at (402) 555-5555.

Thank you for taking the time to assist me in my job search. Best of luck in all
your future endeavors!

Yours sincerely,

Chris Smith

Enc. business profile

- Letter is brief and concise.
- Letter solicits networking contact's advice rather than assistance with job placement.

NETWORKING LETTER
(International Controller)

178 Green Street
Kilgore, TX 75662
(903) 555-5555

January 16, 1996

Pat Cummings
Finance Manager
Any Corporation
1140 Main Street
Austin, TX 78713

Dear Mr. Cummings:

It was a pleasure meeting you last month while visiting Bob and Cheryl
Maxmillian at their home in Austin. As you may recall, at that time I was working
as an International Controller of Divinex, a multidivision manufacturer of
automatic test equipment. Recent ownership changes have prompted me to seek
another association in finance management. When I updated Bob on my search
recently, he suggested I obtain your assistance.

I possess over sixteen years of experience working with foreign manufacturing
entities and sales/service subsidiaries, which has involved corporate financial
planning and analysis, international reporting, treasury and tax management, and
interactive MIS systems for both corporate and divisional financial operations. I
am searching for a position that would allow me to utilize my diverse background
while providing the opportunity for career growth.

Should you know of any corporations in the Austin area in need of someone with
my qualifications, would you kindly forward my resume to the appropriate
contacts? Also, I will be visiting Bob and Cheryl in two weeks' time, to meet with
industry insiders and continue my search. Should your schedule permit, I would
like to meet, perhaps for lunch or dinner. I would greatly appreciate your input as a
fellow professional in the field. I will contact you next week to find a time that is
good for you.

Thank you for your assistance. I hope to see you again soon.

Sincerely,

Chris Smith

Enc. resume

■ Explaining reason for job search is
optional.

■ Candidate details applicable work
experience.

NETWORKING LETTER
(International Marketing Specialist)

178 Green Street
Stratford, CT 06497
(203) 555-5555

April 10, 1996

Pat Cummings
Senior Marketing Specialist
Any Corporation
1140 Main Street
Middlebury, CT 06762

Dear Ms. Cummings:

My uncle, Joe McGinness, a former Fiji fraternity brother of yours at Worcester Polytechnic Institute, suggested I contact you to explore career opportunities in our mutual field of interest, international marketing.

I graduated from Fairfield University in May 1994, with a Bachelor of Science in Textile Marketing. I feel that through my educational extracurricular programs and work experience, I have gained an outstanding business foundation upon which I can build my professional career. I consider myself to be a determined competitor. Setting high, yet realistic, goals for myself and seeing them through to their completion is something I pride myself in and is a key ingredient in my success to date. I am ambitious and willing to devote the extra time that is usually necessary for worthwhile achievements. Additionally, I would consider travel and/or relocation.

My past experiences have helped me sharpen my interpersonal skills. To me, the marketing field offers unlimited growth potential and a career in which you are directly rewarded for hard work and perseverance. Therefore, I believe marketing is the ideal profession for me, since I am willing to work long and hard to attain success.

I would appreciate a chance to meet with you, at your convenience, to discuss possible career opportunities within your firm or in the greater Connecticut industry. I will call your office during the week of April 17 to confirm an interview time. Thank you for your consideration and any efforts you may extend on my behalf.

Sincerely,

Chris Smith

Enc. resume

■ Discussion of personal qualities reiterates candidate's ability to contribute to potential employer.

■ Letter focuses on acquired skills rather than detailing past employers.

NETWORKING LETTER
(Inventory Control Supervisor)

178 Green Street
Glassboro, NJ 08028

May 24, 1996

Pat Cummings
Inventory Control Coordinator
Any Corporation
1140 Main Street
New Brunswick, NJ 08903

Dear Mr. Cummings:

Beth Monaco, Director of Operations at Welman Industries, suggested I contact you with regard to employment opportunities.

I have enclosed my resume, which outlines my extensive experience in inventory maintenance and control. I am a self-motivated individual who can work well with people, grasp and expand on ideas, tackle and follow through on difficult projects, and achieve or exceed objectives. Although my positions have been fast-paced, challenging, and broad in scope, I feel it is time for a change. Currently, I am investigating new opportunities where my skills can be best utilized to the advantage of the organization.

I feel confident that I can make an immediate as well as long-term contribution to your organization, as I have for my past employers. I will call your office on Friday, May 31, to see if we can schedule a meeting for further discussion.

In the interim, if additional information is required, please contact me at the above address or by phone at (609) 555-5555.

Thank you for your consideration.

Sincerely,

Chris Smith

Enc. resume

- Closing indicates specific date when candidate will follow up inquiry.

- Letter relies on action verbs rather than passive verbs for emphasis.

NETWORKING LETTER
(Legal Assistant)

178 Green Street
Johnson City, TN 37614

June 26, 1996

Pat Cummings
Assistant District Attorney
Any Office
1140 Main Street
Nashville, TN 37203

Dear Ms. Cummings:

Lee Ellis, Director of Career Services at East Tennessee State University, gave me
your name as a valuable contact within the Nashville law enforcement field. I am a
recent graduate of East Tennessee State, which I understand is your alma mater as
well. During the past several years, I have been preparing myself for a career in
law where I can utilize my dual degrees in Criminology and Psychology in the
public or private sector.

As my enclosed resume reveals, in addition to my academic studies in these
fields, I have experience as a student Investigative Assistant with the Memphis
County District Attorney's office, where I was involved in a variety of
investigations and other assigned duties dealing with law enforcement and legal
issues. Based upon my performance in this position, I received the highest possible
evaluation. I consider myself to be dependable, capable of rapid orientation and
training, and skilled at assuming responsibility for assignments as an individual or
as a team member.

I am considering attending law school in several years, and would love the
opportunity to confirm my interest in law and law enforcement through a Legal
Assistant position at an organization such as Any Office. I would greatly
appreciate the opportunity to meet with you to discuss availabilities at your office
or to receive any referrals you might find helpful. Would your schedule permit a
few free moments next week? I will call on Monday to schedule a convenient time
for you.

Should you require additional information prior to our meeting, please
contact me at the above address or by phone at (615) 555-5555.

Sincerely,

Chris Smith

Enc. resume

■ First paragraph introduces
candidate to networking contact.

■ Candidate's most recent position
is outlined in detail.

NETWORKING LETTER
(Leisure Trainer)

178 Green Street
Lincroft, NJ 07738
(908) 555-5555

March 1, 1996

Pat Cummings
President
Any Travel Agency
1140 Main Street
Nyack, NJ 10960

Dear Mr. Cummings:

Anna Murphy, co-owner of Kannenberg Travel, suggested you as a top contact in
the travel industry. I am confident that as an Educator and Staff Trainer with
comprehensive experience in domestic and foreign travel, I have the qualifications
necessary for the position of Leisure Trainer. Do you have a need for a person
with my expertise?

During my seven years in travel, I have been involved in the development, sales,
and marketing of travel products, agency management, and staff development. My
experience encompasses diverse travel packages and customized leisure and
educational travel.

Currently, I am seeking a new association within the travel industry where I can
utilize my combined teaching and travel experience to train new agents in the
nuances of providing clients with a quality travel experience and maintaining the
agency's high standards. I am interested in Any Travel Agency because your
company has committed itself to expanding into Asian travel markets, an area I
was just beginning to explore in my last position.

I would like to speak with you. May we meet?

Sincerely,

Chris Smith

Enc. resume

- ■ Closing reiterates candidate's interest in specific corporation.
- ■ Networking letter establishes candidate's knowledge of his/her field.

NETWORKING LETTER
(Maintenance Supervisor)

178 Green Street
New Castle, DE 19720
(302) 555-5555

April 3, 1996

Pat Cummings
Facilities Manager
Any Country Club
1140 Main Street
New Castle, DE 19720

Dear Ms. Cummings:

I enjoyed playing doubles with you and Brian Fee last week. With regard to the open Maintenance Supervisor position you mentioned, I am forwarding my career history. Pat, I am confident that I can provide your facility with top-notch care and maintenance.

My primary technical skills include plumbing, heating, and the general maintenance of residential and commercial properties. I have broad-based knowledge of and experience in construction and mechanical trades such as electrical work, roofing, painting, carpentry, and other areas essential to the cost-effective upkeep of a quality facility. Presently, I am interested in a position in property management where my skills in these areas can be best utilized.

Please contact me so that we may discuss how my skills can benefit your club. If the Maintenance Supervisor position has been filled, I would appreciate you forwarding my resume to other facility managers or other useful contacts.

Thank you for your time.

Sincerely,

Chris Smith

Enc. resume

■ Personalized tone reinforces candidate's familiarity with addressee.

■ Candidate requests that attached resume be forwarded.

NETWORKING LETTER
(Marketing Assistant)

178 Green Street
Dazey, ND 58428
(701) 555-5555

June 2, 1996

Pat Cummings
Director of Marketing
Any Corporation
1140 Main Street
Chicago, IL 60605

Dear Mr. Cummings:

It was a pleasure talking to you during our flight to Rome last April. I hope you enjoyed your trip!

As you may recall, I was a senior at Harvard University studying marketing and sales. You were kind enough to give me your business card with instructions to contact you once I was "liberated from the fetters of academia." Finally, that day has arrived.

Although I am a recent graduate, I have held several internships at major Boston corporations. As a result, I know how to buy and sell in an aggressive, no-holds-barred manner while retaining the diplomacy necessary to garner respect.

I have enclosed my resume for your reference and file. If you know of anyone seeking a fresh new addition to their marketing team, please let me know.

Thank you for your assistance.

Sincerely,

Chris Smith

Enc. resume

■ Internship experience demonstrates candidate's familiarity with field of work.

■ Reminds networking contact of common experience.

NETWORKING LETTER
(Marketing Specialist)

178 Green Street
Youngstown, OH 44555
(216) 555-5555

March 23, 1996

Pat Cummings
Director, Sales and Marketing
Any Corporation
1140 Main Street
Largo, MD 20772

Dear Ms. Cummings:

Thank you for taking the time to speak with me briefly after your sales presentation on behalf of Any Corporation last Thursday. As you may recall, I am relocating to your area next month and am currently in search of a marketing position within Any Corporation.

During the past five years, my experience in my present position as Marketing Specialist has been focused on product management, strategic planning, marketing, and the sale of equipment, systems, chemicals, and related products and services. Currently, I have responsibility for the worldwide marketing of bio-instrument chemicals sold to biotech markets, pharmaceutical markets, and research laboratories.

As my enclosed resume indicates, my success in product management, new business/market development, and the sales management of national and international markets has provided me with the qualifications I feel would contribute to the growth and profitability of your firm.

At your convenience, I would like to discuss, in detail, the mutual benefit of my joining your management team. I consider myself to be a persistent achiever, and feel confident that I can make a significant difference. I will call your office on March 26 to arrange a meeting time.

I appreciate your consideration and look forward to speaking with you.

Yours sincerely,

Chris Smith

Enc. resume

- ■ Closing reiterates candidate's qualifications for position.
- ■ Letter focuses on functional skills applicable to potential employer.

NETWORKING LETTER
(Medical Sales Representative)

178 Green Street
Odenton, MD 21114
(301) 555-5555

April 20, 1996

Pat Cummings
Sales Director
Any Corporation
1140 Main Street
Emporia, KS 66801

Dear Mr. Cummings:

I write this letter to remind you of our conversation at the Innovex medical sales trade conference in California. As you urged me to forward a summary of my credentials, I have enclosed my resume.

During the past fifteen years, my positions have ranged from Sales Representative to Corporate Vice-President responsible for the sales management of diagnostic imaging equipment and consumables to a $70 million health care market. I have established and maintain excellent contacts with physicians, material management directors, directors of purchasing, and other senior decision-makers. My expertise is in developing and managing key accounts in the medical industry, including major hospitals, imaging centers, HMO's, and group purchasing offices. Salary requirements are negotiable. In addition, I am willing to relocate, given a suitable opportunity.

I am confident that my skills qualify me for a range of senior-level sales positions. Are you aware of any avenues I might pursue to fully utilize my skills? I would appreciate the chance to talk with you. Please contact me in order to tell me when you can take a few moments out of your schedule for a face-to-face discussion.

It was a pleasure meeting you, and I look forward to speaking with you again.

Sincerely,

Chris Smith

Enc. resume

- Discussion of experience clearly spells out candidate's area of expertise.
- Candidate notifies networking contact of travel availability and/or compensation requirements.

NETWORKING LETTER
(Microwave Technician)

178 Green Street
Manchester, NH 03105

January 14, 1996

Pat Cummings
Chief Technician
Any Corporation
1140 Main Street
Keene, NH 03431

Dear Ms. Cummings:

In a recent informational interview, Steven Hague of NewMark Industries referred me to your firm. I am interested in joining an organization where I can utilize my strong technical and leadership skills in microwave or related industries.

I have eleven years of experience in the microwave industry working with state-of-the-art microwave communications antennas. My expertise is in test setups for outdoor and indoor test ranges, as well as the design, manufacturing, and repair maintenance of microwave antennas. In addition, I have extensive experience working with customers and inspectors on final tests to FCC regulations. I am well qualified to assume responsibility for managing projects from initial design to final test and operation.

After you have reviewed my background, please contact me so that we may arrange a personal interview to further expand upon your requirements and my ability to meet them. I can be reached at the above address or (603) 555-5555.

Thank you for your consideration. I await your response.

Sincerely,

Chris Smith

Enc. resume

■ Letter appeals to networking contact's knowledge of industry.

■ Letter focuses on acquired skills relevant to field of interest.

NETWORKING LETTER
(Mortgage/Loan Officer)

178 Green Street
Conway, AR 72032
(501) 555-5555

April 4, 1996

Pat Cummings
Chief Loan Officer
Any Bank
1140 Main Street
Little Rock, AR 72203

Dear Mr. Cummings:

Recently, I ran into an old college roommate and friend, Ellen Barie. As I am currently considering a new association with a bank or corporation in a Mortgage/Loan Officer capacity, Ellen suggested I contact you. She mentioned that she had worked as a Teller at your Little Rock main branch, and thought you might be interested in someone with my qualifications.

As the enclosed resume indicates, my extensive loan experience has encompassed office supervision and general bookkeeping, with a concentration in credit and collections, within the mortgage, insurance, and banking industries. My current position as a Senior Collections Specialist has provided me with the opportunity to accomplish and exceed a set objective of reducing delinquent loans from $24 million to $10 million within six months. At this point, I feel I have successfully surpassed both company and personal goals, and am searching for new and greater challenges.

I am very interested in the opportunities available at Any Bank. Could we meet in a personal interview? I would be happy to make myself available at your convenience.

Sincerely,

Chris Smith

Enc. resume

- Dollar amounts quantify candidate's accomplishments.
- Candidate informs networking contact of mutual acquaintance.

NETWORKING LETTER
(Nurse)

178 Green Street
Kingston, RI 02881
(401) 555-5555

November 19, 1996

Pat Cummings
Nursing Director
Any Hospital
1140 Main Street
Bristol, RI 02809

Dear Ms. Cummings:

Are you in need of a nursing professional with extensive clinical, research, and teaching experience? Laura Fogerty, a nurse in your pediatric unit, suggested that I contact you regarding employment opportunities at Any Hospital.

I possess fifteen years of experience in clinical research and direct patient care with an emphasis on neuroscience intensive care, memory disorders, and brain and cognitive sciences. During the past three years, I have functioned as a Staff Nurse with duties in a neuro-intensive care unit.

I am well qualified to teach, counsel, conduct utilization reviews, or administer programs related to health care, equipment, or human services—all in appropriate settings. I am capable of making presentations to individuals and groups, skilled at conducting meetings and teaching classes, and have the required communication skills necessary to demonstrate as well as instruct medical professions and support staffs.

Enclosed please find my business profile. I would be happy to make myself available for an interview to discuss possible openings matching my qualifications. Please feel free to contact me at the above address or daytime phone, or evenings at (401) 555-4444.

I look forward to your return response.

Sincerely,

Chris Smith, R.N.

Enc. business profile

■ After name, candidate includes professional title.

■ Introductory sentence draws attention.

NETWORKING LETTER
(Paralegal)

178 Green Street
Toledo, OH 44501
(419) 555-5555

March 17, 1996

Pat Cummings
Principal
Any Law Firm
1140 Main Street
Beachwood, OH 44122

Dear Mr. Cummings:

The last time we spoke at the University Club, you urged me to contact you if you could be of assistance. My interest in pursuing and expanding my professional career as a paralegal has prompted me to forward the attached resume for your review and consideration.

Please note that I am a candidate for a certificate in Paralegal Studies, December 1995. While attending college and continuing postgraduate study, I have had hands-on experience in the preparation of litigation, probate, corporate, and real estate documents, as well as with computer system applications for the legal profession. In addition, I have developed strong coaching, training, and leadership skills to handle complex, people-oriented, or detailed assignments as an individual or a team member.

I would appreciate any information you can provide regarding the legal profession and the paralegal's role. May we meet to discuss? I am eager to learn about the job market, career mobility, and about all aspects of the law. I will call your office to schedule a mutually convenient time to talk.

Thank you for your attention in this manner.

Sincerely,

Chris Smith

Enc. resume

■ Continuing education demonstrates candidate's dedication to his/her field.

■ Candidate immediately specifies type of position sought.

NETWORKING LETTER
(Payroll Supervisor)

178 Green Street
Hayward, CA 94541

June 6, 1996

Pat Cummings
Office Manager
Any Corporation
1140 Main Street
Los Angeles, CA 90017

Dear Ms. Cummings:

I received your name as a contact for my job search from a mutual friend, Steve Herson. I was employed at Steve's bank several years ago, and worked closely with him on several projects. In a recent conversation, Steve mentioned that you might be in need of a professional with my qualifications.

As my enclosed resume indicates, in addition to a Bachelor of Arts degree in Economics, my background encompasses eleven years of progressively responsible and sophisticated hands-on experience ranging from Marketing Research Assistant to Union Benefits Coordinator and Human Resources Administrator. In my present position as Payroll Administrator with a special emphasis on the day-to-day details of financial operations and related areas, I have gained valuable experience and training in important organizational and operational areas of a company's general business operation.

I am very interested in investigating opportunities at Any Corporation and believe I could successfully contribute to your staff. Please contact me at the above address or call (415) 555-5555 to arrange a mutually convenient time for an interview.

Thank you for your consideration.

Sincerely,

Chris Smith

Enc. resume

■ Candidate thanks networking contact in advance for his/her assistance.

■ Including a telephone number is essential in a cover letter.

NETWORKING LETTER
(Power Systems Designer)

178 Green Street
Mesa, AZ 85028
(602) 555-5555

August 22, 1996

Pat Cummings
Systems Designer
Any Corporation
1140 Main Street
Tempe, AZ 85284

Dear Mr. Cummings:

Debbie Swanson of Systems Powerphasing recommended I contact you
concerning my interest in locating a position in the field of power systems design.
I understand that your corporation leads the field in power-related emerging
technologies. Debbie spoke highly of your work and thought you could provide
me with some useful information.

My background includes seven years of experience in positions as Technical Sales
Representative and Medical Equipment Technician with a medical equipment
manufacturer, and Power Systems Engineer with a manufacturer of
telecommunications earth stations. My most recent experience involves all phases
of power systems design projects from proposal preparation and specification
phase to on-site installations, customer training, and full operation.

I am very interested in continuing my career in power design with a new firm. I
know that your expertise in the field and knowledge of the current trends would be
very helpful to my search. Would it be possible to meet briefly? I can easily make
myself available at your convenience, and will call you on Monday to see if we
can get together.

Thank you for your generous consideration, Mr. Cummings.

Sincerely,

Chris Smith

Enc. resume

- ■ Introduction expresses candidate's knowledge of firm.
- ■ Candidate informs networking contact of work experience in field of interest.

NETWORKING LETTER
(Production Manager)

178 Green Street
Arlington, VA 22229
(703) 555-5555

July 22, 1996

Pat Cummings
Director of Operations Management
Any Corporation
1140 Main Street
Macon, GA 31201

Dear Ms. Cummings:

As Alex Drumlins may have informed you, I was caught in Timony's recent downsizing. I am writing to inquire if Any Corporation has any openings in production/operations, or if you can provide industry contacts.

My related experience extends throughout the last two decades. In addition to a B.S. in Management, I possess four years of supervisory and production management experience with a large Washington, D.C.-based corporation. While working my way through college, I experienced aspects of many other disciplines and gained valuable insights into corporate structure.

Thank you for your time and consideration. May I hear from you?

Sincerely,

Chris Smith

Enc. resume

■ Part-time work experience during school indicates candidate's strong work ethic.

■ Explanation for unemployment is optional in a networking letter.

NETWORKING LETTER
(Program Coordinator)

178 Green Street
Walnut Creek, CA 94596
(510) 555-5555

July 3, 1996

Pat Cummings
Human Resources Manager
Any Corporation
1140 Main Street
Cupertino, CA 95014

Dear Mr. Cummings:

I write to remind you of our conversation at the Earth Now! environmental services conference. At that time, you urged me to forward a summary of my credentials whenever I began a job search. Although still employed, I have begun to explore new opportunities. I will appreciate any assistance you can provide, whether informing me of positions in your company or forwarding my resume to other industry contacts.

During the past sixteen years, my experience has been in environmental and pest control systems. My past four years as District Manager have encompassed P & L responsibility for sales, service, and public relations, as well as training and awareness programs affecting institutional and commercial markets, community environments, and related government legislation.

I wish to join a company that can benefit from my combined technical, sales/service, and management skills. I am most effective in directing in-house or field activities involving environmental programs for a company or its key accounts in the public or private sector.

I am confident that my experience distinguishes me as a top-notch environmental control systems executive. I look forward to discussing with you how and where I might best utilize my talents.

Thank you.

Sincerely,

Chris Smith

Enc. resume

- Candidate briefly reintroduces himself/herself to networking contact in opening.

- Letter immediately states candidate's purpose.

NETWORKING LETTER
(Project Manager)

178 Green Street
Northridge, CA 91324

November 27, 1996

Pat Cummings
Director
Any Institute
1140 Main Street
Los Angeles, CA 90053

Dear Ms. Cummings:

Pursuant to my conversation with Alex Franks on November 9, I am enclosing my resume as an expressed interest in the position of Project Manager.

Through my education and experience in the transportation field, I have dealt with the public in an assistance capacity in both business and community service environments. In each position I have held, initiative and ability have led to advancement and the assumption of greater responsibilities.

During the preparation of my recently completed thesis, I conducted extensive research on water transportation. (Enclosed please find an abstract from that thesis.) In addition, my current position involves transportation research and computer transportation modeling.

I feel that my skills, eagerness to learn, and motivation to succeed would contribute to a productive association with Any Institute. I would welcome an opportunity to meet with you to discuss ways in which my capabilities may suit your needs. Please consider the enclosed and direct your response to the above address, or phone me at (818) 555-5555.

Your time and consideration are appreciated. I look forward to hearing from you.

Sincerely,

Chris Smith

Enc. resume
    thesis abstract

■ Research projects illustrate candidate's initiative.

■ Candidate immediately specifies type of position sought.

NETWORKING LETTER
(Promotions Representative)

178 Green Street
Bakerton, KY 42711
(606) 555-5555

March 19, 1996

Pat Cummings
Vice-President, Promotions
Any Corporation
1140 Main Street
Knoxville, TN 37902

Dear Mr. Cummings:

Susan Schlegal, Madison Corporation's Promotions Representative, recommended
I contact you about the possibility of an opening with Any Corporation. Please
accept the enclosed resume as an expressed interest in joining your organization.

As you can see from my resume, my diverse experience includes administrative
duties, telemarketing, coaching, and instructing gymnasts. Ideally, I would like to
apply my enthusiasm for athletics, combined with my educational background and
acquired business skills, to an organization where my capabilities would suit their
needs. I feel strongly that Any Corporation is such an organization.

I am confident that my experience and education, coupled with an eagerness to
learn and a motivation to succeed, would contribute to a productive association
with your company. I would value an opportunity to discuss any current or long-
term positions that may be available either at Any Corporation or within the field.

You may contact me at the above address, or I will contact you early next week, to
arrange a meeting at your earliest convenience.

Your time and consideration are very much appreciated. I look forward to
speaking with you in the near future.

Sincerely,

Chris Smith

Enc. resume

- Candidate immediately names referral.
- Letter focuses on filling employer's needs, not the job candidate's.

NETWORKING LETTER
(Property Manager)

178 Green Street
Cocoa Beach, FL 32932
(407) 555-5555

March 3, 1996

Pat Cummings
District Manager
Any Corporation
1140 Main Street
Stamford, CT 06904

Dear Ms. Cummings:

I was glad to meet you last week at the Realtor's Association. Our conversation
has prompted me to write you. As indicated by the enclosed resume, I have
progressively advanced from Property Manager to Senior Area Manager with
multistate, multisite responsibility for full residency and profitability of major
investment properties. At this point in my career, I am seeking a new and
challenging opportunity where these qualifications can be utilized by a progressive
investment property and/or property owner/management organization.

I have a record of cost-effective management for individual, client, and company-
owned properties including high-rise luxury apartment buildings, multibuilding
condominiums converted from apartments, and subsidized housing. I am
accustomed to working with government agencies and associated regulations.

My expertise in troubleshooting, problem-solving, turning serious rental losses
into profitable operations, capital improvement plans, preventive maintenance, and
maintenance management has enabled me to provide harmonious tenant, owner,
and community relationships and trouble-free operation of properties.

If your organization or any of your colleagues can provide someone with my
experience an opportunity, I would like to explore that opportunity in the hope of a
mutually beneficial association. May we meet for discussion?

I look forward to talking to you soon.

Sincerely,

Chris Smith

Enc. resume

■ Candidate reminds networking
contact of last encounter.

■ Qualifications highlight
candidate's problem-solving
ability.

NETWORKING LETTER
(Publicist)

178 Green Street
Woodland Hills, CA 91367

July 9, 1996

Pat Cummings
Publicity Director
Any Corporation
1140 Main Street
Santa Ana, CA 92701

Dear Mr. Cummings:

Lee Cyndis suggested I write you with regards to support areas of advertising and
public relations. I would appreciate any information or advice you can provide
about how to search for a publicity-related support position. I have enclosed a
resume to acquaint you with my background.

I possess comprehensive experience in the support of direct mail fund-raising
activity for a major university. My training and expertise also include areas of
publicity and public relations, staff training and supervision, program coordination
and budget management, market research and copyediting, and management and
administration of related detail.

I have excellent writing skills, work well under pressure, and meet deadlines
consistently. In addition, I have experience with streamlining operations for
enhancing production efficiency at an optimum cost.

I would appreciate the chance to meet with you so that we may discuss how my
abilities prepare me for a position in the advertising world. I can be reached at the
above address or at (818) 555-5555.

I look forward to speaking with you at your earliest convenience. Thank you for
your time.

Sincerely,

Chris Smith

Enc. resume

■ Candidate focuses on relevant
functional skills.

■ Letter solicits networking contact's
advice rather than assistance with
job placement.

NETWORKING LETTER
(Publishing Intern)

178 Green Street
Charleston, SC 29403
(803) 555-5555

July 7, 1996

Pat Cummings
Editor
Any Publishing Company
1140 Main Street
Fairfax, SC 29827

Dear Ms. Cummings:

I am graduating from the College of William and Mary this May, and am searching for an avenue into publishing.

Lee Jones, an Editorial Assistant at Any Publishing, suggested your company as a possible place to gain experience. I will be living in Massachusetts for the summer months and hope you would consider me for a summer internship. I would welcome the opportunity to work several days a week in order to better understand the workings of a publishing house.

As an intern, I could contribute excellent editing, researching, and writing skills. I am familiar with computers and the general library cataloging systems. Additionally, I am an eager and quick learner, and an observer with a creative eye for detail.

My resume is enclosed; writing samples and references are available upon request. I look forward to hearing from you.

Thank you for your consideration.

Sincerely,

Chris Smith

Enc. resume

■ Candidate requests addressee's return response.

■ First paragraph introduces candidate to networking contact.

NETWORKING LETTER
(Quality Control Engineer)

178 Green Street
Daytona Beach, FL 32117
(904) 555-5555

January 24, 1996

Pat Cummings
Production/Operations Manager
Any Corporation
1140 Main Street
Long Grove, IL 60047

Dear Mr. Cummings:

I enjoyed talking with you on the plane from Denver. I only wish that we had met a little earlier, on the slopes of Winter Park. Enclosed is the resume you asked to see. I am very interested in discussing opportunities within Any Corporation.

As a Quality Control Engineer, I played a key role in the growth of Victor, Inc., where I interfaced with all departments including sales, purchasing, manufacturing, and inventory. I am knowledgeable in quality functions and have experience bringing product lines through the transitional stages from research/prototype to full production.

During the past seven years, I implemented and audited clean room contamination control, electrostatic discharge, and internal auditing programs for semiconductor and engineering facilities.

I am interested in joining the professional staff of a firm where I can apply my experience in quality control engineering and manufacturing. I am innovative, productive, accurate, and work well as an individual or as a team member.

I will be in Chicago for a training conference from April 10 to April 17. I would enjoy meeting with you at that time to talk further. Please let me know if this would be a good time to schedule a meeting.

I look forward to hearing from you soon.

Sincerely,

Chris Smith

Enc. resume

■ Networking letter may allow for personal discussion.

■ Discussion of personal qualities reiterates candidate's ability to contribute to potential employer.

NETWORKING LETTER
(Record Manager)

178 Green Street
Kent, OH 44243

October 15, 1996

Pat Cummings
Senior Vice-President, Artists and Repertoire
Any Record Company
1140 Main Street
Dayton, OH 45402

Dear Ms. Cummings:

It has come to my attention, via industry sources, that you have recently assumed the position of Senior Vice-President of the artist and repertoire department for Any Record Company. As it is common practice for new administrators to acquire their own personnel, I am enclosing my resume for your consideration. I have been observing some very positive changes occurring within Any Record Company and I would very much like to become part of your team.

My experience includes the discovery and management of the Escalator Rise (Islo), of which Steve Kline is acquainted, and co-management of Sligo Blue, of which Rick Mavan is quite familiar. I have also managed two independent labels, one of which originally signed Pain Cave (Addison). Accordingly, as I feel I have accumulated extensive experience in artist development and product management, I am confident I could become a valuable asset to your department.

Should you like to review a resume tape, please do not hesitate to contact me at (216) 555-5555. I would appreciate the opportunity to speak with you personally, at your earliest convenience.

Thank you for your time. I look forward to hearing from you in the near future.

With best regards,

Chris Smith

Enc. resume

■ Letter incorporates industry knowledge into discussion of qualifications.

■ Candidate familiarizes networking contact with relevant skills and experiences.

NETWORKING LETTER
(Research Assistant)

178 Green Street
Elgin, IL 60123

July 20, 1996

Pat Cummings, M.D.
Director of Pharmaceutical Research
Any Hospital
1140 Main Street
Cicero, IL 60650

Dear Dr. Cummings:

Susan Burwen of your human resources department recently informed me of an
opening for a Research Assistant (Allergic Diseases) in your pharmaceutical
division. Susan and I have been longtime friends, and she felt that my
qualifications as a Researcher would match ideally with your job requirements.
Although I have submitted my resume to Susan, I would like to introduce myself
to you as well.

As a graduate of the Massachusetts College of Pharmacy and Allied Health
Science, where I earned my Pharmacy degree, I have had the opportunity to
perform research in laboratory facilities where I received instruction and hands-on
experience in the use of state-of-the-art research techniques and equipment. As a
member of a family who, for generations, has been severely affected by allergic
diseases, it has always been my professional objective to either research a cure or
contribute to discovering a method that alleviates the discomfort of allergy
sufferers.

Given the opportunity to become a part of your pharmaceutical laboratory,
I will apply my education, laboratory training, and technical skill toward the
achievement of your research objectives dealing with gene regulation and allergic
diseases. I would very much like the opportunity to meet with you for further
discussion. I will call your office early next week to arrange a time that is
convenient for you.

Should you require additional information, please feel free to contact Susan
Burwen. Also, I can be reached at the above address or (705) 555-5555.

Thank you for your time.

Sincerely,

Chris Smith, Ph.G.

Enc. resume

- Personal experience with industry
strengthens candidacy.

- Closing invites addressee to
inquire about additional
information.

NETWORKING LETTER
(Restaurant Manager)

178 Green Street
Glen Burnie, MD 21060

April 26, 1996

Pat Cummings
Regional Manager
Any Restaurant Chain
1140 Main Street
Silver Spring, MD 20901

Dear Ms. Cummings:

I am writing in response to a referral from a colleague of yours, Jim Murray. Jim
was the Assistant Manager of your Baltimore location in 1991, when I worked
there as a waitress. When I expressed my desire to return to your organization in a
managerial position, Jim enthusiastically responded with several contact names,
including yours.

I have enclosed my resume as an expressed interest in exploring available
management opportunities at Any Restaurants. In addition to an Associate degree
in Hotel/Restaurant Management, I have five years of experience ranging from
Roving Manager with a multiunit restaurant operation to General Manager of
a full-service restaurant, lounge, and multiple function/banquet facility. My
experience encompasses front- and back-of-the-house management, food and
beverage preparation, and personnel training and supervision.

I feel confident of my potential to make a significant contribution to your
restaurant chain. My previous experience as a waitress not only provided specific
insight into your management operations, but was very rewarding personally.

After you have reviewed my qualifications, please do not hesitate to contact me
at the above address or call (301) 555-5555. I would like to arrange a mutually
convenient time for a meeting to discuss your current or anticipated needs in terms
of my qualifications.

I greatly appreciate your consideration.

Sincerely,

Chris Smith

Enc. resume

- Candidate's practical experience outweighs his/her education.
- Candidate immediately introduces purpose for writing.

NETWORKING LETTER
(Retail Sales Manager)

178 Green Street
Berkeley, CA 94710

May 7, 1996

Pat Cummings
Regional Manager
Any Corporation
1140 Main Street
Carson City, NV 89706

Dear Mr. Cummings:

I am currently considering a change of position and am launching a campaign to find a new opportunity in a growth-oriented retail company. At the suggestion of your colleague Maureen Dodge, I have enclosed my professional profile and would appreciate any assistance you may be able to provide.

My objective is to join the management staff of a medium-sized retail chain that is at a stage in its growth where it needs experienced leaders to help it successfully reach new expansion goals. With my experience and successful achievements within domestic and international operations, I can provide the impetus to enhance the revenue stream and profit margins through staff development, product diversification, quality services, customer satisfaction, and cost control.

My professional experience with Martins Fashions and the entrepreneur-type environment of Dressing for Success is a valuable resource for moving a company through the next plateau of growth. My successes in all aspects of operations further underscore the valuable contribution I could make to an innovative firm such as yours. Although my geographic preference is the West Coast, I will consider a move for an enterprising company that views experience and capabilities essential to achieving their goals.

Should you know of any organizations searching for a professional with my qualifications, please contact me at the above address or by phone at (510) 555-5555. As I have not yet discussed a potential move with my current employer, I would like to request your confidentiality.

Sincerely,

Chris Smith

Enc. professional profile

■ Candidate informs networking contact of all relevant information, including geographical preference.

■ Closing informs addressee of need for confidentiality.

NETWORKING LETTER
(Sales Director)

178 Green Street
Sumas, WA 98295
(604) 555-5555

February 7, 1996

Pat Cummings
Eastern District Manager
Any Corporation
1140 Main Street
New York, NY 10028

Dear Ms. Cummings:

It was great to meet you at the DeLux Designer's conference. I hope we have the chance to speak again soon. As you may remember, I am looking for a new opportunity where my excellent sales skills, strong work ethic, and initiative would directly correlate to my growth, advancement, and future within a company.

During the past six years I have had experience in new business development, negotiations, proposal and contract preparation, and interfacing with banks and attorneys.

Throughout my career, I have worked well independently or as a member of a team. I possess sound knowledge of and experience with the sales of tangible and intangible products as indicated in the enclosed resume. I feel confident that I can be an asset to your company as I have for my present and past employers.

My strong interest in Any Corporation makes relocation feasible and salary issues negotiable.

I look forward to our next discussion.

Sincerely,

Chris Smith

Enc. resume

■ Reminds networking contact of common experience.

■ Closing is straightforward and concise.

NETWORKING LETTER
(Sanitarian)

178 Green Street
Rockville, MD 20850

May 6, 1996

Pat Cummings
Director
Any Health Department
1140 Main Street
Baltimore, MD 21207

Dear Mr. Cummings:

As per your request at last week's district meeting, I am enclosing my updated resume so that I may be considered for the position of Sanitarian with Any Health Department.

During the past seventeen years, I have been professionally associated in various capacities with private and public health care facilities and educational institutions. My activities have not only involved health care provider services, but also required extensive involvement with individuals and groups, both of which required direct interfacing with community, municipal, and public health agencies.

A prime interest for me is to work in an area where my recommendations can make a difference in the quality of care and in the environmental surroundings of people dependent on the decisions made by the staff of Any Health Department. I am equally effective working independently as I am in a team effort, and I hope to be able to apply my skills toward achieving the objectives of the department.

I want to thank you for the opportunity to be considered for the position. Should you require any additional information prior to a personal interview, please contact me at the above address or by phone at (301) 555-5555.

Yours sincerely,

Chris Smith

Enc. resume

■ Networking letter establishes candidate's knowledge of his/her field.

■ Candidate thanks networking contact in advance for his/her assistance.

NETWORKING LETTER
(Secretary)

178 Green Street
Birmingham, AL 35294
(205) 555-5555

November 15, 1996

Pat Cummings
Personnel Director
Any Corporation
1140 Main Street
Mobile, AL 36630

Dear Ms. Cummings:

Maureen Deegan suggested I speak with you regarding a secretarial position with
Any Corporation. Enclosed is my resume for your consideration. I hope, in
reviewing my background, you will find that my qualifications suit your needs.

During the last five years with Stuart Photographers, my responsibilities included
assisting on shoots, handling incoming calls, arranging appointments, and light
typing. As Service Representative for the Dalton Corporation, I dealt with all
customer inquiries and resolved problems in shipping and billing. I am
accustomed to working closely with staff and management in a fast-paced
environment and enjoy the satisfaction of doing a job well.

Also enclosed is my resume for your review. I am eager to join the staff of Any
Corporation and would be glad to make myself available for an interview. I look
forward to hearing from you at your earliest convenience.

Sincerely,

Chris Smith

Enc. resume

■ Letter focuses on candidate's
most relevant qualifications.

■ Basis for referral is immediately
established.

NETWORKING LETTER
(Special Agent)

178 Green Street
Wayne, NJ 07866

April 15, 1996

Pat Cummings
Special Agent
Any Bureau
1140 Main Street
Washington, DC 20036

Dear Mr. Cummings:

At the request of Ms. Morrow, Special Agent in Charge, I am enclosing my profile
in consideration for a position as Special Agent with Any Bureau.

Prior to my recent tour of duty in the Gulf War, I planned to separate from my
position as Group Targeting Officer, attached to special forces, for a position with
an investigations bureau. However, my involvement in Desert Storm and related
on-going assignments have made it necessary for me to put my earlier plan, for a
June 1995 transition, on hold. Unfortunately, I will not be able to attend the
session at the Employment Release Force Center at Fort Dix, March 30, and ask
that you review this application in my absence. At this writing, I hope to be able to
accept a new position during the first quarter of 1997.

I am free to travel and relocate within the United States, as assignments require,
and I am confident that I can provide the skills and quality of performance
required of its Special Agents by Any Bureau. As soon as it is mutually
convenient, I would like to arrange for a meeting to discuss bureau requirements
and my ability to handle the responsibilities of the position.

Please contact me at the above address or leave a message by phone at (201) 555-
5555 should you require additional information prior to our meeting.

I look forward to your return response.

Sincerely,

Chris Smith

Enc. professional profile

■ Candidate informs networking
contact of mutual acquaintance.

■ Candidate informs networking
contact of all relevant information,
including geographical preference.

NETWORKING LETTER
(Staff Accountant)

178 Green Street
Newport, RI 02840

November 12, 1996

Pat Cummings
Director, Career Services
Any College
1140 Main Street
Smithfield, RI 02917

Dear Ms. Cummings:

It was nice meeting you at the alumni luncheon last Monday. If you recall, at that time you offered your assistance in my job search. I would greatly appreciate any assistance you might be able to offer.

During the past three years, I have been employed as a Staff Accountant with a major corporation with responsibility for maintaining financial statements and monthly closings, and preparing financial reports using Lotus 1-2-3. During the prior four years, while attending college, I held positions of increasing responsibility in areas ranging from auditing to accounts payable in corporate and nonprofit environments.

These positions have been fast-paced and challenging, and the experience I gained is broad in scope. However, to further my career in accounting and finance, I am investigating new opportunities where I can apply my experience to benefit a company that offers room for advancement based on personal preference.

Should you know of any corporation in need of an experienced accountant, please do not hesitate to forward the attached resume. Also, if you have any questions or can provide any further guidance, I can be reached at (401) 555-5555 or (401) 555-4444.

I appreciate your time, Ms. Cummings.

Sincerely,

Chris Smith

Enc. resume

■ Candidate reminds networking contact of last encounter.

■ Candidate requests that attached resume be forwarded.

NETWORKING LETTER
(Teacher: Secondary Level)

178 Green Street
Atlanta, GA 30303
(904) 555-5555

June 4, 1996

Pat Cummings
Headmaster
Any Academy
1140 Main Street
Sarasota, FL 34236

Dear Mr. Cummings:

Diego Arrigo suggested I contact you in reference to teaching positions in the fields of history and social studies. I am not sure if openings currently exist with your school, but I would appreciate any advice or information you could provide about career opportunities in the academic world. As a recent graduate with a Master of Education degree in Secondary History, and a Bachelor of Arts degree in History, my goal is to become associated with a university or private school where I can apply my education and experience in the field of education.

From 1992 to June 1994, I worked as a permanent Substitute Teacher with responsibility for teaching various secondary-level history and other courses. I possess superior research, computer, leadership, and organizational skills, and I am capable of working independently or as a team member in an educational, administrative, or research environment.

I would appreciate the chance to meet with you. As a young academic, I am interested to hear how your career has progressed to its current point. Please contact me at your convenience so that we may schedule a time to meet.

I look forward to hearing from you.

Sincerely,

Chris Smith

Enc. resume

■ Letter appeals to networking contact's knowledge of industry.

■ Educational credentials accentuate candidate's qualifications.

NETWORKING LETTER
(Telecommunications Specialist)

178 Green Street
Savage, MT 59262
(406) 555-5555

September 26, 1996

Pat Cummings
Telecommunications Consultant
Any Corporation
1140 Main Street
Chicago, IL 60605

Dear Ms. Cummings:

Several years ago, I was your son Dan's classmate at the University of Miami.
When I bumped into him last week in Billings, Montana, of all places, he informed
me that you deal closely with several leading specialists in the telecommunications
field and suggested I contact you immediately.

I am interested in joining a company where I can contribute strong skills and
education in communications. I offer:

- A Bachelor of Arts degree in Communications
- Familiarity with all areas of marketing, public relations, and advertising
- One year experience as a promotions intern at a radio station
- Fluency in German

I would greatly appreciate any advice and/or referrals you might be able to give
me. I will call you in a few days to follow up.

Thank you for your time.

Sincerely,

Chris Smith

Enc. resume

■ Bullets in networking letter draw
attention to candidate's
accomplishments.

■ Candidate requests additional
referrals from networking contact.

NETWORKING LETTER
(Telemarketer)

178 Green Street
Wooster, OH 44691
(216) 555-5555

December 4, 1996

Pat Cummings
Director, Telemarketing
Any Corporation
1140 Main Street
Columbus, OH 43216

Dear Mr. Cummings:

Your name was given to me by Leanne Marquis, who I understand has worked
with you on several promotional projects. Leanne is a close friend of my mother's,
and has been very helpful in assisting me obtain an entry-level position in the
telemarketing field. Leanne felt that I would benefit from your extensive industry
experience.

I possess four years of successful part- and full-time employment in sales
administration and support, and have worked most recently in telemarketing,
direct mail, marketing, and sales for a variety of product and/or service-orientated
companies.

I would like to meet with you briefly to discuss your insight into the industry. Any
referrals or advice you could provide for my job search would be greatly
appreciated. I will contact your office on Friday morning to see if I could schedule
a few moments at your convenience.

Thank you for your consideration.

Sincerely,

Chris Smith

Enc. resume

■ Closing suggests a meeting to
follow letter.

■ Candidate immediately names
referral.

NETWORKING LETTER
(Transportation Coordinator)

178 Green Street
Batesville, MS 38606
(601) 555-5555

January 11, 1996

Pat Cummings
Operations Manager
Any Campaign
1140 Main Street
Tupelo, MS 38802

Dear Ms. Cummings:

I recently completed an extended association with the campaign team to elect
Congressman Bob Millis. Now that the election is over, Campaign Director
Marsha Herns suggested I contact your office to offer my services as
Transportation Coordinator.

I have spent the last eleven years owning and operating my own business—
coordinating limousine and luxury car services for business professionals and
politicians, entertainment celebrities, foreign dignitaries, and the general public. I
have the stamina and enthusiasm to work long hours, possess the experience and
ability to handle crisis situations, and am known to be responsible and innovative
when it comes to getting the job done as planned and on schedule.

Enclosed please find my business profile. If you are need of a competent,
experienced Transportation Coordinator, I would like to meet for further
discussion. I could be available for an interview at your convenience, and would
be happy to supply references at that time.

I look forward to hearing from you.

Sincerely,

Chris Smith

Enc. business profile

■ Candidate immediately specifies type of position sought.

■ Candidate emphasizes how past business experience can benefit potential employer.

NETWORKING LETTER
(Victim Witness Advocate)

178 Green Street
Pawtucket, RI 02860

December 1, 1996

Pat Cummings
Bureau Chief
Any Agency
1140 Main Street
Providence, RI 02902

Dear Mr. Cummings:

In a recent telephone conversation, Marcie Waters of the Children's Protectorate Agency suggested I submit my resume for your review regarding the position of Victim Witness Advocate.

Please note that, in addition to a Bachelor of Arts degree in Psychology and fluency in English, Spanish, and French, my most recent experience has been as a Special Police Officer/Security Officer for Puttnicks Department Store. During this employment, I have, on a daily basis, been called upon to employ skillful, sensitive interviewing and counseling techniques during the detention/arrest procedure from initial apprehension through court appearances. In addition, for more than three years, I have had the opportunity to interact extensively with personnel, clientele, and families at all levels.

My experience has provided me with the ability to motivate others toward achieving personal objectives while promoting human dignity. I would welcome the chance to discuss available or anticipated professional opportunities within Any Agency. Should you require additional information, I can be reached at the above address or by phone at (401) 555-5555.

Thank you for your attention to this matter.

Sincerely,

Chris Smith

Enc. resume

■ Foreign language skills strengthen candidate's qualifications.

■ Candidate informs networking contact of work experience in field of interest.

NETWORKING LETTER
(Writer/Reporter)

178 Green Street
Holdrege, NE 68949

April 9, 1996

Pat Cummings
Managing Editor
Any Newsletter
1140 Main Street
Omaha, NE 68102

Dear Ms. Cummings:

At the suggestion of a member of your staff, I am writing you to express my
interest in a position with your writing/reporting team.

As a recent college graduate, class of 1995, with a major in political science and
minor in English, I have extensive experience in researching, abstracting, and
writing accurate, detailed papers on topical issues, using journalistic techniques.

Currently, I am seeking a career opportunity with a publication, such as *Any
Newsletter*, where I can combine my writing skills with my keen interest in
ecology to research, and report on discoveries and events dealing with the
environment on a local or international level. Also, based on my interest in
providing effective pollution awareness materials to the general public, I consider
myself to be a viable candidate for the position.

Enclosed are my resume and samples of my writing skills. I am confident of my
ability to handle the responsibilities of the position offered. Should you wish to
schedule a personal interview, please contact me by phone between 5:30 and 10 p.m.
at (308) 555-5555.

I look forward to your return response.

Sincerely,

Chris Smith

Enc. resume
    writing samples

- Candidate familiarizes networking contact with relevant skills and experiences.
- Closing cites specific times candidate may be reached.

NETWORKING LETTER
(X-Ray Technician)

178 Green Street
Allentown, PA 18105
(215) 555-5555

May 31, 1996

Pat Cummings, M.D.
Director of Radiology
Any Hospital
1140 Main Street
Philadelphia, PA 19106

Dear Dr. Cummings:

Your name comes highly recommended to me as an expert in the field of
radiology from your associate, Dr. Richard Meyer of Northwest Hospital. Dr.
Meyer has been gathering contacts to assist me in investigating employment
opportunities, and informs me that you are seeking additional X-Ray Technicians
for your team.

In addition to Associate degrees in Liberal Arts, May 1993, and Radio
Technology, May 1994, I have two years of academic and clinical intern
experience which covers a wide range of radiographic services including the
operation of equipment, associated clinical materials and supplies, and
radiographic procedures. I also gained experience with film processing,
documentation, patient records, and patient relations.

The attached resume summarizes my background. I would greatly appreciate a
personal interview in which I could further outline my potential to make a
significant contribution to your facility.

If you will please contact me at the above address or phone, I would like to
arrange a mutually convenient time for such a meeting.

Thank you for your consideration.

Yours sincerely,

Chris Smith

Enc. resume

■ Candidate informs networking
contact of mutual acquaintance.

■ Relevant internship bolsters
otherwise limited work experience.

16
Broadcast Letter

With a broadcast letter, well-qualified candidates can advertise their availibility to top-level professionals in a particular field. The candidate attempts to entice the potential employer to consider his or her impressive qualifications for available positions. Although the broadcast letter discusses a candidate's background in detail, a resume is usually included. Since this type of letter is used primarily by seasoned executives, its tone should reflect the candidate's experience, knowledge, and confidence in his or her capabilities.

A candidate using the broadcast letter format might begin, "Are you in need of a Management Accountant who, in her most recent association, contributed to productivity improvements resulting in an annual savings of $20 million?" This attention-grabbing opening is effective only if the reader understands the significance of such an accomplishment. For this reason, broadcast letters are not recommended for those candidates conducting widespread job searches, where cover letters may end up in the human resources department, rather than in the hands of a fellow industry executive.

BROADCAST LETTER
(Account Executive)

178 Green Street
Knoxville, TN 37902

July 16, 1996

Pat Cummings
Managing Director
Any Theater
1140 Main Street
Nashville, TN 37203

RE: Account Executive

Dear Mr. Cummings:

Please note that I have ten years of progressively responsible experience which includes management positions in hospitality services, marketing, promotion, corporate communications, and public and media relations. My focus has been on event planning, press relations, and the implementation of image-building, attention-getting public relations operations and events for several nationally recognized companies. My accomplishments include:

- Increased paid attendance for special events by more than 31 percent as Marketing and Promotions Coordinator.
- Development of city/corporate transportation programs which substantially increased employee participation.
- Prepared and made presentations as Public Relations Representative and Lecturer before Chambers of Commerce and Convention/Tourist Bureaus, as well as group sales to private, professional corporate organizations.

My current responsibilities encompass hosting a weekly, international program on TV Channel 38 and three out-of-state cable stations. My responsibility involves research, script preparation, on-site taping coordination, and on-air interviews.

I have enclosed my resume. My prime interest is in the challenge and personal satisfaction I will derive from achieving the company's objectives. The compensation package is negotiable. To arrange for a meeting, please contact me at the above address or call (615) 555-5555.

Sincerely,

Chris Smith

Enc. resume

■ Candidate limits experiences discussed to significant accomplishments.

■ Candidate quantifies extensive experience.

BROADCAST LETTER
(Account Manager)

178 Green Street
Burlington, VT 05401
(802) 555-5555

January 18, 1996

Pat Cummings
Accounting Supervisor
Any Corporation
1140 Main Street
Montpelier, VT 05602

Dear Ms. Cummings:

Throughout my extensive experience in the field of accounting, I have been aware of, and impressed by, the growth and national reputation of Any Corporation. If your firm is in need of a qualified, seasoned Account Manager, I would welcome the opportunity to meet with you.

I offer over twenty years of experience as a hands-on manager in all areas of accounting including general ledger, accounts payable, payroll, budgeting/forecasting/analysis, and management reporting. I possess a strong background in cost accounting, inventory control, and supervision. Some of my accomplishments include:

- Initiating a department analysis which increased productivity by 20 percent.
- Implementing a strong system of internal controls which resulted in a reduction of inventory write-offs from $300,000 per year to $0.
- Revising and implementing a revenue accounting system in support of the direct end customer sales of a European subsidiary, which resulted in a cost savings of $150,000 per year.
- Negotiating policy decisions regarding expenditures and investments across multiple businesses and disciplines.
- Writing policies to govern worldwide fiscal processes throughout the company.

Thank you for your consideration of this matter. I look forward to speaking with you further concerning possible openings at Any Corporation.

Sincerely,

Chris Smith

Enc. resume

■ Statistics and dollar amounts quantify candidate's accomplishments.

■ Candidate customizes broadcast letter to meet needs of potential employer.

BROADCAST LETTER
(Chiropractor)

178 Green Street
Chicago, IL 60601
(312) 555-5555

April 9, 1996

Pat Cummings
Chairperson of the Board
Any Clinic
1140 Main Street
Chicago, IL 60601

Dear Mr. Cummings:

I am a certified Chiropractor currently exploring affiliations with established clinics. I have worked in the Chicago area for over twenty years and, as a result, my reputation for quality care is well-known.

Currently, I work as a Chiropractic Therapist with the Chicago Chiropractic Center, a position I have held for the past fifteen years. In this capacity I provide spinal manipulation and handle necessary musculoskeletal needs of sports injury patients, alleviate pain in elderly and work-related patients, and assist the industrial accident injured in regaining strength and stamina.

I am also an active member of the following associations:

* American Chiropractic Association
* Illinois Chiropractic Society
* Chicago Chiropractic Society
* Sports Injury Council of the American Chiropractic Association

If my qualifications are of interest to you, I can be reached at the phone number and address above.

Sincerely,

Chris Smith

Enc. resume

■ Professional memberships show candidate's commitment to his/her field.

■ Letter details how candidate's most recent experience will benefit potential employer.

BROADCAST LETTER
(Corporate Salesperson)

178 Green Street
Newberg, OR 97132
(503) 555-5555

February 9, 1996

Pat Cummings
Vice-President, Sales
Any Corporation
1140 Main Street
Portland, OR 97201

Dear Ms. Cummings:

For more than ten years, I have been instrumental in opening, selling to, and servicing accounts as well as establishing corporate accounts in a multistate region. Some of my accomplishments include:

- Opening and servicing accounts which resulted in an increase in volume from $50,000 to $500,000.
- Successful sales exceeding 20 percent of entire account inventory.
- Increasing customer accounts by 10 percent in six month period.

Currently, I am seeking a new association with a company that can benefit from the efforts of a self-starter who has not only developed new approaches to sales and has experience with customer controlled computer inventories, but also has motivated individuals and groups to achieve desired objectives or quotas as independent contributors or team producers.

I am a dedicated, highly productive, hard-working individual with the kind of persistence that gets results. I work best in a competitive environment and prefer working with an incentive package.

I would be happy to meet in a personal interview to provide you with more detail as to my qualifications and how they can best serve your company.

Thank you for your consideration and early response.

Sincerely,

Chris Smith

Enc. resume

- Broadcast letter includes only experience most relevant to position sought.

- Bulleting draws attention to major accomplishments.

BROADCAST LETTER
(Credit Manager)

178 Green Street
Dickinson, ND 58601

May 10, 1996

Pat Cummings
President
Any Corporation
1140 Main Street
Jamestown, ND 58405

Dear Mr. Cummings:

My current position as Credit Manager with a $20 million manufacturing and distribution firm, has, during the past ten years, been challenging and gratifying. In my association with this firm, I have successfully set up and enforced credit controls which resulted in reducing DSO from sixty to thirty-three days. I am continually involved in training personnel in credit/collection policies and procedures, troubleshooting and resolving sales/customer disputes, and making credit/collection decisions to reduce bad debt risk and increase cash flow.

However, it is time for me to make a change, and I am investigating new opportunities where my expertise can make a bottom-line difference. I can offer a firm, such as Any Corporation, twenty years of successful credit management experience. Based on my contribution to the credit profession, I received recognition, through NACM New England, as Credit Executive of the Year, 1991, and was elected the first woman president of the same professional credit association for the 1992-93 term.

I would appreciate scheduling a mutually convenient time to discuss your requirements for a truly competent Credit Manager and my ability to handle the responsibilities of that position.

My compensation requirement is in the $65,000–$75,000 range. Should you require additional information prior to our meeting, please contact me at the above address or by phone at (701) 555-5555.

I look forward to your return response.

Sincerely,

Chris Smith

Enc. resume

- Impressive credentials and awards further enhance candidate's qualifications.

- Broadcast letters often suggest a salary range.

BROADCAST LETTER
(Entrepreneur)

178 Green Street
Washington, DC 20013
(202) 555-5555

June 26, 1996

Pat Cummings
Chief Executive Officer
Any Company
1140 Main Street
Arlington, VA 22234

Dear Ms. Cummings:

I am a successful entrepreneur with fifteen years' experience in areas which include planning, organization, setup, start-up, and management of unique and successful retail sales, product development, manufacturing, and marketing ventures.

Most recently, I have been involved in the launching of a gourmet food product within retail accounts and the hospitality industry. This new venture has given me the opportunity to participate, first-hand, in product formulation, development, and package design. And, under my direction, the product increased its distribution by 52 percent and averaged $150 million in sales.

Although these positions have been broad in scope, requiring the skills of a well-organized, innovative individual, I am seeking a new association where there is an opportunity to participate in high-level decision-making processes and to contribute to the company's growth and success.

I look forward to a new challenge. Please call with questions.

Sincerely,

Chris Smith

Enc. resume

- Candidate selects only most impressive accomplishments to describe.
- Job descriptions indicate how candidate contributed to his/her previous employers.

BROADCAST LETTER
(Fashion Designer)

178 Green Street
Colorado Springs, CO 80903

May 13, 1996

Pat Cummings
Manager
Any Corporation
1140 Main Street
Jacksonville, FL 32231

Dear Mr. Cummings:

I am a veteran of the fashion industry seeking a position with an aggressive, cutting-edge design team. Any Corporation's recent, extensive marketing campaign has confirmed my interest in the company.

I possess three years of diverse experience as an Art Director and Fashion Designer working with a screen printing company. In these capacities, my principal responsibility has been creating the art and fashion design of clothing lines for national mass markets.

I feel that my creative skills and experience in dealing with sales and buyers can be effectively utilized with a firm such as yours. If you have the need for a highly motivated achiever in your firm, then we have good reason to meet.

Please respond at the above address or by phone at (719) 555-5555 to arrange a mutually convenient time for a meeting to discuss my qualifications. A portfolio of my creative work is available for your review.

Thank you for your consideration.

Sincerely,

Chris Smith

Enc. resume

■ Letter incorporates company knowledge into discussion of qualifications.

■ Stating that a portfolio is available on request is beneficial for certain positions.

BROADCAST LETTER
(Financial Consultant)

178 Green Street
Casper, WY 82604
(307) 555-5555

January 11, 1996

Pat Cummings
Communications Services Specialist
Any Corporation
1140 Main Street
Des Moines, IA 52401

Dear Ms. Cummings:

During the past fifteen years, I have held senior-level positions ranging from Senior Consultant with a Big-8 CPA firm, where I specialized in corporate financial planning and control, to my current activity as Chief Financial Officer/Consultant for investment banking and venture capital groups.

Although I am presently involved in interesting and challenging projects, I am ready for a change. I feel that my experience in financial management and administration can better be utilized in a firm that requires a high-energy, self-starter for its management team—in short, a professional who can impact a positive bottom line.

I have established a fine track record in financial and strategic planning which produced high-profit results and encompassed:

- Multimillion dollar improvement in cash flow.
- Reduction in operating costs and increased profitability of a rapid growth service organization ($15 million to $28 million within two years).
- Profit and business planning, financial evaluation, and long-range financial forecasting for a $140 million group of operating companies.
- Negotiation for public and private funding totaling $35 million.

I feel that a meeting to discuss both the opportunities available at Any Corporation and my capabilities would be mutually beneficial. For a phone interview, or to arrange for a meeting, please contact my office phone at (307) 444-4444.

Sincerely,

Chris Smith

Enc. resume

■ Bulleting the broadcast letter brings immediate attention to candidate's accomplishments.

■ Including a business number is optional in a cover letter.

BROADCAST LETTER
(Fleet and Transportation Manager)

178 Green Street
Altus, OK 73521
(918) 555-5555

April 25, 1996

Pat Cummings
Executive Vice-President
Any Corporation
1140 Main Street
Tulsa, OK 74106

Dear Mr. Cummings:

If your firm can benefit from a committed professional with general, financial, fleet, and transportation management, then we have good reason to meet.

In addition to a Master's in Business Administration, summa cum laude, from Harvard University and advanced study in dealer management, I offer:

- More than sixteen years of senior-level management experience with P & L responsibility for a composite automotive dealership with new and used car/truck sales, service, and rental/leasing operations.
- Eight years of additional experience in banking as an investment officer with investment analysis and portfolio management responsibility.
- Expertise in the design, implementation, and installation of computerized accounting systems, as well as extensive experience with financial analysis, budgets, and cost-effective corporate operations.
- Skill in the selection and development of management teams, incentive, and benefit programs to retain the most capable personnel in management and support activities.
- Knowledge of developing cash management and financial programs to provide funding for new or continuing operations to maximize returns on investment and increase productivity in sales and service.
- Qualifications to function as controller, financial analyst, operations, or administrative manager where corporate management is interested in achieving its objectives of cost-effective operations and increased profitability.

I am in search of a fast-paced, aggressive company that could benefit from my ability to quickly increase growth and profitability. Relocation and travel would be considered. Thank you for your time.

Sincerely,

Chris Smith

Enc. resume

- Educational honors are emphasized.
- Broadcast letter effectively highlights candidate's significant accomplishments.

BROADCAST LETTER
(Freight Supervisor)

178 Green Street
Raleigh, NC 27611

September 1, 1996

Pat Cummings
District Supervisor
Any Corporation
1140 Main Street
Fayetteville, NC 28302

Dear Ms. Cummings:

During the past thirteen years, I have been actively involved in positions as Field
Manager of Contained Operations and Night Operations Supervisor of freight
stations and service centers dealing with domestic and international freight
deliveries.

In addition to the supervision of day-to-day operations, my experience
encompasses hiring, training and supervision of drivers, office and support
personnel, and the provision of cost-effective quality service within a multiple
service network. I have sound knowledge of computer systems design for freight
movement management, and am skilled in both troubleshooting and resolving
problems relative to the movement or transfer of materials.

Although my present situation is challenging and diverse, I feel that it is time for
me to make a change. I am looking for a new association with a firm that can
benefit from my extensive experience with import/export traffic. Depending on the
benefits package, salary is negotiable.

I would welcome the opportunity to discuss your requirements and further outline
my qualifications. Should you require additional information, please contact me at
the above address or by phone at (919) 555-5555.

Thank you for your consideration.

Sincerely,

Chris Smith

Enc. resume

■ Specific contributions emphasize
candidate's achievements and
problem-solving abilities.

■ Compensation requirements are
often discussed in a broadcast
letter.

BROADCAST LETTER
(Legal Associate)

178 Green Street
St. Louis, MO 63135

August 26, 1996

Pat Cummings
Attorney-at-Law
Any Law Firm
1140 Main Street
Detroit, MI 48221

Dear Mr. Cummings:

As a newly arrived St. Louis Attorney in the Detroit area, who is now a permanent resident of Michigan, I am interested in a position as a First Year Associate with a firm that has a need for strong legal support in the areas of litigation, trade regulation, corporate, or general practice of law.

During my three and a half years as a Legal Assistant with Murphy, Smith, and Murray, I was actively involved in researching and drafting memoranda in areas of trade regulations, copyrights, and trademarks. I managed the discovery process, handled the deposition process, and provided litigation support during trials.

My experience as Contract Consultant/Assistant to a Vice-President of Elliot Fashions involved extensive research, contract negotiations, and the review, from a legal perspective, of all written, printed, advertising, or other materials relative to nonapparel products for this international conglomerate. I have worked in close cooperation with all departments and prepared materials for final approval by the corporate legal department.

The enclosed resume is a summary of my experience for your review. I was admitted to the Missouri Bar, January 1995, and to further my legal career, I plan to sit for the February 1996 Michigan Bar exams.

I am anxious to discuss with you how my credentials might benefit your firm. Should you require additional information as to my ability and interests or can advise me as to other possible avenues of employment in the legal profession, please contact me at the above address or phone at (314) 555-5555.

Thank you in advance for your interest and assistance.

Sincerely,

Chris Smith

Enc. resume

■ Professional accreditation enhances candidate's qualifications.

■ Relevant work experience is emphasized while other positions are omitted.

BROADCAST LETTER
(Marketing/Sales Executive)

178 Green Street
Cedar Rapids, IA 54201
(319) 555-5555

April 10, 1996

Pat Cummings
Chief Account Executive
Any Corporation
1140 Main Street
Wichita, KS 67202

Dear Ms. Cummings:

I am a seasoned Marketing/Sales Executive seeking an association with an aggressive, young firm such as Any Corporation. I offer extensive experience and achievements in marketing, business development, and product management at national and international levels.

During the past ten years, some of my successes include:

- Development of sales programs and new businesses to increase penetration, market share, and revenue through advanced, technically sophisticated systems management services.
- Team participation in the development and marketing of new service products for a service business generating $3.7 billion worldwide.
- P & L responsibility for an added-value services business generating $90 million.
- An established record of achievement for producing positive bottom-line results in a high-tech service-oriented business with worldwide markets.

I am well-qualified to direct areas that are key to achieving your business objectives. I am prepared to play an integral role in the profitable management of corporate programs designed to broaden your business opportunities on national or international levels.

My salary range is in the mid-$70,000 range. However, as my primary interest is in the challenge of the position and your goals, this figure is negotiable.

Sincerely,

Chris Smith

Enc. resume

■ Broadcast letter often separates major accomplishments for emphasis.

■ Broadcast letter emphasizes candidate's strong record of success.

BROADCAST LETTER
(Multimedia Specialist)

178 Green Street
Chicago, IL 60611
(312) 555-5555

June 13, 1996

Pat Cummings
Executive Director
Any Corporation
1140 Main Street
Des Moines, IA 50309

Dear Mr. Cummings:

During the past three years I have been actively involved in research, development, and demonstration projects that have focused on the introduction of interactive multimedia instructional methodologies into both corporate training programs and university curriculum.

My participation in these projects has been primarily in the areas of concept development and marketing, proposal writing, and project management. I offer experience in curriculum analysis and design, human factors research, instructional design, and media production. In addition, I am capable of operating a wide variety of authoring and development tools on both PC-compatible and Macintosh platforms.

I am currently looking for an opportunity to work in an organization that is introducing or developing plans to introduce interactive multimedia instruction techniques as components of its corporate training program.

I believe that my comprehensive knowledge of interactive multimedia technology, my vision for its application in corporate training, and my experience as a Senior Human Resources Manager offer a unique mix of credentials—all summarized in the enclosed resume.

I would be delighted to discuss my qualifications with you at your convenience. Thank you for your consideration.

Sincerely,

Chris Smith

Enc. resume

■ Candidate refers to attached resume in closing.

■ Letter details how candidate's most recent experience will benefit potential employer.

BROADCAST LETTER
(Program Manager)

178 Green Street
Tulsa, OK 74117
(918) 555-5555

August 12, 1996

Pat Cummings
Director
Any Company
1140 Main Street
Anadarko, OK 73005

Dear Ms. Cummings:

An article in the July issue of *Oklahoma Business Journal* featured Any Company's recent success and growth. As a Program Manager interested in establishing connections with a new, up-and-coming firm, I submit the enclosed resume for your review.

My qualifications include over twelve years' managing experience with Ricochet Data. In this capacity I developed and coordinated short- and long-range plans for the design and introduction of four new microcomputer products. I also created master charts to track major milestones and critical path activities, directed a management task force to develop a set of work instructions for the introduction of out-sourced products, and reduced product time to market by 25 percent.

My work in retail management might also be of interest to you. While employed at Lorenz Company, I generated gross annual sales in excess of $2 million for four consecutive years, managed a sales and service team of twenty people, and provided superior customer service and support.

Should my qualifications match your current or anticipated needs, I can be reached at the telephone number and address above.

Sincerely,

Chris Smith

Enc. resume

■ Candidate customizes broadcast letter to meet needs of potential employer.

■ Qualifications highlight candidate's leadership skills.

BROADCAST LETTER
(Real Estate Executive)

178 Green Street
Appleton, WI 54912

December 14, 1996

Pat Cummings
President
Any Corporation
1140 Main Street
Madison, WI 53713

Dear Mr. Cummings:

During the past thirteen years, working with a full-service real estate and consulting firm, I have acted as:

- Director of Development for consulting services generating $1.8 million in fees.
- Project Manager overseeing major additions and renovations for corporate and institutional clients involving 1.2 million square feet.
- Property/Asset Manager of one-half million square feet of company developed, owned, and managed real estate.

My position has been one of diverse responsibilities and challenges. However, I feel it is time for me to make a change to a larger, more aggressive firm where my comprehensive experience in development, property/asset management, and related consulting skills can be better utilized.

In prior positions, as Regional Manager and Loan Officer, I gained broad experience and insight into residential and commercial financing with emphasis on the mortgage and mortgage insurance industries involving institutions and private investors. I am confident that this combination of varied and successful experience can be effectively applied to a firm competing against other major full-service real estate operations.

Should you require additional information, please contact me at the above address or by phone at (414) 555-5555. Since my present employer is not aware of my intent to make a change, I would appreciate you holding this correspondence in the strictest confidence. Thank you.

Sincerely,

Chris Smith

Enc. resume

- Letter suggests discretion.
- Broadcast letter includes only experience most relevant to position sought.

BROADCAST LETTER
(Senior Vice-President)

178 Green Street
Bridgeton, MO 63044
(314) 555-5555

January 3, 1996

Pat Cummings
President
Any Bank
1140 Main Street
St. Louis, MO 63146

Dear Ms. Cummings:

I am currently the Senior Vice-President at Central St. Louis Bank where I have
been for the past twenty-five years. Please note my credentials:

- Fifteen years of diverse experience ranging from Acting Branch Manager
  and District Manager to my present position as Vice-President.
- Supervision of all internal departments including sales/account
  development, human resources, customer relations and customer service
  supervision, and product and sales support.
- Increased new business by 25 percent in one year through extensive
  interface with clients, decision-makers, and support personnel.

Although my present position is challenging, I am looking to associate with a
progressive firm that addresses both national and international banking markets. I
offer both experience and enthusiasm.

I look forward to hearing from you.

Sincerely,

Chris Smith

Enc. resume

■ Broadcast letter often separates
major accomplishments for
emphasis.

■ Closing reiterates candidate's
interest in position.

BROADCAST LETTER
(Senior-Level MIS Operator)

178 Green Street
Birmingham, AL 35266

September 5, 1996

Pat Cummings
Controller
Any Corporation
1140 Main Street
Mobile, AL 36630

Dear Mr. Cummings:

I am currently seeking a position change and would like to meet with you to discuss senior-level opportunities within your firm's MIS department. I am interested in applying my combined technical knowledge and experience to create and implement innovative concepts for greater information systems efficiency.
I can offer your firm:

1. Seventeen years of experience with corporate information systems.

2. Experience in the operation and supervision of administrative functions of UNIX systems using AT&T System V (release 3.0) operating software.

3. Skill in communicating with domestic/international networks, mainframes, and network system support.

4. Ability to work as a team member, team leader, and/or independent contributor working off-site via modem and data network, to assist users in sales, finance, manufacturing, and production.

5. Effective interface for mainframe/network and UNIX systems problems involving either hardware or software.

6. Techniques to teach the cost-effective utilization of multifunctioning systems from mainframe to PC, and instruct system operators in system problem identification and resolution.

This list summarizes my experience. However, during a comprehensive interview we could further discuss your requirements and expand on my ability to handle the responsibilities of the position under consideration. Please contact me at the above address or by phone at (205) 555-5555.

Yours sincerely,

Chris Smith

Enc. resume
Internet: csmith@service.com

■ Avoid technical jargon unless it is specific to candidate's field.

■ Including an e-mail address may be advantageous for certain fields of work.

BROADCAST LETTER
(Vice-President of Administration)

178 Green Street
Dodge City, KS 67801
(316) 555-5555

July 26, 1996

Pat Cummings
Chief Executive Officer
Any Corporation
1140 Main Street
Wichita, KS 67226

Dear Ms. Cummings:

I have served as Vice-President of Administration and Finance at Third Bank of Kansas for the past eighteen years. Although this position has been very challenging, I am interested in a change and feel that my background might be of interest to you.

Please consider the following qualifications:

- Provided handling and record-keeping services for corporate, fiduciary, and personal custody accounts with assets totaling $20 billion dollars.

- Managed administrative sales which totaled over $500,000 dollars.

- Directed administrative processes for 56 percent of the department's largest and most complex accounts.

- Analyzed new accounting systems to determine customers needs.

- Developed and maintained strong securities operational knowledge.

In addition to my extensive experience, I am also a member and past president of the Securities Operations Association of the Heartland, speaker/panel member of the Kansas Bankers Association, and past president of the Bank of Heartland Supervisors' Association.

I look forward to hearing from you in the near future.

Sincerely,

Chris Smith

Enc. resume

■ Candidate selects only most impressive accomplishments to describe.

■ Job-related affiliations demonstrate candidate's active participation in his/her field.

BROADCAST LETTER
(Warehouse Operator)

178 Green Street
Indianapolis, IN 46206

July 15, 1996

Pat Cummings
Controller
Any Corporation
1140 Main Street
South Bend, IN 46626

Dear Mr. Cummings:

My broad-based experience in state-of-the-art warehousing and distribution systems and procedures, with operations ranging from $7 million to $160 million, can be of immeasurable value to a company interested in cost-cutting, expansion, or greater efficiency and improved service.

My prior positions have been challenging and provided me with both responsibility for reorganizing, restructuring, and upgrading systems, and controls for cost-effective, efficient, and productive warehousing operations. Currently, I am seeking a new association with a firm that can benefit from my experience.

Should you wish to discuss my credentials further, I can be reached during business hours at (317) 555-5555 or evenings at (317) 444-4444.

Your return response is appreciated.

Sincerely,

Chris Smith

Enc. resume

■ Broadcast letter emphasizes candidate's strong record of success.

■ Including an evening telephone number is optional in a cover letter.

BROADCAST LETTER
(Zoologist)

178 Green Street
Lexington, KY 21345
(606) 555-5555

June 26, 1996

Pat Cummings
Director
Any Stable
1140 Main Street
New York, NY 10153

Dear Ms. Cummings:

I am a Zoologist with eight years of experience working primarily with race horses. I am currently seeking a position in a stable where my expertise in genetics and breeding will contribute to the success of the organization. Perhaps my credentials will interest you.

First, my most recent experience includes work with the following:

- Center for DNA Research, Cambridge, MA; Spring 1990
- Truman Thoroughbred Stables, Hamilton, MA; Spring 1992
- Center for Genetic Research, New York, NY; Summer 1993

Currently I serve as Genetics/Breeding Specialist for the Uphill Thoroughbred Stables and Stud. In this position, I work directly with doctors of veterinary medicine and race horse trainers in breeding and grooming top-quality thoroughbreds for racing and dressing. I also investigate genetic factors, forecast cross breeding, and evaluate artificial insemination considerations of specific mares and studs.

Although I am quite happy with my present employer and the work is challenging, I am interested in a position where I can research more closely in a laboratory environment. If my qualifications meet your needs, please call.

I look forward to hearing from you.

Sincerely,

Chris Smith, D.V.M.

Enc. resume

- Valuable research experience is highlighted in detail.

- Broadcast letter effectively highlights candidate's extensive experience.

17
Resume Letter

The resume letter combines your cover letter and resume. So, you may be wondering, why use this format if you've already completed your resume? The resume letter enables you to customize your inquiry to meet the needs of a specific employer, position, or industry. For instance, if your printed resume emphasizes your sales experience, a resume letter would quickly allow you to tailor your response to an advertisement for a Computer Programmer.

As with a resume, the resume letter should include all relevant information including education, work experience, and functional skills. The resume letter offers a convenient way to apply to a position, but remember, a resume will be required as the hiring process progresses.

RESUME LETTER
(Business Manager)

178 Green Street
Hillsboro, MO 63050
(314) 555-5555

January 12, 1996

Pat Cummings
President
Any Corporation
1140 Main Street
Columbia, MO 65211

Dear Mr. Cummings:

I am a seasoned professional offering over twenty-one years of extensive experience in business and corporate administrative responsibilities in the following areas:

- Cost engineering and estimating
- Accounting and financial analysis
- Planning and scheduling
- Personal computers and microsystems
- Procurement and contact administration
- Claim preparation and pricing
- Documentation and negotiations
- Mainframe computers and systems

In addition to the above, I have worked with construction managers, project managers, project engineers, project accountants, discipline engineers and designers, quality assurance and other technical and support personnel. I am able to establish effective rapport with supervisors, colleagues, and subordinates and have "hands-on" knowledge of computer services and office procedures.

During seventeen years with Picciano & Houllahan Engineering, Inc., I have put together a record of which I am quite proud. I have assumed positions of increasing responsibility, and I am now ready for a greater challenge. I believe you will agree that my record justifies the expectation of seeking a staff-level position with the opportunity to fully utilize my experience and potential for advancement to a line-management position.

On both a day-to-day and long-range basis, I have participated in the cost and scheduling activities of both large and small projects, and a number of various types: fuel, fossil, nuclear, process, pulp and paper, industrial, infrastructure, and environmental. My strengths include a heavy background in project controls, budget forecast and maintenance, staff supervision, and problem-solving. I have the respect of colleagues and clients in terms of overall effectiveness, on-schedule and under-budget performance, and quality of final product and/or reports.

My goal is to join a firm that requires the immediate use of these skills to either increase a rate of established growth, or to effect a turnaround situation.

Within the next week or so, I will call to see whether you agree that our mutual interests would be served by exploring this matter further, and if so when your calendar might permit time for a personal interview.

Thank you for your time and consideration.

                Sincerely,

                Chris Smith

■ Resume letter format combines cover letter and resume into one.

■ Background summary accentuates candidate's acquired professional skills and impressive track record.

RESUME LETTER
(Cardiologist)

178 Green Street
Payne Gap, KY 41537
(606) 555-5555

April 30, 1996

Pat Cummings
Chief Administrator
Any Hospital
1140 Main Street
Sandy Springs, SC 29677

Dear Ms. Cummings:

I recently read about your need for a Cardiologist in the May edition of the bulletin published by the South Carolina Medical Association. Please accept the following summary of accomplishments as application for this opportunity.

- Two years as Cardiology Fellow with extensive experience covering the full spectrum of clinical cardiology.
- Experience encompasses: cardiac catheterization and angioplasty, cardiac pacing and electrophysiology, echocardiography, exercise testing and nuclear imaging, in- and out-patient hospital care of cardiac patients.
- Two years of experience as a Clinical Instructor in Medicine at St. Martha's Hospital teaching interns, residents, and medical students.
- Board certified—Internal Medicine, board eligible in Cardiology.

In my current position as Cardiology Fellow at St. Martha's, I have had the opportunity to utilize state-of-the-art systems, procedures, and techniques covering the full spectrum of clinical cardiology. I am also presently involved in research encompassing clinical evaluation of the bundeen cross-coronary stent, and have just completed a review article dealing with ventricular arrhythmias. Additionally, I received my Doctor of Medicine degree from the Boston College School of Medicine, and a Bachelor of Science degree in Preprofessional Studies from the University of Pennsylvania.

I am planning to move to South Carolina shortly, and was very excited to see that you needed a qualified Cardiologist to fill your vacancy. Would you have a few moments to speak with me next week during a scheduled visit to your area? I am sure I could convince you that I have the capabilities and the motivation to join your staff.

I will call your office on Friday to follow up on this inquiry.

Sincerely yours,

Chris Smith, M.D.

■ Advanced degrees add weight to cover letter.

■ After name, candidate includes professional title.

RESUME LETTER
(Community Center Director)

178 Green Street
West Chester, PA 19380
(800) 555-5555

February 29, 1996

Pat Cummings
President and Executive Director
Any Community Center
1140 Main Street
Philadelphia, PA 19114

Dear Mr. Cummings:

I was sorry to hear about your retirement in the article "Community Top Gun to Step Down" featured in the February 28 edition of the *Philadelphia Enquirer*. Your accomplishments as Executive Director at Any Community Center speak for themselves, and I am sure your dedication and vision will sorely be missed.

I understand from your statement that you will be personally choosing your successor prior to retirement. As a seasoned Community Center Director myself, I would be honored if you would consider me worthy of continuing your work. Presently, I am working as the Associate Executive Director of the Westchester YMCA.

My responsibilities encompass all aspects of operations:

Supervision: Supervise seven full-time program directors and nonexempt administrative staff. Recruit, hire, train, and evaluate full- and part-time staff. Organize and conduct staff meetings and training events. Responsible for career development for full-time professional staff.

Management: Financial management of $2 million multidepartment annual budget. Developed and projected new annual budget, balanced and allocated funds, and ensured branch departments met financial goals. Operations management of all program areas, member services, office administration, and facility maintenance. Administered safety and risk-management procedures for the branch.

Fundraising: Chaired 1994 Annual Support Campaign and Community Gifts Chair of the 1995 Annual Support Drive. Organized campaign activities, recruited and trained volunteers, managed telephone solicitations, developed prospects, and implemented related administrative procedures.

Programs/Services: Managed multiprogram areas, scheduling, enrollment, and member evaluations. Established program guidelines and criteria. Managed and supervised membership department and front desk area, program registration, and member services/relations.

Community Relations: Responsible for administration and allocation of scholarship/financial aid funds. Assisted in volunteer development program. Direct responsibility to branch board of directors and program committees. Responsible for public service announcements and public relations via presentations at various community organizations.

I would be very interested in talking with you about your requirements for the position. When would be a convenient time to meet?

Sincerely,

Chris Smith

■ Categorizing qualifications adds strength to cover letter.

■ Letter focuses on the needs of the employer, not the job candidate.

RESUME LETTER
(Construction Manager)

178 Green Street
Forth Worth, TX 76104
(817) 555-5555

June 16, 1996

Pat Cummings
Principal Engineer
Any Corporation
1140 Main Street
Arlington, TX 76004

Dear Ms. Cummings:

During the past eighteen years, I have developed the professional skills that are the essential building blocks for successful project and construction management. Currently, I am looking for a new association with a firm, such as yours, where I can apply these skills to increasingly complex and challenging projects with profitable bottom-line results.

After earning my Bachelor of Science degree in Civil Engineering from the University of Austin, Texas, and competing in the Olympics in 1980, I joined B.R. Rice, Inc. as a Construction Engineer managing construction on major power plant sites in Mexico, Texas, and California. From 1982 to 1991, I was responsible as Senior Project Manager for project engineering and design/build project management assignments in the power, environmental, and commercial process industries. This included both field and home office desk assignments for both public and private sector companies.

Since 1991, I have been the Director of Engineering and Principal Engineer for an engineering and environment consulting company. My responsibilities also include marketing, proposal preparation, and project management. I serve as a consultant to public and private sector clients in business planning, environmental permitting, financing, design/construction management, and start-up of environmental and waste management building projects.

To date, I have managed the design and construction of projects representing over 32 million cubic feet of building volume, 200 megawatts of power, and nearly $275 million in financing.

My projects have been varied and complex. Some of my prior project management accomplishments include:

- The design and construction of a four-year, $52 million coal conversion project in Austin, Texas. Completed the project on schedule and $500,000 under budget.

- Process, site, and building designs—a $30 million portion of the largest waste-to-energy facility in the world, Cincinnati, Ohio. Managed a $3.5 million design, field engineering, and a start-up assistance contract. Directed a project team that issued twenty-five individual construction contract bid packages, each one on schedule. Recommended $1 million in value engineering cost savings to the client, and closed out the contract $500,000 under budget.

- Provision of constructability review and pricing for an advanced energy research project for the U.S. Department of Energy and NASA.

- Direction of the development, planning, and implementation of a $1.3 billion, twenty-three-year engineering and construction program extending the lives of fourteen power plants for a large electric utility company.

As an Engineering Management Professional, I am technically proficient; apply creative solutions to complex problems; encourage team building among project participants; maintain constant communication both up and down the ladder; set and ensure achievement of total quality management objectives; and closely monitor resource allocations and expenditures, goal attainments, and project team performance.

I am keenly interested in suitable availabilities at Any Corporation and am immediately available pending adequate prior notice to my current employer. The reason for leaving my current employment is the desire to join a larger company where I can put all of my knowledge to use and be deeply involved in all phases of complex, construction projects.

I look forward to meeting with you, in confidence, to discuss my experience and the mutual benefits of my joining your company.

Sincerely,

Chris Smith, P.E.

- Two pages is an acceptable length for top positions.

- Letter emphasizes achievements, and does not simply list job responsibilities.

RESUME LETTER
(Director of Information Services)

178 Green Street
Clearfield, UT 84016

November 5, 1996

Pat Cummings
Vice-President, Operations
Any Corporation
1140 Main Street
Salt Lake City, UT 84104

Dear Mr. Cummings:

I am interested in your advertisement for a Director of Information Services as published in the November 4 edition of the *Salt Lake Tribune*. Several of the qualifications I could bring to this position include:

- Extensive experience in Cobol Programming.

- Proven managerial abilities.

- Self-motivation; able to set effective priorities to achieve immediate and long-term goals and meet operational deadlines.

- Development of interpersonal skills, having dealt with a diversity of professionals, clients, and staff members.

- Ability to function well in fast-paced, high-pressure atmosphere.

For the past eleven years I have had the opportunity to progress in positions of responsibility at my current employer from Programmer to Director of Information Services. In this capacity, I control programming and systems, computer operations, data entry, membership records, and membership promotion and retention departments. I have successfully implemented complete financial reporting systems, inventory, accounts receivable, computerized production of publications, and applications.

In addition to my work experiences, I hold both a Bachelor's and Master's degree in Business Administration. I am proficient in Burroughs B-2900 computer systems, with various peripheral equipment and 35 on-line CRT terminals (COBOL).

I am very interested in learning more about your work at Any Corporation and how I might best apply my skills to your advantage. Please contact me to schedule a meeting at (801) 555-5555.

Sincerely,

Chris Smith

- Including computer skills may be advantageous for certain fields of work.

- Letter's format outlines all relevant information to field of interest including, qualifications, achievements, and education.

RESUME LETTER
(District Manager)

178 Green Street
Long Beach, CA 90802

December 27, 1996

Pat Cummings
Vice-President, Pacific Region
Any Restaurant Chain
1140 Main Street
Los Angeles, CA 90010

Dear Ms. Cummings:

I would like to express my sincere interest in the District Manager position you advertised in the December 26 edition of the *Los Angeles Times*. I have taken the liberty of summarizing my background in the restaurant franchise industry for your consideration:

- Fifteen years of successful experience in the management of three franchise restaurants, including financing, contractual agreements, corporate and personnel relations, property management, facilities design and layout, advertising, promotion, and community relations.

- Experience also includes purchasing, inventory control and management, personnel hiring, training, scheduling and evaluation, security, policy and procedure.

- Proven record as top salesperson. Consistently awarded top sales manager honors.

For the past ten years, I have succeeded in increasingly responsible positions with the Pizza Palace franchise. In my current position as Branch Manager, I am responsible for managing a work force of over 250 employees, while generating annual sales of over $3.5 million. I am actively involved in all aspects of successful business operations, including sales, finance, and personnel management, property maintenance, and associated aspects of administrative detail.

I would be happy to supply several excellent references at your request. Additionally, I would be available at your convenience to meet for an interview. Please contact me at (203) 555-5555, or evenings at (203) 444-4444.

I appreciate your consideration, Ms. Cummings.

Sincerely,

Chris Smith

- Career objective is supported by awards and accomplishments.
- Candidate tailors resume letter to his/her field of interest.

RESUME LETTER
(Hospital Administrator)

178 Green Street
Norwalk, CT 06856
(203) 555-555

August 12, 1996

Pat Cummings
Chairperson, Board of Directors
Any Hospital
1140 Main Street
Bridgeport, CT 06605

Dear Mr. Cummings:

Thank you for speaking with me this morning regarding the Hospital Administrator position available at Any Hospital. Per your request, please allow me to present several of my most relevant experiences and accomplishments in health care management/administration.

For the past year, I have been working as Acting Director of the Norwalk Medical Center. In this capacity, I am responsible for the supervision/coordination of all administrative services for the city's public health care program. This includes the health care and hospitalization for indigents, low-income, and welfare patients, consistent with care afforded insurance and fee-for-service patients. In addition, I troubleshoot staff and general administration conflicts and resolve policy issues, as well as develop reports for budgeting proposals and expenditure control.

Previous to my current position, I spent six years as Central Administrator of Emergency Services for the same institution. I coordinated all administrative details of the department, prepared the department budget, and monitored expenditures. As Administrator, I also supervised ward secretaries, interpreters, and ancillary personnel. This same duty was performed in the position of Unit Manager, which I held from 1987 to 1989. This experience exposed me to several aspects of administrative support, vendor relations, and inventory control.

This experience is supported by a Master of Science degree in Health Service Administration, a certificate in Management Development from the Connecticut Hospital Association, and a Bachelor or Arts degree in English.

I am very eager to apply my acquired knowledge of health care administration to the position at Any Hospital. I hope my qualifications match your requirements, and that I will have the opportunity to speak with you again in a personal interview.

Thank you for your consideration.

Sincerely,

Chris Smith

■ Specific contributions emphasize candidate's achievements and problem-solving abilities.

■ Resume format is particularly effective for top-level positions.

RESUME LETTER
(Manufacturing Manager)

178 Green Street
Lake City, FL 32056
(904) 555-5555

May 8, 1996

Pat Cummings
Chief Executive Officer
Any Corporation
1140 Main Street
Chicago, IL 60611

Dear Ms. Cummings:

I discovered Any Corporation through your listing in the *Chicago Job Bank*. I am an experienced executive with a broad technical as well as management background in the machining and manufacturing fields. Next month, I will be moving permanently to Illinois, and would be very interested in learning of suitable management opportunities at your firm.

With more than sixteen years of training in the manufacturing industry, I possess a proven track record of accomplishment. Some of the experiences I could bring to Any Corporation include:

Manufacturing Manager; Gladstone Motor Company, Lake City, VT

- Oversaw modernization and reorganization of engine plant contracted for remanufacture of Dane Motor Company engines.

- Set up controls for workers in manufacturing departments and the machine shop which included grinding, boring, and honing operations.

- Initiated an improved quality control system to meet Dane specifications for full-year warranty. System resulted in reduction of rejects to less than 4 percent on 500 to 600 engines completed monthly.

- Classified purchasing details on 80 different production engines; implemented inventory control; greatly improved ordering efficiencies; and set up effective marketing service policies.

Manufacturing Manager; P.I.L. Engineering Company, Tampa, FL

- Supervised the production of a machine shop that subcontracted to manufacture precision machine parts and assemblies for the electronic industry.

- Developed and implemented manufacturing, cost control, and quality control programs; successfully developed business to $8.2 million in annual sales.

General Manager; Ferou Maintenance, Tampa, FL

- Shouldered full responsibility for tractor-trailer maintenance company servicing the Shaw Line Hault Fleet consisting of 500 trailers and 200 tractors traveling Florida and the Mid-Atlantic.

- Initiated many vehicle design changes that were adopted by the Stanza Motor Company.

- Designed unique field service trucks on which specifications were written for national application.

I will be in the Chicago area during the week of May 20 to 24, and would be very interested in meeting with you at that time regarding possible openings appropriate for my qualifications. Perhaps I could share several of my design and organizational ideas, which I feel might benefit operations at Any Corporation. I will contact you next week to find a convenient meeting time.

Sincerely,

Chris Smith

■ Resume letter includes all pertinent information that would appear on a resume.

■ Candidate's work experience reads like a series of accomplishments, not just a list of job duties.

RESUME LETTER
(Real Estate Director)

178 Green Street
Hunt Valley, MD 21030
(301) 555-5555

March 3, 1996

Pat Cummings
President
Any Corporation
1140 Main Street
Landover, MD 20785

Dear Mr. Cummings:

Are you searching for an Executive Director to supervise operations, stimulate development, and increase your market edge? As a seasoned professional in the field of real estate management, I have the ability to quickly and significantly contribute to Any Corporation in an executive position.

I have selected several career highlights to demonstrate my abilities:

- **Multidisciplined Professional:** Possess real estate background encompassing business development, strategic planning, marketing, and construction project management.

- **Marketing Edge:** While with current employer, Raze Realty and Construction Company, Inc., developed a vital network of business and industry contacts instrumental to the acquisition of key contracts with the China Society, Jen Bright, and Weld Corporations.

- **Technical Expertise:** Offer a Bachelor of Science in Mechanical Engineering from the Massachusetts Institute of Technology. Possess proven abilities to estimate costs, design and install electrical, telecommunications, fire and safety, and related technological systems.

- **Project Executive:** Managed full profit and loss accountability for key client projects involving scheduling, cost accounting, cash flow analysis, purchasing, and professional relations.

- **Human Resources Management:** Able to recruit, assign, motivate, and evaluate management and support staff. Developed and implemented progressive policy for 500 employees.

- **Cost Conscious:** Developed innovative cost-savings programs including cellular telephone service and Raze T-Bar Systems.

- **Sales Achiever:** Reputation for excellent sales presentations. Closed the largest single sale within Meyer for an infrared lighting control system.

- **Skilled Negotiator:** Deal successfully with U.S. and Asian corporate representatives. Handled contractor negotiations, secured an equity position with RSSO for Raze's 1,500-room Manhattan Ritz Hotel.

Let's get together to further discuss your needs in terms of my qualifications. Please contact me with a tentative interview time that is convenient for you.

I look forward to your response.

Sincerely,

Chris Smith

- Candidate carefully details all relevant experience, accomplishments, and educational credentials.

- Closing is straightforward and concise.

RESUME LETTER
(Vice-President, Sales and Marketing)

178 Green Street
Pigeon Forge, TN 37868
(615) 555-5555

October 14, 1996

Pat Cummings
Chief Executive Officer
Any Corporation
1140 Main Street
Nashville, TN 37211

Dear Ms. Cummings:

In a phone conversation Friday, my neighbor and your Senior Sales Representative, Milton Farley, informed me of the newly vacant position of Vice-President, Sales and Marketing at Any Corporation. Milton felt that my extensive experience as an executive in this area would make me an excellent candidate for this opportunity. In this regard, please allow me to introduce my background to you.

<u>Experience: Vice-President; Littleton and Shelley, Nashville, TN</u>

Company is a $10 million, industry-leading producer of toys and related items manufactured and sold internationally. Started as Purchasing Manager, assuming additional responsibilities for outside sales, and, on basis of outstanding success in the development and handling of key accounts and general operations, advanced to current position of Vice-President in charge of sales and product development.

<u>Accomplishments:</u>

- Personal sales over $4 million a year, while managing/working with network of over 46 sales organizations employing 150 sales representatives.

- Managed development, sourcing, manufacturing, and importation of total doll and doll accessory product lines from Far East and Europe. Reduced cost of manufacture by 15 percent.

- Added $350,000 at significant margin to gross sales through establishment of new division marketing line of doll accessories. Developed new fashions projected at $600,000 first-year sales.

- Developed new sales accounts, through establishment of national representative/distributor organization, from annual sales of $250,000 to current volume of $850,000.

Although my time at Littleton and Shelley has provided me with a great deal of challenge and satisfaction, I would like to apply my experience to a new environment. I am familiar with your products and services, and am confident I could provide innovative and cost-effective supervision of your sales and marketing team. Based on my experience, my compensation requirements are between $100,000-115,000.

Could we meet for further discussion?

Sincerely,

Chris Smith

- Statistics and dollar amounts quantify candidate's accomplishments.

- Resume letter often includes salary range.

18
Follow-Up Letter (After Telephone Conversation)

Immediately after a telephone conversation with a potential employer, you should send a cover letter expressing your gratitude for his or her time. You should use this opportunity to reiterate your qualifications and continued interest in the position. Be sure to send your resume along with the letter. Doug B., an Accountant, followed his initial inquiry with a phone call and was lucky enough to speak with the Accounting Manager. After discussing the position for several minutes, Doug was able to schedule an interview. Immediately after the call, he sent a polite thank you letter that reiterated his qualifications and confirmed their meeting time. Doug's letter set him apart from the competition.

FOLLOW-UP LETTER (AFTER TELEPHONE CONVERSATION)
(Acquisitions Manager)

178 Green Street
Brookings, SD 57006

July 2, 1996

Pat Cummings
Land Acquisitions Supervisor
Any Corporation
1140 Main Street
Yankton, SD 57078

Dear Mr. Cummings:

The opportunity to talk with you on a one-on-one basis gave me a positive feeling about the caliber of your company and its managers, and increased my interest in joining your firm. Per your request, I am enclosing my resume which briefly outlines my qualifications for a position involving right-of-way and land acquisition transactions.

I offer eleven years of progressively responsible experience acquired during roadway, civil, site, hazardous waste, and waterfront projects. This is supported by a Bachelor of Science degree in Forest Resource Management, certification as Land Surveyor-in-Training, and the competition of Hazardous Site Activities courses. As a Surveyor, I have broad experience in researching deeds, and land and legal descriptions for commercial, industrial, and residential applications.

Currently, I am investigating new opportunities where my technical and supervisory skills can be effectively utilized and expanded upon. I am not opposed to learning new systems and procedures or accepting a support position leading to advancement within the company. If relocation is a requirement, then I am ready to make that commitment to achieve my career objectives.

I am confident of my ability to make a positive and immediate contribution to Any Corporation, and would welcome the opportunity to meet with you at your convenience. I can be reached at the above address or by phone at (605) 555-5555. Thank you for the chance to discuss available opportunities. I anticipate your response.

Yours sincerely,

Chris Smith

Enc. resume

■ Date of telephone conversation is noted immediately.

■ Introduction refers to attached resume.

FOLLOW-UP LETTER (AFTER TELEPHONE CONVERSATION)
(Arbitrator)

178 Green Street
Yorktown Heights, NY 10598
(914) 555-5555

September 24, 1996

Pat Cummings
Director of Regional Administration
Any Corporation
1140 Main Street
Port Chester, NY 10573

Dear Ms. Cummings:

As per our conversation and your request, I am enclosing my business profile for
your review in consideration for the position of Arbitrator with Any Organization.

In addition to a Bachelor of Arts degree and study in arbitration, I have been
actively involved as an Arbitrator for the Better Business Bureau for the past four
years. My activities during the past thirteen years, as a licensed Auctioneer and
Night Club Manager, have consistently involved skill in new business
development, negotiating, listening, weighing facts, and making decisions to
resolve disputes in the best interest of all parties concerned.

I have successfully arbitrated cases involving manufacturers, vendors, and
customers, chaired arbitration panels, and established a reputation for being able to
make fair decisions under stressful conditions.

The enclosed document summarizes my experience. If you feel that my
qualifications match your needs, I would like to speak with you further in an
interview. I can be reached at the above address and phone or a message can be
left at (914) 555-4444.

Thank you for your consideration of my application. I look forward to your return
response.

Yours sincerely,

Chris Smith

Enc. business profile

■ Letter allows candidate
opportunity to suggest personal
interview as next step.

■ Qualifications highlight
candidate's problem-solving
ability.

FOLLOW-UP LETTER (AFTER TELEPHONE CONVERSATION)
(Assistant Engineer)

178 Green Street
Rogers, AR 72757
(501) 555-5555

September 18, 1996

Pat Cummings
Executive Assistant
Any Shipbuilder
1140 Main Street
Little Rock, AR 72203

Dear Mr. Cummings:

Thank you for extending your time to me this morning over the phone. I am glad
to hear that Mr. Gulesarian is still looking for an Assistant Engineer. I understand
the expertise you are in search of, and I believe I possess it. To this position, I
would bring:

- More than five years of progressively responsible, hands-on, management
  experience in the maintenance, repair, modification, overhaul, and
  installation of heavy marine equipment and machinery.

- Expertise with electrical, water, fuel, lubrication, hydraulic, power plant,
  motor control, and related systems and major components.

- Experience that includes AC/DC light and power systems, generators,
  controllers, starters, transformers, communications systems, general
  electronics, consoles, and computers.

I would be able to provide further testimony of my skills during the course of a
meeting with Mr. Gulesarian. I will call his office late next week to see when his
schedule would allow a few moments to speak with me. In the interim, I have
enclosed a professional profile for his consideration.

Again, I enjoyed our conversation and hope to speak with you again as the hiring
process continues.

Sincerely,

Chris Smith

Enc. professional profile

- Candidate expresses gratitude for
  addressee's consideration.

- Letter tailors experience and skills
  to position applied for.

FOLLOW-UP LETTER (AFTER TELEPHONE CONVERSATION)
(Assistant Portfolio Manager)

178 Green Street
Parsippany, NJ 07054
(201) 555-5555

March 28, 1996

Pat Cummings
Director of Finance
Any Firm
1140 Main Street
Morristown, NJ 08057

Dear Ms. Cummings:

Our phone conversation yesterday was both informative and valuable for my job search. Thank you for your help. As you know, I am very interested in joining Any Firm, whose progressive approach to financial planning and management has prompted me to forward the enclosed resume.

As I mentioned while speaking with you, I offer considerable work experience ranging from Promotional Sales Representative, Assistant Campaign Manager, and Assistant Budget Analyst to my present position as Assistant Portfolio Manager. I would like to meet and discuss further my qualifications and the opportunities available.

Thank you again for your time. I look forward to your reply.

Sincerely,

Chris Smith

Enc. resume

■ Follow-up letter briefly reiterates relevant experience.

■ In closing, candidate specifically requests interview.

FOLLOW-UP LETTER (AFTER TELEPHONE CONVERSATION)
(Associate Editor)

178 Green Street
Marylhurst, OR 97036
(503) 555-5555

January 4, 1996

Pat Cummings
Managing Editor
Any Corporation
1140 Main Street
Portland, OR 97201

Dear Mr. Cummings:

Thank you for taking the time to speak with me on the phone yesterday. As requested, I am sending my resume for your review.

As previously mentioned, I am currently an Editorial Intern at the Portland State University Press. My career goal is to become a Managing Editor. I proofread and copyedit on a regular basis at work using *The Chicago Manual of Style,* and recently completed a course in copyediting. I also help our Production Editor prepare manuscripts for turnover to the production department. I am eager to apply my knowledge, develop new skills, and contribute to a growing company.

I plan to contact you again before the summer, when you predicted there could be job openings. In the meantime, I hope that 1996 is a successful year for you and your growing company.

Sincerely,

Chris Smith

Enc. resume

■ Internship experience is valuable for candidates with little job experience, particularly if it corresponds to the position sought.

■ Candidate expresses gratitude for addressee's consideration.

FOLLOW-UP LETTER (AFTER TELEPHONE CONVERSATION) (COBOL Programmer)

178 Green Street
Norfolk, VA 23510
(703) 555-5555

February 14, 1996

Pat Cummings
Director of Human Resources
Any Corporation
1140 Main Street
Casper, WY 82604

Dear Ms. Cummings:

Thank you for taking the time from your schedule on Friday to speak with me regarding available COBOL Programmer positions with your clients. Please accept the enclosed resume as an expressed interest in joining your organization to contribute and develop my skills and abilities.

As you can see from my resume, my hardware exposure has included Suzuki and HyTech, and I have had substantial experience in implementing both batch and on-line computer systems using COBOL. Initiative and ability in each position I have held has led to advancement and the assumption of greater responsibilities.

I feel that I have acquired valuable experience and education and the skills that I have developed, coupled with an eagerness to learn and a motivation to succeed, would contribute to a productive association with your company.

I would welcome the opportunity to meet with you to discuss ways in which my capabilities may suit your needs or those of your clients. I would also like to reiterate my willingness to relocate, given a suitable opportunity. Please consider the enclosed and direct your response to the above address.

I appreciate your time and consideration. I look forward to hearing from you.

Sincerely,

Chris Smith

Enc. resume

- Willingness to relocate can be advantageous.
- Technical language is acceptable when it relates to candidate's field.

FOLLOW-UP LETTER (AFTER TELEPHONE CONVERSATION)
(Concierge)

178 Green Street
Warren, MI 48091
(313) 555-5555

July 23, 1996

Pat Cummings
Executive Manager
Any Hotel
1140 Main Street
Port Huron, MI 48060

Dear Mr. Cummings:

I appreciate the time you took yesterday to speak with me concerning the Concierge position at Any Hotel. Your description of the position and its responsibilities was most helpful. I would like to take this opportunity to review my qualifications:

- Promoted to establish concierge department in 350-room luxury hotel.

- Responsible for setting tone and image of hotel through providing guest services, including tourist information, tour arrangements, and hotel and airline reservations.

- Supervise and manage 40-person hotel staff including concierge department assistants, mail and information clerks, bell staff, doormen, valet parking and hotel garage staff, and telephone operators.

- Diplomatically and effectively resolve guests' grievances/problems; compose responses and make follow-up phone contact.

In addition to the outlined experience, I would bring to the position an intimate knowledge of the area and its offerings and the ability to work well under pressure. My formal education includes dual degrees in Restaurant and Hotel Management and in French from Marquette University, as well as a year of study at the Sorbonne University, Paris, France.

After you have reviewed the enclosed resume, I would appreciate the opportunity to continue our phone conversation in person. Thank you.

Sincerely,

Chris Smith

Enc. resume

- Foreign language skills and international exposure, in exchange programs and/or internships, are valuable assets in today's global market.

- Candidate reiterates qualifications discussed in telephone conversation.

FOLLOW-UP LETTER (AFTER TELEPHONE CONVERSATION)
(Department Manager)

178 Green Street
Tacoma, WA 98416
(206) 555-5555

February 10, 1996

Pat Cummings
Chief Administrator
Any Hospital
1140 Main Street
Spokane, WA 99201

Dear Ms. Cummings:

It was a pleasure speaking with you today in connection with your search for a
Department Manager. I feel my experience and achievements are well within the
required qualifications set forth in your detailed job description, and I am
confident of my ability to provide your department with the same dedication and
capability as I exercise in my present position.

As outlined in my resume, I have extensive administrative and fiscal management
experience working with all departments on nonmedical aspects in a health care
environment. The challenges associated with the above position are of great
interest to me and I would like the opportunity to meet with you, at your
convenience, to further discuss my candidacy for this position.

Yours sincerely,

Chris Smith

Enc. resume

■ Closing reiterates candidate's
  interest in position.

■ Candidate immediately reviews
  circumstances of most recent
  contact.

FOLLOW-UP LETTER (AFTER TELEPHONE CONVERSATION)
(Executive Marketing Director)

178 Green Street
Boise, ID 83725
(208) 555-5555

August 3, 1996

Pat Cummings
Vice-President
Any Corporation
1140 Main Street
Chicago, IL 60605

Dear Mr. Cummings:

I am forwarding my resume with regard to the opening we discussed in your
marketing department.

Although I am currently employed in a management position, I am interested in a
career change, especially one where I can combine a thorough knowledge of
boating with my sales, marketing, and communication skills. I am an imaginative,
well-organized self-starter with a strong interest in boating. As a semi-professional
sailboat racer, I twice won national honors and participated in the races at Cape
Cod. In addition, I have made lasting contacts with owners and officials.

After you have had the chance to review my resume, please contact me so that we
can further discuss the possibility of my joining your staff. I am confident that my
business background and knowledge of boats will enable me to have a favorable
impact on both your sales and image.

Thank you for your attention, and I look forward to speaking with you again to
learn more about this opportunity.

Sincerely yours,

Chris Smith

Enc. resume

- Career objective is supported by awards and accomplishments.
- Candidate expresses knowledge in his/her field of interest.

FOLLOW-UP LETTER (AFTER TELEPHONE CONVERSATION)
(Export Manager)

178 Green Street
New York, NY 10027
(212) 555-5555

July 1, 1996

Pat Cummings
Controller
Any Corporation
1140 Main Street
Chicago, IL 60605

Dear Ms. Cummings:

Thank you for taking time out of your busy schedule to speak with me yesterday
regarding the Export Manager position. My interest in this position and in Any
Corporation is stronger than ever, particularly because it would afford me the
opportunity to become less desk-bound—an occupational hazard in my most
recent employment.

Pursuant to our conversation, I have compiled a supplement to my resume,
detailing my experience relevant to the position of Export Manager. As I explained
to you, my family has been involved in the fashion industry for most of my life. I
have actively assisted/advised both my mother and my uncle with their European
outlets, acquiring considerable expertise and knowledge of the fashion accessory
and perfume industry.

With regard to salary requirements, I did a brief cost survey of the Chicago area
and happily discovered a favorable difference between that area and where I reside
in New York. I would, therefore, be able to consider a salary somewhat lower than
we discussed—perhaps in the low fifties—since my living expenses would be so
significantly decreased.

I am very enthusiastic about the prospect of re-entering a field where my
interpersonal skills and familiarity with European culture and fashion will be more
fully utilized. I look forward to hearing from you again in the near future.

Sincerely,

Chris Smith

Enc. resume

■ Letter expresses commitment to
field of interest.

■ Including compensation
requirements is optional.

FOLLOW-UP LETTER (AFTER TELEPHONE CONVERSATION)
(Flight Attendant)

178 Green Street
Mountain View, CA 94039

February 5, 1996

Pat Cummings
Director of Human Resources
Any Airline
1140 Main Street
San Francisco, CA 94104

Dear Mr. Cummings:

I appreciate the time you took to speak with me today regarding the Flight Attendant opening advertised in the *San Francisco Chronicle*. After considering the requirements you outlined, I am even more confident of my ability to meet your needs:

You require:
- Communication skills
- Customer service aptitude
- Specialized training

I offer:
- A Bachelor of Arts degree in Communications.
- Developed interpersonal skills, having dealt with a diversity of professionals, clients, and associates.
- Fluency in Spanish; a knowledge of German.
- Over five years' experience in retail/sales, dealing with a wide variety of clients.
- Skill at handling customer complaints and problem-solving.
- Flight Attendant certification.
- CPR training.
- Participation in three-day intensive seminar, "Reacting in an Emergency."

I have enclosed a resume for your review. I would welcome the chance to address my skills and enthusiasm for this position in a personal meeting. Please contact me at the above address or (415) 555-5555.

Sincerely,

Chris Smith

Enc. resume

- Format is neat and professional.
- Continuing education indicates candidate's ongoing commitment to his/her field.

FOLLOW-UP LETTER (AFTER TELEPHONE CONVERSATION)
(Head Coach)

178 Green Street
Rutland, VT 05701

September 27, 1996

Pat Cummings
Athletic Director
Any High School
1140 Main Street
Bennington, VT 05201

Dear Ms. Cummings:

Per your suggestion during our recent discussion, I am enclosing my updated
resume as a means of expressing my continued interest in the position of Head
Varsity Baseball Coach at Any High School.

As I stated during our discussion, I have successfully established myself as a
winning coach in a comprehensive seasonal sports program encompassing six
major sports and numerous minor sports in a co-ed environment. In baseball, I
have consistently built highly competitive winning teams that have achieved
championship status.

I consider myself to be a dedicated coach who has the ability to recognize young
talent and develop a player's natural talent and competitive spirit for the makings
of a winning team. I would like to bring my coaching skills to Any High School,
and hope you will consider my qualifications in keeping with your expectations
for the position.

Should you wish to arrange a meeting for further discussion, please call me at my
home, (802) 555-5555, or write me at the above address. I enjoyed talking with
you and look forward to the opportunity to work with you at Any High School.

Sincerely,

Chris Smith

Enc. resume

■ Follow-up letter confirms
candidate's enthusiasm for
desired position.

■ Experiences are tailored to
employer's needs.

FOLLOW-UP LETTER (AFTER TELEPHONE CONVERSATION)
(Laboratory Technician)

178 Green Street
Weymouth, MA 02190
(617) 555-5555

September 12, 1996

Pat Cummings
Human Resources Director
Any Corporation
1140 Main Street
Chicago, IL 60605

Dear Mr. Cummings:

It was nice talking with you again today. As promised, I am enclosing my resume for your information.

In addition to a Bachelor of Science degree in Biology, I have five years of experience in a laboratory setting. This includes preparation and performance of experiments, as well as analysis, writing, and presentation of results.

Currently, I am investigating new opportunities where I can continue to develop my skills and apply my knowledge toward broader responsibilities and advancement. I look forward to our meeting on September 18, and learning more about the industry's forecast.

Again, thank you for taking time out of your busy schedule to aid me in my job search. Your confidence in my abilities is greatly appreciated.

Sincerely,

Chris Smith

Enc. resume

■ Candidate confirms meeting time established during previous telephone conversation.

■ Including a telephone number is essential in a cover letter.

FOLLOW-UP LETTER (AFTER TELEPHONE CONVERSATION)
(Magazine Publishing Intern)

178 Green Street
Phoenix, AZ 85004
(602) 555-5555

March 30, 1996

Pat Cummings
Editor-in-Chief
Any Magazine
1140 Main Street
Little Rock, AR 72203

Dear Ms. Cummings:

Thank you for your time and courtesy during our telephone conversation on
Friday, March 26. As I mentioned to you, I am very interested in the summer
internship at *Any Magazine*.

I am currently participating in a senior-year internship at a Tucson publishing firm,
Baker Communications Group. After my graduation, I want to expand my
experience in the publishing and public relations fields. I feel the *Any Magazine*
internship provides that opportunity, and that I can make a valuable contribution as
a summer Intern.

I am most interested in discussing the possibility of working for *Any Magazine* this
summer. I have enclosed my resume for your review, and I look forward to
hearing from you.

Sincerely,

Chris Smith

Enc. resume

■ Relevant internship bolsters
otherwise limited work experience.

■ Date of telephone conversation is
noted immediately.

FOLLOW-UP LETTER (AFTER TELEPHONE CONVERSATION)
(Mailroom Supervisor)

178 Green Street
Carey, OH 43316
(419) 555-5555

March 23, 1996

Pat Cummings
Director of Human Resources
Any Corporation
1140 Main Street
Galion, OH 44833

Dear Mr. Cummings:

I enjoyed speaking with you over the phone yesterday and appreciate your consideration of my resume for the Mailroom Supervisor position.

I believe I possess the specific experience you require for this position. As I mentioned during our conversation, I have direct experience in mailroom management. In my current position at O'Keefe and Murphy, my responsibilities include:

- Coordinating all incoming mail, dispersing interbuilding correspondence, managing courier services, and shipping/receiving.

- Researching and accounting for certified, registered, and express mail.

- Administering employee evaluations/appraisals, and scheduling hours.

- Obtaining/maintaining lease agreements for electronic masonry and equipment.

I am very interested in applying my skills as your new Mailroom Supervisor. Could we meet for a personal interview? Please contact me when your schedule permits a meeting.

Thank you for your courtesy yesterday. I look forward to speaking with you further.

Sincerely,

Chris Smith

Enc. resume

■ Type of position desired is clearly stated.

■ Candidate expresses gratitude for addressee's consideration.

FOLLOW-UP LETTER (AFTER TELEPHONE CONVERSATION)
(Manager of Patient Services)

178 Green Street
Miami, FL 33054

September 15, 1996

Pat Cummings
Director of Patient Services
Any Hospital
1140 Main Street
Princeton, NJ 08540

Dear Ms. Cummings:

Thank you for a most interesting and enlightening discussion during our recent telephone interview pertaining to the position of Manager of Patient Services at Any Hospital. I am gratified to hear that Kelly Merke, currently interim Manager of Patient Services, was so thoughtful as to recommend me to you for the above position.

As I previously mentioned, my interest is in the clinical aspect of the health care profession — an area in which my education, training, and experience is comprehensive. I am a skilled, dedicated professional with the ability to supervise a cost-effective clinical, patient, or support services activity.

My present position is diverse and represents the broad scope of clinical responsibility I am capable of handling. However, I am presently planning to relocate and I am seeking a new association, with a hospital such as Any Hospital, where I can continue to apply my clinical and supervisory expertise toward providing cost-effective, quality health care.

The enclosed resume summarizes my background and experience. After you have reviewed my qualifications, I would appreciate hearing from you so that we may discuss travel arrangements and a mutually convenient time for our one-on-one meeting. I can be reached by phone at (305) 555-5555 between 9 a.m. and 2 p.m.

Thanks again for the opportunity to discuss the position, and I hope to hear from you soon.

Yours sincerely,

Chris Smith

Enc. resume

- Candidate discusses pertinent information received during telephone conversation.
- Candidate expresses best time of day to be reached in closing.

FOLLOW-UP LETTER (AFTER TELEPHONE CONVERSATION)
(Nanny)

178 Green Street
Boise, ID 83730
(208) 555-5555

July 6, 1996

Pat Cummings
1140 Main Street
Boise, ID 83757

Dear Mr. Cummings:

Per your request during our recent phone conversation, I have enclosed several excellent references attesting to my abilities as a Nanny.

Also attached is a professional profile listing relevant activities that might be of interest to you. In addition to my experience as a private day-care provider, I have taught in infant, toddler, and preschool programs which involved planning curriculums, organizing activities, and communicating regularly with parents and staff.

I have made children's growth and development my career, and would very much like to apply my skills as your Nanny. I would appreciate the opportunity to speak with you further after you have verified my references, and would love to meet your children!

I hope to hear from you soon.

Sincerely,

Chris Smith

Enc. professional profile
    references

■ Enclosure line refers to all attached materials.

■ Dedication to candidate's field of interest is emphasized.

FOLLOW-UP LETTER (AFTER TELEPHONE CONVERSATION)
(Precision Inspector)

178 Green Street
Horsham, PA 19044
(215) 555-5555

October 14, 1996

Pat Cummings
Vice-President
Any Corporation
1140 Main Street
Reading, PA 19612

Dear Ms. Cummings:

Per our phone conversation this morning, I would like to confirm an interview
time of 9:00 a.m., October 18, for the Precision Inspector position.

In preparation for our meeting, I would like to reiterate my qualifications for this
position. I offer more than ten years' experience in:

* First-piece, in-process, and other phases of precision inspection.

* A wide variety of production manufacturing departments shops and
  associated inspection areas.

* Inspection procedures and methods pertaining to machined and fabricated
  complex parts from in-plant and vendors.

* Working to industrial and government specifications, and interpreted
  drawings.

* Making complicated setups and using tools and techniques to inspect with
  a maximum amount of efficiency and minimum supervision.

I look forward to our interview and the opportunity to discuss the mutual benefit
of our working together.

Sincerely,

Chris Smith

Enc. resume

■ Candidate confirms meeting time
established during previous
telephone conversation.

■ Closing is brief and to the point.

534

FOLLOW-UP LETTER (AFTER TELEPHONE CONVERSATION)
(Principal)

178 Green Street
Atlanta, GA 30378
(404) 555-5555

February 5, 1996

Pat Cummings
Superintendent
Any School System
1140 Main Street
Mobile, GA 31776

Dear Mr. Cummings:

Thank you very much for taking the time to speak with me today regarding the Principal position available in your district. As you suggested, I have enclosed a resume for your consideration.

I would be very interested in meeting with you and learning more about the position and its requirements. Should you require any additional information, please do not hesitate to contact me.

I look forward to pursuing the next step in the application process.

Sincerely,

Chris Smith

Enc. resume

■ Closing suggests a meeting to follow letter.

■ Introduction refers to attached resume.

FOLLOW-UP LETTER (AFTER TELEPHONE CONVERSATION)
(Production Assistant)

178 Green Street
Tulsa, OK 74103
(918) 555-5555

January 24, 1996

Pat Cummings
Human Resources Director
Any Publishing Company
1140 Main Street
Philadelphia, PA 19130

Dear Ms. Cummings:

Thank you for taking the time to talk with me on Friday, January 21 about the present opening for a Production Assistant. I am very interested in this position and believe it would be an appropriate place to learn more about the publishing field.

I enjoyed our conversation and look forward to hearing more about this opportunity. Thank you for your time and consideration.

Sincerely,

Chris Smith

Enc. resume

■ Follow-up letter confirms candidate's enthusiasm for desired position.

■ Letter uses short sentences and common words.

FOLLOW-UP LETTER (AFTER TELEPHONE CONVERSATION)
(Protection Professional)

178 Green Street
Boulder, CO 80301
(303) 555-5555

May 1, 1996

Pat Cummings
Human Resources Director
Any Corporation
1140 Main Street
Englewood, CO 80112

Dear Mr. Cummings:

As you suggested during our recent conversation, I am enclosing a summary of my education, training, and experience in security services management. Thank you for taking the time to discuss your requirements for the Certified Protection Professional position. I am very interested in applying my skills to meet your needs.

As I briefly explained, my experience in industry is with a multisite, 2,800-person division of a high-tech firm requiring strict adherence pertaining to security as well as physical accountability, safety, and environmental concerns. During the past seven years, I have played a key role in developing and installing cost-effective internal and off-site systems and controls essential for sophisticated, high-risk industries.

I feel that I have much to offer Any Corporation relative to directing a safe and secure environment. After you have reviewed my qualifications, I would like to arrange a personal meeting for further discussion. Please call me at your convenience.

Sincerely,

Chris Smith

Enc. professional profile

■ Candidate reiterates qualifications discussed in telephone conversation.

■ Letter allows candidate opportunity to suggest personal interview as next step.

FOLLOW-UP LETTER (AFTER TELEPHONE CONVERSATION)
(Psychiatric Nurse)

178 Green Street
Racine, WI 53406
(414) 555-5555

May 2, 1996

Pat Cummings
Director of Human Resources
Any Hospital
1140 Main Street
Milwaukee, WI 53203

Dear Ms. Cummings:

Thank you for taking the time yesterday to discuss the Psychiatric Nursing
position. I am excited about the opportunity and I am confident that I could make a
positive contribution.

As mentioned during our phone conversation, some of my relevant experiences
include:

- Work in diverse hospital and human service environments in a range of
  units from pediatric and medical/surgical, to handling mixed
  adults/adolescents, manic depressive individuals, and borderline/acute
  personality patients.

- Crisis intervention, case management, working with conduct disorders,
  sexual and physical abuse patients, acute or chronic psychiatric distress,
  substance abuse, and work with the physically challenged.

- Ssupervising three nurses and associated staff, assigning patients for
  evaluation, working with social service representatives, patients' family
  and/or guardians, distributing medications, providing emergency medical
  assistance, and handling associated details of medical administration.

I would like the opportunity to continue our discussion in person. Perhaps we
could arrange a mutually convenient time to meet. I will contact your office
Monday, May 6, to set up an appointment.

Sincerely,

Chris Smith

Enc. resume

■ Bullets provide a clear and crisp
presentation.

■ Letter allows candidate follow-up
opportunity to discuss his/her
skills and accomplishments.

FOLLOW-UP LETTER (AFTER TELEPHONE CONVERSATION)
(Purchasing Agent)

178 Green Street
Carlsbad, NM 88220
(505) 555-5555

December 5, 1996

Pat Cummings
Supervisor, Order Entry Department
Any Store
1140 Main Street
Albuquerque, NM 87106

Dear Mr. Cummings:

As you requested during our recent discussion, I am enclosing my resume for you
to review and distribute to the administration services department. My interest is in
a position where I can utilize, and the company can benefit from, my strong
purchasing and inventory skills.

Although my present position is diverse and secure, there seems to be little room
for further growth within the company and I think it is time for a change. I would
like the opportunity to rejoin Any Store and I feel that my diverse purchasing,
inventory, and traffic skills can be well utilized within the new administration
services department.

I want to thank you in advance for your interest and your time, and look forward to
a meeting to further discuss opportunities with Any Store. Should you require
additional information or like to set up an interview, please contact me. I have
enjoyed working at Any Store in the past and would like to join the company on a
full-time basis.

Thanks again for your interest and assistance.

Sincerely,

Chris Smith

Enc. resume

■ Personalized tone reinforces
candidate's familiarity with
addressee.

■ Candidate indicates type of
employment desired.

FOLLOW-UP LETTER (AFTER TELEPHONE CONVERSATION)
(Regional Sales/Product Trainer)

178 Green Street
West Bend, IN 53095

June 3, 1996

Pat Cummings
National Sales Trainer
Any Corporation
1140 Main Street
Green Bay, WI 54307

Dear Ms. Cummings:

Per your request during our recent phone conversation, I am enclosing my resume for your review and to initiate a meeting to discuss the position of Regional Sales/Product Trainer for Any Corporation.

Audio/video equipment and systems have been an integral part of my life as both a vocation and avocation. Based on my experience and accomplishments as a top producer in conceptual sales and technical training management, I am confident of my ability to contribute, through dealer training and motivation, to a substantial increase in sales of your product line. I feel that the combination of my knowledge of, and belief in, the quality of your products can only assist me in an exceptional performance of training for Any Corporation.

I would welcome a personal interview in which we would have the opportunity to discuss, in detail, your requirements and my ability to handle the responsibilities of the Regional Sales/ Product Trainer position.

Should you have any further questions, please do not hesitate to contact me at the above address or by phone at (414) 555-5555.

I look forward to your return response.

Sincerely,

Chris Smith

Enc. resume

■ Candidate highlights areas of expertise.

■ Follow-up letter briefly reiterates relevant experience.

FOLLOW-UP LETTER (AFTER TELEPHONE CONVERSATION)
(Teacher)

178 Green Street
Akron, OH 44316

August 5, 1996

Pat Cummings, M.D.
Director
Any School for the Deaf
1140 Main Street
Dayton, OH 45404

Dear Dr. Cummings:

Thank you for the opportunity, during our recent phone conversation, to discuss
the teaching position available at Any School for the Deaf. As you suggested,
I am enclosing my resume which reflects my dedication to teaching and
counseling hearing-impaired children.

In addition to a Bachelor of Arts degree in Human Development, which includes
coursework in child development, psychology of learning, and counseling
theories, I have four years' experience working with the severely handicapped.
This background, combined with my many years of personal experience as a hard-
of-hearing person, can be successfully drawn upon in a teaching capacity to
motivate and benefit hearing-impaired children at your institution.

After you have reviewed my qualifications, I would appreciate meeting with you
to further explain my interest in working within the deaf community. I feel I have
the expertise, willingness for further personal development, interest, and patience
required to work with your students.

Should you require additional information prior to our meeting, I can be reached at
the above address or phone at (216) 555-5555. I plan to make a follow-up call
within a few days.

Once again, thank you for your courtesy.

Sincerely,

Chris Smith

Enc. resume

- Courses listed are related to candidate's field of interest.
- Candidate immediately reviews circumstances of most recent contact.

19
Follow-Up Letter (After Job Interview)

Presumably, if your initial cover letter is well written, it should open the door for future communication with a potential employer. Ideally, you would land a job interview! Should you reach this stage, it is courteous to send a follow-up letter within one day of your conversation. Not only will you appear thoughtful and detail-orientated, but your follow-up letter can give you a considerable edge over candidates who neglect this important step.

A follow-up letter expresses thanks to the employer for his or her time, and emphasizes your continued interest in the available position. Follow-up letters can also provide a convenient opportunity to reiterate your unique qualifications for the position. Simply stating something like, "I would like to reiterate my strong interest in this position. I believe that it would be an exciting opportunity, and feel that my track record shows I would be a successful candidate," can enhance your candidacy dramatically.

542

FOLLOW-UP LETTER (AFTER JOB INTERVIEW)
(Administrative Assistant)

178 Green Street
Neptune, NJ 07754
(908) 555-5555

January 22,1996

Pat Cummings
Hiring Officer
Any Corporation
1140 Main Street
Passaic, NJ 07055

Dear Ms. Cummings:

Thank you for the opportunity to interview for the Administrative Assistant
position Friday. Our meeting was as informative as it was enjoyable.

I was impressed with your product lines and position in the marketplace, as well as
your vitality and commitment to growth, and I hope to contribute to the continued
growth of Any Corporation.

To this end, I would like to meet Richard Griffin to discuss how I may be of
assistance. Organization and administration are two of my strongest skills, and I
believe my experience in these areas would be beneficial to your company.

Thank you again for your time and consideration. I look forward to hearing from
you.

Sincerely,

Chris Smith

■ Letter immediately expresses
candidate's gratitude for the
interview.

■ Candidate clearly expresses
eagerness to work for specific
employer.

FOLLOW-UP LETTER (AFTER JOB INTERVIEW)
(Assistant Editor)

178 Green Street
Fargo, ND 58102

June 22, 1996

Pat Cummings
Editor
Any Publication
1140 Main Street
Nashua, NH 03061

Dear Mr. Cummings:

I want to thank you for interviewing me yesterday for the Assistant Editor position. I enjoyed meeting you and learning more about your company.

My enthusiasm for the position and my interest in working for Any Publication were strengthened as a result of our meeting. I am confident that my education and experience fit nicely with the job requirements, and I am sure I could make a significant contribution to the company over time. In short, you offer the opportunity I seek.

I am still planning on relocating to the Northeast. If, in the interim, I can provide you with any additional information, please feel free to contact me at (701) 555-5555.

Again, thank you for the interview and your consideration.

Sincerely,

Chris Smith

■ Letter immediately restates position candidate interviewed for.

■ Candidate highlights pertinent information discussed during interview.

FOLLOW-UP LETTER (AFTER JOB INTERVIEW)
(Bank Manager)

178 Green Street
Pullman, WA 99164
(509) 555-5555

June 20, 1996

Pat Cummings
Vice-President, Northwest Region
Any Bank
1140 Main Street
Sumas, WA 98295

Dear Ms. Cummings:

Thank you for the quality time you extended me during our meeting June 17 to discuss management opportunities with Any Bank.

I want to express my appreciation to you for providing an overview of the various responsibilities associated with management positions in Any Bank's northwest division. I am confident of my ability to meet your requirements for efficient and quality performance in any position for which I am considered.

Management opportunities with Any Bank are of great interest to me, and I look forward to hearing from your human resources representative for further discussion.

Thanks again for a most pleasant and informative interview.

Sincerely,

Chris Smith

■ Candidate refers to information received during interview.

■ Candidate uses opportunity to restate his/her interest in position.

FOLLOW-UP LETTER (AFTER JOB INTERVIEW)
(Business Manager)

178 Green Street
Hickory, NC 28603
(704) 555-5555

July 10, 1996

Pat Cummings, M.D.
Director of Retinopathy
Any Hospital
1140 Main Street
Raleigh, NC 27607

Dear Dr. Cummings:

Thank you for the time you took out of your busy schedule on Tuesday to discuss the requirements of the position of Business Manager. I hope I was able to convince you of my capability to cost-effectively execute the responsibilities of the position.

I would like to stress that my experience with Blue Cross/Blue Shield has involved interfacing and dealing with all operations and administrative departments on matters pertaining to financial and business reporting. As previously stated, I have broad experience with Lotus 1-2-3 as well as other sophisticated programs designed for the health care industry. This knowledge and experience are essential requirements of the position under discussion.

From my initial interview on July 2nd with Douglas Antonucci of your human resources department through my final interview with you today, my interest in the position of Business Manager has strengthened. I sincerely feel that I am right for the job and hope that you and your associates have come to the same conclusion.

Thank you again for the time and courtesies extended to me by you, Dr. Martins, and Ms. D'Isidori. I look forward to joining your management team.

Sincerely,

Chris Smith

■ Candidate refers to all employees involved in interview process.

■ Computer experience calls attention to candidate's technical knowledge.

FOLLOW-UP LETTER (AFTER JOB INTERVIEW)
(Computer Operator)

178 Green Street
Baldwyn, MS 38824
(601) 555-5555

August 28, 1996

Pat Cummings
Manager, Billing Department
Any Corporation
1140 Main Street
Jackson, MS 39217

Dear Mr. Cummings:

Thank you for a most enjoyable interview in reference to the Computer Operator
position at Any Corporation. It was a pleasure meeting you and Robert Richmond
and learning more about the operations of your billings department.

I am very interested in contributing my seven years of experience operating
computer systems to the success of your firm. Per your suggestion, I will call your
office next week to check the status of the hiring process.

Again, thank you for your time and consideration.

Sincerely,

Chris Smith

■ Candidate establishes when
follow-up contact will take place.

■ Letter is easy and quick to read,
and only relevant details are
included.

FOLLOW-UP LETTER (AFTER JOB INTERVIEW)
(Conference Coordinator)

178 Green Street
Fort Smith, AR 72902
(501) 555-5555

August 5, 1996

Pat Cummings
Executive Director
Any Corporation
1140 Main Street
Little Rock, AR 72219

Dear Ms. Cummings:

Thank you for allowing me the opportunity to interview for the Conference
Coordinator position. As the result of our informative discussion, my interest in
the position has been strengthened substantially.

As I mentioned during our interview, I can bring eight years of diverse part-time
and full-time experience in positions which required flexibility and the ability to
accept and follow through on new assignments and responsibilities. I have had the
opportunity to deal with people on all levels in the workplace as an Instructor and
Event Coordinator in hospitality and related businesses.

Based on my past work experience, as well as my Master's degree in
Administration, I feel confident that I have the qualifications for the position under
discussion. Please let me know if there is anything I can do to assist you further in
your hiring process.

Thank you again for a most enjoyable interview.

Sincerely,

Chris Smith

■ Letter highlights candidate's
acquired professional and
educational training.

■ Candidate expresses his/her
continued interest in desired
position.

FOLLOW-UP LETTER (AFTER JOB INTERVIEW)
(Distribution Coordinator)

178 Green Street
Flint, MI 48501
(313) 555-5555

December 4, 1996

Pat Cummings
Vice-President, Operations
Any Corporation
1140 Main Street
East Lansing, MI 48824

Dear Mr. Cummings:

It is not often that a candidate has a company and its position responsibilities presented as clearly as you did during our conversation last Friday. The opening of Distribution Coordinator sounds like an ideal opportunity for which I consider myself to be well-qualified, and I appreciated the opportunity to discuss my credentials with you in so much detail.

As we discussed, I possess seven years' experience managing a successful and profitable wholesale seafood company which has expanded into retail seafood sales and seafood restaurant operations. In addition, I have since been involved in multistate, retail operations that require cost-effective management of sales and operational activities from development of start-up locations to multistate distribution using all forms of transportation.

My combined experience with fresh seafood, distribution, planning, and scheduling can be successfully applied to areas of interest to you and to the benefit of Any Corporation. I am excited about the challenge the position presents, and look forward to your return response.

Thank you again for the gracious invitation to your offices. I enjoyed my stay and I hope to return soon.

Yours sincerely,

Chris Smith

■ Experience reinforces candidate's professional objective.   ■ Candidate uses opportunity to reiterate qualifications.

FOLLOW-UP LETTER (AFTER JOB INTERVIEW)
(District Sales Supervisor)

178 Green Street
Wicomico, VA 23184
(804) 555-5555

July 4, 1996

Pat Cummings
Human Resources Director
Any Corporation
1140 Main Street
Chicago, IL 60605

Dear Ms. Cummings:

I enjoyed meeting with you yesterday. Thank you for taking the time out of your busy schedule to talk with me about the current Sales Supervisor position available with Any Corporation.

I would like to stress my interest in this position. The prospect of having the freedom to run my own sales territory like my own business is exciting and appealing to me.

My background includes extensive team selling, and I would like to emphasize that all decisions regarding the structure of presentations, targets, and general selling strategy within the downtown Lynchburg territory were principally my responsibility. I had the freedom to set pricing structure and tailor product packages as I saw fit to best make the sale. I thrived on that freedom and was successful.

As a follow-up to our meeting, I will write a rough business plan, as we discussed, and I will contact Jordan Banks for further insight into the position.

Thank you again for your time. I look forward to meeting with you again in August at the Chicago office.

Sincerely,

Chris Smith

cc. J. Banks

- Letter highlights candidate's significant accomplishments.
- Letter avoids abbreviations and slang.

FOLLOW-UP LETTER (AFTER JOB INTERVIEW)
(Doctor)

178 Green Street
Luna, NM 87824
(505) 555-5555

December 2, 1996

Pat Cummings, M.D.
Director, Emergency Medicine Fellowship Program
Any Hospital
1140 Main Street
Chicago, IL 60605

Dear Dr. Cummings:

Thank you for allowing me to interview for the fellowship position in your
department at Any Hospital. I appreciated the opportunity to meet with the faculty
and the staff; everyone was most hospitable.

I was impressed with the program and in particular the thought that has gone into
the fellowship curriculum development and research guidance. I came away very
enthusiastic about the position.

Please extend my thanks to Dr. Lee, Dr. Murphy, and Dr. Sloat for a thoughtful
discussion relative to the Emergency Medicine Fellowship Program. Being part of
such a team is, indeed, an enticing prospect.

If you have any further questions please do not hesitate to contact me. I look
forward to hearing from you.

Sincerely,

Chris Smith, M.D.

cc. Joan Lee, M.D.
    Brian Murphy, M.D.
    Susan Sloat, M.D.

■ Candidate highlights pertinent
information discussed during
interview.

■ Follow-up letter thanks addressee
for enjoyable interview.

FOLLOW-UP LETTER (AFTER JOB INTERVIEW)
(Editorial Assistant)

178 Green Street
Kingston, MA 02364

July 1, 1996

Pat Cummings
Editor
Any Publishing Company
1140 Main Street
Boston, MA 02106

Dear Mr. Cummings:

I want to thank you for interviewing me yesterday for the Editorial Assistant
position. I enjoyed meeting you and learning more about Any Publishing
Company and your work on the *Internet Primer*.

This position offers an incredible opportunity to learn the entire editorial and
production processes involved in creating a book. I think my education as well as
written and editorial skills fit ideally with the job requirements outlined. Above
all, I am very eager to learn and I know that I could make a significant
contribution to the project.

I would like to reiterate my strong interest in the position and in working with you
and Daniel Connelly. This is the ideal opportunity I seek. Please feel free to call
me at (617) 555-5555 if I can provide you with any additional information.

Again, thank you for the interview and your consideration.

Sincerely,

Chris Smith

■ Follow-up letter further illustrates candidate's suitability for available position.

■ Closing reiterates candidate's interest in position.

FOLLOW-UP LETTER (AFTER JOB INTERVIEW)
(Engineering Consultant)

178 Green Street
Geismar, LA 70734
(504) 555-5555

January 18, 1996

Ms. Pat Cummings
Vice-President
Any Corporation
1140 Main Street
Lafayette, LA 70504

Dear Ms. Cummings:

It was a sincere pleasure making your acquaintance Tuesday regarding the position of Engineering Consultant. The personal dynamics that you exude, the predicted corporate growth, and the position's promised personal fulfillment, have left me very enthused.

Thank you for the consideration. I look forward to meeting with you again in the near future.

Sincerely,

Chris Smith

■ Day of interview is generally included in follow-up letter.

■ Letter is brief and concise.

FOLLOW-UP LETTER (AFTER JOB INTERVIEW)
(Executive Assistant)

178 Green Street
West Hazelton, PA 18201
(717) 555-5555

July 18, 1996

Pat Cummings
Hiring Manager
Any Corporation
1140 Main Street
Pittsburgh, PA 15222

Dear Mr. Cummings:

It was a pleasure meeting you and Joyce Duncan last Friday and learning more
about the products and services provided by Any Corporation. The Executive
Assistant position sounds like the ideal opportunity to apply my administrative and
organizational skills to the overall operations of your firm.

The qualifications I would bring to the position include:

- Nine years' experience handling all office functions, including preparing
  and generating letters and reports, payroll, accounts payable/receivable,
  and customer service.

- Organizational proficiency with Quicksilver Metro, Inc., reflected in my
  revamping of a records storage system to reduce records access time by
  over 60 percent from the previous system.

- A scrupulous attention to detail which led me to discover and correct over
  $125,000 in duplicated and incorrectly assigned labor charges.

- Experience working with a variety of both IBM/PC and Macintosh
  applications, including Microsoft Word, WordPerfect, Excel, and Lotus
  1-2-3.

I am confident these skills could be successfully applied in the position of
Executive Assistant. Thank you for considering my candidacy. I look forward to
meeting with you.

Sincerely,

Chris Smith

Enc. resume

- Letter highlights candidate's
  significant accomplishments.

- Computer skills listed are related
  to candidate's field of interest.

FOLLOW-UP LETTER (AFTER JOB INTERVIEW)
(Export Manager)

178 Green Street
Mill Valley, CA 94941
(414) 555-5555

March 22, 1996

Pat Cummings
Vice-President, Exports
Any Corporation
1140 Main Street
Minneapolis, MN 55404

Dear Ms. Cummings:

Thank you for taking time out of your schedule to speak to me yesterday regarding the position as Export Manager. My interest in this position, and in Any Corporation, is stronger than ever, particularly because it would afford me the opportunity of becoming less desk-bound—an occupational hazard in my most recent employment.

I will contact your offices on March 29 to determine the next stage of the application process. In the interim, any questions can be addressed to my business phone, (414) 444-4444, or FAX, (414) 333-3333.

Sincerely,

Chris Smith

■ Candidate indicates time frame for follow-up contact.

■ Including a FAX number is optional in a cover letter.

FOLLOW-UP LETTER (AFTER JOB INTERVIEW)
(Finance Executive)

178 Green Street
Casper, WY 82604

November 15, 1996

Pat Cummings
Hiring Manager
Any Corporation
1140 Main Street
Charleston, WV 25301

Dear Mr. Cummings:

Thank you for a most informative and enjoyable discussion during our recent meeting. The knowledge I gained during the interview has certainly enhanced my interest in joining Any Corporation.

With my expertise in strategic planning, international finance, marketing, and general management, I feel confident that I can meet those expectations and significantly contribute to your company's objectives as a member of your management staff.

I want to thank you again for the time and courtesy you extended to me. I look forward to meeting with you again for a continued discussion of marketing opportunities available with your company.

Should you require additional information prior to a second meeting, please contact me at the above address or by phone at (307) 555-5555.

Sincerely,

Chris Smith

■ Candidate reminds addressee of how his/her qualifications will benefit potential employer.

■ Language is straightforward and understandable.

FOLLOW-UP LETTER (AFTER JOB INTERVIEW)
(Fundraiser)

178 Green Street
Baltimore, MD 21217

November 9, 1996

Pat Cummings
Vice-President
Any Organization
1140 Main Street
Silver Spring, MD 20910

Dear Ms. Cummings:

I wish to thank you and Shannon Rickle for the opportunity to discuss the fundraiser position advertised by your firm. As you requested, I am enclosing a writing sample for your review, and I would like to emphasize that the orientation and purpose of this campaign, as I understand it, is of great interest to me.

I feel that my experience, as outlined below, ideally matches your needs:

Requirements of the position:

- Extensive service and administrative experience.

- Ability to effectively manage personnel.

- Specific fundraising accomplishments.

My qualifications:

- More than eighteen years of strategic planning, administrative, and sales experience in a major service-intensive industry.

- As Director of Agencies, National Sales Trainer, Sales Manager, and Administrator, responsibilities encompassed the development and management of personnel recruitment, orientation, training, telemarketing, data collection, and motivational programs, seminars, and workshops which generated dedicated, highly productive teams.

- During the three years served as Vice-President of Wing Industries, was responsible for the organization and planning of fund-raising campaigns which successfully raised an excess of $800,000 for the reconstruction of a $1.2 million auditorium which had been destroyed by arson.

Based on this background, I feel confident that I have the principal qualifications to manage and administer programs and provide meaningful support to campaigns that require strong organizational and motivational skills. If I can provide any additional information to assist you in your decision, please do not hesitate to contact me at (301) 555-5555.

Thank you again for a most enjoyable interview. I look forward to hearing from you.

Sincerely,

Chris Smith

Enc. writing sample

■ Unique format demonstrates candidate's ability to meet advertised job requirements.

■ Summary of experience highlights candidate's achievements.

FOLLOW-UP LETTER (AFTER JOB INTERVIEW)
(Hotel Manager)

178 Green Street
Fort Wayne, IN 46803
(219) 555-5555

January 23, 1996

Pat Cummings
Executive Director
Any Hotel Chain
1140 Main Street
Chicago, IL 60605

Dear Mr. Cummings:

I would like to thank you for meeting with me on Friday regarding the Hotel
Manager availability. I enjoyed learning more about this opportunity and Any
Hotel Chain.

I would also like to reiterate my interest in the position. I feel that it would be an
exciting opportunity and believe my track record shows I would be a successful
candidate.

I am looking forward to hearing your final decision. Thank you again.

Sincerely,

Chris Smith

■ Follow-up letter should be no
longer than one page.

■ Candidate thanks addressee for
continued consideration.

FOLLOW-UP LETTER (AFTER JOB INTERVIEW)
(Human Resources Representative)

178 Green Street
Gardner, MA 01440
(508) 555-5555

November 15, 1996

Pat Cummings
Director of Human Resources
Any Corporation
1140 Main Street
Winchester, MA 01890

Dear Ms. Cummings:

I would like to thank you for extending your time to interview me yesterday for
the Representative position. I was very impressed by the large staff size you work
with, and I certainly understand how demanding such a position would prove to
be.

Ms. Cummings, after speaking with you, I am even more eager to join the ranks of
your qualified representatives. I believe my education, training, and strong
motivation would assist me in successfully completing all aspects of the position.

Thank you again for meeting with me. I hope your hiring decision will result in
our meeting again!

Yours sincerely,

Chris Smith

■ Closing reiterates candidate's
gratitude to interviewer.

■ Letter immediately restates
position candidate interviewed for.

FOLLOW-UP LETTER (AFTER JOB INTERVIEW)
(Inventory Control Analyst)

178 Green Street
Little Rock, AK 72203
(501) 555-5555

November 19, 1996

Pat Cummings
President
Any Corporation
1140 Main Street
Chicago, IL 60605

Dear Mr. Cummings:

It was a pleasure meeting you today. I appreciate you taking the time from your hectic schedule to speak with me about your opening for an Inventory Control Analyst.

The position is exciting and seems to encompass a number of diverse responsibilities. I believe that with my experience and skills, I would be able to contribute significantly to your business.

I look forward to hearing from you in the near future. If you need further information, please feel free to call me.

Sincerely,

Chris Smith

■ Follow-up letter thanks addressee for enjoyable interview.

■ Letter uses short sentences and common words.

FOLLOW-UP LETTER (AFTER JOB INTERVIEW)
(Legal Intern)

178 Green Street
Boston, MA 02215
(617) 555-5555

April 19, 1996

Pat Cummings, J.D.
Principal
Any Law Firm
1140 Main Street
Woodland Hills, CA 91367

Dear Ms. Cummings:

Thank you for taking the time to interview me Thursday. I enjoyed meeting with you to discuss the internship at Any Law Firm. I also enjoyed the tour of the office, which I found to be interesting and informative.

Thank you again for your time and consideration. If you have any questions, I would be happy to provide any additional information. I look forward to hearing from you soon.

Sincerely,

Chris Smith

■ Day of interview is generally included in follow-up letter.

■ Candidate thanks addressee for continued consideration.

FOLLOW-UP LETTER (AFTER JOB INTERVIEW)
(Materials Manager)

178 Green Street
Chicago, IL 60605
(312) 555-5555

August 5, 1996

Pat Cummings
Vice-President of Operations
Any Corporation
1140 Main Street
Chicago, IL 60605

Dear Mr. Cummings:

I greatly enjoyed our meeting yesterday. I would like to reiterate my interest in
Any Corporation's opening for a Materials Manager.

As I explained during our conversation, I feel confident that my qualifications
match the requirements of the position. I offer twelve years' experience working
as Manager of Warehousing and Distribution and as Senior Buyer for a large
metropolitan hospital. Briefly, my accomplishments include:

- Reducing expenditures of all in-house medical and nonmedical supplies
  by 20 percent through cost-effective negotiations, purchasing, and control.

- Automating inventories which increased efficiency and decreased costly
  errors, thus saving over $10,000 annually.

- Designing a functional warehouse layout which effectively reduced the
  selection and distribution process for warehoused materials and provided
  more stringent controls.

- Reducing shrinkage, damage, and obsolescence of inventory by 33
  percent.

Thank you for the time and courtesy you and your associates extended to me. I
look forward to hearing from you.

Sincerely,

Chris Smith

■ Separating major
accomplishments from body
provides emphasis.

■ Candidate's most relevant work
experience is prioritized.

FOLLOW-UP LETTER (AFTER JOB INTERVIEW)
(Personal Secretary)

178 Green Street
Nashua, NH 03060
(603) 555-5555

July 15, 1996

Pat Cummings
President
Any Corporation
1140 Main Street
Manchester, NH 03103

Dear Ms. Cummings:

I found our interview this morning to be most refreshing. Your staff was
hospitable, your facilities impressive, and our discussion informative. I am very
interested in becoming your Personal Secretary.

You mentioned during our meeting that you are looking for an assistant with
extensive knowledge of computer systems and applications. My computer literacy
includes proficiency in WordPerfect, Lotus 1-2-3, dBase 111, DOS, DisplayWrite,
desktop publishing, and experience with spreadsheets inventory management.

I believe I have much to offer this position, and I hope I will receive the
opportunity to prove my worth to you. Thank you for extending me your time, Ms.
Cummings.

Sincerely,

Chris Smith

■ First paragraph is short and hard-hitting.

■ Valuable computer skills are highlighted.

FOLLOW-UP LETTER (AFTER JOB INTERVIEW)
(Personnel Manager)

178 Green Street
Halifax, MA 02338
(617) 555-5555

March 11, 1996

Pat Cummings
President
Any Corporation
1140 Main Street
Lynn, MA 01903

Dear Mr. Cummings:

I am grateful for the time you took this morning to interview me for the Personnel Manager position. Any Corporation sounds like an exciting, fast-growing construction firm; I would very much like to apply my skills to your continued success.

During our conversation, you mentioned that you were looking for a professional who could adjust human resources policy to the needs of an expanding company. I believe I possess just the qualifications to do this. My prior experience in human resources management has provided me with extensive experience in all aspects of policy conception and implementation. My skills range from training and program development to budget management and employee relations.

If given the chance, I am confident I could restructure your department to meet, and exceed, your expectations. I hope I will be offered that chance!

Thank you again for a most enjoyable interview.

Sincerely,

Chris Smith

■ Follow-up letter demonstrates candidate's acquired company knowledge.

■ Candidate highlights pertinent information discussed during interview.

FOLLOW-UP LETTER (AFTER JOB INTERVIEW)
(Product Design Engineer)

178 Green Street
Clarkston, MI 48346
(313) 555-5555

January 31, 1996

Pat Cummings
Chief Engineer
Any Corporation
1140 Main Street
Huron, MI 48060

Dear Ms. Cummings:

I would like to thank you for extending your time to interview me yesterday. Any Corporation is an impressive, innovative manufacturing site, one which I would be very interested in joining as a Product Design Engineer.

Please be assured of my abilities to perform the responsibilities of the position as you outlined them:

Your requirements:

1.   Oversee product design and assembly.

2.   Prepare and monitor expense and capital budgets.

3.   Monitor product safety.

4.   Generate product revenue.

My relevant experiences:

1.   Oversaw design engineering for over 200 consumer and PC products, both in assembled and kit form.

2.   Managed $600,000 in expense budget, plus $2 to 9 million in preproduction engineering prototypes per year.

3.   Regularly monitored product safety and regulatory compliance.

4.   Responsible for adding $9 million of new product revenue out of $90 million total business.

I look forward to hearing your hiring decision. Thank you again for considering my qualifications.

Sincerely,

Chris Smith

■ Candidate reminds addressee of how his/her qualifications will benefit potential employer.

■ Statistics and dollar amounts quantify candidate's accomplishments.

566

FOLLOW-UP LETTER (AFTER JOB INTERVIEW)
(Production Assistant)

178 Green Street
Rapid City, SD 57709

September 9, 1996

Pat Cummings
Station Manager
Any Television Station
1140 Main Street
Sioux Falls, ND 57117

Dear Mr. Cummings:

Thank you for meeting with me yesterday. I appreciate your thorough explanation
of the Production Assistant position and, knowing exactly what the position
entails, I am confident that I can make a positive contribution to the station.

I want to reemphasize my strong interest in joining your team. I believe my degree
in Mass Communications, my internship experience, and my winning attitude
make me a suitable candidate for this position.

Please feel free to contact me at (605) 555-5555 with any questions, and I look
forward to your reply.

Sincerely,

Chris Smith

- Letter immediately expresses candidate's gratitude for the interview.

- Candidate expresses his/her continued interest in desired position.

FOLLOW-UP LETTER (AFTER JOB INTERVIEW)
(Public Records Analyst)

178 Green Street
Long Beach, CA 90840
(310) 555-5555

May 28, 1996

Pat Cummings
Senior Analyst
Any Corporation
1140 Main Street
Thousand Oaks, CA 91362

Dear Ms. Cummings:

Thank you for speaking with me Friday regarding the Public Records Analyst
position. I am convinced my experience and training would benefit a progressive
firm such as yours.

Please let me reiterate my qualifications:

- Twelve years' professional experience as a Marine Information Specialist
  and Public Records Analyst.

- Skilled in working with automated and manual record management
  systems.

- Increased corporation's efficiency by 84 percent with development of
  broad-based management programs for electronic records.

- Regarded as a specialist in records management systems analysis.

- Conducted workshops and seminars explaining records management and
  all phases of its practices.

Again, I appreciate your time and consideration. Please contact me at the above
address or phone number with any further questions. I look forward to your reply.

Sincerely,

Chris Smith

- Letter highlights candidate's
  significant accomplishments.

- Letter highlights candidate's
  management skills.

FOLLOW-UP LETTER (AFTER JOB INTERVIEW)
(Publisher's Assistant)

178 Green Street
Albuquerque, NM 87109
(505) 555-5555

January 20, 1996

Pat Cummings
Human Resources Director
Any Publication
1140 Main Street
Albuquerque, NM 87109

Dear Mr. Cummings:

I very much enjoyed talking with you today about the position of Publisher's Assistant. I was particularly interested in the position's variety of tasks, which would make the day's work challenging. My experience at Malkmus Press is an excellent foundation for the work required at *Any Publication*.

I was glad to be able to meet Mr. Poska, and have no doubt that I would be an excellent assistant to him. I recognize the importance of making his day more productive; I could help to do that.

I am looking forward to hearing from you next week. Thank you for taking the time out of your busy schedule to talk with me. I found it to be a rewarding afternoon.

Sincerely,

Chris Smith

■ Follow-up letter further illustrates candidate's suitability for available position.

■ Closing reiterates candidate's gratitude to interviewer.

FOLLOW-UP LETTER (AFTER JOB INTERVIEW)
(Real Estate Salesperson)

178 Green Street
Camden, SC 29020

June 19, 1996

Pat Cummings
General Manager
Any Corporation
1140 Main Street
Hilton Head, SC 29928

Dear Ms. Cummings:

It is not very often that an interview can be a relaxing and pleasant experience, but I found our discussion to be the exception. If anything, it has increased my interest in and enthusiasm for a position in real estate sales, as well as my confidence that I can do an outstanding job for Any Corporation.

As I explained, I have several years of successful experience in promoting and selling high-priced commercial properties to clients in the upper income bracket. I consider the sale of exclusive, residential properties to require the same capability as making effective presentations, conversing, and negotiating with decision-makers in upper economic levels. I am sure that I will, through my persistent efforts, meet mutual sales objectives.

Once again, my thanks for a fine interview and I hope that you feel as I do—that I am the right person for the position. Please contact me at the above address or at (803) 555-5555.

Sincerely,

Chris Smith

■ Candidate uses opportunity to restate his/her interest in position.

■ Follow-up letter should be no longer than one page.

FOLLOW-UP LETTER (AFTER JOB INTERVIEW)
(Recycling Manager)

178 Green Street
Warsaw, IN 46580
(219) 555-5555

December 10, 1996

Pat Cummings
Director
Any Corporation
1140 Main Street
Crane, IN 47522

Dear Mr. Cummings:

My time spent at Any Corporation yesterday was thoroughly enjoyable. Thank you for taking the time to discuss the position of Recycling Manager with me. After carefully reviewing its requirements, I have composed a brief list of my matching qualifications:

- Sixteen years' broad experience in recycling programs, recyclable materials, and spin-off industries using materials to manufacture products for industrial and consumer markets.

- Solid experience in sales, customer service, and relations.

- Ability to promote and/or market products or services provided or produced by related recycling industries.

- Skill as an accomplished communicator who can effectively work with individuals and groups in educational or sales environments.

I am very interested in joining Any Corporation in this capacity. I know I can meet and exceed your expectations.

I look forward to hearing your decision.

Yours sincerely,

Chris Smith

- Candidate uses opportunity to reiterate qualifications.

- Letter emphasizes achievements, and does not simply list job responsibilities.

FOLLOW-UP LETTER (AFTER JOB INTERVIEW)
(Restaurant Manager)

178 Green Street
Mobile, AL 35202
(205) 555-5555

August 17, 1996

Pat Cummings
Chief Executive Officer
Any Restaurant Franchise
1140 Main Street
Birmingham, AL 35201

Dear Ms. Cummings:

I enjoyed speaking with you last week. You were most helpful in describing the opportunities available at Any Company. And, as promised, an additional copy of my resume is enclosed for your consideration.

As I mentioned during our conversation, I am confident my seventeen years' experience owning and operating a string of franchise restaurants would contribute substantially to the success and growth of the company. I offer a strong professional background that encompasses the full range of financial, legal, and operational responsibilities including personnel, property, and general operations management, advertising and promotion, community and public relations, and the financial details of administrative management.

Again, thank you for the time and courtesy you and your associates extended toward me. On Thursday, August 22, I will contact your office to review my candidacy.

Sincerely,

Chris Smith

Enc. resume

■ Candidate indicates time frame for follow-up contact.

■ Enclosure line suggests candidate is a meticulous, detail-oriented professional.

FOLLOW-UP LETTER (AFTER JOB INTERVIEW)
(Retail Sales Associate)

178 Green Street
Gary, IN 46402
(219) 555-5555

February 1, 1996

Pat Cummings
Retail Sales Manager
Any Store
1140 Main Street
South Bend, IN 46626

Dear Mr. Cummings:

I want to thank you for meeting with me on January 28 regarding the position of Sales Associate. I enjoyed the opportunity to learn more about the responsibilities and opportunities available at Any Store.

I also want to reiterate my interest in the position. I feel confident that my seven years of acquired sales experience, combined with well-seasoned communication and interpersonal skills, would make me an ideal candidate for this position.

Thank you again. I look forward to hearing your final decision.

Sincerely,

Chris Smith

■ Letter is short and to the point.

■ Follow-up letter briefly reiterates relevant experience.

FOLLOW-UP LETTER (AFTER JOB INTERVIEW)
(Sales Representative)

178 Green Street
Metairie, LA 70001
(504) 555-5555

January 5, 1996

Pat Cummings
Regional Sales Supervisor
Any Airline
1140 Main Street
Baton Rouge, LA 70803

Dear Ms. Cummings:

I appreciate you taking the time to interview me for the position of Sales
Representative with your organization. I found your discussion of the operational
procedures of Any Airline, as well as your expectations of the sales staff, to be
very informative as well as interesting. I am confident that, as Sales Associate, I
would make a strong contribution to your staff by increasing profits and expanding
your market.

I would like to reiterate my qualifications which would contribute directly to your
organization:

- Over twelve years of broad-based experience in travel, hospitality, and
  retail environment industries.

- Positions in Air Travel ranging from Customer Service Representative to
  Director of Regional Sales.

- Extensive responsibility handling major corporate accounts on both
  domestic and international levels.

Again, thank you for taking the time to consider my candidacy. I look forward to
hearing your final decision.

Sincerely,

Chris Smith

■ Candidate refers to information
received during interview.

■ Letter focuses attention on
candidate's major skills and
accomplishments.

FOLLOW-UP LETTER (AFTER JOB INTERVIEW)
(Staff Accountant)

178 Green Street
Eugene, OR 97401
(503) 555-5555

July 21, 1996

Pat Cummings
Human Resource Manager
Any Corporation
1140 Main Street
Portland, OR 97204

Dear Mr. Cummings:

I would like to thank you for meeting with me Friday regarding the Staff
Accountant position. After considering your needs, as we discussed them, I am
even more convinced of my ability to make a valuable contribution to your firm.

For your consideration, I have taken the liberty to match my qualifications with
the requirements of the position offered:

Solid Accounting Background:
Experience in excess of five years with all facets of accounting, including financial
statements, budgeting, payroll, and accounts receivable.

Business Office Operation:
Broad experience supervising personnel at all levels. Maintained excellent banking
relationships.

Computer Experience:
Broad knowledge of accounting software and PC-based applications including
Lotus 1-2-3. Experience with mainframe systems and payroll service.

If I can be of additional assistance, please do not hesitate to contact me. I am very
eager to apply my skills to the successful ranks of your accounting team, and I
look forward to hearing your final decision.

Yours truly,

Chris Smith

■ Letter allows candidate follow-up
opportunity to discuss his/her
skills and accomplishments.

■ Closing emphasizes candidate's
enthusiasm for desired position.

FOLLOW-UP LETTER (AFTER JOB INTERVIEW)
(Talent Agent)

178 Green Street
Chandler, AZ 85244
(602) 555-5555

March 12, 1996

Pat Cummings
Personal Manager
Any Talent Agency
1140 Main Street
Carefree, AZ 85377

Dear Ms. Cummings:

Thank you for the courtesy you extended to me during a most pleasant meeting, and for the time you took, on my behalf, to arrange a meeting with Roger Fallings. I came away feeling that both sessions were most interesting and informative.

My discussion with Mr. Fallings was quite enlightening and, as I expressed in my recent letter to him, I was very impressed not only with the portfolio of artists/label signings he outlined but also the professional image of Any Talent Agency as a marketing firm.

Based on this information and the materials I came away with, it is quite evident to me that your firm can provide the challenging environment in which I function best, and I, in turn, would like to provide the experience and skills necessary to achieve our mutual goals.

Once again, my thanks for your assistance in setting up a most productive meeting. I am certainly interested in exploring the position of Talent Agent further.

With best regards,

Chris Smith

■ Follow-up letter demonstrates candidate's acquired company knowledge.

■ Powerful adjectives, when used sparingly, ensure maximum impact.

FOLLOW-UP LETTER (AFTER JOB INTERVIEW)
(Teacher)

178 Green Street
Loganville, GA 30249
(404) 555-5555

April 23, 1996

Pat Cummings
Principal
Any Elementary School
1140 Main Street
Norcross, GA 30071

Dear Mr. Cummings:

I thoroughly enjoyed my afternoon at Any Elementary School and our interview for the sixth grade teaching position. Thank you for taking time out of your day to speak with me.

It was also a pleasure meeting Richard Morrison and observing his classroom for an hour. His dedication to the children he teaches is evident, and I would be honored to instruct room 160 during his leave of absence.

Thank you again for inviting me to your school. I hope that your hiring decision will result in my returning to Any Elementary in the fall!

Sincerely,

Chris Smith

■ Candidate immediately reviews circumstances of most recent contact.

■ Letter immediately expresses candidate's gratitude for the interview.

FOLLOW-UP LETTER (AFTER JOB INTERVIEW)
(Writer/Researcher)

178 Green Street
Middletown, CT 06457
(203) 555-5555

January 14, 1996

Pat Cummings
Staff Writer
Any Publications
1140 Main Street
Waterbury, CT 06723

Dear Ms. Cummings:

Thank you for the opportunity to meet with you again today. It was a pleasure to learn more about the position and your goals for continuing the success of the *Inside Connecticut* publications.

I am very excited about the potential the Writer/Researcher position has to offer. I am confident that my skills, abilities, and interest would contribute to enhance the productivity of this publication.

I hope that you find me a qualified candidate for this position, and I would enjoy the opportunity to contribute to your organization. Thank you for your consideration, and I look forward to hearing your decision.

Sincerely,

Chris Smith

■ Letter immediately restates position candidate interviewed for.

■ Candidate uses opportunity to reiterate qualifications.

20
Information Request

Requests for information are formal inquires to organizations or potential employers to assist you in your job-hunting research. Common inquiries include requests for membership listings, annual reports, company brochures, and alumni data. When writing an information request, job seekers should be brief and to the point.

In your cover letter, simply state who you are and ask politely for the information you are requesting. For example, "I am an experienced Paralegal searching for a list of firms specializing in international law," is sufficient. It is always best to include a self-addressed stamped envelope to help expedite the process.

INFORMATION REQUEST
(Alumni Network)

178 Green Street
Jackson Center, OH 45334
(513) 555-5555

August 10, 1996

Pat Cummings
Director of Career Planning
Any University
1140 Main Street
Richmond, VA 23298

Dear Mr. Cummings:

I am a 1989 graduate of Any University, who has been employed in the social services industry for the last six years. Budgetary cuts within the local youth services agency have prompted me to begin searching for a new association in case management.

Does the University provide a network of alumni in my field? Perhaps there is a local chapter of graduates I can contact. Gaining several new contacts in the Ohio area especially would be a valuable asset to my job-hunting research.

Please forward a directory of names, or information on how to contact other professionals in social services. Thank you for your assistance.

Sincerely,

Chris Smith

■ Candidate briefly introduces himself/herself to addressee.

■ Citing reason for job search is optional.

INFORMATION REQUEST
(Annual Report)

178 Green Street
San Jose, CA 95134
(408) 555-5555

January 27, 1996

Pat Cummings
Director, Public Relations
Any Corporation
1140 Main Street
San Francisco, CA 94120

Dear Ms. Cummings:

I am currently investigating career opportunities in the San Francisco area. In the course of my research, I found Any Corporation to be an industry leader in accounting and financial planning.

Could you send me information concerning your services? I would be especially interested in an annual report and company roster. I have enclosed a self-addressed stamped envelope for your convenience.

I appreciate your attention to my request.

Sincerely,

Chris Smith

■ Candidate specifies geographic preference for job-search assistance.

■ Candidate courteously includes a self-addressed stamped envelope.

INFORMATION REQUEST
(Career Planning Services)

178 Green Street
Arlington Heights, IL 60004
(708) 555-5555

November 7, 1996

Pat Cummings
Director
Any Woman's Bureau
1140 Main Street
Chicago, IL 60603

Dear Mr. Cummings:

I am an accomplished loan officer who is finding it very difficult to obtain gainful employment in my field. My resources in the Chicago area have been exhausted and relocation is not an option. In this respect, I would like to ask for your help.

I would be very eager to participate in any career planning or placement services you might offer. Please send any relevant information to the above address.

Many thanks for your assistance. I look forward to hearing from you.

Sincerely,

Chris Smith

■ Candidate includes all information necessary for response.

■ Candidate thanks addressee in advance for his/her assistance.

INFORMATION REQUEST
(Company Catalog)

178 Green Street
Washington, DC 20071
(202) 555-5555

March 25, 1996

Pat Cummings
Publisher's Assistant
Any Publisher
1140 Main Street
New York, NY 10108

Dear Ms. Cummings:

I am writing to inquire about Any Publisher. Please send me information regarding your company size and target markets, as well a catalog of your recent publications.

I have enclosed a self-addressed stamped envelope for your convenience. Thank you for your attention.

Sincerely,

Chris Smith

■ Letter briefly inquires about desired information.

■ Candidate immediately states letter's purpose.

INFORMATION REQUEST
(Course Registration)

178 Green Street
Olympia, WA 98507
(206) 555-5555

May 30, 1996

Pat Cummings
Director, Continuing Education
Any Community College
1140 Main Street
Seattle, WA 98119

Dear Mr. Cummings:

A friend of mine recently completed a course at your college focusing on career planning and job-hunting techniques. I have been unemployed for several months and feel that I could benefit greatly from such instruction.

Is such a course being offered during the upcoming semester? Please send me information on enrollment costs, course dates and times, and whatever application materials need to be completed.

Thank you for your kind assistance.

Sincerely,

Chris Smith

■ Candidate names basis for referral.

■ Information request is direct and concise.

INFORMATION REQUEST
(Grants Listing)

178 Green Street
Worcester, MA 01610
(508) 555-5555

April 13, 1996

Pat Cummings
Director
Any Research Agency
1140 Main Street
New York, NY 10017

Dear Ms. Cummings:

I would like to request information on current research projects being conducted in the area of molecular biology.

I will complete a Doctor of Physiological Chemistry degree from Worcester Polytechnic Institute in May and am searching for a new research association. My doctoral thesis focused on DNA sequence analysis and S1 mapping.

Do you possess a listing of all grants conferred in related areas within the last two years? Any information you could provide would greatly assist me in my search.

Thank you.

Sincerely,

Chris Smith

■ Candidate briefly introduces himself/herself to addressee.

■ Candidate thanks addressee in advance for his/her assistance.

INFORMATION REQUEST
(Industry Directory)

178 Green Street
Heston, KS 67062
(316) 555-5555

September 25, 1996

Pat Cummings
President
Chamber of Commerce
1140 Main Street
Topeka, KS 66612

Dear Mr. Cummings:

I am currently conducting a job search in the greater Kansas area and would appreciate any assistance you could provide me.

My interest is in the field of computer programming, and I am wondering if you publish a Directory of Members, especially listing the major employers in the technology industry.

If so, could you possibly send me this information? I have attached an self-addressed stamped envelope for your use.

Sincerely,

Chris Smith

■ Candidate specifies geographic preference for job-search assistance.

■ Candidate includes all information necessary for response.

INFORMATION REQUEST
(Industry Newsletter)

178 Green Street
St. Louis, MO 63146
(314) 555-5555

October 11, 1996

Pat Cummings
Executive Officer
Any Association of Legal Services
1140 Main Street
Dallas, TX 75201

Dear Ms. Cummings:

I am in the process of conducting a job search in the Dallas area, to which I will be relocating next month.

Does your association publish a newsletter listing employment opportunities for legal professionals? If so, I would appreciate a copy and have enclosed a self-addressed stamped envelope for your convenience. I would also be interested in any type of placement service you provide to members, and the application process for membership.

Thank you for your assistance. I look forward to learning more about the services your association offers.

Sincerely,

Chris Smith

■ Citing reason for job search is optional.

■ Candidate courteously includes a self-addressed stamped envelope.

INFORMATION REQUEST
(Membership Listing)

178 Green Street
Tempe, AZ 85285
(602) 555-5555

July 18, 1996

Pat Cummings
Director
Any Association of Zoologists
1140 Main Street
Denver, CO 80205

Dear Mr. Cummings:

I am writing to inquire if your association provides a mailing list of member organizations.

I am currently conducting a job search within the Midwest, and would appreciate any assistance you could provide regarding organization names, personnel titles, addresses, and other relevant information.

Please forward any appropriate materials to the above address.

I look forward to your return response.

Sincerely,

Chris Smith

■ Information request is direct and concise.

■ Candidate immediately states letter's purpose.

INFORMATION REQUEST
(Subscription Information)

178 Green Street
Everett, MA 02149
(617) 555-5555

February 5, 1996

Pat Cummings
Subscription Manager
Careers in Psychology
1140 Main Street
Boston, MA 02118

Dear Ms. Cummings:

I heard about your publication through the National Association of Psychologists. I understand that *Careers in Psychology* publishes an "Advertised Openings" section at the close of each edition. Could you possibly send me information on subscription prices and an order form?

I have enclosed a self-addressed stamped envelope for your convenience. Thank you.

Sincerely,

Chris Smith

Enc.

- Candidate names basis for referral.

- Letter briefly inquires about desired information.

21
Address/Phone Number Change

In today's tough market, the job-search process is often lengthy. If your personal situation has changed since your last correspondence (i.e., a geographical move, and/or phone number change), you must *always* inform a potential employer. Keep your correspondence brief. This is a courtesy letter, not a full-page reiteration of your qualifications.

To begin, remind the employer of the position you applied for, and when. State the change in your circumstances and thank the reader for his or her continued consideration. Be sure to send along another, updated copy of your resume for the employer's convenience. Remember that this letter is not optional. An employer will not waste time trying to track you down!

ADDRESS/PHONE NUMBER CHANGE
(Laboratory Assistant)

178 Green Street
Shawnee Hills, OH 43965
(216) 555-5555

May 31, 1996

Pat Cummings
Research Scientist
Any Medical Association
1140 Main Street
Chicago, IL 60605

Dear Mr. Cummings:

I am writing to inform you that I have moved to the above address and telephone listing. Enclosed is an updated copy of my resume for your files. I am looking forward to hearing more about any Laboratory Assistant positions you may have available.

Thank you for your time.

Sincerely,

Chris Smith

Enc. resume

■ Address-change letter is accompanied by updated resume.

■ Letter immediately states candidate's purpose.

ADDRESS/PHONE NUMBER CHANGE
(Musician)

178 Green Street
Winston-Salem, NC 27113

July 21, 1996

Pat Cummings
Agent
Any Production Studio
1140 Main Street
Durham, NC 27702

Dear Ms. Cummings:

I recently received your kind letter in response to my audition for the lead guitarist position. Since you mentioned that you would be keeping my resume and demo tape on file, I wanted to let you know that my address will change on August 1 to the address listed above. My phone number is (919) 555-5555.

Until August 1, you can reach me at (708) 444-4444 in Aurora, IL.

I am still very interested in the position, and look forward to hearing from you soon.

Sincerely,

Chris Smith

■ Candidate uses opportunity to restate his/her interest in position.

■ Candidate notifies addressee of specific date when changes will go into effect.

ADDRESS/PHONE NUMBER CHANGE
(Pet Groomer)

178 Green Street
Baltimore, MD 21210
(410) 555-5555

September 21, 1996

Pat Cummings
Owner
Any Pet Salon
1140 Main Street
College Park, MD 20742

Dear Mr. Cummings:

Thank you for speaking with me last week regarding the Pet Groomer position. I remain very interested in this opportunity and, for this reason, wanted to alert you to my address change. Beginning October 1, I can be reached at the address and telephone number above.

I look forward to hearing from you.

Sincerely,

Chris Smith

■ Candidate is careful to specify date of address change.

■ Candidate expresses gratitude for addressee's consideration.

ADDRESS/PHONE NUMBER CHANGE
(Staff Nutritionist)

178 Green Street
Tampa, FL 33681
(813) 555-5555

April 6, 1996

Pat Cummings
Human Resources Manager
Any Hospital
1140 Main Street
Ocala, FL 32674

Dear Ms. Cummings:

Last month, I sent my resume in response to your advertisement in the Monday, March 11, edition of the *Tampa Tribune* for Staff Nutritionist. I am still very interested in this or similar openings at Any Hospital.

For this reason, I would like to make you aware of an address change from my previous inquiry. I have since moved from Jacksonville to the address listed above. I have enclosed an updated resume for your convenience.

Thank you. I look forward to hearing from you in the future.

Sincerely,

Chris Smith

Enc. resume

- Address-change letter should be brief and direct.
- Letter cites advertisement's specific publication and date.

ADDRESS/PHONE NUMBER CHANGE
(Wholesale Buyer)

178 Green Street
Greenbelt, MD 20770

February 23, 1996

Pat Cummings
Senior Buyer
Any Corporation
1140 Main Street
Landover, MD 20785

Dear Mr. Cummings:

I want to thank you for a pleasant and informative interview last week in reference to the Wholesale Buyer position. I enjoyed meeting with you and Richard Mayes and learning more about your department's successful track record of commercial negotiations.

I would also like to alert you to a change in my phone number. The new listing is (301) 555-5555. My address remains the same.

Please be assured of my continued interest. I look forward to hearing your decision.

Sincerely,

Chris Smith

■ In addition to including address change, candidate reiterates interest in position.

■ Candidate refers to all employees involved in interview process.

22
Thank You Letter (For Good Reference)

During the course of your job search it may be necessary to call upon personal and professional references to support your credentials. These people are doing you a favor and deserve your written thanks. Thank you letters also allow you to keep your contacts current. When Rick R. requested a reference from a former employer, he sent a timely letter of thanks. Six months later when Rick needed another reference, that same employer was more than happy to help him out.

When writing your letter, you might want to remind the person why you needed the reference and the outcome of his or her efforts. Keep your comments brief and your tone polite.

THANK YOU LETTER (FOR GOOD REFERENCE)
(Biomedical Researcher)

178 Green Street
Hanover, NH 03755
(603) 555-5555

March 4, 1996

Pat Cummings
Department Head, Biology
Any University
1140 Main Street
Florham Park, NJ 07932

Dear Ms. Cummings:

I understand that you recently provided Helmut Industries with a reference
attesting to my research abilities. During my interview this morning, Fredrick
Jonns praised my senior thesis work as you described it. Thank you so much for
your enthusiasm regarding my work!

I believe that my interview at Helmut went well, and I will keep you posted when
a decision is reached. I hope all is going well at the lab!

Sincerely,

Chris Smith

■ Candidate begins letter by thanking addressee for good reference.

■ Personalized tone reinforces candidate's familiarity with addressee.

THANK YOU LETTER (FOR GOOD REFERENCE)
(Bookkeeper)

178 Green Street
Washington, DC 20016
(202) 555-5555

November 11, 1996

Pat Cummings
Bookkeeper
Any Corporation
1140 Main Street
Washington, DC 20001

Dear Mr. Cummings:

Thank you so much for your great reference regarding my application for the Bookkeeping position at The Baldwin Company.

I have since been offered, and have accepted, the position. I appreciate your efforts on my behalf.

Sincerely,

Chris Smith

■ Candidate informs addressee of application's outcome.

■ Letter uses short sentences and common words.

THANK YOU LETTER (FOR GOOD REFERENCE)
(Broker)

178 Green Street
Sidney, MT 59270
(406) 555-5555

April 26, 1996

Pat Cummings
Investment Broker
Any Corporation
1140 Main Street
Missoula, MT 59807

Dear Ms. Cummings:

I want to thank you for the excellent reference you provided Denmark Associates. With your generous help, I was offered a position as a Broker.

I am excited about this opportunity and I appreciate your assistance. I look forward to returning the favor.

Sincerely,

Chris Smith

■ In closing, candidate offers to reciprocate addressee's generosity.

■ Including telephone number is necessary in a cover letter.

THANK YOU LETTER (FOR GOOD REFERENCE)
(Fashion Designer)

178 Green Street
Sandy, UT 84070
(801) 555-5555

February 23, 1996

Pat Cummings
Designer
The Brittney Collection
1140 Main Street
Ogden, UT 84401

Dear Mr. Cummings:

I would like to thank you for speaking to the design staff at Edge Fashions on my behalf. I appreciate your support of my work in fashion design.

I hope that the new spring collection is going well. I am very interested in seeing its premiere in late February.

Thank you again. I promise to keep in contact as my job search continues.

Sincerely,

Chris Smith

■ In closing, candidate promises to keep addressee informed of job search progress.

■ Candidate thanks addressee for his/her assistance in job search.

THANK YOU LETTER (FOR GOOD REFERENCE)
(Government Intern)

178 Green Street
Albany, GA 31701
(912) 555-5555

November 29, 1996

Pat Cummings
Assistant to the President
Any University
1140 Main Street
Doraville, GA 30340

Dear Ms. Cummings:

I am writing to express my thanks for your kind reference regarding my summer
internship application. The selection committee at the State House informs me that
you were contacted, and spoke highly of my work in the President's office.

I will contact you in early January when my application is processed and I hear a
decision. Once again, I am very grateful for your help.

Best wishes,

Chris Smith

■ Candidate begins letter by
thanking addressee for good
reference.

■ Candidate establishes when
follow-up contact will take place.

THANK YOU LETTER (FOR GOOD REFERENCE)
(Nurse)

178 Green Street
Mount Vernon, NY 10550
(914) 555-5555

April 14, 1996

Pat Cummings
Nursing Administrator
Any Hospital
1140 Main Street
New York, NY 10001

Dear Mr. Cummings:

Kathy Mohagan at West Side Hospital mentioned that she contacted you as a reference and you spoke very highly of my work at Any Hospital.

Thanks so much for your assistance, Pat. Please let me know if I can do anything in return.

With best regards,

Chris Smith

■ Good reference letter sometimes
assumes an informal tone.

■ Candidate includes only relevant
information.

THANK YOU LETTER (FOR GOOD REFERENCE)
(Retail Store Manager)

178 Green Street
Golden, CO 80401
(303) 555-5555

July 21, 1996

Pat Cummings
Manager
Any Clothing Store
1140 Main Street
Ft. Lauderdale, Fl 33310

Dear Ms. Cummings:

I am happy to say that my job search has come to an end! Delightful Duds, the retail clothing chain in Colorado, has offered me a position as Assistant Branch Manager. I am arranging for a move to Golden within the next two weeks.

Ms. Cummings, thank you so much for offering to act as a reference for my job search, and for all the assistance that you provided. Your support is greatly appreciated!

Please keep in touch and let me know how things are going at the store. I have listed my new address and phone number above.

I hope to hear from you soon.

Sincerely,

Chris Smith

■ Candidate informs addressee of application's outcome.

■ Closing encourages reader to respond to letter.

THANK YOU LETTER (FOR GOOD REFERENCE)
(Surgeon)

178 Green Street
Santa Clara, CA 95054
(408) 555-5555

June 11, 1996

Pat Cummings, M.D.
General Surgeon
Any Hospital
1140 Main Street
Palo Alto, CA 94304

Dear Dr. Cummings:

Thank you for speaking to Dr. Griffin and supporting my credentials. As you
know, getting established in the medical community is not easy and I appreciate
the confidence you have in my abilities.

I have since been called back to interview with the Board of Directors. I will keep
you updated on my progress.

Thank you again for all your help.

Sincerely,

Chris Smith

■ In closing, candidate promises to
keep addressee informed of job
search progress.

■ Closing is brief and to the point.

THANK YOU LETTER (FOR GOOD REFERENCE)
(Teacher)

178 Green Street
Triangle Park, NC 27709
(919) 555-5555

May 29, 1996

Pat Cummings
Principal
Any High School
1140 Main Street
Raleigh, NC 27695

Dear Mr. Cummings:

Thank you for agreeing to act as a reference for my teaching application at Martin
Luther King High School. I greatly appreciated your assistance, Pat.

I have been offered the position, and have gladly accepted. I will be teaching two
sections of remedial english and one special topics course in journalism. They
have also asked me to act as faculty moderator for the school newspaper. My year
should be very busy, yet also very enjoyable.

Enjoy the remainder of your summer vacation. I hope to see you at association
meetings in the Fall.

Sincerely,

Chris Smith

■ Candidate thanks addressee for
his/her assistance in job search.

■ Good reference letter sometimes
assumes an informal tone.

THANK YOU LETTER (FOR GOOD REFERENCE)
(Technical Writer)

178 Green Street
Marshaltown, IA 50158
(515) 555-5555

January 3, 1996

Pat Cummings
Editor/Technical Writer
Any Corporation
1140 Main Street
Des Moines, IA 50303

Dear Ms. Cummings:

While interviewing at McErney Associates yesterday, I was informed that you provided an excellent reference for me.

Thank you for your kind words. My meeting for the Technical Writer position with McErney resulted in an invitation for a second interview!

I appreciate your assistance. Would you let me know when I could return the favor?

With best regards,

Chris Smith

■ In closing, candidate offers to reciprocate addressee's generosity.

■ Candidate includes only relevant information.

23
Thank You Letter (For Letter of Recommendation)

Potential employers sometimes require written letters of recommendation to complete the application process. These letters may be written by previous employers or, for those with little professional experience, by college professors. Since you requested this person's time, it is only courteous to express your written thanks. By doing so, he or she will be more likely to remember you, should you require further assistance in the future.

Kim W., a recent college graduate, submitted a letter of recommendation from an English professor when applying for a proofreading position. Despite her lack of experience, Kim's letter attested to her superior writing and editing skills and greatly improved her candidacy.

THANK YOU LETTER (FOR LETTER OF RECOMMENDATION)
(Accountant)

178 Green Street
Hobbs, NM 88240
(505) 555-5555

May 31, 1996

Pat Cummings
Account Manager
Any Corporation
1140 Main Street
Santa Fe, NM 87504

Dear Mr. Cummings:

I appreciate the kind letter of recommendation you wrote to assist me in my job search. Yesterday, I received an offer to begin work as a Staff Accountant with Enstel and Yang. Your praise of my internship work at Any Corporation definitely contributed to my success.

If there is anything I can do in return, please contact me. Thank you again.

Sincerely,

Chris Smith

- Candidate begins letter by thanking addressee for recommendation.

- Candidate informs addressee of application's outcome.

THANK YOU LETTER (FOR LETTER OF RECOMMENDATION)
(Art History Student)

178 Green Street
Washington, DC 20007
(202) 555-5555

September 6, 1996

Pat Cummings
Professor of Art History
Any College
1140 Main Street
Worcester, MA 01610

Dear Dr. Cummings:

Knowing how busy you are with different projects, I really appreciate the time you took to write a recommendation for my graduate school applications. I have since received three letters of acceptance and I am confident that your letter contributed to my success.

Again, thank you for your continued support. I will be sure to keep in touch as I pursue my degree.

Sincerely,

Chris Smith

■ Recommendation letters are not restricted to job-search process.

■ Letter is easy and quick to read, and only relevant details are included.

THANK YOU LETTER (FOR LETTER OF RECOMMENDATION)
(Chemical Engineer)

178 Green Street
Medford, WI 54451
(715) 555-5555

October 29, 1996

Pat Cummings
Distinguished Professor of Chemistry
Any University
1140 Main Street
West Bend, MI 53095

Dear Dr. Cummings:

Thank you for your excellent recommendation for my job-search applications. I feel confident that your acknowledgment of my abilities will contribute to the strength of my candidacy.

I will keep you informed as the selection process comes to a close next week.

Sincerely,

Chris Smith

■ Candidate begins letter by thanking addressee for recommendation.

■ Candidate indicates time frame for follow-up contact.

THANK YOU LETTER (FOR LETTER OF RECOMMENDATION)
(Human Resources Representative)

178 Green Street
Hesston, KS 67062
(316) 555-5555

April 3, 1996

Pat Cummings
Assistant Director, Career Services
Any University
1140 Main Street
Topeka, KS 66612

Dear Mr. Cummings:

I received your letter of recommendation in this morning's mail. Thank you for your kind words, and the effort you extended to mail it to me before my interview on April 12.

I am sure that your letter will greatly assist me in presenting myself as a qualified candidate for the Human Resources Representative position with Any Corporation. I will be sure to inform you of the outcome of my interview.

Thank you again.

Sincerely,

Chris Smith

- Candidate confirms receipt of recommendation letter.

- Letter avoids abbreviations and slang.

THANK YOU LETTER (FOR LETTER OF RECOMMENDATION)
(Restaurant Manager)

178 Green Street
Augusta, ME 04336
(207) 555-5555

July 1, 1996

Pat Cummings
Manager
Any Restaurant
1140 Main Street
Kennebunk, ME 04043

Dear Ms. Cummings:

Thank you so much for taking the time to write me a letter of recommendation for
my job search. As you know, I had an interview for the Management Training
Program with Fat Dickie's restaurant chain last week.

I have since been asked back for a second interview. I will keep you posted as to
the outcome of my application.

Thank you again, Ms. Cummings. I hope that everything is going well at the
restaurant.

Sincerely,

Chris Smith

■ Candidate thanks addressee for
his/her assistance in job search.

■ Personalized tone reinforces
candidate's familiarity with
addressee.

24
Thank You Letter (For Referral)

As we mentioned in Chapter 8, many jobs are found with the assistance of a networking contact or referral. Throughout your job search keep track of all your referrals, and be sure to send each one a personalized thank you note for his or her assistance. In your letter, briefly express sincere gratitude for the referral's help on your behalf. If his or her efforts directly led to a positive outcome for you, let the person know. It may be advantageous to offer your return assistance. In any event, sending a thoughtful thank you letter is an invaluable career move. If you recognize someone's assistance on your behalf, he or she may be more likely to help you again in the future.

THANK YOU LETTER (FOR REFERRAL)
(Acquisitions Editor)

178 Green Street
Twodot, MT 59085
(406) 555-5555

October 14, 1996

Pat Cummings
Managing Editor
Any Press
1140 Main Street
Chicago, IL 60605

Dear Ms. Cummings:

I am happy to inform you that I have just accepted an offer for employment as an Acquisitions Editor at Dandelion Publishing Group. I should begin work there the first week of November.

I would like to thank you for all of your help during my job search, specifically for putting me in touch with Ninona Punder at Dandelion's billings office.

If there is ever anything that I can do for you, please do not hesitate to contact me. Yours was a favor I shall not soon forget.

Again, many thanks and best wishes.

Sincerely,

Chris Smith

■ Candidate indicates willingness to return favor.

■ Letter demonstrates referral's positive results.

THANK YOU LETTER (FOR REFERRAL)
(Bank Manager)

178 Green Street
Tacoma, WA 98477
(206) 555-5555

June 4, 1996

Pat Cummings
Assistant Vice-President
Any Savings Bank
1140 Main Street
Spokane, WA 99201

Dear Mr. Cummings:

I received your letter dated June 2, regarding my initial inquiry for job placement assistance. Thank you so much for providing several names for contact purposes.

I have enclosed another copy of my resume. Please feel free to pass it on to any colleagues searching for a new Branch Manager.

Once again, your assistance is greatly appreciated!

Sincerely,

Chris Smith

Enc. resume

■ Candidate requests that attached resume be forwarded.

■ Candidate expresses appreciation to addressee for referral.

THANK YOU LETTER (FOR REFERRAL)
(Computer Application Programmer)

178 Green Street
Lamar, CO 81052
(719) 555-5555

March 5, 1996

Pat Cummings
Vice-President of Human Resources
Any Corporation
1140 Main Street
Englewood, CO 80111

Dear Ms. Cummings:

Thank you for taking several moments to assist me with my job search last week.
Although you indicated there were no vacancies at Any Corporation, the referrals
you provided have been extremely useful.

In fact, I have been able to schedule two informational interviews with computer
applications programmers at EMP and Stide and Huston. I hope to learn more
about specific projects and innovations to keep me updated on industry trends.

Thank you again for your time. I am still very interested in pursuing opportunities
at Any Corporation. I have enclosed another resume for your review should you
anticipate a need for someone with my qualifications.

With best regards,

Chris Smith

Enc. resume

■ Closing informs addressee that resume is enclosed.

■ Candidate informs addressee of referral's outcome.

THANK YOU LETTER (FOR REFERRAL)
(Fitness Instructor)

178 Green Street
Van Nuys, CA 91411
(818) 555-5555

February 16, 1996

Pat Cummings
General Manager
Any Fitness Center
1140 Main Street
Van Nuys, CA 91411

Dear Mr. Cummings:

I am writing to thank you for your wonderful referral to Dani Johnson with Body Beautiful. When I called Ms. Johnson two weeks ago while on a visit to California, she invited me to interview for a Fitness Instructor position. Yesterday, she called to offer me the job!

Thank you so much for your assistance. If there is ever anything I can do in return, please do not hesitate to contact me. I have listed my new address and phone number above, effective March 1.

With best regards,

Chris Smith

- Candidate is careful to specify date of address change.
- Letter expresses usefulness of referral.

THANK YOU LETTER (FOR REFERRAL)
(Medical Assistant)

178 Green Street
Richardson, TX 75083
(214) 555-5555

September 19, 1996

Pat Cummings, M.D.
Optometrist
Any Hospital
1140 Main Street
Irving, TX 75038

Dear Dr. Cummings:

Although I regret that you did not have a need for an Assistant, I would like to thank you for referring me to Dr. Wilson in Richardson. I met with him on Tuesday, and received further contact names, as well as learned a great deal about his work.

Should you become aware of any opportunities for a Medical Assistant, please let me know. I am still very interested in gaining hands-on experience before I begin graduate study in the field.

I hope to speak with you in the future.

Sincerely,

Chris Smith

- Candidate indicates specific referral who assisted him/her in job search.

- Candidate asks for addressee's further job-search assistance.

THANK YOU LETTER (FOR REFERRAL)
(Nurse)

178 Green Street
Ketchikan, AK 99901
(907) 555-5555

August 26, 1996

Pat Cummings
Nursing Administrator
Any Hospital
1140 Main Street
Anchorage, AK 99515

Dear Mr. Cummings:

Thank you for the wonderful referrals you provided for my job search. I called
Michelle Peters as you suggested yesterday and was invited to interview for a
nursing position!

Several of the other contacts you gave me very graciously offered their personal
insight and/or further referrals.

I will keep you informed as my search for a position progresses. Thank you again.

Sincerely,

Chris Smith, R.N.

■ Candidate indicates specific
referral who assisted him/her in
job search.

■ After name, candidate includes
professional title.

THANK YOU LETTER (FOR REFERRAL)
(Photographer)

178 Green Street
Monroe, LA 71209
(318) 555-5555

November 1, 1996

Pat Cummings
Director
Any Corporation
1140 Main Street
New Orleans, LA 70130

Dear Ms. Cummings:

Thank you for referring me to the resources available at the New Orleans
Photography Center and especially to its Director, Peter O'Sullivan. The job
listings he provided have been invaluable for my career search. I have since made
numerous contacts as well as scheduled two interviews.

Thank you again and I would appreciate any assistance you might provide in the
future.

Sincerely,

Chris Smith

- In closing, candidate offers to reciprocate addressee's generosity.
- Candidate asks for addressee's further job-search assistance.

THANK YOU LETTER (FOR REFERRAL)
(Publicist)

178 Green Street
Anniston, AL 36202
(205) 555-5555

March 4, 1996

Pat Cummings
Director of Public Relations
Any Heart Association
1140 Main Street
Montogomery, AL 36102

Dear Mr. Cummings:

I enjoyed meeting with you Friday at your Montgomery headquarters. Your work for the Heart Association seems very rewarding.

I would also like to thank you for referring me to Beth Holmes with the Committee on Social Awareness. My discussions with both Ms. Holmes and yourself have definitely confirmed my interest in public relations work for a non-profit organization.

Good luck with your new television campaign.

Sincerely,

Chris Smith

■ Candidate immediately thanks addressee for pleasurable meeting.

■ Candidate refers to information received during interview.

THANK YOU LETTER (FOR REFERRAL)
(Software Technician)

178 Green Street
El Segundo, CA 90245
(310) 555-5555

December 22, 1996

Pat Cummings
Software Engineer
Any Corporation
1140 Main Street
Chicago, IL 60605

Dear Ms. Cummings:

I am pleased to inform you that my job search has come to a successful conclusion. Yesterday, I was offered a position with L. GWA PO Inc., a Japanese software conglomerate that has recently opened a branch office in Los Angeles. I am delighted to be able to participate once again in the fast-paced world of computer technology.

I would like to extend my warmest thanks to you for your encouragement and the excellent referrals you provided for my job search. The next time you visit L.A., please be sure to let me know.

Happy holidays and best wishes for the New Year!

Sincerely,

Chris Smith

■ Letter demonstrates referral's positive results.

■ Candidate indicates willingness to return favor.

THANK YOU LETTER (FOR REFERRAL)
(Teacher)

178 Green Street
Wilmington, DE 19803
(302) 555-5555

January 4, 1996

Pat Cummings
Principal
Any School
1140 Main Street
New Castle, DE 19720

Dear Mr. Cummings:

Thank you for putting me in touch with Steven Simons and the Wilmington School District. A number of opportunities were available and I was fortunate enough to be offered a forth grade teaching position.

Again, I appreciate your assistance.

Sincerely,

Chris Smith

■ Candidate informs addressee of referral's outcome.

■ Candidate expresses appreciation to addressee for referral.

25
Thank You Letter (After Informational Interview)

Thank you letters are not restricted to potential employers. Everyone who assists you in any way during the course of your job search deserves written thanks for his or her efforts. Even in the case of an informational interview, a letter is required. Although you are not asking for a job, you have taken a person's time and should thank the person accordingly.

Consider Susan B., who wrote a timely thank you letter to an industry executive with whom she met in an informational interview. The executive, impressed by her considerate attention to detail, heard about an appropriate employment opportunity several weeks later and recommended Susan for the job!

THANK YOU LETTER (AFTER INFORMATIONAL INTERVIEW)
(Art Designer)

178 Green Street
Radnor, PA 19087
(215) 555-5555

March 25, 1996

Pat Cummings
Art Director
Any Advertising Agency
1140 Main Street
York, PA 17402

Dear Ms. Cummings:

It was a pleasure meeting with you Tuesday and learning about your work at Any Agency. I especially enjoyed watching you design the promotional sample for Smithe and Resin's new copier.

After spending the day with an art team at an actual agency, I am sure that I want to pursue a career in art design. I will be sure to contact you upon graduation to follow up on your offer of placement assistance.

Good luck in your future endeavors at Any Agency, and thank you again for your kindness.

Sincerely,

Chris Smith

■ Letter outlines candidate's course of action resulting from informational interview.

■ Candidate establishes when follow-up contact will take place.

THANK YOU LETTER (AFTER INFORMATIONAL INTERVIEW)
(Benefits Coordinator)

178 Green Street
Doraville, GA 30340
(404) 555-5555

March 21, 1996

Pat Cummings
Director
Any Corporation
1140 Main Street
Bainbridge, GA 31717

Dear Mr. Cummings:

The information you offered me yesterday concerning opportunities for Benefits
Coordinators was most helpful. Thank you for the time you took to meet with me.

Prior to our discussion, I had no idea of the diverse opportunities someone with
my experience could explore. I have already begun to research some of the
companies you suggested and I am hopeful that I will find a position in the near
future.

Again, thank you. Your assistance was most helpful.

Sincerely,

Chris Smith

■ Candidate expresses gratitude for
new knowledge obtained during
informational interview.

■ Letter clarifies candidate's career
goals.

THANK YOU LETTER (AFTER INFORMATIONAL INTERVIEW)
(Child Psychologist)

178 Green Street
Toast, NC 27049
(919) 555-5555

July 26, 1996

Pat Cummings
Associate Professor of Psychology
Any University
1140 Main Street
Chicago, IL 60605

Dear Ms. Cummings:

It was a pleasure seeing you again today. I appreciate the time you found in your busy schedule to meet with me.

It was interesting to learn about the use of interactive toys and models in child psychology. I have already been to the library to borrow the book by Leonard Finn that you recommended so highly. I am looking forward to reading about his ideas on child's play before the latency period.

I will be contacting Mr. Hayden within the next few days to set up an appointment. I will let you know how everything is progressing after I have met with him.

Again, thank you for your assistance. You will hear from me soon.

Sincerely,

Chris Smith

■ Candidate highlights pertinent information discussed during interview.

■ Letter expresses candidate's continued commitment to field of interest.

THANK YOU LETTER (AFTER INFORMATIONAL INTERVIEW)
(High School Administrator)

178 Green Street
Grand Forks, ND 58201
(701) 555-5555

January 18, 1996

Pat Cummings
Assistant Superintendent
Any School System
1140 Main Street
Fargo, ND 58107

Dear Mr. Cummings:

I wish to thank you for speaking with me yesterday concerning my interest in
obtaining a high school administration position. I have revised my resume
according to your suggestions, and have enclosed a copy for your review.

I am planning to contact Daniel Conner as you suggested, and have already
scheduled a meeting with Stephanie Birch with Bismarck Public Schools. I am
sure these meetings will prove to be as insightful and enjoyable as our discussion.

I will keep you informed as my search progresses. If you think of any more
information that might be helpful, or contacts I should be speaking with, please do
not hesitate to give me a call. Thank you again.

Sincerely,

Chris Smith

Enc. resume

■ In closing, letter refers to updated resume attached.

■ In closing, candidate promises to keep addressee informed of job search progress.

THANK YOU LETTER (AFTER INFORMATIONAL INTERVIEW)
(Hotel Clerk)

178 Green Street
Newark, DE 19713
(302) 555-5555

September 22, 1996

Pat Cummings
General Manager
Any Inn
1140 Main Street
Wilmington DE 19801

Dear Ms. Cummings:

Thank you for being so gracious with your time Friday. I found your description of current trends in hospitality very enlightening.

I appreciate the suggestions you made regarding my resume. I think the new version is much improved. Please feel free to make any further comments on the enclosed revision or to share it with anyone in the industry you feel might be interested in someone with my qualifications.

I will contact James Moller with Daylight Hotels this week. Again, thank you for all of your assistance.

Sincerely,

Chris Smith

Enc. resume

■ Candidate requests addressee's future consideration for available opportunities.

■ Candidate expresses appreciation to addressee for referral.

THANK YOU LETTER (AFTER INFORMATIONAL INTERVIEW)
(Marketing Assistant)

178 Green Street
Exeter, NH 03833
(603) 555-5555

December 3, 1996

Pat Cummings
Director, Marketing
Any Corporation
1140 Main Street
Keene, NH 03431

Dear Mr. Cummings:

I appreciate you taking a few moments to meet with me yesterday. I realize that, as Marketing Director of a large support staff, your time is very valuable.

After visiting Any Corporation and hearing about your experiences, I am even more confident that I would like to pursue a career in marketing upon my graduation next year. In the meantime, I will follow your advice on course selection and summer employment.

Thank you again for your time, Mr. Cummings. I plan to keep in touch throughout the year, as my job-hunting strategy becomes more focused.

Sincerely,

Chris Smith

■ Candidate highlights aspects of informational interview that were especially helpful.

■ Letter is short and to the point.

THANK YOU LETTER (AFTER INFORMATIONAL INTERVIEW)
(Mechanical Engineer)

178 Green Street
Norman, OK 73019
(405) 555-5555

November 4, 1996

Pat Cummings
Mechanical Engineer
Any Corporation
1140 Main Street
Tulsa, OK 74102

Dear Ms. Cummings:

Thank you for speaking with me yesterday regarding your work at Any
Corporation. Your new design plans for coal-fired boilers sound very exciting. I
wish you much success.

As you know, I have been considering a shift in focus within the field of
mechanical engineering. Although I have enjoyed my training in costing and
standards, my greatest interest has always been transportation. I am sure your
insight will help me determine the smoothest transition into this new line of
design.

As you requested, I will keep in contact as I pursue new opportunities.

Sincerely,

Chris Smith

■ Interest in new field is
emphasized.

■ Letter refers to specific topics
discussed during informational
meeting.

THANK YOU LETTER (AFTER INFORMATIONAL INTERVIEW)
(Meteorologist)

178 Green Street
New Rochelle, NY 10801
(914) 555-5555

April 22, 1996

Pat Cummings
Meteorologist
Any Television Station
1140 Main Street
Dobbs Ferry, NY 10522

Dear Mr. Cummings:

I thoroughly enjoyed my day at Any Television Station. Thank you for allowing
me to assist you as you tracked the day's weather.

As a result of our time together, I now have a much better understanding of the
immense time and skill necessary to interpret even the smallest piece of data. I
certainly agree that broadcast forecasting is not just a "glamorous" profession.

I am still very interested in pursuing a career as a Meteorologist. I am sure the
knowledge I gained from observing you will prove valuable in my studies.

Best of luck in your future endeavors.

Sincerely,

Chris Smith

■ Candidate immediately thanks
addressee for pleasurable
meeting.

■ In closing, letter refers to updated
resume attached.

THANK YOU LETTER (AFTER INFORMATIONAL INTERVIEW)
(Occupational Therapist)

178 Green Street
Downers Grove, IL 60515
(708) 555-5555

May 12, 1996

Pat Cummings
Occupational Therapist
Any Rehabilitation Center
1140 Main Street
Evanston, IL 60201

Dear Ms. Cummings:

Thank you for taking the time to meet with me on Friday. I enjoyed meeting with
you and learning about the programs offered at Any Rehabilitation Center.

Our discussion definitely strengthened my interest in occupational therapy as a
career path. I am planning to take your advice and enroll in a graduate program in
September. In the interim, I will contact the referrals you provided to inquire about
summer internship possibilities.

Thank you again for your assistance.

Sincerely,

Chris Smith

- Candidate thanks addressee for
  time extended.

- Candidate confirms his/her
  commitment to field of interest.

THANK YOU LETTER (AFTER INFORMATIONAL INTERVIEW)
(Social Worker)

178 Green Street
Jacksonville, FL 32256
(904) 555-5555

February 20, 1996

Pat Cummings
Social Worker
Any Agency
1140 Main Street
Clearwater, FL 34625

Dear Mr. Cummings:

Speaking with you yesterday was very helpful. Thank you for rearranging your busy schedule to offer your advice and experience.

Although I am considering a career in social work, I had not given thought to working exclusively with young adults until I visited your offices. The Early Intervention Program you direct is an amazing venture and I am now very interested in becoming involved with an agency that targets at-risk youth.

Currently, I am applying for an internship with the Jacksonville Teen Clinic. I will keep you updated on the status of my application.

Thank you again for the interest you expressed in my career search. I appreciate your help.

Sincerely,

Chris Smith

■ Letter outlines candidate's course of action resulting from informational interview.

■ Candidate confirms his/her commitment to field of interest.

26
Resurrection Letter

 If several weeks or even months have passed since you mailed your initial inquiry and you have not received a response, your candidacy may be in need of a jump start. Sending a resurrection letter informs an employer of your continued interest in, and suitability for, a desired position. Begin by reminding the employer of your initial reason for writing. Next, reiterate your most relevant qualifications, and stress your desire to join the employer's organization. Be sure to close your letter by clearly stating how and when you can be reached, and enclose another resume for the employer's convenience.

Sometimes writing for a response to your application can be frustrating. If you feel this way, don't let it reflect in your resurrection letter. A hiring manager is more likely to respond to a polite, upbeat letter.

RESURRECTION LETTER
(Advertising Assistant)

178 Green Street
Parsippany, NJ 07054
(201) 555-5555

July 18, 1996

Pat Cummings
Senior Vice-President
Any Advertising Agency
1140 Main Street
Ridgefield Park, NJ 07660

Dear Ms. Cummings:

Congratulations on your recent write-up in the *Advertising Advantage*. Your innovative marketing campaign for Hi-land products sounds very intriguing. I have no doubt it will be a huge success.

I am writing to inquire about joining your talented staff. I have sent a resume in response to the position of Assistant that you advertised in the *New York Times* on May 27, 1996. Although I did not receive a response, I am sure I would make a valuable addition to Any Advertising Agency. If any entry-level openings occur, please reconsider my qualifications. I have included a copy of my resume for your convenience.

Sincerely,

Chris Smith

Enc. resume

■ Introduction expresses candidate's knowledge of firm.

■ Resurrection letters generally include an additional resume.

RESURRECTION LETTER
(Assistant Regional Manager)

178 Green Street
Beaverton, OR 97005

July 22, 1996

Pat Cummings
Hiring Director
Any Retail Chain
1140 Main Street
Portland, OR 97204

Dear Mr. Cummings:

Since first sending my application materials in response to your advertisement for an Assistant Regional Manager, my interest in the position has continued to strengthen. In an effort to convince you of my capability to handle its responsibilities, I have prepared a comparison of my qualifications and the requirements you outlined in the July 14 edition of the *Oregonian*:

Your requirements:

- At least five years' experience in retail management.

- Ability to effectively deal with employees at all levels.

- Extensive experience in problem resolution.

- Knowledge of all aspects involved in retail operations.

My qualifications:

- Over ten years working in all areas of store management for several nationally recognized chains.

- Selection by current management for a highly sensitive headquarters position which requires the ability to deal with field and management personnel at all levels.

- As Problem Resolution/Communication Coordinator, responsibilities encompass troubleshooting and resolving conflicts in field operations affecting a 500-unit retail chain and several distribution centers.

- Experience handling issues pertaining to sales, distribution, personnel performance, corporate communications, customer satisfaction, and corporate image.

I am a well-organized, innovative assistant capable of providing management with efficient follow-through and skillful support. My interest in contributing to the growth of Any Retail Chain is sincere, and I look forward to hearing from you regarding my candidacy. I can be contacted either at home at (503) 555-5555, or confidentially at my current employer at (503) 444-4444.

Sincerely,

Chris Smith

■ Specific contributions emphasize candidate's achievements and problem-solving abilities.

■ Candidate assures potential employer that his/her interest in position has strengthened since first inquiry.

RESURRECTION LETTER
(Bank Administrator)

178 Green Street
Knoxville, TN 37921

May 27, 1996

Pat Cummings
Division Head, Banking
Any Corporation
1140 Main Street
Memphis, TN 38103

Dear Ms. Cummings:

Approximately two weeks ago, I submitted a resume for your review and consideration. As I have yet to receive a response, I am enclosing a second copy of my resume in the event that my previous correspondence did not reach your company.

As indicated, I am interested in making a new association with a company where I can apply the knowledge I acquired during my employment and academic endeavors, as well as exceptional management and administration skills, to a career in the banking industry.

I have seven years' experience in the marketing and management divisions of banking, involving every aspect of the administration, planning, and direction necessary for success. Accordingly, I feel I could become a valuable asset to your company.

I would appreciate the opportunity for a personal interview, at your convenience. Please contact me at (615) 555-5555 during the day and at (615) 444-4444 during evening hours.

Thank you for your time. I look forward to hearing from you soon.

With best regards,

Chris Smith

Enc. resume

■ Candidate immediately states date of initial application.

■ Candidate uses closing to suggest possibility of interview.

RESURRECTION LETTER
(Billings Clerk)

178 Green Street
Elko, NV 89801

July 27, 1996

Pat Cummings
Billings Supervisor
Any Corporation
1140 Main Street
St. Louis, MO 63121

Dear Mr. Cummings:

Thank you for considering my resume. Your time is greatly appreciated.

I wanted to inform you that I will be relocating to Missouri in the near future. My plans are to further my career in the accounting and finance industry in the St. Louis area. Just an added note: I am taking a computer spreadsheet course, which should further enhance my skills in the field.

I am still very interested in progressing my career at Any Corporation and would ask for your consideration regarding any future availabilities. Until my move to St. Louis on August 28, I can be reached by phone at (702) 555-5555. I will call again in six weeks' time.

Thank you again. I look forward to speaking with you.

Sincerely,

Chris Smith

■ Letter details continuing education completed since initial application.　■ Candidate establishes when follow-up contact will take place.

RESURRECTION LETTER
(Business Manager)

178 Green Street
Dunnellon, FL 34433
(813) 555-5555

November 14, 1996

Pat Cummings
President
Any Corporation
1140 Main Street
Fort Lauderdale, FL 33301

Dear Ms. Cummings:

In a recent letter, David Kipler, Group Vice-President with your company, indicated that my resume and letter regarding employment with Any Corporation were being forwarded for your review.

At this time, I have not had a response from you and am enclosing the attached resume to reiterate my interest in becoming a member of your firm.

I offer seven years' experience and the qualifications that could be well utilized in a managerial position with your firm. In addition to a Master's degree in Business Administration, I offer experience in relevant positions ranging from Product Management Trainee to Clinical Service Manager of five company-operated, out-patient treatment centers.

I am very much interested in the opportunity to join Any Corporation and look forward to hearing from you.

Sincerely,

Chris Smith

Enc. resume

- Resurrection letter is often used to reiterate candidate's qualifications.

- Four short paragraphs is the ideal length for a resurrection letter.

RESURRECTION LETTER
(Commercial Photographer)

178 Green Street
Baltimore, MD 21214
(301) 555-5555

April 20, 1996

Pat Cummings
Hiring Manager
Any Advertising Agency
1140 Main Street
Wheaton, MD 20902

Dear Mr. Cummings:

After speaking with your colleague Michael Hicks yesterday, I understand that your search for a Commercial Photographer is still on. Please allow me to express my continued interest in the position, and to reiterate my qualifications.

In addition to having graduated from a two-year program in all aspects of professional photography, at the Ziegler School of Photography, I have additional training in graphic and liberal arts, as well as in related areas of advertising and promotion (examples of my work are currently on exhibit in London, Canada, and the United States). My experience also includes diverse aspects of both large and small business operations, which is of great value in selecting subjects and backgrounds appropriate to commercial advertising and promotion, or personnel and public relations.

I have assembled a portfolio of relevant work that I think would be of interest to you. Will you be scheduling interviews soon? I would like to show you my work and express my sincere interest in producing quality products for Any Advertising Agency.

I will follow up this inquiry with a phone call next week. In the interim, I have enclosed another copy of my resume for your review.

Thank you very much for your time.

Sincerely,

Chris Smith

Enc. resume

- Candidate includes training pertinent to his/her field of interest.

- Stating that a portfolio is available on request is beneficial for certain positions.

RESURRECTION LETTER
(Computer Programmer)

178 Green Street
St. Paul, MN 55164
(612) 555-5555

September 2, 1996

Pat Cummings
Systems Programmer
Any Corporation
1140 Main Street
Minnetonka, MN 55343

Dear Ms. Cummings:

Thank you for taking the time to speak with me in late May regarding entry-level, computer programming positions at Any Corporation. Although you explained your hiring freeze at that time, I would like to update you on several newly acquired skills I thought would be of interest.

During the past summer at the University of Minnesota's Studio, I worked as both a Programmer and Research Assistant, successfully meeting a variety of technical and intellectual challenges. As a Programmer, I learned Windows programming and implemented improvements to ConStats, a Windows-based package of educational software teaching introductory statistics. As a Research Assistant, I used the SAS statistical language to produce analyses regarding how ConStats was being used by students. This work resulted in a published journal article, an excerpt of which is enclosed.

I am very interested in applying my newly acquired skills to your organization and would appreciate the opportunity to talk with you in a personal interview. Thank you for your time and consideration.

Sincerely,

Chris Smith

Enc. resume
      excerpt from *Computer Programmer*, December

■ In effort to improve his/her candidacy, applicant mentions newly acquired skills.

■ Technical language is acceptable when it relates to candidate's field.

RESURRECTION LETTER
(Correctional Officer)

178 Green Street
Butte, MT 59404
(406) 555-5555

January 18, 1996

Pat Cummings
Director of Security
Any State Prison
1140 Main Street
Billings, MT 59104

Dear Mr. Cummings:

This letter regards a resume I faxed to your offices Thursday, January 4. I have not heard if the Correctional Officer position has been filled. I remain very interested in the opportunity and look forward to your reply. Please feel free to contact me with any additional questions concerning my qualifications.

An additional copy of my resume is enclosed for your review.

Sincerely,

Chris Smith

Enc. resume

■ Candidate indicates date and nature of initial inquiry.

■ Closing informs addressee that resume is enclosed.

RESURRECTION LETTER
(Field Engineer)

178 Green Street
Jacksonville, FL 32207
(904) 555-5555

March 17, 1996

Pat Cummings
Vice-President, Field Engineering
Any Corporation
1140 Main Street
Ocala, FL 32672

Dear Ms. Cummings:

Thank you very much for talking with me regarding the Field Engineer position I applied for on March 4. I am glad to hear that the position is still available.

I would like to ask that you keep me in mind when considering candidates for the position. To make this easier, I have highlighted several of my most relevant experiences and accomplishments:

- More than six years' experience with an internationally recognized field engineering corporation.
- Maintenance and operation of UNIVAC and special purpose computers.
- Implementation of various cost-reduction programs resulting in over $150,000 savings in reduced labor and material costs.
- Supervision and coordination of all field engineering functions.

I look forward to hearing from you to schedule an interview. Thank you for your time.

Sincerely,

Chris Smith

■ In a resurrection letter, bullets provide a unique way to restate relevant qualifications.

■ Closing encourages reader to respond to letter.

RESURRECTION LETTER
(Foreign Language Teacher)

178 Green Street
Hapeville, GA 30354
(404) 555-5555

May 20, 1996

Pat Cummings
Principal
Any High School
1140 Main Street
Warner Robins, GA 31088

Dear Mr. Cummings:

On May 6, I wrote you regarding your anticipated opening for a Foreign Language Teacher to be filled in the 1996-97 school year.

In the event that my original application was not received, I have enclosed a packet containing an additional professional profile, proof of certification, and letters of recommendation.

I would appreciate the opportunity of an interview to further discuss my qualifications and enthusiasm for this or other available positions. I will follow up this letter with a phone call in a few days.

Sincerely,

Chris Smith

Enc. professional profile
    certification
    recommendations

■ Candidate encloses all pertinent information, in the event that first inquiry was not received.

■ In addition to initial position sought, candidate expresses willingness to fill other suitable positions.

RESURRECTION LETTER
(Freelance Copy Editor)

178 Green Street
Shawnee, OK 74801

November 21, 1996

Pat Cummings
Vice-President, Editorial
Any Publishing Company
1140 Main Street
Oklahoma City, OK 73125

Dear Ms. Cummings:

Please allow me to update my previous letter to Any Corporation with regard to your search for a position as Freelance Copy Editor. You will notice my resume has been revised to include more relevant experience.

My most recent assignment for Southwestern Publications involved copyediting material intended for educational television, geared for a high school audience. Many of my line corrections, as well as my editorial suggestions for improvements, were used in final versions. I was thorough, precise, and consistent in this work.

I also edited a Master's thesis in Business Administration for a Langston University student. The text needed many spelling, grammar, usage, and style corrections. I offered suggestions for improving content as well. The feedback on my work was quite good.

You may also recall that I am proficient in desktop publishing. I print high-quality resumes, essays, and formal letters for clients who need my services. I apply strict standards to my own work and operate in a thoroughly professional manner.

Thank you again, Ms. Cummings, for considering me as a potential freelancer for Any Corporation. I will be following up this letter with a phone call in the next few weeks. Should you wish to contact me sooner, my phone number is (405) 555-5555. I look forward to communicating with you in the near future.

Sincerely,

Chris Smith

Enc. resume

■ In a resurrection letter, candidate restates relevant skills and accomplishments regarding position.

■ Telephone number included in closing is omitted in return address.

RESURRECTION LETTER
(Fundraising Coordinator)

178 Green Street
Idaho Falls, ID 83415
(208) 555-5555

August 15, 1996

Pat Cummings
Senior Vice-President
Any Corporation
1140 Main Street
Boise, ID 83706

Dear Mr. Cummings:

I am very much interested in becoming your new Fundraising Coordinator.

In the weeks since I mailed my original application, I have given much thought to
how closely my skills meet your requirements. I am confident that I could make a
significant contribution to your corporation.

Knowing that you prefer not to take telephone inquiries, and that mail sometimes
does not reach its destination, I am taking this opportunity to provide you with an
additional copy of my resume, and to ask for your continued consideration of my
candidacy.

If you have questions regarding my resume or the skills I would bring to this
position, I would appreciate an opportunity to talk with you.

Sincerely,

Chris Smith

Enc. resume

■ Candidate assures potential
employer that his/her interest in
position has strengthened since
first inquiry.

■ Position applied for is clearly and
immediately defined.

RESURRECTION LETTER
(Jewelry Designer)

178 Green Street
Norman, OK 73019
(405) 555-5555

August 5, 1996

Pat Cummings
Owner
Any Jewelry Maker
1140 Main Street
Edmond, OK 73034

Dear Ms. Cummings:

On July 12, I sent a resume and small portfolio of samples in application for a position as a Designer for your jewelry line. Since I have not received a response, I can only assume that you did not have any suitable vacancies at that time. Please allow me to highlight my qualifications again, as I am very interested in joining your design team:

- Eight years' experience as a model maker and designer for several prominent competitors in the jewelry industry.

- Honors graduate of the National School of Jewelry Design, including an award for outstanding achievement.

- Three years of additional, diverse experience as a Customer Service Representative in the industry.

Would it be possible to meet with you next week to discuss your needs and present several examples of my past design work? I will call you this Friday to schedule a time that is convenient for you.

Thank you for your continued consideration. I hope that our future discussions will result in our working together.

Sincerely,

Chris Smith

Enc. resume

■ Phrasing request in question form is a strong closing.

■ Candidate immediately states date of initial application.

RESURRECTION LETTER
(Physical Therapist)

178 Green Street
Somerville, MA 02145
(617) 555-5555

November 16, 1996

Pat Cummings
Rehabilitation Coordinator
Any Clinic
1140 Main Street
Mansfield, MA 02048

Dear Mr. Cummings:

In a letter dated August 12, I expressed my interest in obtaining a staff position as a Physical Therapist at Any Clinic. Although I realize that there may not have been any suitable availabilities at that time, I have enclosed a second resume for continued consideration.

Since my initial application, I have been working on an independent research project while continuing my job search. My study evaluated back and shoulder strength of athletes suffering from tendinitis and bursitis. Last week, my results were accepted for publication with the *National Journal of Rehabilitation*.

I have enclosed an excerpt of my article for your review. I hope this strengthens my candidacy for a position at Any Clinic. I would welcome the chance to meet with you should any opportunities for a Physical Therapist become available.

Sincerely,

Chris Smith

Enc. resume
    excerpt from "XYZ"

■ Publications are impressive and add weight to cover letter.

■ Letter provides additional information not stated in initial inquiry.

RESURRECTION LETTER
(Purchasing Agent)

178 Green Street
Peoria, IL 61643

February 22, 1996

Human Resource Director
Any Corporation
P.O. Box 7777
Alton, IL 62002

Dear Human Resources Director:

I am writing this letter to follow up on the resume I sent you on February 14. I am very interested in talking with you about the Purchasing Agent position. If you have any questions please do not hesitate to call me anytime at (309) 555-5555.

I have enclosed another resume for your consideration.

Thank you for your time.

Sincerely,

Chris Smith

Enc. resume

- Candidate indicates date and nature of initial inquiry.

- Candidate invites addressee to respond to inquiry since specific employer is unknown.

RESURRECTION LETTER
(Radio Announcer)

178 Green Street
New Rochelle, NY 10801

January 4, 1996

Pat Cummings
Production Manager
Any Radio Station
1140 Main Street
Garden City, NY 11530

Dear Mr. Cummings:

Last week, I spoke with your assistant, Linda McMillian, regarding the initial resume and demo tape I sent for the On-Air Announcer vacancy. Although Ms. McMillian could not confirm whether you had had the chance to review my application materials, she did inform me that the position is still available.

I would like to take this opportunity to express my continued interest in becoming an Announcer at Any Radio Station. Ever since I moved to New York three years ago, I have listened to, and admired, your station's broadcasts. I would love to contribute to the success of what *Radio NY* considers to be "Westchester's Best News Station."

As your newest Announcer, I would bring almost thirteen years of experience in diverse areas of AM and FM announcing, newscasting, and audio production, including current responsibility for a regular on-air shift with WJBF AM (1170), New Rochelle, NY.

I enclosed second copies of my resume and tape. After you have listened to my tape, I would like to arrange a meeting to further discuss the position. I can be reached at (914) 555-5555.

I look forward to speaking with you.

Sincerely,

Chris Smith

Enc. resume
      demo tape

- Letter incorporates company knowledge into discussion of qualifications.

- In a resurrection letter, candidate restates relevant skills and accomplishments regarding position.

RESURRECTION LETTER
(Sales Representative)

178 Green Street
Yuma, AZ 85365
(602) 555-5555

November 7, 1996

Pat Cummings
Vice-President of Industrial Relations
Any Corporation
1140 Main Street
Helena, MT 59601

Dear Ms. Cummings:

On October 3, I sent you a letter expressing my interest in a position in professional sales and enclosed my resume for your review. As of today, I have not received a response and I am writing again to reiterate my interest in becoming a member of your sales staff.

My objective is to remain in the health care field with a company that is consistently developing, marketing, and promoting products to help those with chronic and other diseases. I would like to re-emphasize my education, clinical experience as a medical student, and practical experience in medical research, as well as direct patient care. Each of these experiences has given me the skills and sincerity to introduce and sell health care products, equipment, instruments, or services to medical professionals and administrators.

I have taken the liberty to enclose a second copy of my resume. I am free to relocate and/or travel. I hope to hear from you so that I can convince you that I have the qualifications and motivation to effectively represent your company.

Thank you again for reviewing my material. I look forward to your return response.

Sincerely,

Chris Smith

Enc. resume

- Candidate thanks potential employer for consideration of initial inquiry.
- Discussion details how candidate's qualifications will benefit potential employer.

RESURRECTION LETTER
(Sanitation Inspector)

178 Green Street
Conshohocken, PA 19428
(215) 555-5555

May 23, 1996

Pat Cummings
Chief Inspector
Any Office
1140 Main Street
Lewisburg, PA 17837

Dear Mr. Cummings:

I am writing to express my continued interest in the position of Sanitation Inspector advertised in the May 8 edition of the *Express-Times*.

In the event that you did not receive my original mailing, I have enclosed a second copy of my resume for your deliberation. I feel that this position provides the ideal opportunity to apply my thirteen years of experience in the public health and safety industry. I am confident that, given the opportunity, I could effectively maintain your strict inspection standards.

I would be happy to further discuss my qualifications for this position in a personal interview. I am available at your convenience, and look forward to hearing from you.

In the interim, be assured of my enthusiasm and competence.

Sincerely,

Chris Smith

Enc. resume

- Resurrection letters generally include an additional resume.

- Follow-up letter confirms candidate's enthusiasm for desired position.

RESURRECTION LETTER
(Shipping/Receiving Expediter)

178 Green Street
Anchorage, AK 99502
(907) 555-5555

April 15, 1996

Pat Cummings
Supervisor
Any Company
1140 Main Street
Fairbanks, AK 99701

Dear Ms. Cummings:

This letter follows a resume I mailed to your offices last Monday. I am very
interested in the Shipping/Receiving Expediter position you advertised in the
Sunday, April 7, edition of the *Anchorage Daily News*.

Please note I offer twelve years' experience with The Alpha Corporation as an
Expediter. In this capacity I entered packing slips, invoices, and other material
control information into the computer through CRT, compared and identified
contents to packing slips, scheduled daily deliveries of incoming traffic, and
created and implemented an inventory system.

I am confident I can make an immediate contribution to Any Company. If you
have any questions, I can be reached at the address and telephone number above.

Thank you for your consideration and I look forward to hearing from you.

Sincerely,

Chris Smith

- ■ Resurrection letter is often used to reiterate candidate's qualifications.
- ■ Closing invites addressee to inquire about additional information.

RESURRECTION LETTER
(Social Worker)

178 Green Street
Baltimore, MD 21218
(301) 555-5555

June 1, 1996

Pat Cummings
Director
Any Agency
1140 Main Street
Landover, MD 20785

Dear Mr. Cummings:

Please accept this updated version of my letter addressing the Social Worker position. I remain very interested in the opportunity and my revised resume is enclosed for your consideration.

Recently, I worked as an Intern at the Baltimore Community Center. My responsibilities included intake, evaluation, and treatment of individuals, couples, and families in a medical and social service setting. The experience also entailed volunteering at the Andrew T. Ferris Children's Clinic two days a week. There my primary duties covered diagnostic evaluation and treatment of children, adolescents, adults, and families, and investigation of care and protection petitions within a multidisciplinary team.

I hope these experiences strengthen my candidacy for the position. I look forward to your reply.

Sincerely,

Chris Smith

Enc. resume

■ Letter provides additional information not stated in initial inquiry.

■ Activities highlight candidate's involvement in local community.

RESURRECTION LETTER
(Staff Accountant)

178 Green Street
Parsippany, NJ 07054

August 4, 1996

Pat Cummings
Director of Human Resources
Any Corporation
1140 Main Street
New York, NY 10019

Dear Ms. Cummings:

Last year I spoke with Susan Rutter, the Director of Human Resources with your Chicago office, about the possibility of working within that division of Any Corporation as a Staff Accountant.

Since that conversation, a change in my personal situation has necessitated a move to the New York area. Consequently, I would like to continue my application process with Any Corporation in your office. I have enclosed a resume for your consideration.

I was graduated from the University of Chicago in May with a Bachelor's degree in Accounting and Economics. Both my education and my internship at Gunn and Millstreet have adequately prepared me to begin a career in the corporate arena, and I am very eager to apply this preparation to a position at Any Corporation.

I would be happy to further outline my capabilities and learn more about your prestigious training program during the course of a personal interview. I can be reached at the above address or by phone at (201) 555-5555. I look forward to your reply.

Sincerely,

Chris Smith

Enc. resume

■ Letter details continuing education completed since initial application.

■ Candidate clearly expresses eagerness to work for specific employer.

RESURRECTION LETTER
(Systems Analyst)

178 Green Street
Schenectady, NY 12305

March 2, 1996

Pat Cummings
Supervisor
Any Company
1140 Main Street
Olympia, WA 98505

Dear Mr. Cummings:

Last week I interviewed with Pisces Data Systems, Inc. for a Systems Analyst position. Although there were no openings with the company, Matthew Pratt faxed my resume to your offices since he was aware of a number of openings there. I am unsure if you received the information so I have enclosed an additional copy. I am very interested in opportunities at Any Company.

Please let me review my qualifications:

- Set up the interfacing of a mini-computer to a PC in order to archive daily receipts onto optical disks.
- Created a device driver for a new disk system, and developed a new operating system to handle the new driver.
- Qualified all of Devlin software onto a new computer system.
- Built a new method of handling orders into the system.
- Rewrote accounts receivable program system to handle long-term notes.

I will contact your offices this Wednesday to discuss how my skills can benefit your company. If you have any further questions before this time, please feel free to call me at (508) 555-5555.

Sincerely,

Chris Smith

Enc. resume

- In a resurrection letter, bullets provide a unique way to restate relevant qualifications.
- Candidate encloses all pertinent information, in the event that first inquiry was not received.

RESURRECTION LETTER
(Telemarketer)

178 Green Street
Grace City, OH 58445
(216) 555-5555

February 19, 1996

Hiring Manager
P.O. Box 7777
Kent, OH 44242

RE: Advertisement in the February 2 edition of the *Sun Newspapers*

Dear Hiring Manager:

Please consider this letter as a follow-up inquiry regarding my resume sent on February 4, 1996 for the telemarketing position.

Should the advertised position still be available, I would be very interested in discussing my qualifications with you in a personal interview. As the enclosed copy of my resume reflects, I have a proven track record of selling and closing capabilities as a Telemarketer. Last year, I independently generated over $1.5 million in sales for my employer through cold-calling techniques. I would like to apply the same successful telemarketing abilities to your firm.

When could we meet for an interview?

Sincerely,

Chris Smith

Enc. resume

■ Job descriptions indicate how candidate contributed to his/her previous employers.

■ In closing, candidate specifically requests interview.

RESURRECTION LETTER
(Translator)

178 Green Street
New Haven, CT 06511
(203) 555-5555

May 23, 1996

Pat Cummings
Director
Any Program
1140 Main Street
Meriden, CT 06450

Dear Mr. Cummings:

Recently I applied for a Translator position with Any Program. I am aware that you hire sporadically depending on the needs of your clients and, for this reason, I am enclosing an updated resume for your review. If any positions are currently available, please consider my qualifications.

As you may recall, I have a working knowledge of written and spoken Japanese, as well as the following relevant experience:

- Served as liaison between Japanese diplomats and the Japanese-American relations group, and with the Japanese press during the prime minister's stay.

- Translated correspondence and filed inquiries from the Japanese population in the Hartford business community.

- Designed and circulated posters, banners, and invitations in order to introduce the Japanese community to New England.

- Organized travel itineraries for Japanese officials visiting the New England area.

I would welcome the opportunity to discuss how my background can benefit your program. I will contact your offices early next week to arrange a mutually convenient meeting time.

Thank you for your consideration.

Sincerely,

Chris Smith

Enc. resume

- Letter stresses candidates' foreign language skills and international exposure.

- In addition to initial position sought, candidate expresses willingness to fill other suitable positions.

RESURRECTION LETTER
(Typist)

178 Green Street
Gaithersburg, MD 20879
(301) 555-5555

March 3, 1996

Pat Cummings
Executive Hiring Officer
Any Corporation
1140 Main Street
Potomac, MD 20854

Dear Ms. Cummings:

On February 15 I sent my resume via fax to your office. Since then I have not received any response. I am very interested in the typing position you were offering, and if it has not been filled, I would welcome the opportunity to discuss the position with you. However, if this position has been filled, I would appreciate your input as to how I might further my job search. I have enclosed a SASE for your convenience.

I am also enclosing another resume with references, for any other opportunities you may offer in the future.

Thank you for your time.

Sincerely,

Chris Smith

Enc. resume
    references
    SASE

■ Candidate encloses all pertinent information, in the event that first inquiry was not received.

■ Closing is straightforward and concise.

27
Response to Rejection

 A well-written thank you note, mailed within one or two days of receiving notice of rejection, makes a positive statement. Admittedly, this technique is less widely used than other thank you letters, but it can be equally effective. When Danny P. was turned down for a position as Publicity Director, he quickly wrote his interviewer a letter which expressed his disappointment at not being offered the job, but also his thanks for the company's consideration of his qualifications. The interviewer, impressed by his initiative, provided Danny with several contact names to assist in his search.

When writing your letter, emphasize an on going interest in being considered for future openings. Also, be careful to use an upbeat tone. Although you may be disappointed, you don't want to imply that you don't respect the employer's hiring decision.

RESPONSE TO REJECTION
(Administrative Assistant)

178 Green Street
Shawnee, OK 74801
(405) 555-5555

February 27, 1996

Pat Cummings
President
Any Corporation
1140 Main Street
Oklahoma City, OK 73101

Dear Mr. Cummings:

Thanks to you and your enthusiastic staff for all the help offered me while visiting your offices last week. Although I was not selected for the Administrative Assistant position, I would appreciate detailed feedback on how to improve my candidacy for future openings at Any Corporation. Yours is a team I hope to someday join. Let me know how to achieve this goal.

Again, thank you for your consideration. I look forward to your response.

Sincerely,

Chris Smith

■ Letter expresses candidate's continued interest in working for the company.

■ Candidate requests addressee's return response.

RESPONSE TO REJECTION
(Architect)

178 Green Street
Middletown, RI 02840
(401) 555-5555

July 10, 1996

Pat Cummings
President
Any Firm
1140 Main Street
Providence, RI 02912

Dear Ms. Cummings:

Again, thank you for meeting with me last week to discuss the opportunities for Architects at Any Firm. I admire the innovative work you and your staff produce and, although I was not chosen for the position, I would like to be considered for upcoming projects.

I have enclosed an additional copy of my resume for your files. Thank you for your attention and I hope to hear from you in the near future.

Sincerely,

Chris Smith

Enc. resume

■ Candidate refers to attached resume in closing.

■ Candidate recalls enjoyable interview process.

RESPONSE TO REJECTION
(Assistant Editor)

178 Green Street
White Plains, NY 10604
(914) 555-5555

July 1, 1996

Pat Cummings
Editor
Any Publication
1140 West 43rd Street
New York, NY 10036

Dear Mr. Cummings:

Once again, I would like to thank you for the chance to interview for the Assistant Editor position with *Any Publication*. Although I am disappointed I was not chosen for the position, I enjoyed meeting with you and your staff and learning more about your company.

I am still interested in opportunities with Any Publication and would appreciate it if you would keep me in mind for future openings in either your magazine or book divisions. Thank you again for your consideration.

Sincerely,

Chris Smith

■ Candidate begins letter by thanking addressee for previous consideration.

■ Closing thanks addressee in advance for attention.

RESPONSE TO REJECTION
(Counselor)

178 Green Street
Wadesboro, NC 28170
(704) 555-5555

September 5, 1996

Pat Cummings
Head Counselor
Any Center
1140 Main Street
Charlotte, NC 27706

Dear Ms. Cummings:

Thank you for meeting with me last Friday regarding your current vacancy.
Although I regret not being chosen for the Counselor position, I found the
interview process very informative.

Please note that I have applied for a Master's degree in Social Work program to
begin in January of 1997. I would be very interested in pursuing the field work
required for my M.S.W. degree in a counseling capacity at Any Center.

I will contact you again in the future to inquire about suitable opportunities.

Thank you again for your consideration.

Sincerely,

Chris Smith

■ Letter provides additional
information not stated in initial
inquiry.

■ Type of position desired is clearly
stated.

RESPONSE TO REJECTION
(Telemarketer)

178 Green Street
Ontario, OR 97914
(503) 555-5555

March 2, 1996

Pat Cummings
Human Resources Director
Any Corporation
1140 Main Street
Albany, OR 97321

Dear Mr. Cummings:

Per receipt of your letter dated March 1, I understand that your search for a Telemarketing Professional has come to an end. Although I am disappointed that I was not chosen for the position, I appreciate your taking the time to interview me. I was impressed by both Any Corporation's products and its friendly staff.

I am still very interested in applying for any current or anticipated availabilities at Any Corporation. I have enclosed another copy of my resume for your convenience. Please consider my qualifications in the future.

I look forward to speaking with you again.

Sincerely,

Chris Smith

Enc. resume

■ Candidate relays enthusiasm for future opportunities.

■ Candidate refers to information received during interview.

28
Withdrawal from Consideration

If you must withdraw your application from consideration at any point in the hiring process, it is best to inform the employer in writing. This will establish you as a courteous individual worthy of consideration should you reapply for a position in the future. In general, a withdrawal letter should be concise. If you choose to include a reason for your withdrawal, phrase it briefly and in positive terms.

WITHDRAWAL FROM CONSIDERATION
(Coach)

178 Green Street
Orono, ME 04473
(207) 555-5555

October 12, 1996

Pat Cummings
Head Coach
Any High School
1140 Main Street
Portland, ME 04104

Dear Ms. Cummings:

Thank you for the time you spent with me last week discussing coaching opportunities. I enjoyed meeting both you and the players. You have a great team.

As we discussed, my most recent experience has been with college-level teams and yesterday I was offered an excellent opportunity at the University of Maine. Although I am confident I would have enjoyed working with your players, I must withdraw from consideration.

Again, thank you and best of luck in the upcoming season.

Sincerely,

Chris Smith

- Candidate may include a brief explication when withdrawing from consideration.

- Candidate immediately thanks addressee for pleasurable meeting.

WITHDRAWAL FROM CONSIDERATION
(Firefighter)

178 Green Street
Decatur, IL
(217) 555-5555

December 12, 1996

Pat Cummings
Captain
Any Fire Department
1140 Main Street
Palos Heights, IL 60455

Dear Mr. Cummings:

Last week I met with you to discuss the opening for a Firefighter. I was very impressed by the team of people working at Any Fire Department and the facility itself was one of the most technologically advanced I have seen.

Although I am convinced I would have enjoyed the position, I must withdraw my candidacy. My family and I are presently relocating and the move will take us out of state.

Thank you again and best wishes.

Sincerely,

Chris Smith

■ Withdrawal letter is brief and to the point.

■ Language is straightforward and understandable.

WITHDRAWAL FROM CONSIDERATION
(Freelance Textbook Editor)

178 Green Street
Boca Raton, FL 33486
(407) 555-5555

August 22, 1996

Pat Cummings
Vice-President, Promotion
Any Corporation
1140 Main Street
Pensacola, FL 32520

Dear Ms. Cummings:

On August 8, I responded to your advertisement in the *Florida Times-Union* for a Freelance Textbook Editor.

I am not aware whether this position has been filled, but I would like to inform you that I no longer wish to be considered. I have accepted an offer from Holden Press to work as Project Manager on a new series of elementary grammar textbooks.

This new position was offered on a contractual basis, to last three months. Should your company need a freelance writer for similar projects in the future, I would appreciate your consideration.

Sincerely,

Chris Smith

■ Candidate indicates date and nature of initial inquiry.

■ Letter expresses candidate's continued interest in working for the company.

WITHDRAWAL FROM CONSIDERATION
(Hair Stylist)

178 Green Street
Carthage, MS 39051
(601) 555-5555

June 4, 1996

Pat Cummings
Owner
Any Boutique
1140 Main Street
Jackson, MS 39205

Dear Mr. Cummings:

I would like to express my appreciation for the time you extended to me during our interview on May 30 for the Hair Stylist position. I have rarely seen such a friendly and enthusiastic staff, and your customers certainly seem satisfied with your work!

Although the position sounds wonderful, I am writing to withdraw my name from consideration. Since our meeting, my current employer has offered me a promotion that I cannot turn down. I hope my decision does not hinder your hiring process: I know that whomever you chose will prove to be an excellent Hair Stylist.

Once again, thank you for your consideration.

Sincerely,

Chris Smith

■ Follow-up letter thanks addressee for enjoyable interview.

■ Candidate apologizes for inconvenience to potential employer.

WITHDRAWAL FROM CONSIDERATION
(Legal Assistant)

178 Green Street
Ann Arbor, MI 48108
(313) 555-5555

October 9, 1996

Pat Cummings
Principal
Any Law Firm
1140 Main Street
Sterling Heights, MI 48314

Dear Ms. Cummings:

I enjoyed meeting with you over lunch Friday to discuss the possibility of my working as a part-time Legal Assistant with your firm. Your insight into the legal field and description of your own experiences were very insightful. Any Law Firm sounds like an ideal environment in which to gain experience.

Unfortunately, I must withdraw my candidacy to assist you this fall. As you know, I am completing my law degree, and my schedule next semester does not permit the flexibility that the position would demand.

Thank you for the assistance you graciously extended. I hope that we can work together in the future.

Sincerely,

Chris Smith

- Letter expresses candidate's appreciation for addressee's consideration.

- Candidate refers to information received during interview.

WITHDRAWAL FROM CONSIDERATION
(Nurse's Aide)

178 Green Street
Denver, CO 80239
(303) 555-5555

March 11, 1996

Pat Cummings
Nursing Director
Any Hospital
1140 Main Street
Stratford, CT 06497

Dear Mr. Cummings:

I regret to inform you that I am withdrawing my application from the pool of applicants for the Nurse's Aide position. An abrupt change in my personal situation has made relocation to your area impossible at the present time.

I wish you the best of luck as your search continues.

Sincerely,

Chris Smith

■ When withdrawing from consideration, providing a specific reason is optional.

■ Letter immediately states candidate's purpose.

WITHDRAWAL FROM CONSIDERATION
(Preschool Instructor)

178 Green Street
Newnan, GA 30265
(404) 555-5555

December 12, 1996

Pat Cummings
Owner
Any Preschool
1140 Main Street
Macon, GA 31297

Dear Ms. Cummings:

I would like to thank you for interviewing me last Thursday for the part-time Preschool Instructor position. It was a pleasure meeting you and Jennifer Hedge, as well as the wonderful children you have the opportunity to work with.

As I mentioned during our conversation Thursday, my prime interest is in obtaining full-time teaching work. Therefore, I have decided to accept a position as a Pre-Kindergarten Teacher in an elementary school near my home. Although I would have enjoyed working with your fine staff, I feel that this position provides an ideal opportunity for me to pursue my goals.

I have no doubt that you will find an qualified instructor to fill your vacancy, as you manage an excellent developmental facility for children. Thank you again for considering my candidacy.

Best of luck in your future endeavors.

Sincerely,

Chris Smith

■ Candidate may include a brief explication when withdrawing from consideration.

■ Candidate refers to all employees involved in interview process.

WITHDRAWAL FROM CONSIDERATION
(Regional Sales Manager)

178 Green Street
Kennelworth, NJ 07033
(201) 555-5555

July 1, 1996

Pat Cummings
Human Resources Director
Any Corporation
1140 Main Street
New Brunswick, NJ 08933

Dear Mr. Cummings:

As you may recall, I spoke with you over the phone several weeks ago regarding the status of my application for the Regional Sales Manager position. Thank you for the time you extended to inform me of the hiring process.

While I understand that you are still in the process of sorting through resumes, I wanted to notify you that I no longer wish to be considered as an applicant. I have just accepted another offer for a similar position.

I wish you the best of luck in your search for a qualified candidate.

Sincerely yours,

Chris Smith

- Letter expresses candidate's appreciation for addressee's consideration.
- Follow-up letter confirms candidate's enthusiasm for desired position.

WITHDRAWAL FROM CONSIDERATION
(Systems Analyst)

178 Green Street
Melville, NY 11754
(516) 555-5555

February 13, 1996

Pat Cummings
Custom Products Engineer
Any Corporation
1140 Main Street
Cleveland, OH 44112

Dear Ms. Cummings:

It was a pleasure meeting with you and touring your corporate headquarters last week. Thank you for extending me the invitation to fly out to Ohio; I thoroughly enjoyed my first stay in Cleveland!

During my visit, I was continually impressed by your innovations in product development and testing. Your organization's reputation is certainly well deserved.

Unfortunately, I feel I must withdraw from further consideration for the Systems Analyst position. After thoroughly weighing my options, I have decided that it is not in the best interest of my family to relocate at this time. I apologize for the seemingly sudden nature of my resolution; I hope that I have not caused too much inconvenience.

Congratulations on your continued success. I wish you all the best in the future.

Sincerely,

Chris Smith

■ Candidate apologizes for inconvenience to potential employer.

■ Follow-up letter demonstrates candidate's acquired company knowledge.

WITHDRAWAL FROM CONSIDERATION
(Travel Agent)

178 Green Street
Lexington, MA 02173
(617) 555-5555

December 11, 1996

Pat Cummings
President
Any Travel Agency
1140 Main Street
Allston, MA 02134

Dear Mr. Cummings:

I enjoyed meeting with you yesterday to discuss the Travel Agent availability. The prospect of working with you and your staff in such a fast-paced environment was very exciting.

However, after much thought, I have decided to withdraw my candidacy. The extensive travel the position involves is not well suited to my present situation.

Again, thank you for your consideration and best of luck with your search.

Sincerely,

Chris Smith

- When withdrawing from consideration, providing a specific reason is optional.

- Withdrawal letter is brief and to the point.

29
Rejection of Offer

If you decide to reject an employment offer, inform the employer through a formal letter. Even if you rejected the offer over the phone, you should confirm your decision in writing. Begin by thanking the interviewer for both the offer and the time extended to your candidacy. Stating a reason for rejection is optional. Above all, keep your letter upbeat—you never know if you'll reapply to the company in the future!

REJECTION OF OFFER
(Archivist)

178 Green Street
Rogers, AR 72757
(501) 555-5555

May 22, 1996

Pat Cummings
Executive Director
Any University Library
1140 Main Street
Little Rock, AR 72211

Dear Ms. Cummings:

I received your letter dated May 20, and would like to thank you for offering me
the Archivist position at Any University Library.

Although the prospect of working with such a prestigious reference collection is
very enticing, I must decline your offer. I have accepted a position assisting a local
historian on a book project. Since this opportunity requires only a part-time
commitment, I feel it is better suited to my personal situation.

You manage a wonderful facility, Ms. Cummings. I am confident that you will
have no trouble finding a professional eager to join your staff.

Best regards,

Chris Smith

■ When rejecting an offer, providing a reason is optional.

■ Candidate indicates type of employment desired.

REJECTION OF OFFER
(Assistant Art Director)

178 Green Street
Rupert, ID 83350
(208) 555-5555

May 15, 1996

Pat Cummings
Art Director
Any Corporation
1140 Main Street
Chicago, IL 60605

Dear Mr. Cummings:

I would like to use this opportunity to thank you for taking the time to meet with me last week.

However, after careful thought and consideration, I must decline your tempting offer for the position of Assistant Art Director. I have decided that my interests and career goals lie elsewhere at this point in my life. Perhaps our needs will coincide at a later date.

Thank you again. Best wishes for your continued success.

Sincerely,

Chris Smith

■ Letter clarifies candidate's career goals.

■ Candidate's explication of rejection is concise.

REJECTION OF OFFER
(Dental Hygienist)

178 Green Street
Terre Haute, IN 47804
(812) 555-5555

May 12, 1996

Pat Cummings, D.M.D.
Any Dental Center
1140 Main Street
Wayne, IN 46802

Dear Dr. Cummings:

I received your letter dated May 8, offering me the Dental Hygienist position at Any Dental Center. The compensation and benefits of the position sound very tempting, and I am confident I would enjoy working with your staff.

However, shortly before receiving your letter, I was offered, and accepted, another position. Thank you for your time and consideration of my candidacy.

Best wishes,

Chris Smith

■ Letter confirms candidate's receipt of offer.

■ Letter uses short sentences and common words.

REJECTION OF OFFER
(Editor)

178 Green Street
Bartow, FL 33830
(813) 555-5555

September 17, 1996

Pat Cummings
Senior Editor
Any Publishing Company
1140 Main Street
Miami, FL 33173

Dear Mr. Cummings:

Thank you so much for your generous offer of employment, and for your confidence in my abilities as an Editor.

As I explained during our phone conversation, a newly arisen personal situation has caused me to rethink my plans to relocate to Miami. After much deliberation, I have decided that I must postpone my plans. I apologize for informing you of this change on such short notice, and I regret not being able to seize the opportunity to work for such a distinguished organization.

I hope that we will be able to join forces in the future.

Sincerely,

Chris Smith

- Letter's tone is both courteous and appreciative.
- Candidate begins letter by thanking addressee for previous consideration.

REJECTION OF OFFER
(Law Enforcement Officer)

178 Green Street
Chalmette, LA 70043
(504) 555-5555

January 5, 1996

Pat Cummings
Police Chief
Any Police Department
1140 Main Street
Broussard, LA 70518

Dear Ms. Cummings:

I would like to extend my thanks to you and your squad for speaking with me about the Law Enforcement Officer availability. I enjoyed the time I spent at the station. You have a great group of people working with you.

Although I know I would be proud to serve on your team, I must decline your generous offer. I have accepted a position in a neighboring town.

Thank you again and best of luck for a safe New Year.

Sincerely,

Chris Smith

■ Candidate expresses gratitude for addressee's consideration.

■ Candidate recalls enjoyable interview process.

REJECTION OF OFFER
(Marine Biologist)

178 Green Street
Tacoma, WA 98411
(206) 555-5555

November 4, 1996

Pat Cummings
Environmental Scientist
Any Corporation
1140 Main Street
Seattle, WA 98188

Dear Mr. Cummings:

I want to thank you for considering me qualified to represent your organization in the development and testing of aquatic toxicity. I consider Any Corporation to be a leader in the field of environmental testing, and am continually impressed by your work.

While I have enjoyed my work in toxicity, at this point in my career, I have decided to shift focus. I have accepted a position researching aquaculture survival techniques in the Pacific Ocean. I feel this position will ideally lend itself to my career goals.

Thank you again for your confidence in my abilities as a Marine Biologist. Best of luck with your current aquatic testing project.

Sincerely,

Chris Smith

■ Candidate closes letter on a positive note.

■ Dedication to candidate's field of interest is emphasized.

REJECTION OF OFFER
(Paralegal)

178 Green Street
Woodbridge, NJ 07095
(908) 555-5555

March 4, 1996

Pat Cummings
Hiring Manager
Any Law Firm
1140 Main Street
Cherry Hill, NJ 08034

Dear Ms. Cummings:

Thank you very much for offering me the chance to work as a full-time Paralegal at Any Law Firm next fall. I realize what a challenging and gainful experience this opportunity represents.

As I explained in our interview on February 28, I had also submitted law school applications for the upcoming year. Early this week, I received an acceptance notification from Fordham University.

After weighing my choices, I realized that the best decision would be to begin school without delay. However, I sincerely wish to thank you for your trust in my skills.

Should you need a summer intern or part-time Law Clerk within the next three years, I would welcome the opportunity to work for your firm.

Sincerely,

Chris Smith

■ Candidate relays enthusiasm for future opportunities.

■ When rejecting an offer, providing a reason is optional.

REJECTION OF OFFER
(Production Assistant)

178 Green Street
Belair, TX 77401
(713) 555-5555

May 27, 1996

Pat Cummings
Producer
Any Production Company
1140 Main Street
Dallas, TX 75227

Dear Mr. Cummings:

It was a pleasure meeting with you last week and learning more about the current film projects underway at Any Production Company. I was pleased to receive your generous offer to assist you on a part-time basis as a Production Assistant.

Since that time, however, I have received an opportunity to pursue a documentary film project of my own. As you may recall, I was waiting for a decision on a grant proposal; I have now been granted funding.

I am afraid this project will consume my energies on a full-time basis, so I must decline the opportunity to work with you on your new film. I admire your work greatly, Mr. Cummings, and know that I would have enjoyed assisting you.

Good luck on your project!

Sincerely,

Chris Smith

■ Letter confirms candidate's receipt of offer.

■ One page is standard length for cover letters.

694

REJECTION OF OFFER
(Program Coordinator)

---

178 Green Street
Carlsbad, NM 88220
(505) 555-5555

April 5, 1996

Pat Cummings
Resort Director
Any Resort
1140 Main Street
Albuquerque, NM 87121

Dear Ms. Cummings:

Thank you very much for your employment offer extended during our meeting on April 2. I appreciate your confidence in my ability to perform the duties of Program Coordinator.

After careful deliberation, however, I am going to have to decline the position. As I previously mentioned, I have been considering a career in the hospitality industry for some time, and thought that the Program Coordinator position would provide exactly the type of entry-level experience I needed. I now realize that my true ambition is to follow in your footsteps, by becoming a Resort Director. Therefore, I have enrolled in a graduate program in Hospitality Management to begin this month.

I wish you continued success at Any Resort. I was very impressed by your resort and would like to apologize for any inconvenience my decision may cause.

Sincerely,

Chris Smith

■ Candidate thanks addressee for employment offer.

■ Letter provides additional information not stated in initial inquiry.

REJECTION OF OFFER
(Publishing Intern)

178 Green Street
Youngstown, OH 44501
(216) 555-5555

July 24, 1996

Pat Cummings
Editor
Any Publishing Company
1140 Main Street
Easton, PA 18044

Dear Mr. Cummings:

I would like to thank you for taking the time to talk to me about Any Publishing Company and offering me an internship position. I enjoyed meeting both you and Lee Jones and was very enthusiastic about the type of company Any Publishing appears to be. Being able to participate in the writing process as well as the editorial process of publishing is quite appealing to me, and I realize how unique the opportunity is. I feel that the internship position and I would have been a perfect fit.

As you know, and abrupt change in my personal circumstances necessitated turning down your offer. I want you to know that I sincerely regret this, as I know it would have been a pleasure to work for you as well as a challenging experience. I hope I have not inconvenienced you. Thank you again for your time.

Sincerely,

Chris Smith

- Candidate apologizes for inconvenience to potential employer.
- Candidate's explication of rejection is concise.

REJECTION OF OFFER
(Researcher)

178 Green Street
Winterthur, DE 19735
(302) 555-5555

February 14, 1996

Pat Cummings
Vice-President, Research and Development
Any Corporation
1140 Main Street
Chicago, IL 60605

Dear Ms. Cummings:

Thank you for taking the time to meet with me on Friday to discuss the opportunities for employment within your research and development department.

While I appreciate your generous offer, I have decided to decline the position. I have accepted a position elsewhere which I feel is better suited to my long-term needs.

Again, many thanks for your time. I wish you the best of luck in your future endeavors at Any Corporation.

Sincerely,

Chris Smith

■ Candidate closes letter on a positive note.

■ Letter expresses candidate's appreciation for addressee's consideration.

REJECTION OF OFFER
(Sales Representative)

178 Green Street
Menomonee Falls, WI 53051
(414) 555-5555

January 30, 1996

Pat Cummings
Vice-President, Sales
Any Corporation
1140 Main Street
Milwaukee, WI 53202

Dear Mr. Cummings:

I truly enjoyed our meeting Friday to discuss the possibility of my joining Any Corporation in a sales position. Your staff seems very enthusiastic, and I was impressed by your semiannual sales record. That is quite an achievement.

Although I greatly appreciate your confidence in my abilities, I must decline your employment offer. I realize that in order to generate the quantity of sales necessary to reach mutual goals, I would have to invest a great deal of time in travel. At this point, that is not an allowance I am able to make.

Once again, thank you for your consideration. Best of luck in the future.

Sincerely,

Chris Smith

■ Candidate highlights pertinent information discussed during interview.

■ Letter's tone is both courteous and appreciative.

REJECTION OF OFFER
(Systems Representative)

178 Green Street
Newnan, GA 30265
(404) 555-5555

July 5, 1996

Pat Cummings
Director of Information Services
Any Corporation
1140 Main Street
Houston, TX 77030

Dear Ms. Cummings:

It was a pleasure talking with you Monday concerning the Systems Representative position. I appreciated the opportunity to meet and talk with several members of your staff; everyone was very courteous and helpful.

I would also like to thank you for offering me employment at that meeting. However, I have decided to accept another position more in keeping with my specific career goals. Please accept my apology for having to decline your invitation.

I wish you the best of luck in the future.

Sincerely,

Chris Smith

■ Candidate expresses gratitude for addressee's consideration.

■ Day of interview is generally included in follow-up letter.

REJECTION OF OFFER
(Teacher)

178 Green Street
Canton, MA 02024
(617) 555-5555

June 19, 1996

Pat Cummings
Principal
Any Elementary School
1140 Main Street
Billerica, MA 01821

Dear Mr. Cummings:

Thank you for taking the time to meet with me regarding teaching positions at Any Elementary School, and for consequently offering me your vacant fourth grade classroom.

As you know, my prime interest is in securing a position where I may apply my newly acquired skills in ESL instruction. I understand that budgetary constraints will not allow you to offer that opening for the upcoming school year. However, I feel that this is where my interests and abilities best lie.

I appreciate your offer, and although I cannot join your school at this time, I hope that our paths will cross in the future.

Sincerely,

Chris Smith

■ Candidate thanks addressee for employment offer.

■ Candidate confirms his/her commitment to field of interest.

REJECTION OF OFFER
(Veterinary Assistant)

178 Green Street
Kingston, RI 02881
(401) 555-5555

December 5, 1996

Pat Cummings, D.V.M.
Veterinarian
1140 Main Street
Warwick, RI 02888

Dear Dr. Cummings:

Thank you very much for offering me the opportunity to intern at your office for the upcoming semester.

Unfortunately, I have not been able to come to an agreement with the internship coordinator's office at the University of Rhode Island to work the twenty hours per week the position would demand. The University strictly adheres to its maximum commitment of fifteen hours per week.

I truly regret not being able to work with you. I hope that, in the future, circumstances will allow me to be of your assistance.

Again, my thanks for your generous offer.

Sincerely,

Chris Smith

■ Letter is brief and concise.

■ Candidate requests addressee's future consideration for available opportunities.

30
Resignation Letter

 Always send a formal resignation letter two weeks before terminating your present employment. Many resignation letters simply state your last day of employment and a willingness to assist in the transition process. Other letters may personally thank the employer and/or explain your reasons for departure. Whatever the circumstances may be, take care to phrase your resignation letter in a positive way. Your past employer might be called on to provide a reference for you in the future.

RESIGNATION LETTER
(Architect)

178 Green Street
Greenwich, CT 06830
(203) 555-5555

March 25, 1996

Pat Cummings
Head Architect
Any Corporation
1140 Main Street
Hartford, CT 06106

Dear Ms. Cummings:

Effective April 8, 1996, I will be terminating my employment with Any
Corporation. I have allowed two weeks prior to my departure for assisting in the
transition process.

I have recently accepted a position as Head Architect with a local office in the
public sector. I feel that this new opportunity is well suited to my long-term career
goals.

I would be happy to train and assist my replacement, as well as complete any other
organizational matters that need my attention.

Sincerely,

Chris Smith

■ Letter indicates employee's
willingness to help with departure
preparations.

■ Employee immediately specifies
last date of employment.

RESIGNATION LETTER
(Environmental Consultant)

178 Green Street
Southfield, MI 48075
(313) 555-5555

April 8, 1996

Pat Cummings
Vice-President of Environmental Affairs
Any Corporation
1140 Main Street
Detroit, MI 48208

Dear Ms. Cummings:

I am writing to inform you that I will be leaving Any Corporation permanently
on April 22, 1996. After much deliberation, I have decided to move out of the
Michigan area.

Thank you for allowing me the opportunity to work with and learn from such an
outstanding staff. The knowledge I have gained in my year at Any Corporation
will surely aid me in my future endeavors. I am especially grateful for your close
and patient supervision of my training. Your kind encouragement assured me of
my ability to handle all aspects of the environmental consulting business.

If there is anything I can do to make my departure easier, please let me know.

Sincerely,

Chris Smith

- Letter indicates employee's willingness to help with departure preparations.
- Resignation letter should be dated two weeks prior to departure.

RESIGNATION LETTER
(Forester)

178 Green Street
Cheyenne, WY 82001
(504) 555-5555

February 15, 1996

Pat Cummings
Executive Director
Any State Park
1140 Main Street
Cheyenne, WY 82001

Dear Mr. Cummings:

As of March 5, I will be terminating my employment at Any State Park.

As you know, my goal has always been to work full-time as an advocate for forestry preservation. Recently, I have been offered, and accepted, a year's appointment with the International Forestry Preservation Corps in Brasilia, Brazil. The chance to work and live among the rain forests of Brazil is a unique and exciting opportunity that I could not turn down.

I have thoroughly enjoyed my time at Any State Park, and regret having to abandon my work. Please be assured that I will extend every effort to make my departure as smooth as possible.

I appreciate your understanding.

Sincerely,

Chris Smith

■ Letter briefly describes reason for departure.

■ Tone is both polite and somewhat formal.

RESIGNATION LETTER
(Hotel Manager)

178 Green Street
London, NWI 4SA UK
(44) 71 555 55 55

October 21, 1996

Pat Cummings
Vice-President, International Division
Any Corporation
1140 Main Street
Los Angeles, CA 90071

Dear Ms. Cummings:

I am writing to inform you that I have decided to return to the United States or
Canada to establish a more permanent base for my family as of November 11.

While I regret leaving Any Corporation, I have asked several times, without
success, for relocation to a position with the North American division. I enjoyed
working for Any Corporation and would have liked to continue. However, I have
established an excellent reputation and the credentials for quality and profitability
of food and beverage, as well as general hotel operations over the years and I am
confident these will assist me in securing a new position within the industry.

Once again, I regret having to resign from my position. I wish you much success
in the future.

Sincerely,

Chris Smith

- In a rejection letter, stating reason for departure is optional.
- Letter's purpose is immediately stated.

RESIGNATION LETTER
(Marketing Director)

178 Green Street
Houston, TX 75217
(713) 555-5555

March 17, 1996

Pat Cummings
President
Any Company
1140 Main Street
Addison, TX 75001

Dear Mr. Cummings:

Regretfully, I must offer you my resignation effective April 1. Although I have enjoyed watching Any Company grow from its beginnings to its present, formidable size in my capacity as your Marketing Director, my ability to contribute to its future success is past. For this reason, I have accepted a position with a smaller company that offers the potential for growth.

I am grateful for the experience you allowed me. If there is anything I can do to make my departure a smooth one, please let me know.

Sincerely,

Chris Smith

■ Employee expresses regret for departure.

■ Resignation letters are generally short and to the point.

RESIGNATION LETTER
(Medical Technologist)

178 Green Street
West Fargo, ND 58078
(701) 555-5555

May 31, 1996

Pat Cummings
Senior Medical Technologist
Any Hospital
1140 Main Street
West Fargo, ND 5878

Dear Ms. Cummings:

Friday, June 14, will be my last day of employment at Any Hospital.

I have accepted a research position in a private laboratory setting. While I have enjoyed working as a member of your staff, my new employment will allow me to pursue an area of real interest for me, hematology.

Please let me know if there is anything I can do to assist you in locating a replacement.

Sincerely yours,

Chris Smith

- Resignation letter should be dated two weeks prior to departure.
- Employee offers his/her assistance in securing a replacement.

RESIGNATION LETTER
(Production Assistant)

178 Green Street
Pittsburgh, PA 15222
(412) 555-5555

August 5, 1996

Pat Cummings
Internship Coordinator
Any Television Coordinator
1140 Main Street
Allentown, PA 18101

Dear Mr. Cummings:

I would like to offer you notice of the termination of my production assistantship. As I am preparing to return to school, August 16 will be my last day of employment.

My experience at Any Television Station has been both educational and enjoyable. I know that the production work I have done will continue to benefit me in the future.

Thank you for affording me this experience. I am grateful to have contributed to Any Television Station in return for the skills and knowledge I have gained.

Yours truly,

Chris Smith

■ Employee immediately specifies last date of employment.

■ Letter briefly describes reason for departure.

RESIGNATION LETTER
(Speech Pathologist)

178 Green Street
Santa Fe, NM 87504
(505) 555-5555

July 3, 1996

Pat Cummings
Principal
Any School
1140 Main Street
Deming, NM 87199

Dear Ms. Cummings:

I am writing to inform you of my resignation, effective July 15. Although I have enjoyed my position as Speech Pathologist, I have accepted another position where I feel my diverse skills are more fully utilized.

I want to thank you for the wonderful experience I had with Any School. Both the staff and the students were great to work with. I wish you much luck with the approaching academic year.

Sincerely,

Chris Smith

- Tone is both polite and somewhat formal.

- In a rejection letter, stating reason for departure is optional.

RESIGNATION LETTER
(Transaction Processing Supervisor)

178 Green Street
St. Louis, MO 63090
(314) 555-5555

December 12, 1996

Pat Cummings
Operations Manager
Any Corporation
1140 Main Street
St. Louis, MO 63102

Dear Mr. Cummings:

Please accept this as formal notification of my resignation from Any Corporation.
I am fully prepared to offer the customary two weeks notice. My last day of
employment with you will therefore be December 30.

While I have found my experience at Any Corporation to be very rewarding, I
have accepted another position which I feel is better suited to my career goals.
In my current role as Supervisor of Transaction Processing, I have successfully
restructured processing procedure, increased profiting procedure, and supervised a
sizable staff. I am ready to move forward, confident of the superior skills I have
acquired under your competent management.

Thank you for your confidence in my abilities. I hope I have succeeded in
contributing to your long-term goals.

Sincerely,

Chris Smith

■ Letter's purpose is immediately
stated.

■ Resignation letters are generally
short and to the point.

RESIGNATION LETTER
(Vice-President, Sales)

178 Green Street
Falls Church, VA 22043
(703) 555-5555

August 22, 1996

Pat Cummings
President
Any Company
1140 Main Street
Alexandria, VA 22312

Dear Ms. Cummings:

I have enjoyed serving as Vice-President of Sales, but I have received an offer from another pharmaceuticals company that I feel is better suited to my career objectives. Regrettably, I submit this letter as notice of my resignation.

My last day will be September 6. If I can be of any assistance in recommending potential candidates for my position, I would be more than happy to help.

I wish you the best of luck and future success.

Sincerely,

Chris Smith

■ Employee offers his/her assistance in securing a replacement.

■ Employee expresses regret for departure.

31
Acceptance Letter

Even if you've been offered the position of your choice, no hiring decision is final until it is in writing. Confirm your acceptance of a job offer with a brief, but gracious letter. Express thanks for the organization's decision and your enthusiasm for the new position. You also might confirm terms of the agreement, including start date, salary, and benefits. Ken O. sent a polite thank you letter one day after receiving an employment offer from A&R Mitchell Design Company. When he began work, his employer remembered his letter and Ken started off his new association on the right foot.

ACCEPTANCE LETTER
(Accountant)

178 Green Street
Cedar City, UT 84720
(801) 555-5555

December 4, 1996

Pat Cummings
Account Manager
Any Corporation
1140 Main Street
Salt Lake City, UT 84110

Dear Mr. Cummings:

Please receive this letter as my formal acceptance of your employment offer. I am very excited to join the ranks at Any Corporation, and I hope to quickly make a contribution to your qualified accounting staff.

Yesterday, I submitted a formal resignation notice to my current employer, and have arranged a start date of December 9. I will contact you this week to confirm this date, and provide any additional information you might need.

In the interim, be assured of my enthusiasm to join Any Corporation.

Sincerely,

Chris Smith

■ Candidate confirms termination of previous employment.

■ Candidate expresses confidence in his/her ability to fulfill employer's expectations.

ACCEPTANCE LETTER
(Benefits Administrator)

178 Green Street
Weeping Water, NE 68463
(402) 555-5555

May 21, 1996

Pat Cummings
Human Resources Director
Any Corporation
1140 Main Street
Chicago, IL 60605

Dear Ms. Cummings:

I would like to express my enthusiasm for my new position as Benefits
Administrator. This is an exciting opportunity, and I am eager to join your ranks.

I have turned in my resignation to my present employer, and I will begin working
for you three weeks from today. During the interim, I will remain in contact with
both you and Rick Starchon in order to ensure that my initiation is a smooth one.

Again, thank you for your confidence and support. I look forward to fulfilling your
expectations.

Sincerely,

Chris Smith

■ Letter cites specific start date.

■ In closing, candidate suggests
follow-up contact to finalize terms
of agreement.

ACCEPTANCE LETTER
(Contractor)

178 Green Street
Mayville, WI 53050
(414) 555-5555

May 1, 1996

Pat Cummings
Principal Architect
Any Corporation
1140 Main Street
Columbia, SC 29208

Dear Mr. Cummings:

I am pleased to accept the offer to assist you on the Glendale Shopping Complex project. The proposal you gave me sounds very exciting, and I am pleased to be given the chance to add my expertise to such a challenging endeavor.

As you know, I am in the process of securing housing to facilitate my move to Columbia. I expect to be settled in your area by the end of the month, in plenty of time to start work in mid-June. Should this arrangement present a conflict, please let me know.

I will keep in touch as my start date nears. Thank you again for your kind offer.

Sincerely,

Chris Smith

- Candidate invites employer to inquire about additional information.

- Candidate accepts terms of employment offer.

ACCEPTANCE LETTER
(Customer Service Representative)

178 Green Street
South Pasadena, CA 91030
(213) 555-5555

April 1, 1996

Pat Cummings
Customer Service Manager
Any Corporation
1140 Main Street
Los Angeles, CA 90010

Dear Ms. Cummings:

I would like to thank you and Donald Grasier for offering me the position of Customer Service Representative during our meeting on Friday. As you suggested, I took the weekend to consider your offer, and am pleased to accept its terms.

This morning I gave notice to my current employer and should be able to begin work at Any Corporation on April 15. Please let me know if there are any papers we need to go over before my start date.

Thank you again for providing me with this opportunity. I am very excited to join your sales team!

Sincerely,

Chris Smith

- Letter includes reference to all involved in hiring process.

- Candidate expresses willingness to complete necessary preparations before start date.

ACCEPTANCE LETTER
(Editorial Assistant)

178 Green Street
Halifax, MA 02338

July 6, 1996

Pat Cummings
Editor
Any Publishing Company
1140 Main Street
Port Chester, NY 10573

Dear Mr. Cummings:

Per our telephone conversation, I would like to confirm my acceptance of your employment offer. This position as Editorial Assistant provides exactly the kind of experience I hoped to find. I feel confident that I can make a significant contribution to Any Publishing Company, and I am grateful for the opportunity you have given me.

As we discussed, I will report to work at 8:00 a.m. on Monday, July 18. I will be moving to New York on July 11. Until then, I can be reached in Massachusetts at (617) 555-5555. Again, I appreciate your confidence in me and look forward to beginning work.

Sincerely,

Chris Smith

■ Candidate provides any additional information needed before start date.

■ Candidate reiterates terms of agreement previously discussed.

ACCEPTANCE LETTER
(Geographer)

178 Green Street
St. Paul, MN 55104
(612) 555-5555

May 12, 1996

Pat Cummings
Hiring Coordinator
Any Government Agency
1140 Main Street
Minneapolis, MN 55413

Dear Ms. Cummings:

I am grateful for the opportunity to be part of such an esteemed department in the agency. I look forward to assuming my post as Geographer, and I am happy to accept the terms of our agreement.

As discussed, my graduation date is set for May 31, and I will be available to begin the following Monday, June 3. I will contact your offices early next week to schedule my training session.

Again, thank you. I am very excited to begin.

Sincerely,

Chris Smith

■ In closing, candidate suggests follow-up contact to finalize terms of agreement.

■ Candidate reiterates terms of agreement previously discussed.

ACCEPTANCE LETTER
(Group Leader)

178 Green Street
Simons Island, GA 31522
(912) 555-555

November 25, 1996

Pat Cummings
Program Director
Any Treatment Center
1140 Main Street
Moultire, GA 31776

Dear Mr. Cummings:

It is with great expectation that I accept your offer of employment with Any Treatment Center. The prospect of working as a Group Leader at such a progressive and reputable center is very exciting to me.

The terms of your invitation are very generous, and I will immediately make plans to facilitate a start date within the next two weeks. As requested, I will call your office on Friday to finalize arrangements.

Thank you very much for your trust in my capabilities, Mr. Cummings. I am very eager to begin training and prove my worth.

Sincerely,

Chris Smith

■ Candidate suggests time frame for follow-up contact.

■ Letter expresses candidate's enthusiasm for new position.

ACCEPTANCE LETTER
(Statistician)

178 Green Street
Kingston, RI 02881
(401) 555-5555

February 25, 1996

Pat Cummings
Chief Statistician
Any Corporation
1140 Main Street
Pawtucket, RI 02862

Dear Ms. Cummings:

I received your letter, and I am very pleased to accept your offer of employment as a Statistician at Any Corporation. I appreciate your trust in my skills, and will make every effort to contribute to your team.

I have given notice of my resignation at my current employer and intend to start at Any Corporation on March 11. Per your request, I have scheduled a physical exam for this week, and will submit the appropriate materials on my first day of work.

I am very excited to begin working with you and your statistical staff.

Sincerely,

Chris Smith

■ Candidate confirms termination of previous employment.

■ Candidate expresses willingness to complete necessary preparations before start date.

ACCEPTANCE LETTER
(Underwriter)

178 Green Street
Batavia, IL 60510
(708) 555-5555

October 16, 1996

Pat Cummings
General Manager
Any Insurance Agency
1140 Main Street
Decatur, IL 62526

Dear Mr. Cummings:

I received your letter dated October 14, and am pleased to accept your employment offer. I am very excited to begin work as an Underwriter for such a prestigious organization.

I would like to confirm my start date of October 28. I have already given notice to my current employer, and expect a smooth transition to Any Insurance Agency.

Should you require any additional information, please do not hesitate to contact me. Once again, I would like to thank you and Frank Russo for your positive response to my candidacy.

Sincerely,

Chris Smith

■ Candidate refers to favorable aspect of new environment.

■ Letter includes reference to all involved in hiring process.

32
Resumes and Cover Letters in the Electronic Age

Welcome to the electronic age! As computers have impacted many other aspects of our lives, they have dramatically changed the way we go about job hunting, too. With companies slashing recruiting budgets and trimming hiring staffs, they rely increasingly on automated applicant tracking systems to process and sort employment applications. Other companies hire electronic employment database companies to fill specific openings. This means that your resume will be read by more computers and fewer people. Your resume, therefore, must be in a format that is easy for a computer to recognize and understand. Otherwise, your application will quickly begin collecting dust.

Basically, this is how it works: Your resume is fed through a scanner, which sends an image of the document to a computer. The computer then "reads" your resume, looking for key words, and then files your resume accordingly in its database. When an employer has an opening to fill, he or she will search the database for applications that have key words associated with the requirements of the position.

The good news about this technology is that it enables you to market your resume to hundreds of thousands of employers very easily. The bad news is that you must create an "electronic resume" in order to take advantage of the technology. But don't panic! An electronic resume is simply a modified version of your conventional resume. And though an electronic resume is very different from other types of resumes, it's easy to create. Here's how.

Content

Name. Your name should appear at the top of your resume, with your address following underneath.

Abbreviations. Most resume scanning systems will recognize a few common abbreviations like BS, MBA, and state names. Widely used acronyms for industry jargon, such as A/R and A/P on an accounting resume, are also generally accepted. But if there's any question of whether an abbreviation is a standard one, play it safe and spell it out.

Key Words. Using the right key words or key phrases in your resume is critical to its ultimate success—or lack thereof. Key words are usually nouns or short phrases that the computer searches for when scanning your resume. They usually refer to experience, training, skills, and abilities. For example, let's say an employer searches an employment database for a sales representative with the following key word criteria:

> sales representative
> BS/BA
> exceeded quota
> cold calls
> high energy
> willing to travel

Even if you have the right qualifications, if you don't use these key words on your resume, the computer will pass over your application.

To complicate matters further, different employers search for different key words. These are usually buzzwords common to your field or industry that describe your experience, education, skills, and abilities. Though there is no way to know for sure which key words employers are most likely to search for, you can make educated guesses. Check the classified ads for job openings in your field. What terms do employers commonly use to describe their requirements? Executive recruiters who specialize in your field are also a good source of this kind of information. Of course, you'll want to use as many key words in your resume as possible to maximize your chances.

Key-Word Summary. This is a compendium of your qualifications, usually written in a series of succinct key-word phrases, that immediately follows your name and address.

Experience and Achievements. Your professional experience should immediately follow the key-word summary, beginning with your most recent position. (If you are a recent college graduate, however, you should list your education before your experience.) Be sure that your job title, employer, location, and dates of employment are all clearly displayed. Highlight your accomplishments and key responsibilities with bullets.

Education. This section immediately follows the experience section. List your degrees, licenses, certifications, relevant course work, and academic awards or honors. Be sure to clearly display the name of the schools, locations, and years of graduation.

References. Don't waste valuable space with statements like "References available upon request." Though this section was standard fare for resumes of old, it won't win you any points on an electronic resume.

Format

Length of the Resume. Ideally your resume should be one to two pages in length. If you go over one page, make sure your name appears on the top of each subsequent page. Do not staple or fold your resume.

Paper. Don't bother with expensive papers or fancy colors. Use standard, twenty pound, 8½-by-11-inch paper. Because your resume needs to be as sharp and legible as possible, your best bet is black ink on white paper.

Font. Choose a non-decorative font with clear, distinct characters, such as Helvetica or Times.

Font Size. A font size of 12 points is ideal. Don't go below 10 or above 14 points, as type that is too small or too large is difficult for the scanner to read.

Font Style. Most scanners will accept boldface, but if an employer specifically tells you to avoid it, you can substitute boldface with all capital letters. Boldfacing and all capitalization are best used only for major section headings, such as "Experience" and "Education."

Graphics, Lines, and Shading. A resume scanner will try to "read" graphics, lines, and shading as text, resulting in computer chaos. You should also avoid using nontraditional layouts for your resume, such as two-column.

Printing. Whatever type of printing process you use, make sure the end result is letter quality. Ideally, you should have it printed at your local copy shop. Otherwise, a laser printer is perfectly acceptable. Avoid typewriters and dot matrix printers, since the quality of type they produce is inadequate for most scanners. Because your resume needs to be as sharp and legible as possible, you should always send originals, not photocopies. For the same reason, you should always mail, not fax, your resume.

Should You Include a Cover Letter with Your Electronic Resume?

Yes. Though cover letters are generally not scanned, some systems will take a "photograph" of it, and store it electronically with your resume. And while your cover letter will not help you in the initial selection process, it can help distinguish you from the competition in the final rounds of elimination. If you've taken the time to craft a letter that reiterates a couple of your strongest qualifications, you'll have the edge over other contenders who skipped this important step.

As with your resume, your cover letter should contain key words reflecting your strongest qualifications. If you're responding to a classified ad, be sure to echo as many of the key words mentioned in the ad as possible. And if you're sending your resume to a new networking contact, be sure to mention who referred you. Even in this anonymous electronic age, the old adage "It's all in who you know" still holds true.

ELECTRONIC COVER LETTER

47 Lake Shore Drive
Cambridge, MA 02138
(617) 555-5555

September 3, 1996

Ms. Pat Cummings
Controller
Any Corporation
1140 Main Street
Boston, MA 02215

Dear Ms. Cummings:

This letter is in response to your September 2 advertisement in the *Boston Globe* for the position of Assistant Controller. I am very interested in the position and believe I have the qualifications you are looking for. Please consider the following:

- Over twenty years experience in Accounting and Systems Management, Budgeting, Forecasting, Cost Containment, Financial Reporting, and International Accounting.
- Implemented "team-oriented" cross-training program within accounting group, resulting in timely month-end closings and increased productivity of key accounting staff.
- MBA in Management from Northeastern University.
- Results-oriented professional and proven team leader.

These are only a few of my credentials that may be of interest to you. I look forward to discussing them with you further in a personal interview. Thank you for your consideration.

Sincerely,

Chris Smith

Enc. Resume

■ Letter echoes the key words used in the employment ad.

■ Candidates uses bullets to emphasize his/her key credentials.

ELECTRONIC RESUME

CHRIS SMITH
47 Lake Shore Drive
Cambridge, MA 02138
(617) 555-5555

KEY WORD SUMMARY
Senior financial manager with over twenty years experience in Accounting and Systems Management, Budgeting, Forecasting, Cost Containment, Financial Reporting, and International Accounting. MBA in Management. Proficient in Lotus, Excel, Solomon, Real World, Windows.

EXPERIENCE
COLWELL CORPORATION, Wellesley, MA
$100 Million Division of Bancroft Corporation

Director of Accounting and Budgets, 1988 to present
Directed staff of 20 in General Ledger, Accounts Payable, Accounts Receivable, and International Accounting. Facilitated month-end closing process with parent company and auditors.

- Implemented "team-oriented" cross-training program within accounting group, resulting in timely month-end closings and increased productivity of key accounting staff.
- Developed and implemented a strategy for Sales and Use Tax Compliance in all 50 states with 100% compliance for both parent company and subsidiaries.
- Prepared monthly financial statements and analyses for review by management executive board.

Accounting Manager, 1985-1988
Managed a staff of 6 in General Ledger and Accounts Payable. Responsible for the design and refinement of financial reporting package. Assisted in month-end close.

- Established guidelines for month-end closing procedures, thereby speeding up closing by 5 business days.
- Promoted to Director of Accounting and Budgets.

FRANKLIN AND DELANY COMPANY, Melrose, MA

Senior Accountant, 1979-1985
Managed A/P, G/L, transaction processing, and financial reporting. Supervised staff of two.

- Developed Management Reporting package, including variance reports and cash flow reporting.

■ Resume contains many key words such as Budgeting, Forecasting, and MBA.

■ Format is "computer-friendly:" non-decorative font, traditional layout, no italics or special graphics.

CHRIS SMITH
(page 2)

Staff Accountant, 1975-1979
Managed A/P, including vouchering, cash disbursements, and bank reconciliation. Wrote and issued policies. Maintained supporting schedules used during year-end audits. Trained new employees.

Junior Accountant, 1973-1975
Assisted in general ledger closing. Monitored cash collections and accounts receivable.

EDUCATION

MBA in Management, Northeastern University, Boston, MA, 1985
BS in Accounting, Boston College, Boston, MA, 1973

ASSOCIATIONS

National Association of Accountants

Index

Account Executive (Broadcast Letter), 476
Account Manager (Broadcast Letter), 477
Account Manager (No Clear Career Path), 108
Accountant ("Cold" Letter to a Potential Employer), 244
Accountant (Acceptance Letter), 714
Accountant (Immigrant), 105
Accountant (Thank You Letter [For Letter of Recommendation]), 610
Accounting Manager (Letter to an Employment Agency), 346
Accounts Receivable Clerk ("Cold" Letter to a Potential Employer), 245
Acquisitions Editor (Thank You Letter [For Referral]), 616
Acquisitions Manager (Follow-Up Letter [After Telephone Conversation]), 516
Administrative Assistant ("Cold" Letter to a Potential Employer), 246
Administrative Assistant (Follow-Up Letter [After Job Interview]), 542
Administrative Assistant (Letter to an Employment Agency), 347
Administrative Assistant (Networking Letter), 400
Administrative Assistant (Response to a Classified Advertisement), 132
Administrative Assistant (Response to Rejection), 668
Administrative Assistant (Temporary Employment History), 125
Administrative Director ("Cold" Letter to a Potential Employer), 247
Administrative Judge (Response to a Classified Advertisement), 133
Administrator (Displaced Homemaker), 96
Administrator: Parks and Recreation Department (Response to a "Blind" Advertisement), 212
Advertising Assistant (Career Changer), 86
Advertising Assistant (Resurrection Letter), 640
Advertising Executive ("Cold" Letter to a Potential Employer), 248
Advertising Executive (Networking Letter), 401
Advertising Sales Associate ("Cold" Letter to a Potential Employer), 249
Advertising/Graphic Design Assistant (Letter to an Employment Agency), 348
Advisor (Networking Letter), 402
Airline Caterer (Recent Graduate), 114
Alumni Network (Information Request), 580
Alumni Relations Coordinator ("Cold" Letter to a Potential Employer), 250
Analyst (Response to a Classified Advertisement), 134
Annual Report (Information Request), 581
Applications Programmer (Response to a "Blind" Advertisement), 213

Arbitrator (Follow-Up Letter [After Telephone Conversation]), 517
Architect (Resignation Letter), 702
Architect (Response to Rejection), 669
Architectural Designer (Networking Letter), 403
Architectural Engineer ("Cold" Letter to a Potential Employer), 251
Archivist (Rejection of Offer), 686
Art Designer (Thank You Letter [After Informational Interview]), 628
Art Director ("Cold" Letter to a Potential Employer), 252
Art History Student (Thank You Letter [For Letter of Recommendation]), 611
Art Instructor (Part-Time Employment History), 110
Arts Administrator ("Cold" Letter to a Potential Employer), 253
Assistant Art Director (Rejection of Offer), 687
Assistant Curator (Gaps in Employment History), 103
Assistant Curator (Response to a Classified Advertisement), 135
Assistant Editor (Follow-Up Letter [After Job Interview]), 543
Assistant Editor (Response to a Classified Advertisement), 136
Assistant Editor (Response to Rejection), 670
Assistant Engineer (Follow-Up Letter [After Telephone Conversation]), 518
Assistant Hospital Administrator (Networking Letter), 404
Assistant Hospital Supervisor (Response to a Classified Advertisement), 137
Assistant Museum Director (Recent Graduate), 115
Assistant Personnel Officer (Response to a "Blind" Advertisement), 214
Assistant Portfolio Manager (Follow-Up Letter [After Telephone Conversation]), 519
Assistant Regional Manager (Resurrection Letter), 641
Associate Desktop Publisher (Response to a Classified Advertisement), 138
Associate Editor ("Cold" Letter to a Potential Employer), 254
Associate Editor (Follow-Up Letter [After Telephone Conversation]), 520
Athletic Director (Response to a Classified Advertisement), 139
Audio-Visual Specialist ("Cold" Letter to a Potential Employer), 255
Auto Salesperson (Networking Letter), 405
Automated Systems Specialist ("Cold" Letter to a Potential Employer), 256
Aviation Specialist ("Cold" Letter to a Potential Employer), 257
Bank Administrator (Resurrection Letter), 643

Bank Manager (Follow-Up Letter [After Job Interview]), 544

Bank Manager (Networking Letter), 406

Bank Manager (Thank You Letter [For Referral]), 617

Banking/Finance Professional ("Cold" Letter to a Potential Employer), 258

Benefits Administrator (Acceptance Letter), 715

Benefits Coordinator (Thank You Letter [After Informational Interview]), 629

Beverage Manager (Networking Letter), 407

Billings Clerk (Resurrection Letter), 644

Biomedical Researcher (Thank You Letter [For Good Reference]), 598

Bookkeeper (Letter to an Employment Agency), 349

Bookkeeper (Thank You Letter [For Good Reference]), 599

Broadcast Manager (Networking Letter), 408

Broker (Thank You Letter [For Good Reference]), 600

Business Consultant ("Cold" Letter to a Potential Employer), 259

Business Consultant (Career Changer), 87

Business Consultant (Networking Letter), 409

Business Consultant (Response to a "Blind" Advertisement), 215

Business Consultant (Response to a Classified Advertisement), 140

Business Manager (Follow-Up Letter [After Job Interview]), 545

Business Manager (Networking Letter), 410

Business Manager (Resume Letter), 498

Business Manager (Resurrection Letter), 645

Buyer ("Cold" Letter to a Potential Employer), 260

Buyer (Letter to an Executive Search Firm), 378

Campaign Manager ("Cold" Letter to a Potential Employer), 261

Campus Police Officer (Response to a Classified Advertisement), 142

Canine Science Instructor (Response to a Classified Advertisement), 143

Cardiologist (Resume Letter), 500

Career Planning Services (Information Request), 582

Case Manager (Response to a "Blind" Advertisement), 216

Case Manager (Response to a Classified Advertisement), 144

Casino Dealer (Career Changer), 88

Catering Manager (Response to a "Blind" Advertisement), 217

Chef ("Cold" Letter to a Potential Employer), 262

Chemical Engineer (Thank You Letter [For Letter of Recommendation]), 612

Chemist (Letter to an Employment Agency), 350

Chief Executive Officer (Letter to an Executive Search Firm), 379

Chief Executive Officer (Response to a "Blind" Advertisement), 218

Chief Financial Officer (Networking Letter), 411

Chief Financial Officer (Response to a Classified Advertisement), 145

Child Care Director (Response to a Classified Advertisement), 146

Child Psychologist (Thank You Letter [After Informational Interview]), 630

Chiropractor (Broadcast Letter), 478

Civil Engineer ("Cold" Letter to a Potential Employer), 263

Claims Adjuster (Response to a Classified Advertisement), 147

Claims Processor (Letter to an Employment Agency), 351

Clinical Psychologist ("Cold" Letter to a Potential Employer), 264

Clinical Research Nurse (Response to a Classified Advertisement), 148

Clinical Researcher ("Cold" Letter to a Potential Employer), 265

Clinical Service Administrator ("Cold" Letter to a Potential Employer), 266

Coach (Withdrawal from Consideration), 674

COBOL Programmer (Follow-Up Letter [After Telephone Conversation]), 521

Commercial Photographer (Resurrection Letter), 646

Commercial Real Estate Sales Executive (Networking Letter), 412

Commercial Transportation Specialist (Letter to an Executive Search Firm), 380

Communications Consultant ("Cold" Letter to a Potential Employer), 267

Community Center Director (Resume Letter), 501

Community Relations Specialist (Networking Letter), 413

Company Catalog (Information Request), 583

Computer Application Programmer (Thank You Letter [For Referral]), 618

Computer Applications Programmer ("Cold" Letter to a Potential Employer), 268

Computer Operations Supervisor (Letter to an Employment Agency), 352

Computer Operator (Follow-Up Letter [After Job Interview]), 546

Computer Programmer ("Cold" Letter to a Potential Employer), 269

Computer Programmer (Career Changer), 89

Computer Programmer (Resurrection Letter), 647

Computer Software Designer ("Cold" Letter to a Potential Employer), 270

Concierge (Follow-Up Letter [After Telephone Conversation]), 522

Conference Coordinator (Follow-Up Letter [After Job Interview]), 547

Conference Coordinator (Response to a Classified Advertisement), 149

Construction Engineer (Networking Letter), 414

Construction Manager (Networking Letter), 415

Construction Manager (Resume Letter), 503

Consultant (Networking Letter), 416

Consulting/Management Specialist ("Cold" Letter to a Potential Employer), 271

Contracted Typist (Response to a Classified Advertisement), 150

Contractor (Acceptance Letter), 716

Controller ("Cold" Letter to a Potential Employer), 272

Cook (Letter to an Employment Agency), 353

Corporate President (Letter to an Executive Search Firm), 381

Corporate Salesperson (Broadcast Letter), 479

Corporate Treasurer (Networking Letter), 417

Correctional Officer (Resurrection Letter), 648

Cosmetologist (Letter to an Employment Agency), 354

Cosmetologist (Response to a Classified Advertisement), 151

Counselor (Response to Rejection), 671

Country Club Manager ("Cold" Letter to a Potential Employer), 273

Course Registration (Information Request), 584
Credit Analyst (Career Changer), 90
Credit Manager (Broadcast Letter), 480
Credit Officer (Networking Letter), 418
Customer Service Representative (Acceptance Letter), 717
Customer Service Representative (Response to a Classified Advertisement), 152
Customer Support Representative (Networking Letter), 419
Dental Assistant (Letter to an Employment Agency), 355
Dental Hygienist (Rejection of Offer), 688
Dental Hygienist (Response to a Classified Advertisement), 153
Dentistry Department Manager (Response to a Classified Advertisement), 154
Department Manager (Follow-Up Letter [After Telephone Conversation]), 523
Director of Administration (Letter to an Executive Search Firm), 382
Director of College Development (Networking Letter), 420
Director of Information Services (Letter to an Executive Search Firm), 383
Director of Information Services (Networking Letter), 421
Director of Information Services (Resume Letter), 505
Director of Operations (Letter to an Employment Agency), 356
Director of Pharmacy (Letter to an Employment Agency), 357
Director of Public Works (Response to a Classified Advertisement), 155
Distribution Coordinator (Follow-Up Letter [After Job Interview]), 548
District Manager (Resume Letter), 506
District Sales Supervisor (Follow-Up Letter [After Job Interview]), 549
District Supervisor (Application for In-House Position), 83
Doctor (Follow-Up Letter [After Job Interview]), 550
Driver (Networking Letter), 422
Editor (Gaps in Employment History), 104
Editor (Networking Letter), 423
Editor (Rejection of Offer), 689
Editorial Assistant ("Cold" Letter to a Potential Employer), 274
Editorial Assistant (Acceptance Letter), 718
Editorial Assistant (Follow-Up Letter [After Job Interview]), 551
Editorial Assistant (Response to a Classified Advertisement), 156
Editorial/Computer Production Manager (Response to a "Blind" Advertisement), 219
Electrical Engineer (Networking Letter), 424
Electrician ("Cold" Letter to a Potential Employer), 275
Electromechanical Drafter ("Cold" Letter to a Potential Employer), 276
Electronics Supervisor (Military Background), 106
Elementary School Teacher ("Cold" Letter to a Potential Employer), 277
Elementary Teacher (Networking Letter), 425
Engineer ("Cold" Letter to a Potential Employer), 278
Engineering Administrator (Letter to an Executive Search Firm), 384
Engineering Consultant (Follow-Up Letter [After Job Interview]), 552
Engineering Instructor ("Cold" Letter to a Potential Employer), 279

English Teacher (Recent Graduate), 116
Entrepreneur (Broadcast Letter), 481
Environmental Advocate (Former Small Business Owner), 99
Environmental Campaigner (Recent Graduate), 117
Environmental Consultant (Resignation Letter), 703
Environmental Services Director (Networking Letter), 426
Esthetician ("Cold" Letter to a Potential Employer), 280
Events Planner (Response to a Classified Advertisement), 157
Executive Administrator (Letter to an Executive Search Firm), 385
Executive Assistant (Follow-Up Letter [After Job Interview]), 553
Executive Assistant (Letter to an Employment Agency), 358
Executive Marketing Director (Follow-Up Letter [After Telephone Conversation]), 524
Executive Nonprofit Director (Networking Letter), 427
Executive Secretary ("Cold" Letter to a Potential Employer), 281
Executive Sous Chef (Response to a "Blind" Advertisement), 220
Export Manager (Follow-Up Letter [After Job Interview]), 554
Export Manager (Follow-Up Letter [After Telephone Conversation]), 525
Facilities Specialist ("Cold" Letter to a Potential Employer), 282
Fashion Designer (Broadcast Letter), 482
Fashion Designer (Thank You Letter [For Good Reference]), 601
Features Reporter (Response to a Classified Advertisement), 158
Field Coordinator ("Cold" Letter to a Potential Employer), 283
Field Engineer (Resurrection Letter), 649
Field Finance Manager (Response to a "Blind" Advertisement), 221
Field Finance Manager (Response to a Classified Advertisement), 159
Field Service Manager (Networking Letter), 428
Film Archivist (Response to a Classified Advertisement), 160
Finance Assistant (Networking Letter), 429
Finance Broker (Weak Employment Background), 128
Finance Executive (Follow-Up Letter [After Job Interview]), 555
Finance Executive (Networking Letter), 430
Finance Manager (Networking Letter), 431
Financial Administrator (Letter to an Executive Search Firm), 386
Financial Associate ("Cold" Letter to a Potential Employer), 284
Financial Consultant ("Cold" Letter to a Potential Employer), 285
Financial Consultant (Broadcast Letter), 483
Financial Planner ("Cold" Letter to a Potential Employer), 286
Firefighter (Withdrawal from Consideration), 675
Fitness Instructor (Thank You Letter [For Referral]), 619
Fleet and Transportation Manager (Broadcast Letter), 484
Flight Attendant ("Cold" Letter to a Potential Employer), 287
Flight Attendant (Follow-Up Letter [After Telephone Conversation]), 526
Foreign Language Teacher (Resurrection Letter), 650

Foreperson/Ironworker ("Cold" Letter to a Potential Employer), 288

Forester (Recent Graduate), 118

Forester (Resignation Letter), 704

Freelance Copy Editor (Resurrection Letter), 651

Freelance Textbook Editor (Withdrawal from Consideration), 676

Freight Supervisor (Broadcast Letter), 485

Fundraiser ("Cold" Letter to a Potential Employer), 289

Fundraiser (Follow-Up Letter [After Job Interview]), 556

Fundraiser (Response to a Classified Advertisement), 161

Fundraising Coordinator (Resurrection Letter), 652

Gemologist (Response to a Classified Advertisement), 162

Genetic Research Technician (Networking Letter), 432

Geographer (Acceptance Letter), 719

Gerontologist (Recent Graduate), 119

Golf Instructor (Networking Letter), 433

Government Intern (Thank You Letter [For Good Reference]), 602

Grants Listing (Information Request), 585

Graphic Artist ("Cold" Letter to a Potential Employer), 290

Graphic Designer (At-Home Parent Reentering the Work Force), 84

Group Leader (Acceptance Letter), 720

Hair Stylist (Withdrawal from Consideration), 677

Head Coach (Follow-Up Letter [After Telephone Conversation]), 527

Head Nurse ("Cold" Letter to a Potential Employer), 291

Health Services Coordinator ("Cold" Letter to a Potential Employer), 292

High School Administrator (Thank You Letter [After Informational Interview]), 631

Home Economist/Coordinator (Response to a Classified Advertisement), 163

Hospital Administrator (Response to a Classified Advertisement), 164

Hospital Administrator (Resume Letter), 507

Hotel Administrator (Letter to an Employment Agency), 359

Hotel Clerk (Thank You Letter [After Informational Interview]), 632

Hotel Manager (Follow-Up Letter [After Job Interview]), 558

Hotel Manager (Resignation Letter), 705

Hotel Manager (Response to a Classified Advertisement), 165

Housekeeper (Letter to an Employment Agency), 360

Human Resources Manager (Networking Letter), 434

Human Resources Professional ("Cold" Letter to a Potential Employer), 293

Human Resources Representative (Follow-Up Letter [After Job Interview]), 559

Human Resources Representative (Thank You Letter [For Letter of Recommendation]), 613

Human Services Coordinator ("Cold" Letter to a Potential Employer), 294

Industry Directory (Information Request), 586

Industry Newsletter (Information Request), 587

Insurance Account Manager (Letter to an Employment Agency), 361

Insurance Manager (Networking Letter), 435

Insurance Salesperson ("Cold" Letter to a Potential Employer), 295

Insurance Underwriter (Letter to an Employment Agency), 362

Interior Designer ("Cold" Letter to a Potential Employer), 296

International Buyer (Response to a Classified Advertisement), 166

International Controller (Networking Letter), 436

International Marketing Specialist (Networking Letter), 437

International Sales Associate ("Cold" Letter to a Potential Employer), 297

Inventory Control Analyst (Follow-Up Letter [After Job Interview]), 560

Inventory Control Manager (All Employment at One Company), 81

Inventory Control Supervisor (Networking Letter), 438

Jewelry Designer ("Cold" Letter to a Potential Employer), 298

Jewelry Designer (Resurrection Letter), 653

Jewelry Sales/Buyer ("Cold" Letter to a Potential Employer), 299

Labor Relations Specialist (Letter to an Executive Search Firm), 387

Labor Relations Specialist (Response to a "Blind" Advertisement), 222

Laboratory Assistant (Address/Phone Number Change), 592

Laboratory Technician (Follow-Up Letter [After Telephone Conversation]), 528

Landscape Designer ("Cold" Letter to a Potential Employer), 300

Law Enforcement Officer (Rejection of Offer), 690

Lawyer ("Cold" Letter to a Potential Employer), 301

Lawyer: International Law (Letter to an Executive Search Firm), 388

Legal Administrator (Letter to an Employment Agency), 363

Legal Assistant ("Cold" Letter to a Potential Employer), 302

Legal Assistant (Networking Letter), 439

Legal Assistant (Recent Graduate), 120

Legal Assistant (Response to a Classified Advertisement), 167

Legal Assistant (Withdrawal from Consideration), 678

Legal Associate ("Cold" Letter to a Potential Employer), 303

Legal Associate (Broadcast Letter), 486

Legal Associate (Response to a "Blind" Advertisement), 223

Legal Intern (Follow-Up Letter [After Job Interview]), 561

Leisure Trainer (Networking Letter), 440

Librarian ("Cold" Letter to a Potential Employer), 304

Librarian (Response to a "Blind" Advertisement), 224

Librarian (Response to a Classified Advertisement), 168

Loan Officer (Response to a Classified Advertisement), 169

Magazine Publishing Intern (Follow-Up Letter [After Telephone Conversation]), 529

Mailroom Supervisor (Follow-Up Letter [After Telephone Conversation]), 530

Maintenance Supervisor (Networking Letter), 441

Major Account Manager (Response to a "Blind" Advertisement), 225

Management Consultant (Letter to an Executive Search Firm), 389

Manager of Patient Services (Follow-Up Letter [After Telephone Conversation]), 531

Manufacturer ("Cold" Letter to a Potential Employer), 305

Manufacturing Manager (Resume Letter), 508

Manufacturing Test Technician (Response to a "Blind" Advertisement), 226

Marine Biologist (Rejection of Offer), 691

Marketing Analyst (Response to a "Blind" Advertisement), 227

Marketing Assistant (Frequent Job Changer), 102

Marketing Assistant (Networking Letter), 442

Marketing Assistant (Overseas Employment History), 109

Marketing Assistant (Thank You Letter [After Informational Interview]), 633

Marketing Director ("Cold" Letter to a Potential Employer), 306

Marketing Director (Resignation Letter), 706

Marketing Executive (Career Changer), 91

Marketing Intern ("Cold" Letter to a Potential Employer), 308

Marketing Specialist (Networking Letter), 443

Marketing/Development Executive ("Cold" Letter to a Potential Employer), 307

Marketing/Sales Executive (Broadcast Letter), 487

Masonry Supply Manager (Response to a Classified Advertisement), 171

Massage Therapist ("Cold" Letter to a Potential Employer), 309

Materials Manager (All Employment at One Company), 82

Materials Manager (Follow-Up Letter [After Job Interview]), 562

Math Instructor (Retiree Reentering the Work Force), 124

Mechanical Engineer ("Cold" Letter to a Potential Employer), 310

Mechanical Engineer (Thank You Letter [After Informational Interview]), 634

Medical Assistant (Letter to an Employment Agency), 364

Medical Assistant (Response to a "Blind" Advertisement), 228

Medical Assistant (Thank You Letter [For Referral]), 620

Medical Sales Representative (Networking Letter), 444

Medical Technologist (Resignation Letter), 707

Meeting Planner (Physically Challenged), 112

Meeting Planner (Response to a Classified Advertisement), 172

Membership Listing (Information Request), 588

Meteorologist (Thank You Letter [After Informational Interview]), 635

Microwave Technician (Networking Letter), 445

Mortgage/Loan Officer (Networking Letter), 446

Multimedia Manager ("Cold" Letter to a Potential Employer), 311

Multimedia Specialist (Broadcast Letter), 488

Multimedia Specialist (Response to a Classified Advertisement), 173

Musician (Address/Phone Number Change), 593

Mutual Funds Broker ("Cold" Letter to a Potential Employer), 312

Nanny (Follow-Up Letter [After Telephone Conversation]), 532

Newspaper Intern (Response to a Classified Advertisement), 175

Nurse's Aide (Response to a "Blind" Advertisement), 229

Nurse's Aide (Withdrawal from Consideration), 679

Nurse ("Cold" Letter to a Potential Employer), 313

Nurse (Career Changer), 92

Nurse (Networking Letter), 447

Nurse (Thank You Letter [For Good Reference]), 603

Nurse (Thank You Letter [For Referral]), 621

Nurse: Anesthesia ("Cold" Letter to a Potential Employer), 314

Occupational Health Manager (Response to a Classified Advertisement), 176

Occupational Therapist (Thank You Letter [After Informational Interview]), 636

Office Manager ("Cold" Letter to a Potential Employer), 315

Office Manager (Letter to an Employment Agency), 365

Office Receptionist (Response to a Classified Advertisement), 177

Operations Executive ("Cold" Letter to a Potential Employer), 316

Operations Manager ("Cold" Letter to a Potential Employer), 317

Operations Manager (Letter to an Employment Agency), 366

Operations Manager (Letter to an Executive Search Firm), 390

Operations Manager (Response to a "Blind" Advertisement), 230

Optical Manufacturer (Response to a "Blind" Advertisement), 231

Paralegal (Networking Letter), 448

Paralegal (Rejection of Offer), 692

Park Maintenance Supervisor (Response to a Classified Advertisement), 178

Parking Supervisor (Weak Educational Background), 127

Payroll Supervisor (Networking Letter), 449

Payroll Supervisor (Response to a "Blind" Advertisement), 232

Personal Secretary (Follow-Up Letter [After Job Interview]), 563

Personnel Manager (Follow-Up Letter [After Job Interview]), 564

Pet Groomer (Address/Phone Number Change), 594

Pharmaceutical Administrator (Response to a "Blind" Advertisement), 233

Pharmacy Director ("Cold" Letter to a Potential Employer), 318

Photographer (Thank You Letter [For Referral]), 622

Photographer/Writer (Response to a Classified Advertisement), 179

Physical Therapist (Resurrection Letter), 654

Physicist (Recent Graduate), 121

Plant Manager ("Cold" Letter to a Potential Employer), 319

Plant Manager (Letter to an Executive Search Firm), 391

Political Staffer (Response to a Classified Advertisement), 180

Power Systems Designer (Networking Letter), 450

Precision Inspector (Follow-Up Letter [After Telephone Conversation]), 533

Preschool Director (Response to a Classified Advertisement), 181

Preschool Instructor (Withdrawal from Consideration), 680

President/CEO (Letter to an Executive Search Firm), 392

Principal (Follow-Up Letter [After Telephone Conversation]), 534

Printer ("Cold" Letter to a Potential Employer), 320

Product and Services Developer (Career Changer), 93
Product Design Engineer (Follow-Up Letter [After Job Interview]), 565
Product Developer (Response to a Classified Advertisement), 182
Product Manager (50-Plus Job Candidate), 80
Production Assistant (Follow-Up Letter [After Job Interview]), 566
Production Assistant (Follow-Up Letter [After Telephone Conversation]), 535
Production Assistant (Freelancer), 100
Production Assistant (Rejection of Offer), 693
Production Assistant (Resignation Letter), 708
Production Assistant (Response to a Classified Advertisement), 183
Production Controller (Response to a Classified Advertisement), 184
Production Manager ("Cold" Letter to a Potential Employer), 321
Production Manager (Networking Letter), 451
Production/Materials Control Manager (Response to a "Blind" Advertisement), 234
Program Coordinator (Networking Letter), 452
Program Coordinator (Rejection of Offer), 694
Program Coordinator (Response to a Classified Advertisement), 185
Program Manager (Broadcast Letter), 489
Project Manager ("Cold" Letter to a Potential Employer), 322
Project Manager (Networking Letter), 453
Project Manager (Response to a Classified Advertisement), 186
Promotions Representative (Networking Letter), 454
Property Manager ("Cold" Letter to a Potential Employer), 323
Property Manager (Letter to an Employment Agency), 367
Property Manager (Networking Letter), 455
Protection Professional (Follow-Up Letter [After Telephone Conversation]), 536
Psychiatric Nurse (Follow-Up Letter [After Telephone Conversation]), 537
Public Records Analyst (Follow-Up Letter [After Job Interview]), 567
Public Relations Assistant ("Cold" Letter to a Potential Employer), 324
Public Relations Associate (Response to a Classified Advertisement), 187
Publicist (Networking Letter), 456
Publicist (Response to a Classified Advertisement), 188
Publicist (Thank You Letter [For Referral]), 623
Publisher's Assistant (Follow-Up Letter [After Job Interview]), 568
Publisher's Assistant (Response to a Classified Advertisement), 189
Publisher's Assistant (Temporary Employment History), 126
Publishing Intern (Networking Letter), 457
Publishing Intern (Rejection of Offer), 695
Purchasing Agent (Follow-Up Letter [After Telephone Conversation]), 538
Purchasing Agent (Letter to an Employment Agency), 368
Purchasing Agent (Response to a Classified Advertisement), 190
Purchasing Agent (Resurrection Letter), 655
Quality Control Engineer (Networking Letter), 458
Quality Control Specialist ("Cold" Letter to a Potential Employer), 325

Quality Control Specialist (Letter to an Employment Agency), 369
Radio Announcer (Resurrection Letter), 656
Real Estate Banker ("Cold" Letter to a Potential Employer), 326
Real Estate Developer (Career Changer), 94
Real Estate Director (Resume Letter), 510
Real Estate Executive (Broadcast Letter), 490
Real Estate Sales Associate (Response to a Classified Advertisement), 191
Real Estate Salesperson (Follow-Up Letter [After Job Interview]), 569
Record Manager (Networking Letter), 459
Recruiter (Fired/Laid Off), 97
Recycling Manager (Follow-Up Letter [After Job Interview]), 570
Regional Manager (Response to a Classified Advertisement), 192
Regional Sales Manager (Withdrawal from Consideration), 681
Regional Sales/Product Trainer (Follow-Up Letter [After Telephone Conversation]), 539
Repair Technician ("Cold" Letter to a Potential Employer), 327
Research Assistant ("Cold" Letter to a Potential Employer), 328
Research Assistant (Networking Letter), 460
Researcher (Rejection of Offer), 696
Researcher (Response to a Classified Advertisement), 193
Restaurant Manager (Follow-Up Letter [After Job Interview]), 571
Restaurant Manager (Networking Letter), 461
Restaurant Manager (Thank You Letter [For Letter of Recommendation]), 614
Restaurant Manager Trainee (Response to a Classified Advertisement), 194
Retail Manager (Letter to an Employment Agency), 370
Retail Sales Associate (Follow-Up Letter [After Job Interview]), 572
Retail Sales Manager ("Cold" Letter to a Potential Employer), 329
Retail Sales Manager (Networking Letter), 462
Retail Salesperson ("Cold" Letter to a Potential Employer), 330
Retail Store Manager (Thank You Letter [For Good Reference]), 604
Sales Director (Fired/Laid Off), 98
Sales Director (Networking Letter), 463
Sales Executive ("Cold" Letter to a Potential Employer), 331
Sales Manager (Response to a "Blind" Advertisement), 235
Sales Manager (Weak Employment Background), 129
Sales Representative (Career Changer), 95
Sales Representative (Follow-Up Letter [After Job Interview]), 573
Sales Representative (Rejection of Offer), 697
Sales Representative (Response to a Classified Advertisement), 195
Sales Representative (Resurrection Letter), 657
Sales/Customer Service Representative (Letter to an Employment Agency), 371
Salesperson (At-Home Parent Reentering the Work Force), 85
Sanitarian (Networking Letter), 464
Sanitation Inspector (Resurrection Letter), 658

School Administrator: Secondary Level ("Cold" Letter to a Potential Employer), 332

Secretary (Letter to an Employment Agency), 372

Secretary (Networking Letter), 465

Security Guard (Letter to an Employment Agency), 373

Security Specialist ("Cold" Letter to a Potential Employer), 333

Senior Accountant (Letter to an Executive Search Firm), 393

Senior Business Analyst (Letter to an Executive Search Firm), 395

Senior HVAC Technician (Response to a Classified Advertisement), 196

Senior Vice-President (Broadcast Letter), 491

Senior-Level MIS Operator (Broadcast Letter), 492

Set Designer (Recent Graduate), 122

Shipping/Receiving Expediter (Resurrection Letter), 659

Site Location Supervisor (Response to a Classified Advertisement), 197

Social Worker (Response to a Classified Advertisement), 198

Social Worker (Resurrection Letter), 660

Social Worker (Thank You Letter [After Informational Interview]), 637

Social Worker: Counseling ("Cold" Letter to a Potential Employer), 334

Social Worker: Geriatrics ("Cold" Letter to a Potential Employer), 335

Social Worker: Medical ("Cold" Letter to a Potential Employer), 336

Software Technician (Thank You Letter [For Referral]), 624

Special Agent (Networking Letter), 466

Speech Pathologist (Resignation Letter), 709

Staff Accountant (Follow-Up Letter [After Job Interview]), 574

Staff Accountant (Networking Letter), 467

Staff Accountant (Resurrection Letter), 661

Staff Nutritionist (Address/Phone Number Change), 595

Staff Photographer (Response to a "Blind" Advertisement), 236

State Administrator (Response to a Classified Advertisement), 199

Statistician (Acceptance Letter), 721

Stenographer (Letter to an Employment Agency), 374

Store Manager (Part-Time Employment History), 111

Store Manager (Response to a Classified Advertisement), 200

Subscription Information (Information Request), 589

Surgeon (Thank You Letter [For Good Reference]), 605

Systems Analyst (Resurrection Letter), 662

Systems Analyst (Withdrawal from Consideration), 682

Systems Representative (Rejection of Offer), 698

Systems Trainer (Response to a Classified Advertisement), 201

Talent Agent (Follow-Up Letter [After Job Interview]), 575

Teacher (Follow-Up Letter [After Job Interview]), 576

Teacher (Follow-Up Letter [After Telephone Conversation]), 540

Teacher (Rejection of Offer), 699

Teacher (Response to a "Blind" Advertisement), 237

Teacher (Thank You Letter [For Good Reference]), 606

Teacher (Thank You Letter [For Referral]), 625

Teacher: Secondary Level (Networking Letter), 468

Technical Sales Associate (Response to a "Blind" Advertisement), 238

Technical Writer (Response to a Classified Advertisement), 202

Technical Writer (Thank You Letter [For Good Reference]), 607

Telecommunications Specialist (Networking Letter), 469

Telemarketer ("Cold" Letter to a Potential Employer), 337

Telemarketer (Networking Letter), 470

Telemarketer (Physically Challenged), 113

Telemarketer (Response to a Classified Advertisement), 203

Telemarketer (Response to Rejection), 672

Telemarketer (Resurrection Letter), 663

Television Camera Operator (Response to a Classified Advertisement), 204

Television Production Assistant ("Cold" Letter to a Potential Employer), 338

Textile Specialist ("Cold" Letter to a Potential Employer), 339

Transaction Processing Supervisor (Resignation Letter), 710

Translator (Recent Graduate), 123

Translator (Response to a Classified Advertisement), 205

Translator (Resurrection Letter), 664

Transportation Coordinator (Networking Letter), 471

Transportation Operator (Military Background), 107

Travel Agent (Response to a Classified Advertisement), 206

Travel Agent (Withdrawal from Consideration), 683

Typist (Response to a "Blind" Advertisement), 239

Typist (Resurrection Letter), 665

Underwriter ("Cold" Letter to a Potential Employer), 340

Underwriter (Acceptance Letter), 722

Underwriter (Response to a "Blind" Advertisement), 240

Upper-Level Manager: Accounting ("Cold" Letter to a Potential Employer), 341

Veterinarian ("Cold" Letter to a Potential Employer), 342

Veterinary Assistant (Rejection of Offer), 700

Vice-President, Sales and Marketing (Resume Letter), 512

Vice-President, Sales (Resignation Letter), 711

Vice-President of Administration (Broadcast Letter), 493

Vice-President of Banking (Letter to an Executive Search Firm), 396

Vice-President of Nursing (Letter to an Executive Search Firm), 397

Vice-President of Sales (Letter to an Executive Search Firm), 398

Victim Witness Advocate (Networking Letter), 472

Visual Media Production Assistant ("Cold" Letter to a Potential Employer), 343

Wait Person (Letter to an Employment Agency), 375

Warehouse Operator (Broadcast Letter), 494

Wholesale Buyer (Address/Phone Number Change), 596

Writer (Freelancer), 101

Writer/Reporter (Networking Letter), 473

Writer/Researcher (Follow-Up Letter [After Job Interview]), 577

Writer/Researcher (Response to a "Blind" Advertisement), 241

Writing Instructor (Response to a Classified Advertisement), 207

X-Ray Technician (Networking Letter), 474

Yacht Salesperson (Response to a Classified Advertisement), 208

Youth Center Director (Response to a Classified Advertisement), 209

Zoologist (Broadcast Letter), 495